Cinema in the Arab World

Cinema in the Arab World

New Histories, New Approaches

Edited by
Ifdal Elsaket, Daniel Biltereyst and Philippe Meers

BLOOMSBURY ACADEMIC
LONDON • NEW YORK • OXFORD • NEW DELHI • SYDNEY

BLOOMSBURY ACADEMIC
Bloomsbury Publishing Plc
50 Bedford Square, London, WC1B 3DP, UK
1385 Broadway, New York, NY 10018, USA
29 Earlsfort Terrace, Dublin 2, Ireland

BLOOMSBURY, BLOOMSBURY ACADEMIC and the Diana logo are trademarks of
Bloomsbury Publishing Plc

First published in Great Britain 2023
Paperback edition published 2024

Copyright © Ifdal Elsaket, Daniel Biltereyst & Philippe Meers, 2023

Ifdal Elsaket, Daniel Biltereyst & Philippe Meers have asserted their right under the
Copyright, Designs and Patents Act, 1988, to be identified as Editors of this work.

For legal purposes the Acknowledgements on p. xiv constitute an extension of this
copyright page.

Cover design: Ben Anslow
Cover image: Rivoli cinema, Place des Canons, Beirut, 1960 © Marilyn Stafford

All rights reserved. No part of this publication may be reproduced or transmitted
in any form or by any means, electronic or mechanical, including photocopying,
recording, or any information storage or retrieval system, without prior
permission in writing from the publishers.

Bloomsbury Publishing Plc does not have any control over, or responsibility for, any
third-party websites referred to or in this book. All internet addresses given in this
book were correct at the time of going to press. The author and publisher regret any
inconvenience caused if addresses have changed or sites have ceased to exist,
but can accept no responsibility for any such changes.

A catalogue record for this book is available from the British Library.

ISBN: HB: 978-1-3501-6371-3
PB: 978-1-3503-6170-6
ePDF: 978-1-3501-6372-0
eBook: 978-1-3501-6373-7

Typeset by Deanta Global Publishing Services, Chennai, India

To find out more about our authors and books visit www.bloomsbury.com and
sign up for our newsletters.

Contents

List of illustrations	vii
List of contributors	ix
Acknowledgements	xiv
Note on transliteration	xv

Introduction: New histories and approaches to cinema in the Arab world *Ifdal Elsaket, Daniel Biltereyst and Philippe Meers*   1

Part I Arab cinema histories: Distribution, exhibition and audiences

1. Misr abroad: Trading Egyptian films in colonial Maghreb *Morgan Corriou*   27
2. 'Le Roi du Cinéma': Joseph Seibarras and North African film exhibition, 1925–45 *Eric Smoodin*   46
3. Access for the Axis: The battle for ideological supremacy on Middle Eastern, North African and Turkish cinema screens between 1933 and 1945 *Kajsa Philippa Niehusen and Ross Melnick*   62
4. Egyptian women's empowerment and early cinema-going *Mohannad Ghawanmeh*   82
5. Anti-colonial masculinity, the Catholic Film Center and the screening of religious difference in 1950s Egypt: The multiple lives of Husayn Sidqi's *Night of Power* *Rahma Bavelaar*   93
6. Bollywood film traffic: Shaping routes for Hindi films in the Arab world, 1954–2014 *Némésis Srour*   121
7. The business of cinemas in Ismailia with a case study of Ghweba Cinema: An interview with Abbas Ghweba and Tareq Ghweba *Asmaa Gharib*   134
8. Cinema-going in Egypt in the long 1960s: Oral histories of pleasure and leisure *Ifdal Elsaket*   150

Part II Contemporary issues of circulation, experience and memory

9. Film distribution and exhibition in Tunisia since 2011: Is cinema-going back in style? *Patricia Caillé*   177

10	Gatekeepers or facilitators? MAD Solutions and other film distribution networks for Arab cinema *Stefanie Van de Peer*	195
11	A new online cinema audience? An interview on Aflamuna with Jad Abi Khalil *Anaïs Farine*	211
12	A taste for cinema: Saudi Arabia's mediated transitional public film culture *Anne Ciecko*	220
13	The multifunctional cinema exhibition space at the turn of the century: A dialogue *Nour El Safoury and Jowe Harfouche*	244
14	The visual nation: Film, soft power and Egypt as a community of spectators *Iskandar Abdalla*	254

Bibliography 277
Index 295

Illustrations

Figures

1.1	Promotional material for the films *Mughamarat ʿAntar wa-ʿAbla* (Salah Abu Seif, 1948), *Zuhur al-Islam* (Ibrahim ʿIzz al-Din, 1951) and *Lahn al-Khulud* (Henry Barakat, 1952) in a cinema (Centre des archives diplomatiques de Nantes, Protectorat Maroc, série C: section d'iconographie, n° 5602, 1952)	34
1.2	The Donyazad Cinema in Algiers, postcard	38
2.1	Joseph Seibarras, *'le grand animateur du cinéma'*	48
2.2	The Empire cinema in Fez, Morocco	52
2.3	An Algerian helps the French heroine in Jean Renoir's *Le Bled* (1929)	55
3.1	The luxurious Alhambra Cinema towers over the Jaffa, Palestine streetscape in 1937	67
3.2	A box containing a presentation print of the British Ministry of Information-produced *Desert Victory* (1943) sent from Prime Minister Winston Churchill to 'The Spartan General', Field Marshall Bernard Law Montgomery	68
5.1	Husayn Sidqi/Shaykh Hasan in *azhari* garb, featured on the cover of *al-Kawakib* Magazine (October 1951)	98
5.2	Newspaper advertisements for *Laylat al-Qadr* (1952) on the left, and *Shaykh Hasan* (1954) on the right	108
7.1	The entrance of Cinema Al-Taʿawun in Ismailia	136
8.1	Advertisement for a children's 'cinema show' at the Rivoli Cinema	155
8.2	An article about Hollywood musical films in *al-Kawakib* magazine with a focus on *The Sound of Music*	166
8.3	A regular feature in Egyptian magazines and newspapers is the 'Where will you go out this week?' section, which features advertisements for screenings of films	166
8.4	Advertisement for the film *Bayn al-Atlal*	168
9.1	Cinemas in the larger Tunis area	178
9.2	Cinemas in downtown Tunis	180

14.1 Lobby card of *Rasif Nimra Khamsa* or *Platform 5* (1956) featuring Khamis (Farid Shawqi) — 255
14.2 The gathered soldiers watching *Rasif Nimra Khamsa* or *Platform 5* in *The Passage* by Sharif 'Arafa — 256
14.3 Nadia (Fatin Hamama) and Shakir (Mahmud Mursi), her brother-in-law, in *al-Layla al-Akhira* or *The Last Night* (1963) by Kamal al-Shaykh — 261
14.4 Two animated frames from *Sahibet al-Sa'ada*. At the top (Playing with Giants, 1991). At the bottom (Caught in a Honey Trap, 1977) — 266
14.5 Two animated frames from *Sahibet al-Sa'ada*. At the top (An Egyptian Story, 1982). At the bottom (A Wife From The Street, 1960) — 267
14.6 Two animated frames from *Sahibet al-Sa'ada*. At the top (Chitchat on the Nile, 1971). At the bottom (Tit for Tat, 1984) — 268
14.7 Two animated frames from *Sahibet al-Sa'ada*. At the top (A Women who Shook the Throne of Egypt, 1995). At the bottom (The Magician, 2001) — 269

Table

9.1 List of Cinemas Showing Films at the End of 2019 — 186

Contributors

Daniel Biltereyst is a professor of media and film history at Ghent University, Belgium, and director of the Centre for Cinema and Media Studies. Besides exploring new approaches to historical media and cinema cultures, he is engaged in work on film and screen culture as sites of censorship, controversy, public debate and audience engagement. Biltereyst has published widely on these matters in edited volumes and academic journals. He recently published *The Routledge Companion to New Cinema History* (2019, with Richard Maltby and Philippe Meers), *Mapping Movie Magazines* (2020) and a monograph on film control and censorship in Belgium. He recently edited *New Perspectives on Early Cinema History* (2022, with Mario Slugan).

Ifdal Elsaket is assistant-director (Arabic and Islamic studies) at the Netherlands-Flemish Institute in Cairo, Egypt. Her research focuses on Egyptian cinema history with a focus on audiences, industry and broader production contexts. Her work has appeared in the *International Journal of Middle East Studies* and *Arab Studies Journal*. She is currently writing a book on the early cinema in Egypt.

Philippe Meers is a professor of film and media studies at the University of Antwerp, Belgium, where he is director of the Visual and Digital Cultures Research Center (ViDi) and of the Center for Mexican Studies. He has published widely on historical and contemporary film cultures and audiences. With Richard Maltby and Daniel Biltereyst, he co-edited *Explorations in New Cinema History: Approaches and Case Studies* (2011), *Cinema, Audiences and Modernity: New Perspectives on European Cinema History* (2012) and *The Routledge Companion to New Cinema History* (2019). With Annette Kuhn and Daniel Biltereyst, he co-edited a special issue of *Memory Studies* (2017).

Iskandar Abdalla is a curator, researcher and a doctoral fellow at the Berlin Graduate School 'Muslim Cultures and Societies'. Born in Alexandria, Egypt, he studied history and Middle Eastern studies at the Ludwig-Maximilian University of Munich and the Freie Universität Berlin. Since 2014 he is a film curator at the Arab Film Festival Berlin. His research interests encompass secularism, Islam in Europe, queer theory, film and cultural history of the Arab world. In 2020 he produced his first video work titled *Balcony of my Dreams*, which was showcased at the Haus der Kunst in Munich.

Rahma Bavelaar is a doctoral candidate in anthropology at the University of Amsterdam, the Netherlands. Her PhD thesis examines cultural and legal representations and practices around interfaith marriage in modern Egypt. Her research straddles history and ethnography, archives and oral history, and her interests include gender and religion, family law, secularism(s) and anti-colonial movements.

Patricia Caillé is maîtresse de conférences at the Université de Strasbourg and a member of CREM (Centre de recherches sur les médiations EA 3476), France. She is the cofounder of the international and multidisciplinary network HESCALE (History, Economy, Sociology of the Cinemas of Africa and the Middle East). She has recently co-edited the theme issue 'Circulation des films: Afrique du Nord et Moyen-Orient, *Africultures* 101–102 (2016), *Regarder des films en Afriques* (Presses universitaires du Septentrion, 2017), *Pratiques et usages du film en Afriques francophones* (Presses universitaires du Septentrion, 2019), 'Le cinéma européen', *Mise au Point* 13 (2020) and *À l'œuvre au cinéma! Professionnelles en Afrique et au Moyen-Orient* (2022).

Anne Ciecko is an associate professor of international cinema in the Department of Communication at the University of Massachusetts-Amherst, where she directs the interdisciplinary Graduate Film Certificate. Her research, teaching and curatorial activities focus on contemporary emergent, resurgent and underrepresented film industries and cultures. Her work on Arab and Middle Eastern film and media cultures has appeared in *Afterimage: The Journal of Media Arts and Cultural Criticism, Asian Cinema, Continuum: Journal of Media and Cultural Studies, Feminist Media Histories, Wide Screen, The Routledge Companion to World Cinema* and other publications.

Morgan Corriou is an assistant professor in media studies at the University of Paris 8 Vincennes – Saint-Denis, France. Her research focuses on the economic and social history of cinema in colonial Maghreb as well as the correlation of cinephilia and Third World struggles in Africa. She edited the collective volume *Publics et spectacle cinématographique en situation coloniale* (Tunis, IRMC: CERES, 2012).

Anaïs Farine is a film studies scholar living and teaching between Paris and Beirut. She has published in *Ettijahat- Independent Culture, Débordements, The Funambulist Magazine, Africultures* and *Aniki: Portuguese Journal of the Moving Image*, among other journals. Her writing is also included in *Serious Games, Film and Contemporary Art Transform the Essay (Jeux sérieux, Cinéma et art contemporains transforment l'essai*, 2015). As a film curator she has worked with the SILO (a collective exploring the connections between cinema and contemporary art), the Syrian Cine Club in Paris, the University Paris 8 Vincennes – Saint-Denis and the Festival Ciné-Palestine.

Asmaa Gharib is a researcher and cultural worker. Born in Ismailia, Egypt, she graduated from the Faculty of Arts (Mass Communication Department) in 2009 and studied humanities and social sciences for a year-long study programme at the Cairo Institute of Liberal Arts and Sciences (CILAS), Egypt. After years of working on and developing cultural and gender-based activities outside metropolises, Asmaa held the position of Robert Bosch Stiftung and Goethe-Institut cultural manager. Currently, she is the MENA region programme officer at Musawah Global Movement. Her interests include cultural work beyond metropolis, gender, oral history and film studies.

Mohannad Ghawanmeh is a scholar, cineaste, educator and culturist intimately at large. A teacher of communication and media for twenty-five years, Mohannad's instruction has centred on the cinema, for which he has also written, produced, acted, consulted, programmed and curated. He is cofounder of the Twin Cities Arab Film Festival produced by Mizna. Mohannad curated the first editions of the Arab American National Museum's film festival and the Minneapolis/St Paul Italian Film Festival and the series Melnitz Movies at University of California, Los Angeles. Mohannad is well awarded and published, having earned in 2020 his PhD from UCLA in Cinema and Media Studies. His research of the cinema decidedly examines such intersecting fields as governmentality, migration, nativity, religion, theatre, music, literature, industrialization and modernity typically in the mould of cultural history. His dissertation is titled 'Entrepreneurship in a State of Flux: Egypt's Silent Cinema and Its Transition to Synchronized Sound, 1896–1934'.

Jowe Harfouche is the executive director of the Network of Arab Alternative Screens (NAAS), a growing constellation of non-governmental cinema spaces presenting visionary film programmes that engage and challenge audiences across the Arabic-speaking region. He is also a filmmaker.

Ross Melnick is professor of film and media studies at the University of California, Santa Barbara. He is the author of *Hollywood's Embassies: How Movie Theaters Projected American Power around the World* (Columbia University Press, 2022) and *American Showman: Samuel 'Roxy' Rothafel and the Birth of the Entertainment Industry* (Columbia University Press, 2012) and co-editor of *Rediscovering U.S. Newsfilm: Cinema, Television and the Archive* (AFI/Routledge, 2018). He was named an Academy (of Motion Picture Arts and Sciences) Film Scholar and a National Endowment for the Humanities Fellow for his work on Hollywood's expansion into global film exhibition.

Kajsa Philippa Niehusen completed her PhD in film and media studies at the University of California, Santa Barbara. Her work falls at the intersection of film studies, German and German-American studies and history, with a focus on the global distribution of Nazi films in their transnational contexts. Kajsa's dissertation investigated the screening and reception of films produced in Nazi Germany in the United States during the 1930s and 1940s. She holds a master's degree in cultural journalism from the University of the Arts, Berlin, and in film and media studies from UC Santa Barbara.

Nour El Safoury is a cultural worker living in Cairo, Egypt. She has worked as an independent arts and culture editor, an educator, a cinema critic and a public programmes curator. She is editor and co-manager of *Esmat – Publishing List*, a publishing outfit in Cairo dedicated to artist books and alternative texts. Nour is a member of Qaaf. Laam collective, a group of cultural researchers that collects information to develop tools and strategies for more fair and just work conditions in the arts. She holds an MA in film studies from King's College London and a BA from Johns Hopkins University.

Eric Smoodin is a professor of American studies at the University of California, Davis. Most recently, he is the author of *Paris in the Dark: Going to the Movies in the City of Light, 1930-1950* (2020).

Némésis Srour holds a PhD in anthropology from the École des Hautes Études en Sciences Sociales (EHESS) in Paris, France. Her research focuses on the networks of film circulations between India and the Arab-speaking world. She has received the prize for the French-language thesis sponsored by the Agence Universitaire de la Francophonie (AUF) regional office in the Middle East. She teaches film exhibition and distribution at the University of Paris 8 and international relations at ESSCA Business School.

Stefanie Van de Peer is a lecturer in film and media at Queen Margaret University in Edinburgh. Her research specialisms are Arab and African cinema, women's films and film history. She has published articles in *Alphaville, Film Philosophy, Journal for Cultural Research* and others. Some of her books are *Negotiating Dissidence: The Pioneering Women of Arab Documentary* (2017), *Animation in the Middle East* (2017), *Women in African Cinema* (2020) and *ReFocus: The Films of Jocelyne Saab* (2021). She also programmes for film festivals like Africa in Motion (Edinburgh), MONA (Antwerp), REEL Festivals (London) and others.

Acknowledgements

The chapters in this volume constitute a selection of the papers presented at the international conference *Cinema-going in the Arab World: Exhibition, Distribution, and Audiences* held in September 2018 in Cairo, Egypt. The premise of this two-day conference was that although the cinema of the Arab world has been the subject of varied and rigorous study, there is a lack of work on cinema audiences and the economic, social, political and material conditions within which films were produced, distributed and consumed. In this conference we proposed to shift the focus off-screen to examine the history, politics and conditions of distribution, exhibition and cinema-going.

We would like to thank the Netherlands-Flemish Institute in Cairo, especially Anne van Leeuwen, Rudolf de Jong and Tine Lavent, for helping facilitate the organization of the conference, where the seeds of this volume were first planted. In this regard, we are grateful to Luca Brul and Karen Vet for their logistical help. We also express our gratitude to the Research Foundation – Flanders FWO (Belgium) and to the Digital Cinema Studies network for funding some of the workshop participants.

Thanks to all participants of this conference, especially to the authors for their patience and for readily revising and updating their original contributions. We also thank Mélisande Leventopoulos for her constructive comments and suggestions.

Finally, we also want to thank the editors and staff at Bloomsbury Press for their patience, care and work towards bringing this book to fruition.

Note on transliteration

We have followed the *International Journal of Middle East Studies* system of transliteration except for names and words that have common and widely accepted English alternatives (Gamal Abdel Nasser, for example), or in cases where people spell their names a certain way. We have attempted maximum consistency throughout the volume, but accepted alternative spellings where authors deemed them more appropriate.

Introduction

New histories and approaches to cinema in the Arab world

Ifdal Elsaket, Daniel Biltereyst and Philippe Meers

In 1960, the British photographer Marilyn Stafford travelled to Lebanon and collated an intriguing collection of images showcasing everyday life and people.¹ One of her photographs beautifully captures a scene in *Sahat al-Shuhada'* (or Martyr's Square) in downtown Beirut. The photograph features men and women of various ages including a Catholic nun promenading against the dramatic façade of the iconic Rivoli Cinema, which at the time was emblazoned with an advertisement for the 1957 Warner Brothers horror film *The Black Scorpion*. The photograph sits awkwardly in the history of cinema in the Arab world, an aberration to the usual visual cues often associated with cinematic cultures in the region. Yet, the photo raises various questions, takes us in surprising directions and bursts open multiple avenues to examine the vast histories and cultures of film distribution, production and audiences in the country and indeed the entire region. Where did the Rivoli fit in the bustling downtown area that became a central space in Lebanon's tumultuous history? Who were the cinema's audiences? What other films were screened there? What trade networks made possible the screening of *The Black Scorpion*? More contemporarily, what did its demolition in the 1990s (which with three dynamite attempts many read nostalgically as the cinema's last clinging to an old Beirut), and the site's current use as a parking lot, tell us about the fate of cinemas and the destruction of cinematic heritage? How can we apply these questions to cinemas around the Arab world?

Much of the study of cinema in the Arab world tends to neglect these questions and is mostly devoted to the analysis of films, with a heavy focus on modes and issues of representation. It is also bound by rigid geographical parameters. National film production is often prioritized over an exploration of cinematic cultures, where films like *The Black Scorpion* might have circulated, and where questions of audience and context may be raised. Much of the literature probes the motivations of film directors as well as the assumed significance of the film at the time of its release. Many studies are biographies of directors or actors, or encyclopedic compilations of filmmakers and films.[2] In Arabic, celebrity biographies and compilations of anecdotes still dominate the market, as do re-readings of film classics or film adaptations of literature.[3] Coffee table books, collections of film posters and paraphernalia also trend well in the publishing world.[4] No doubt these works have been instrumental in deepening our understanding of filmmaking and indispensable in constructing the broader picture of cinema in the Arab world. But there is a large gap in the scholarship, namely the examination of the history, contexts and logistics of production, distribution, circulation, and especially of audiences.

In this volume we ask: What would happen if cinema scholars of the Arab world (and by this, we mean broadly the Arabic-speaking Middle East and diaspora) looked away from the screen? What would happen if they focused their analytic gaze not on the flickering images, important as they may be, but on the contexts of their production, circulation and exhibition? What if film scholars would argue that films were not that important to people's memories of the cinema as leisure? And that it might be more interesting to focus on people's practices of going to a cinema, on how they chose a particular venue, on how they experienced those places and their ambiance and the movies that were shown there or on the impact of films and cinemas on their imagination and experience of the world? What if scholars gave aspects like distribution, exhibition and programming practices, state policy or business interests more attention? What, in other words, would come out of a shift from investigating films to examining the contexts of their reception, exhibition, distribution or production? One of the assumptions of this volume is that this shift in attention from text to context would contribute to moving film scholarship on cinema in the Arab world from the end product, the film itself, to the many other meanings of cinema—cinema as a place, a space, an experience, a social, cultural and commercial institution.

The study of cinema as a larger societal phenomenon corresponds with some recent (and much older) trends coming out of Arabic and Middle East studies, global cinema studies, especially in the fields of historical sociology and economics, and also new approaches that deal with cinema's past, one of which is known as new cinema history (hereafter NCH).[5]

New cinema history approaches

Inspired by the works of a previous generation of film historians as well as audience studies scholars, new cinema historians call for historical research that takes into account contextual specificities of cinema as a broad sociocultural phenomenon and for taking into account issues of the industry which produced, distributed, promoted and exhibited movies.[6] New cinema historians agree that a purely textual approach too often slides into abstract conjectures about spectator responses or broader claims about a film's allegorical or ideological message.

In asking questions about context, NCH tackles such topics as an audience's cinema-going memories, their engagement with films and their relationship to film venues, not merely as the place where films are shown but as social spaces embedded within local communities and neighbourhoods. The approach also tackles key elements of the industry and its attempts to attract audiences.[7] Besides taking into account broader dimensions of what 'cinema' is, NCH entails the use of other methodologies and other sources than those typically central to film studies. It eschews detached textual analysis of films and promotes the use of archives, trade magazines, newspapers and oral histories. It brings, to quote Richard Maltby, 'uninvited guests into the cloistered halls of an academic culture centred around the close examination of individual filmic texts'.[8]

This volume brings together scholars who are inspired by NCH's broad aims, concepts and methodologies, and it builds on the solid work already taking place in the Arab world to explore historical and current issues of production, distribution, exhibition and reception. Together the contributors to this edited collection offer a unique perspective on cinema's history in the Arab world and contribute to the global conversation about the place and function of the cinema as an interconnected, transnational and multilingual social, cultural and political phenomenon. The chapters in this volume are not only conventional academic work but also include interviews with cinema practitioners, giving readers a rare insight into the bustle of activity that occurs in the background of the cinema industry. Together the chapters are important because they reveal details about specific cinematic cultures. They are also important because they raise broader questions about methods and approaches, and contribute to the wider field of cinema studies and history.

One goal of this volume is to showcase the possibilities that emerge when scholars use sources and methods beyond film analysis. The authors in this volume use memoirs, oral histories and testimonies of cinemagoers (e.g.

chapter by Ifdal Elsaket). They explore magazines (e.g. Mohannad Ghawanmeh's chapter), trade journals and interviews with distributors and exhibitors to examine movies' flow or circulation (e.g. Asmaa Gharib's interview with cinema owners in Ismailia, Stefanie Van de Peer's chapter on Arab film distributors networks, or Némésis Srour on the trade and circulation of Indian films in the Arab world). They also use colonial sources and government reports, and expose the power dynamics at play in local cinema cultures and economies (e.g. Morgan Corriou's and Eric Smoodin's chapters). By using these sources, the authors present analyses more attuned to the practicalities of industry and economics, as well as the importance of audiences and raise questions relevant to a wide array of disciplines by shedding light on aspects such as colonial policy, leisure, business, gender and nationalism.

The use of sources from the region is related to another equally important goal of this volume: to widen the Eurocentric frames around which NCH often functions and inject the field with much-needed views and perspectives from the Arab world. Recently the field has benefited from studies on territories and regions beyond Europe and the anglophone world, with studies on Latin America, Asia and sub-Saharan Africa.[9] But apart from the specific case studies on cinema's past practices and strategies that go beyond European, North American or Australian contexts, there is greater work to be done on questioning epistemologies, concepts, methods and analyses that have dominated the field. The use of Arabic-language sources, interviews with film industry practitioners and the use of memory play a role in shedding new light on cinema cultures and on the social dynamics of cinema. While many of the authors in this volume use non-Arabic-language sources and colonial archives, they do so with deep recognition of their limitations and their epistemic origins.

A crucial aspect in this endeavour, therefore, is to unsettle the Euro-American domination of the NCH field and critically re-examine assumptions on centre-periphery in the power structures related to the production, flow, trade, exhibition and reception of films. Various contributions to this volume deal with issues related to colonialism (e.g. Morgan Corriou on Egyptian films in colonial Maghreb and the French anxieties over Arabic films). They show how colonial powers and structures of control (censorship, access to distribution and production) shaped cinema programming and distribution. A key argument here is to offer other perspectives than those only looking at how the 'West' tried to use movies and cinema in order to control or (politically, ideologically, commercially) exploit Arab societies (e.g. Rahma Bavelaar, or Kajsa Philippa Niehusen and Ross Melnick on the 1933–45 era). The collection showcases how communities carved out spaces for cinema-going, consumed films from all over the world, and built robust cinema infrastructures and facilities – including theatres and fan magazines, all of which spoke to film trends and exhibition practices that traversed national boundaries. They show how cinema-theatre owners negotiated their identities in a changing world and were plugged into a vast cinema network beyond their national borders.

The volume also contains chapters revising dependencies, precisely by offering more complex analyses on issues like contraflow or reverse trade circuits, and by showing the realities of cinema as a transnational phenomenon (e.g. Eric Smoodin's case study on one film distributor in the interwar and the Second World War period who became an important figure in the French, European and Arab film industry). Some contributors deal with crucial issues such as the vibrant distribution in the region, as well as entangled transnational histories of film traffic in and out of the Arab world (e.g. Srour or Niehusen and Melnick). What we get from these chapters is a far more dynamic picture of the relationship between cinema and colonialism, one of unequal power relations no doubt but also one of more complicated global film circuits, negotiations between middlemen and the incredibly diverse programming practices across the region.

Despite the 'Arab world' title of this volume, the following chapters actually point, therefore, to a geographical porosity of cinema circulations and unsettle the frame of 'national cinema'.[10] The national frame, which prioritizes the study of films made by nationals within a defined geographic space, is inadequate for understanding the sprawling global networks and influences that shaped cinematic cultures in the Arab world. Authors show how the distribution of films crossed national and linguistic boundaries. Srour's chapter, for example, follows pirated films from the Bombay markets to Gulf states vis-a-vis Iran and Beirut. Niehusen and Melnick show how Nazi foreign policy related to film circulation in non-Arabic-speaking countries of the region, Turkey in their case, can be read against the grain to decipher broader implications for the distribution of films in the Arabic-speaking world. The evidence they uncover in the German archives, for example, shows how Syrian exhibitors attempted to source films from Turkey as early as the 1930s. While we know little of their success or motives, it presents us with a piece of a puzzle and a step closer to clarifying distribution patterns across the region, and across linguistic lines during the interwar period. Widening the geographical map beyond the Arab world can reveal the robust global South-South distribution and economic lines of film commerce.[11]

Off-screen

As previously mentioned, while off-screen analyses may be less dominant, they are of course not missing. Since widespread academic interest in Arab cinema developed in the English-speaking academy, there has been a tendency, however, to place social and cultural histories of cinema, which rely on archives and primary sources, in the same intellectual field as film studies which rely on films-as-texts.[12] We argue that, while certainly intersecting, these two approaches ask very different questions and deal with very different material. While film studies is interested in the artistry of the film, leaning on art history and philosophy as theoretical frames, cinema history is interested in the social and cultural conditions of the cinema, relying on sociology, history, anthropology, economics and other similar disciplines. Disentangling one approach from the other does not mean that scholars cannot integrate both into their studies (indeed some of the chapters in this volume do precisely that). But we argue that by making the distinction clear, we might be better able to raise new questions about cinema's role in the Arab world and its connection to broader historical and social processes.

For the most part, the scholarship on off-screen dynamics of cinema in the Arab world owes much of its work to political economists and media anthropologists. Walter Armbrust's ground-breaking scholarship has, since the late 1990s, introduced students and researchers to an interdisciplinary mode of writing and research on Egyptian cinema. His work relied heavily on historical artefacts, such as magazines and included interviews.[13] When it comes to publications on popular culture in the Arab world, none have matched Armbrust's edited volume, *Mass Mediations: New Approaches to Popular Culture in the Middle East and Beyond*.[14] The volume's interdisciplinary rigour and directional push towards expanding the methods and sources used to investigate popular culture features a number of chapters on cinema as a social and cultural phenomenon.

Given its dominance in the field of anthropology, the recent upsurge of scholarship on cinema is dominated by anthropological and ethnographic approaches. A notable example is Chihab El Khachab's *Making Film in Egypt*, which takes us behind the scenes to demystify the vast commercial, business, labour and artistic processes that bring a film to fruition.[15] Mariz Kelada's work exposes the labour conditions of the Egyptian film industry, zooming into the unseen workers whose toil is crucial to the production of film.[16] Viviane Saglier's research on cinema infrastructure in Gaza, likewise, broadens the analytic lens by exploring the tensions of cinematic leisure and business in contexts of Israeli oppression and the continued bombardment of Palestinians in Gaza.[17] Terri Ginsberg and Chris Lippard's edited volume *Cinema of the Arab World* also features chapters that analysed the 'larger social enabling conditions' of filmmaking.[18] Kevin Dyer's work on the Moroccan director Muhammad Abderrahman Tazi, which includes a set of interviews, explores key developments in industry and questions of audiences.[19] Outside academic work, the Network of Arab Alternative Screens (NAAS) has also been committed to producing research on aspects of exhibition and audiences. Their recent publication *Mapping Cinema Audiences*, edited by one of the authors in this volume, Nour El Safoury, examined the cinema-going habits of young people across Egypt and the relationship between cinema exhibitors and their audiences.[20]

Historical approaches that rely on archival materials and oral histories are still, however, the most neglected. But while historians in the past ten years have shied away from cinema, this was not always so. In the 1990s and 2000s a group of scholars (including Farida Marʿi,[21] Ahmad al-Hadari,[22] Samir Farid,[23] Andrew Flibbert,[24] Walter Armbrust,[25] Robert Vitalis,[26] Elizabeth Thompson,[27] Manar Hasan and Amy Ayalon[28]) wrote about cinema as a historical phenomenon, diving into the early cinema press and archival materials.[29] Through detailed historical fieldwork, economic analysis and oral histories, they contributed to our understanding of early cinematic cultures across the Arab world. While contributing to the study of history, leisure and industry, a historical trend using similar approaches, however, failed to materialize.

It is not difficult to understand why cinema has been neglected by historians. In 1999, Edward Said, in the context of his paean to the Egyptian dancer and movie-star Tahia Carioca, bemoaned the state of historical documentation of movie stars and the film industry.

> What I have is a sense of a sprawling, teeming history off the page, out of sight and hearing, beyond reach, largely unrecoverable. Our history is mostly written by foreigners – visiting scholars, intelligence agents – while we rely on personal and disorganized collective memory, gossip almost, and the embrace of a family or knowable community to carry us forward in time.[30]

More than two decades since, Said's musings are no less true. Official film archives are non-existent and state archives impenetrable. Cinema paraphernalia and documents circulate in paper markets, often tattered or exorbitantly expensive and are disappearing at a frightening speed.[31] As Ghenwa Hayek points out, the lack of basic infrastructures and investment, not to mention conflict, hampers the efforts of those interested to preserve cinema histories.³² Yet as Hayek also argues, scholars, collectors, preservationists and filmmakers, instead of bemoaning the lack of traditional archives, have found creative and unique ways of piercing together histories of the cinema in the Arab world, inviting us into what she calls 'a methodology of working through the absent archive'.³³ In a recent edition of the journal *Regard*, Hayek brought together a group of scholars to explore the issues of archive making, memory and transnational histories of cinema.³⁴

Digitization projects of key magazines and newspapers, and a shift in the methodologies used – including oral histories (perhaps an attempt to organize the collective memory and gossip that Said referred to) and inventive uses of colonial archives – have facilitated historical research on cinema in recent years. Inspired by new cinema history, Ifdal Elsaket has used archival material, trade and government reports and magazines to trace a history of the cinema in Egypt from 1896, with an examination of cinema-going and broader debates about the role of the cinema.³⁵ Mohannad Ghawanmeh has also explored the silent film era in Egypt using similar sources.³⁶ Recently, Pelle Valentin Olsen has written on histories of cinema-going in Iraq by using material such as magazines, trade reports and literature.³⁷ Olsen reveals transnational lines of distribution and examines the intricacies of exhibition and cinema-going practices in Baghdad. In her work, Hayek emphasizes the importance of 'parafilmic' archives – articles, posters, advertisements – to examine the cultural mood of Lebanon in the 1950s and 1960s. Samhita Sunya has opened up a vast archive of media sources to unravel multilayered South-South distribution circuits and film production processes, especially pertaining to Indian films in the Arab world.³⁸

Also notable are the works of Deborah Starr, on the Jewish director Togo Mizrahi,³⁹ and Hanan Hammad, on Jewish-Egyptian cinema starlet Layla Murad.⁴⁰ Their work goes a long way to rectify the gap in cinema history by using personal papers and the press. Tamara Chahine Maatouk's work on state nationalization of the cinema also provides much-needed economic and structural understanding of the cinema industry in the late 1950s and 1960s.⁴¹ Kay Dickinson's work has also been instrumental to uncover ideological and historical contexts broadly.⁴² Ziad Fahmy, in his work on sound, briefly explores the impact of electrification on the cinema practices of Egyptians in the newly lit cities, opening up issues of infrastructure and urbanization.⁴³ Arthur Asseraf also discusses the role and impact of cinema within a larger discussion of the circulation of news in colonial Algeria.⁴⁴ Through the use of early magazine sources, Raphael Cormack explores the life and work of early cinema pioneer

Aziza Amir and positions cinema within a wider history of celebrity, dance halls and leisure.[45] Nolwenn Mingant's recent work on Hollywood films in the Middle East also significantly contributes to our understanding of the distribution and the role of middlemen in film programming across the region.[46]

The special 2020 fall volume of the journal *Film History: South by South/West Asia* also represents an impactful contribution to the new trend in historical research on cinema. Using colonial archives, material from the Indian film archives and artefacts from various collections, the volume not only engages with important historical questions of exhibition and programming but it also breaks apart the geographic encampment of studies of cinema to explore transregional histories of the Middle East and East Asia, South by South film distribution and production lines, and links between film culture and petromodernity.[47] One scholar whose work features in the special issue, Firat Oruc, has also been pioneering in his examination of 'petrocolonial circulations', and cinema cultures in the Gulf by using colonial and American oil company archives.[48] His work is an intersection between discussions on colonial archives and cinema studies in a new way that speaks to many of the chapters featured here. While colonial archives are rarely a topic of discussion for cinema historians, they actually hold abundant possibilities and stories, which when treated with a sensitivity to their epistemic coloniality, can reveal certain insights into the role of cinema in the colonial period.[49]

The works of these historians have demonstrated the incredibly generative analysis that can emerge when placed in the hands of scholars attuned to the tools of historical research and sensitive to the off-screen politics and history of cinema. Part I of this volume leans into this approach and contributes to our understanding of the histories of cinema in the region, and the economies and cultures of leisure of which it has been a part since the last nineteenth century.

Changing cinema landscapes

As the chapters in Part II of the volume demonstrate, a sensitivity to context, social structures and historical memory can also generate unique perspectives on the role and function of cinema in the Arab world today. Recent opportunities and challenges have changed the exhibition, production and distribution landscape in the region. New initiatives, such as the NAAS (as the dialogue between Nour El Safoury and Jowe Harfouche shows), or Comra Films (which produces films and conducts trainee workshops for Yemeni filmmakers), for example, have worked to cultivate new film cultures and broaden exhibition.[50]

Distributors (as Van de Peer explains) have also played a key role in determining the accessibility of Arab films globally and shaped the film landscape in Arab countries themselves. While cinema theatres have decreased substantially over the years, in places like Tunisia, as Patricia Caillé explores, there are signs of a revival thanks to the emergence of new film cultures and new cultural policies.

Cinema-going may never return to its heyday of the 1950s and the 1960s, but online platforms have contributed to the development of new cinema publics. Online platforms such as Aflamuna (as discussed by Anaïs Farine in her interview with Jad Abi Khalil) have shifted exhibition practices and the way audiences access films. But the very logistics of making this happen is embedded in very complex political and economic environments that cannot be ignored. As Farine and Abi Khalil detail, digital exhibition practices necessarily entail the study of digital infrastructure (access to good internet or lack thereof, and the ability to conduct bank transfers to pay filmmakers), especially in places like Lebanon.

Unlike other majority Arabic-speaking countries, the wealthy Gulf states, especially the United Arab Emirates (UAE) and recently Saudi Arabia, have carved out a large and profitable cinema market, as attested to by Némésis Srour's discussion of Hindi films in the UAE and Anne Ciecko's discussion of Saudi Arabia. As Ciecko's chapter explores, Saudi Arabia has also accelerated its investment in cinema exhibition spaces and the deployment of cinema for global public relations campaigns. The Saudi Arabian General Entertainment Authority, which oversees the expansion of cinema in the country, is directly linked to the broader Saudi Vision 2030 project with an aim to diversify and restructure the country's economy.

International film producers see Saudi Arabia as a profitable market, with Saudi's investment ministry having announced an ambitious goal to have 2,600 screens by 2030.[51] It currently has only 430 screens. International films and studios are keeping a watchful eye as the Gulf cinema market grows. The growth of cinema-going and investment in cinema in the UAE and Saudi Arabia will open up a new vista of study – not only of state deployment of cinema and stars for propaganda, and a broader reckoning with neoliberal policies, corporate film interests and authoritarian state power but of the everyday cinema-going experiences of people living in those countries.

New Arab cinema studies

As the foregoing sketch of recent work on cinema attests, the analytic focus of our volume is, therefore, not so new. But the literature remains disparate and disconnected in a way that diminishes an impactful intervention into the field. The trend to focus 'off-screen' has yet to be intentionally coalesced into an academic direction. As mentioned before, studies of cinema as a social phenomenon are often bundled together with other more traditional film studies perspectives, diminishing their methodological significance. This volume is a call for these disparate projects to engage with each other and to resist the oft-repeated attempts to group them together intellectually with the analysis of films-as-texts. We think a more defined parameter around cinema as 'not just films' would allow scholars to reinstate cinema to its rightful place in the broader study of society, of relations of power and of leisure.

This collection, therefore, not only showcases new scholarship on cinema in the Arab world. It is a call to take historical and contextual approaches to the cinema more seriously. By bringing these works together we hope they help elaborate the parameters of what we might tentatively call 'New Arab Cinema Studies' or 'New Arab Cinema History'. We think that joining these studies under a common conceptual frame may encourage and stimulate a much-needed discussion about new approaches to the study of the cinema and further crystallize the methodological parameters in which these studies operate.

We hope this volume, therefore, is the start of a conversation, whereby each chapter offers new dimensions and/or new perspectives on cinema in the Arab world, reflecting the dynamic diversity typical of NCH approaches. Studies can be either very aligned – a single film, a venue, a professional – or very broad – covering an entire (trans-)national industry; they can be limited in a time frame – a few years in the past or present, or ambitiously overarching – spanning decades. Some are very local, quite regional or national, others transnational and even surpassing the Arab world; the analysis can be on one specific sector of the industry – distribution, exhibition – or taking a transversal view; exploring mainstream commercial cinema or digging into the niche, cultural, arthouse sphere. The focus might be on professionals from the trade, or the flip side of the coin – regular audiences. Finally, studies could expose the political and religious ideologies in their – often hidden or sometimes blatantly overt – attempts at disciplining a medium and its audiences.

In the opening chapter of the historical Part I, Morgan Corriou presents a comprehensive study of the circulation of Egyptian cinema in colonial Maghreb by considering not only the political but also the social and economic dimensions of film trade. Distributors played a central role here, developing expertise for films commonly scorned by French and Maghrebi elites. Egyptian cinema replaced the main enemy of French cinema, Hollywood, and caused a colonial reaction of moral panic and subsequent heavy censorship.

French colonialism is equally present in Eric Smoodin's chapter on Algerian entrepreneur Joseph Seibarras who largely controlled North African film exhibition during the 1920s and 1930s. In the popular, francophone North African press, Smoodin argues, Seibarras's new cinemas signified the possibilities for aesthetic independence from French control and shed light on the racial and ethnic demarcations in Algiers. The chapter shows how Seibarras was a businessman who developed an exhibition empire that made him the 'King of Cinema' in North Africa, while dependent on the structures demanded by colonialism.

Widening the geographical scope towards Middle Eastern, North African and Turkish cinema, Kajsa Philippa Niehusen and Ross Melnick focus on the battle for ideological supremacy between Allied and Axis powers before and during the Second World War. Both powers utilized movies and movie theatres as part of their larger propaganda campaigns in the region. The chapter reveals how Nazi propagandists grouped Turkey with other Middle East countries and developed a region-wide policy. By exploring sources in the German archive, Niehusen and Melnick make a compelling argument for using the Turkish case as a useful launch pad to explore wider Nazi cinema activity in the region.

Taking us to Egypt, Mohannad Ghawanmeh examines the relationship between Egypt's theatre and cinema in the early industrial era (1896–1935). Drawing on the early Egyptian film press and memoirs, he spotlights the rise of female audiences and contributes to our understanding of gender and semi-public leisure in the early twentieth century. He makes original connections between Egyptian women's early cinema-going experiences and their gradual empowerment as audiences and in society. The Ramsis Theatre, led by Yusuf Wahbi, played an important role in this process, as it helped legitimate and promote not only domestic narrative film production but equally women's patronage of the cinema.

Focusing on one film and its surrounding discourses in Egypt, Rahma Bavelaar traces the conflicting audience and official responses to Husayn Sidqi's film *Laylat al-Qadr* (1952), the first feature to treat Muslim-Christian marriage and Christian conversion to Islam. Drawing on the rich archive of the Catholic Film Center in Cairo and contemporary and historical media coverage, she examines censorship practices and public debate around interfaith marriage, love and questions of religious difference. She shows how the debate around *Laylat al-Qadr* became a key site for the postcolonial negotiation of censorship, representations of Christians and anti-colonial masculinities.

In the following chapter, Némésis Srour reconstructs how routes for Bollywood/Hindi films in the Arab world took shape. From the early 1950s, popular Hindi films attracted a wide audience in the Middle East, first on Egyptian and Lebanese screens, then in the Gulf. Srour contextualizes the presence of Hindi films on Arab screens carefully documenting their circulation, interviewing industry insiders, and adding to 'a global history of South-South cinematographic circuits'.

Not only have histories of exhibition been neglected in Egyptian cinema history, but so too the histories of cinema in smaller cities – or those outside the main metropoles. Asmaa Gharib fills part of this gap with a picture of the business of cinemas in the Egyptian city of Ismailia. She interviews Abbas Ghweba and Tareq Ghweba, prominent members of a long-standing exhibitor family. The interviews are unique historical documents and illuminate the relationship between the city and cinemas, and the changes in audience composition. Gharib's piece is particularly important because it sheds light on aspects of the cinema as a business enterprise that we rarely read about. As the interviews show, class and racial segregation played a key role in determining audience makeup as well as business decisions, and shaped experiences of the cinema in the city.

Part I ends with a spotlight on historical audiences, one of the crucial foci of the NCH approach. Ifdal Elsaket reports on cinema-going in Egypt in the 1960s, based on oral history interviews on Cairo and Alexandria. The 'long-1960s' represented the last era of widespread movie-going culture in Egypt. Respondents' memories cast cinemas as transient local playgrounds, at once family spaces and emancipatory adolescent ones. Elsaket shows how cinemas were sociocultural spaces, committed to entertainment and pleasure, in which Egyptians of all classes could find time to socialize, relax and play.

Part II of the volume is more contemporary in its time frame, with a range of studies on the recent cinema landscape in the Arab world, including new platforms and alternative screening spaces. It also connects historical cinema cultures to the present via mediatized collective nostalgia.

Film distribution and exhibition in Tunisia since 2011 is explored by Patricia Caillé. Based on extensive fieldwork and interviews with cinema professionals, she examines how the competition between different conceptions of film exhibition, a changing cultural policy, the institutional visibility of film and the quality of the equipment have led to a revival of cinema-going. As Caillé shows, by 2019, a wide array of cinemas and other venues, ranging from mainstream commercial multiplexes to cultural houses increasingly screened Tunisian films.

Stefanie Van de Peer reconsiders the role of film distribution networks for Arab cinema. In the Middle East, distribution and exhibition are no longer dominated by foreign knowledge. The arrival of Arab regionally based, transnationally oriented distribution companies such as MAD Solutions has turned around the global visibility of Arab cinema. Distributors act as curators, catering to the interests of transnational consumers. At the same time, they facilitate the process for exhibitors worldwide to access the growing catalogues of Arab cinema.

To feel the pulse of very recent media developments, Anaïs Farine talks to Jad Abi Khalil, chairman of Beirut DC. This Lebanon-based organization dedicated to the production and exhibition of films from the Arab world launched the free-of-charge streaming platform Aflamuna // أفلامنا in March 2020. The strategy to diversify its audience and enlarge the life cycle of its films illustrates a rethinking of distribution systems for alternative Arab films and makes clear that any discussion of online cinema exhibition cannot be removed from the political and infrastructural milieu in which it is a part.

It is quite exceptional to witness the reintroduction of cinema in a contemporary media landscape, as is the case in the Kingdom of Saudi Arabia. Anne Ciecko discusses how after the ban on a public exhibition of film, a period of 'transitional public film culture' was installed, from the mid-2000s onwards. Through a critical analysis of English-language media sources, she shows how, in the absence of the officially approved public exhibition of film, the discourse of what cinema is and could be in Saudi Arabia was expanded.

Nour El Safoury and Jowe Harfouche engage in a dialogue on the multi-functional cinema exhibition space at the turn of the century. Harfouche is executive director of NAAS (the Network of Arab Alternative Screens), a regional network for Arab film exhibitors. Within a pan-Arab film market, this coalition among very diverse exhibitors aims to circulate films that are different from the mainstream and to share resources and skills. NAAS aims at reconfiguring the cinema exhibition space, building an alternative Arab film culture.

The last chapter of this volume connects the past of Egyptian cinema to its nostalgic celebration in the televised present. Under the heading of the 'visual nation', Iskandar Abdalla reflects on film as a part of Egypt's soft power, conceptualizing the nation as a community of spectators. The focus is on the TV show *Sahibet al-Sa'ada* where many iconic Egyptian films are honoured. The images and stories offer a platform to comment on political and social events, but foremost, to re-tell the history of the nation.

Challenges and opportunities

Seven of the fourteen chapters featured in this volume focus exclusively or in large part on Egypt. No doubt, Egypt continues to be the centre of filmmaking in the Arab world, with a long history that makes it a natural site of scholarship. But the collection attests that, by shifting methodological gears, by expanding the definitions of cinema studies and by pointing to the historical, the archive and the ethnographical, it can inspire scholarship to emerge from other parts of the region. Not having a robust film industry does not mean that cinema culture did not exist. Lebanon could never compete with Egypt in terms of production, but certainly competed in terms of spectatorship per capita. We hope to show that a study of cinema does not simply rely on film output, but on distribution, circulation and exhibition, on audience experiences, on broader cinema cultures and the economics of cinema business.

To begin with, non-academic works, media clippings, photo essays, memoirs and films have already engaged with questions about the off-screen dynamics of cinema. Arabic news and feature articles litter the internet about cinema cultures and movie theatres. Articles about cinema-going practices in Baghdad[52] and lamentations of lost cinema spaces in Yemen,[53] all highlight neglected topics. Memoirs also can yield results. Margo Kirtikar, who grew up in Baghdad in the 1940s, remembers that cinemas 'played an important role in our family's social life as it did for many Baghdadis'.[54] Suhaib Gasmelbari's 2020 film *Talking about Trees* also engaged with the themes of audiences, exhibitions and the material conditions of cinematic cultures, telling the story of a group of Sudanese filmmakers who attempt, in the midst of dictatorship and conflict, to organize free film screenings in an abandoned cinema.[55] The director's gaze mediates on abandoned open-air cinemas, conjuring histories of bustling cinematic cultures that no longer exist.

Different oral history projects can also reveal cinema-going practices. Dotted through the Palestinian Oral History Archive are references to leisure time at the cinemas.[56] The project *Parallax Haifa*, by Lama Suleiman, also beautifully points to the possibilities of further research of cinema and leisure in the Palestinian city of Haifa.[57] Similarly, the Metropolis Project in Lebanon features interviews with filmmakers that can be used as a launch pad to investigate the cinema-going practices in Lebanon.[58] In its only interview to date, Mounir Maasri, the Lebanese director, speaks of his childhood, sneaking into movie theatres and watching American cowboy films, and sheds light on the Beiruti cinema scene in the 1950s and 1960s. What is clear is that much work is needed on the topic, and an incredibly rich cinema culture across the Arabic-speaking world, past and present, is only beginning to come into view.

But clues and stories also poke out at us from archives and collections that cinema historians would typically not dive into. On histories of the cinema in Palestine, for example the Palestinian Museum Digital Archive has abundant primary source material on cinema and cinema exhibition practices, including rare items such as cinema-theatre tax receipts, film permits and diary entries.[59] Using Israeli place names can yield results in non-Arabic-language collections. The Library of Congress holds one photograph, for example, of a cinema in the city of Jaffa showing the front façade of the cinema, with a promotional display of an Egyptian film.[60] For cinema historians, it raises many questions: Who were the patrons of this cinema theatre? How can we characterize the distribution lines? And what place did Egyptian celebrities hold in the imaginations and lives of Palestinians?

Another collection, 'The First Hebrew City: Early Tel Aviv through the Eyes of the Eliasaf Robinson' at Stanford libraries, holds artefacts that illuminate cinematic cultures in pre-1948 Palestine. Its multilingual cinema advertisements – in Arabic, English or French – suggest diverse cinema audiences in Tel Aviv.[61] Cinema advertisements in newly digitized Arabic newspapers at the National Library of Israel also reveal programming histories that include an array of films from across the globe. One can find advertisements of Egyptian films playing at Zion Hall Cinema in the 1930s, and Arabic and English advertisements promoting a Douglas Fairbanks film at the open-air Eden Cinema in Jerusalem.[62]

Using Israeli sources to recover the history of pre-1948 Palestine is perhaps an act of subverting the erasure of Palestinians from the historic record. Seeing the Arabic language scrolled across 1930s cinema advertisements in Tel Aviv powerfully asserts the presence of Palestinians. There is an inherent coloniality of these archives and collections that we cannot ignore. The historic Palestinian magazines digitized by the National Library of Israel, while a useful resource for historians, expose the colonial logic of collecting and archiving indigenous material. How do we use the collection with the knowledge that much of its material may have been used and embroiled in the surveillance and monitoring of Arab communities in the past; that much of it is now in the hands of a state that denies Palestinians their basic rights? These questions are important for cinema historians to consider because not only are sources we might use embroiled in settler colonialism and surveillance, but they point to broader structures of power that reconfigured aspects of everyday life in which the cinema functioned.

Conclusion

In short, this volume is an invitation to look away from the screen and to consider alternative ways of studying cinema in the Arab world. It is a call to consider seriously contexts in which cinema cultures flourished and represents one step in a potentially much longer journey in which historical and contextual detail lay at the core of scholarly analysis of cinema. We hope that the chapters in this volume encourage more scholars to excavate the histories and contexts of cinema all over the region. We also hope the specifics of production, distribution, and exhibition in the Arab world outlined in the following pages can expose the transnational and global flows of cinematic cultures and cement the region as an important focus of study for cinema historians and other cinema studies scholars. We are convinced that more study of Arabic sources will reveal dynamics that have been hitherto underexplored by scholars of global film distribution and production. Filling in the gap of new cinema histories in the Arab world, the volume adds important pieces to the endless jigsaw puzzle of (trans-)national, regional and global cinema cultures. Each chapter in this volume presents readers with a unique perspective on cinema in the Arab world, past and present, and shows the incredibly rich histories and cultures that flourished.

Notes

1 Marilyn Stafford, *Silent Stories: A Photographic Journey through Lebanon in the Sixties* (London: Saqi Books, 1998).

2 See for example Viola Shafik, *Arab Cinema: History and Cultural Identity* (Cairo: The American University in Cairo Press, 2007); Roy Armes, *New Voices in Arab Cinema* (Bloomington, IN: Indiana University Press, 2015); Roy Armes, *Roots of the New Arab Film* (Bloomington, IN: Indiana University Press, 2018); Gönül Dönmez-Colin (ed.), *The Cinema of North Africa and the Middle East* (London: Wallflower Press, 2007); Malek Khouri, *Arab National Project in Youssef Chahine's Cinema* (Cairo: American University in Cairo Press, 2010); Peter Limbrick, *Arab Modernism as World Cinema: The Films of Moumen Smihi* (Berkeley, CA: University of California Press, 2020); Terri Ginsberg and Chris Lippard (eds), *Historical Dictionary of Middle Eastern Cinema* (Lanham, MD: The Rowman & Littlefield Publishing Group, 2010); Robert Lang, *New Tunisian Cinema* (New York: Columbia University Press, 2014).

3 For the most recent work, see Salma Mubarak and Walid al-Khachab, *al-Iqtibas: Min al-Adab ila al-Sinima* (Cairo: Dar al-Maraya: 2021); Samih Fathi, *Ihsan ʿAbd al-Qaddus Bayna al-Adab wal-Sinima* (Cairo: Self-published, 2018); Mahmud ʿAbd al-Shukur, *Sinima Misr: Ziyara Jadida li Aflam Qadima* (Cairo: Tanmia, 2021).

4 For example, Samih Fathi, *Classic Egyptian Movies: 101 Must-See Films*, trans. Sarah Enany (Cairo: The American University in Cairo Press, 2018); Samih Fathi, *The Art of Egyptian Film Posters*, trans. Siham ʿAbd al-Salam (Cairo: The American University in Cairo Press, 2014); Rasha Azab and Sherif Boraie, *Dream Factory on the Nile. Pierre Sioufi Collection of Egyptian Cinema Lobby Cards* (New York: American University in Cairo Press, 2020); Abudi Abu Jawda, *Hadha Al-Masaʾ, Al-Sinima Fi Lubnan, 1929–1979* (Beirut: al-Furat lil-Nashr wal-Tawziʿ 2015).

5 For theories, concepts and case studies on New Cinema History, see Richard Maltby, Daniel Biltereyst and Philippe Meers (eds), *Explorations in New Cinema History: Approaches and Case Studies* (Malden, MA: Wiley-Blackwell, 2011); Daniel Biltereyst, Richard Maltby and Philippe Meers (eds), *Cinema, Audiences and Modernity: New Perspectives on European Cinema History* (London: Routledge, 2012); Daniela Treveri Gennari, Danielle Hipkins and Catherine O'Rawe (eds), *Cinema Outside the City: Rural Cinema-Going from a Global Perspective* (New York: Palgrave, 2018); Daniel Biltereyst, Richard Maltby and Philippe Meers (eds), *The Routledge Companion to New Cinema History* (London; New York: Routledge, 2019).

6 In English-language scholarship, and especially from the 1970s, there was an increase in the number of social and economic histories of cinema and cinema audiences. A very brief list of examples include Robert Sklar, *Movie-Made America: A Social History of American Movies*, 1st edn (New York: Random House, 1975); Robert Sklar, "'Oh! Althusser!': Historiography and the Rise of Cinema Studies", *Radical History Review* 41 (1988): 10–35; Garth Jowett, *Film: The Democratic Art*, 1st edn, American Film Institute Series (Boston, MA: Little, Brown, 1976); Robert C. Allen, 'Economic and Technological History: Motion Picture Exhibition in Manhattan: Beyond the Nickelodeon', *Cinema Journal* 18, no. 2 (1979): 2–15; Tino Balio, *Grand Design: Hollywood as a Modern Business Enterprise, 1930–1939* (New York; Toronto: Scribner; Maxwell Macmillan Canada; Maxwell Macmillan International, 1993); Miriam Hansen, *Babel and Babylon: Spectatorship in American Silent Film*, Acls Humanities E-Book (Cambridge, MA: Harvard University Press, 1991). These studies of course did not emerge in a vacuum, but were part of a wider reassessment of popular culture. See as a case in point Stuart Hall, 'Notes on Deconstructing "the Popular" [1981]', in *Essential Essays*, vol. 1, ed. David Morley (New York: Duke University Press, 2020), 347–61.

7 See for a special issue dealing with historical cinema audiences, Annette Kuhn, Daniel Biltereyst and Philippe Meers (eds), 'Memories of Cinema-Going and Film Experience', *Memory Studies* 10, no. 1 (2017): 1–104.

8   Richard Maltby, 'How Can Cinema History Matter More?', *Screening the Past* 22 (2007), http://www.screeningthepast.com/issue-22-tenth-anniversary/how-can-cinema-history-matter-more/ (accessed 27 February 2022).
9   See for example Añulika Agina, 'Cinema-Going in Lagos: Three Locations, One Film, One Weekend', *Journal of African Cultural Studies* 32, no. 2 (2020): 131–45; Laura Fair, *Reel Pleasures: Cinema Audiences and Entrepreneurs in Twentieth-Century Urban Tanzania*, New African Histories Series (Athens, OH: Ohio University Press, 2018); Laura Fair, '"They Stole the Show!": Indian Films in Coastal Tanzania, 1950s–1980s', *Journal of African Media Studies* 2, no. 1 (2010): 91–106; Megan Feeney, *Hollywood in Havana: US Cinema and Revolutionary Nationalism in Cuba before 1959* (Chicago: The University of Chicago Press, 2019); Dafna Ruppin, 'The Emergence of a Modern Audience for Cinema in Colonial Java', *Bijdragen Tot de Taal-, Land- En Volkenkunde* 173, no. 4 (2017): 475–502; Brigitte Reinwald, '"Tonight at the Empire": Cinema and Urbanity in Zanzibar, 1920s to 1960s', *Afrique & Histoire* 5, no. 1 (2006): 81–109; Gareth McFeely, '"Gone Are the Days": A Social and Business History of Cinema-Going in Gold Coast/Ghana, 1910–1982', (ProQuest Dissertations Publishing, 2015). Jennifer Coates, 'Rethinking the Young Female Cinema Audience: Postwar Cinema-Going in Kansai, 1945–1952', *U.S.-Japan Women's Journal* 54, no. 1 (2018): 6–28.
10 Andrew Higson, 'The Concept of National Cinema', *Screen* 30, no. 4 (1989): 36–47.
11 The circulation of Egyptian films is a case in point. The trade networks of the Egyptian cinema industry reveal a vast global empire that is only beginning to be pieced together. See the following for references to Egyptian film circulation: Odile Goerg, *Tropical Dream Palaces: Cinema in Colonial West Africa* (London: Hurst & Company, 2020); Laura Fair, *Reel Pleasures: Cinema Audiences And Entrepreneurs In Twentieth-Century Urban Tanzania* (Athens, OH: Ohio University Press, 2018); Ahmet Gürata, 'Tears of Love: Egyptian Cinema in Turkey (1938–1950)', *New Perspectives on Turkey* 30 (2004): 55–82.
12 This especially happens in conferences where it seems cinema sociologists and historians do not have an intellectual home. As a less popular topic of research in Middle East studies, film analysis and cinema histories are also often placed in the same field in edited books. See for example Terri Ginsberg and Chris Lippard (eds), *Cinema of the Arab World: Contemporary Directions in Theory and Practice* (Cham: Springer International Publishing, 2020).
13 Walter Armbrust, *Mass Culture and Modernism in Egypt* (Cambridge: Cambridge University Press, 1996); Walter Armbrust (ed.), *Mass Mediations New Approaches to Popular Culture in the Middle East and Beyond* (Berkeley, CA: University of California Press, 2000).
14 Joel Gordon, 'Pop Culture Roundup', *International Journal of Middle East Studies* 50, no. 4 (2018): 787–94.

15 Chihab El Khachab, *Making Film in Egypt: How Labor, Technology, And Mediation Shape The Industry* (Cairo: American University in Cairo Press, 2021). See also Chihab El Khachab, 'The Sobky Recipe and the Struggle over "the Popular" in Egypt', *Arab Studies Journal* 27, no. 1 (2019): 34–61.

16 Bahira Amin, 'The Shoot Stops for No One: The Labor Behind the Camera in Egyptian Film and T.V.', *Mada Masr*, 13 July 2021, https://www.madamasr.com/en/2021/07/13/feature/culture/the-shoot-stops-for-no-one-the-labor-behind-the-camera-in-egyptian-film-and-tv/ (accessed 1 March 2022). See also Mariz Kelada, 'Letting Fieldwork Speak Back', *SYNOPTIQUE*, 43 (2019), https://www.synoptique.ca/_files/ugd/811df8_fb55e7e8409c442f8dbce84d881cd315.pdf#page=49 (accessed 1 March 2022).

17 Viviane Saglier, '"Not-Yet" an Industry: The Temporalities of Contemporary Palestinian Cinema', in *Cinema of the Arab World: Contemporary Directions in Theory and Practice*, ed. Terri Ginsberg and Chris Lippard (Cham: Springer International Publishing, 2020), 125–46.

18 Terri Ginsberg and Chris Lippard (eds), *Cinema of the Arab World: Contemporary Directions in Theory and Practice* (Cham: Springer International Publishing, 2020).

19 Kevin T. Dwyer, *Beyond Casablanca. M.A. Tazi and the Adventure of Moroccan Cinema* (Bloomington, IN: Indiana University Press, 2004).

20 Nour El-Safoury (ed.), *Mapping Cinema Audiences* (Cairo: Network of Arab Alternative Screens, 2018).

21 Farida Mar'i (ed.), *Sihafat al-Sinima fi Misr: al-Nisf al-Awwal min al-Qarn al-'Ishrin* (Cairo: Egyptian Film Centre, 1996); Farida Mar'i (ed.), *Turath al-Nuqqad al-Sinima'iyyin fi Misr: Kitabat al-Sayyid Hassan Jum'a, Vol 1–3* (Cairo: Markaz al-Qawmi lil-Sinima, 1997).

22 Ahmad al-Hadari, *Tarikh al-Sinima fi Misr: al-Juz' al-Awwal (Vol.1) min Bidayat 1896 li- Akhir 1930* (Cairo: Nadi al-Sinima, 1989).

23 Samir Farid, *Tarikh al-Raqaba 'ala al-Sinima fi Misr* (Cairo: al-Maktab al-Misri li-Tawzi' al-Matbu'at, 2002).

24 Andrew Flibbert, 'State and Cinema in Pre-Revolutionary Egypt, 1927–52', in *Re-Envisioning Egypt 1919–1952*, ed. Arthur Goldschmidt, Amy J. Johnson, and Barak A. Salmoni (Cairo: American University in Cairo Press, 2005), 448–65; Andrew Flibbert, *Commerce in Culture: States and Markets in the World Film Trade*, 1st edn (New York: Palgrave Macmillan US, 2007).

25 See Armbrust, *Mass Culture and Modernism in Egypt*; Walter Armbrust, 'The Golden Age before the Golden Age: Commercial Egyptian Cinema Before the 1960s', in *Mass Mediations New Approaches to Popular Culture in the Middle East and Beyond*, ed. Walter Armbrust (Berkeley, CA: University of California Press, 2000), 292–327; Walter Armbrust, 'The Rise and Fall of Nationalism in the Egyptian Cinema', in *Social Constructions of Nationalism in the Middle East*, ed. Fatma Müge Göçek (Albany, NY: State University of New York Press, 2002), 217–50; Walter

Armbrust, 'New Cinema, Commercial Cinema, and the Modernist Tradition in Egypt', *Alif: Journal of Comparative Poetic*, Arab Cinematics: Towards the New and the Alternative 15 (1995): 81–129; Walter Armbrust, 'Audiovisual Media and History of the Arab Middle East', in *Middle East Historiographies: Narrating the Twentieth Century*, ed. Israel Gershoni, Amy Singer and Y. Hakan Erdem (Seattle and London: University of Washington Press, 2006), 288–313; Walter Armbrust, 'Colonizing Popular Culture or Creating Modernity? Architectural Metaphors and Egyptian Media', in *Middle Eastern Cities, 1900–1950*, ed. Hans Chr. Korsholm Nielsen and Jakob Stovgaard-Petersen (Gylling: Aarhus University Press, 2001), 20–43; Walter Armbrust, 'The Ubiquitous Nonpresence of India: Peripheral Visions from Egyptian Popular Culture', in *Global Bollywood: Travels of Hindi Song and Dance*, ed. Sangita Gopal and Sujata Moori (Minneapolis, MN: University of Minnesota Press, 2008), 200–20.

26 Robert Vitalis, 'American Ambassador in Technicolor and Cinemascope: Hollywood and Revolution on the Nile', in *Mass Mediations New Approaches to Popular Culture in the Middle East and Beyond*, ed. Walter Armbrust (Berkeley, CA: University of California Press, 2000), 269–91.

27 Elizabeth F. Thompson, 'Politics by Other Screens: Contesting Movie Censorship in the Late French Empire', *Arab Media and Society* 7 (January 2009): 1–23; Elizabeth F. Thompson, *Colonial Citizens: Republican Rights, Paternal Privilege and Gender in French Syria and Lebanon* (New York: Columbia University Press, 2000), 197–210; Elizabeth F. Thompson, 'Sex and Cinema in Damascus: The Gendered Politics of Public Space in a Colonial City', in *Middle Eastern Cities, 1900–1950: Public Spaces and Public Spheres in Transformation*, ed. Hans Chr. Korsholm Nielsen and Jakob Skovgaard-Petersen (Gylling: Aarhus University Press, 2001), 89–111.

28 Manar Hasan and Ami Ayalon, 'Arabs and Jews, Leisure and Gender, in Haifa's Public Spaces', in *Haifa Before & After 1948 - Narratives of a Mixed City*, ed. Mahmoud Yazbak and Yfaat Weiss (Dordrecht: Republic of Letters, 2011), 69–98.

29 See also Muhammad Khidr, *al-Kiyanat al-Sinimaiya al-Kubra fi Misr ba'da al-Khaskhasa* (Giza: Akadimiyat al-Funun, 2006).

30 Edward Said, 'In Memory of Tahia', *London Review of Books* 21, no. 21 (28 October 1999), https://www.lrb.co.uk/the-paper/v21/n21/edward-said/in-memory-of-tahia (accessed 15 February).

31 Lucie Ryzova, 'The Good, the Bad, and the Ugly: Collector, Dealer and Academic in the Informal Used-paper Markets of Cairo', in *Archives, Museums and Collecting Practices in the Modern Arab World*, ed. Sonia Mejcher-Atassi and John-Pedro Schwartz (London: Ashgate, 2011), 93–120.

32 Ghenwa Hayek, 'Locating the Lost Archive of Arab Cinema', *Regards – Revue Des Arts Du Spectacle* 26 (30 October 2021): 16.

33 Hayek, 'Locating the Lost Archive of Arab Cinema', 17.

34 Hayek, 'Locating the Lost Archive of Arab Cinema'.

35 Ifdal Elsaket, 'Projecting Egypt: The Cinema and the Making of Colonial Modernity, 1896–1952', (PhD. Thesis, University of Sydney, 2013).
36 Mohannad Ghawanmeh, *Entrepreneurship in a State of Flux: Egypt's Silent Cinema and Its Transition to Synchronized Sound, 1896–1934* (PhD. Dissertation, UCLA, 2020).
37 Pelle Valentin Olsen, 'Al-Qahira-Baghdad: The Transnational and Transregional History of Iraq's Early Cinema Industry', *Arab Studies Journal* 29, no. 2 (Fall 2021): 8–33.
38 See for example, Samhita Sunya, "On Location: Tracking Secret Agents and Films, between Bombay and Beirut," Film History (New York, N.Y.) 32, no. 3 (2020): 105–40.
39 Deborah A. Starr, *Togo Mizrahi and the Making of Egyptian Cinema* (California: University of California Press, 2020).
40 Hanan Hammad, *Unknown Past: Layla Murad, the Jewish-Muslim Star of Egypt* (Redwood City: Stanford University Press, 2022).
41 Tamara Chahine Maatouk, *Understanding the Public Sector in Egyptian Cinema: A State Venture* (Cairo: American University in Cairo Press, 2019).
42 See for example Kay Dickinson, *Arab Cinema Travels. Transnational Syria, Palestine, Dubai and Beyond* (London: BFI, 2016); Kay Dickinson, *Arab Film and Video Manifestos Forty-Five Years of the Moving Image Amid Revolution* (Cham: Springer International Publishing, 2018).
43 Ziad Fahmy, *Street Sounds: Listening to Everyday Life in Modern Egypt* (Stanford, CA: Stanford University Press, 2020).
44 Arthur Asseraf, *Electric News in Colonial Algeria* (Oxford; New York: Oxford University Press, 2019).
45 Raph Cormack, *Midnight in Cairo: The Divas of Egypt's Roaring '20s* (New York: W. W. Norton & Company, Inc., 2021), 226–44.
46 Nolwenn Mingant, *Hollywood Films in North Africa and the Middle East: A History of Circulation* (Albany, NY: SUNY Press, 2022).
47 Kaveh Askari and Samhita Sunya, 'Introduction: South by South/West Asia: Transregional Histories of Middle East–South Asia Cinemas', *Film History (New York, N.Y.)* 32, no. 3 (2020): 1–9.
48 Firat Oruc, 'Petrocolonial Circulations and Cinema's Arrival in the Gulf', *Film History (New York, N.Y.)* 32, no. 3 (2020): 10–42; see also Firat Oruc, '"Cinema Programmes" of the British Public Relations Office in the Persian Gulf, 1944–1948', *Film History (New York, N.Y.)* 32, no. 3 (2020): 197–209.
49 Ann Laura Stoler, *Along the Archival Grain: Epistemic Anxieties and Colonial Common Sense* (Princeton, NJ: Princeton University Press, 2010).
50 Comra Films website, https://www.comrafilms.com/ (accessed 1 February 2022).

51 Nick Vivarelli, 'Saudi Arabia Box Office Increases 95% in 2021 as Theaters Grow', *Variety*, 11 January 2022 https://variety.com/2022/film/news/saudi-arabia-box-office-2021-1235151010/ (accessed 16 February 2022).
52 Ali Abdulameer, 'Fi Madih Dar lil-Sinima bi Baghdad', *Jadaliyya*, 23 January 2013, https://www.jadaliyya.com/Details/27866 (accessed 16 February 2022).
53 'Abd al-Hakim al-Salmi, 'al-Sinima fil Yaman', *Manasati30*, 31 May 2020, https://manasati30.com/culture/12029/ (accessed 16 February 2022); Khawla Fu'ad, 'Dur al-Sinima fil-Yaman', *Khuyut*, 11 May 2020, https://www.khuyut.com/blog/7180 (accessed 16 February 2022).
54 Margo Kirtikar, *Once Upon a Time in Baghdad* (Bloomington, IN: Xlibris, 2011), 110.
55 Suhaib Gasmelbari (2020) *Talking about Trees*.
56 See collection at Palestinian Oral History Archive, American University of Beirut, https://libraries.aub.edu.lb/poha/ (accessed 16 February 2022).
57 Parallax Haifa project, http://parallaxhaifa.com/ (accessed 2 March 2022).
58 *Cinematheque Beirut Project*, Metropolis, https://www.metropoliscinema.net/page/videoarchives/ (accessed 16 February 2022).
59 The Palestinian Museum, Digital Archive. https://palarchive.org/
60 American Colony. Photo Department, photographer. *Jaffa. Alhambra Cinema. Arab Cinema in Jaffa 'Alhambra', Entrance*. Tel Aviv Israel, 1937. Photograph. https://www.loc.gov/item/2019707809/ (accessed 16 February 2022).
61 Eliasaf Robinson Tel Aviv collection, circa 1909–68, Stanford University Libraries, https://exhibits.stanford.edu/tel-aviv (accessed 16 February 2022).
62 Jrayed – Arabic Newspaper Archive of Ottoman and Mandatory Palestine, https://jrayed.org/en/newspapers/home (accessed 16 February 2022).

Part I

Arab cinema histories
Distribution, exhibition and audiences

1

Misr abroad

Trading Egyptian films in colonial Maghreb

Morgan Corriou

The history of the international circulation of films seems to reduce itself, after the First World War, to a history of Hollywood exports, dominated by the question of cultural imperialism.[1] Cultural studies and new cinema history have made it possible, however, to emphasize the diversity of spectatorship and the consumption of non-Hollywood films.[2] These practices cannot, of course, be detached from the particular conditions governing the international trade of non-dominant cinemas. While the development of a dynamic Egyptian film industry from the 1930s onwards has drawn much attention, the distribution of these films abroad remains less known. For many decades, however, Egyptian films were the only Arabic-language films available to North African and Middle Eastern audiences. The French colonial empire, in particular, represented an important export market and played a key role in the internationalization of Egyptian production. The political stakes of these screenings have been discussed in a few studies.[3] Researchers have highlighted the moral panic that seized the colonial administration and the strict control imposed on these films. But, even before the intervention of censorship, the distribution of Egyptian films faced a series of economic obstacles, partly erected by the French authorities. It is therefore important to consider not only the political but also the economic and social dimensions of this trade.

In this chapter, I will focus on the circulation of Egyptian films in the Maghreb from the turn of the 1930s until independence. Be it on the political, economic or cultural level, Egyptian cinema represented for the Algerians, the Moroccans and the Tunisians an opportunity for cinematic independence in a repressive context that prevented the birth of national cinemas. While the predominance of foreign films on North African screens has been often dubbed as 'Western neo-colonialism' and 'imperialism of international money',[4] these 'South-South' circulations demonstrate the diverse cultural and/or political meanings of foreign films. The colonizers treated Egyptian cinema as both a dangerous and despised adversary, replacing Hollywood as the new nemesis of French cinema. For North African audiences, Egyptian films depicted a world that was both exotic and familiar and could shape pan-Arab or even national identity. From an economic standpoint, the trade of Egyptian films reflected the maintenance of cultural relations between Egypt and the Maghreb, as well as their colonial reconfiguration in the context of French Occupation.

This chapter draws not only on the records of the colonial administration, trade journals, interviews and memoirs but also on hitherto underexplored sources such as printed lyrics and the private archives of the distributor Films Régence.[5] I wish indeed to emphasize the figure of the distributor, too often neglected in a history that, as highlighted by Jean-Marc Leveratto, tends to concentrate on the auteur's sole competence and describe producers and distributors as mere 'obstacles to the development of the Seventh Art'.[6]

The jewels of the Nile

Egyptian cinema appeared on North African screens in the early 1930s.[7] In Tunis, *Unshudat al-Fu'ad* (*The Song of the Heart*, Mario Volpe, 1932) was the first Egyptian feature film to be exhibited. It played to full houses for four weeks, attracting the attention of the Direction de la Sûreté publique (Directorate for Public Security), dumbfounded.[8] Foreign films seemed to foster a plurality of identities and allegiances that for long had threatened France's hegemony.[9] Even the very concept of foreign film could take on several meanings in a region where Muslims, Jews, Italians, Spaniards and French coexisted. In the absence of a domestic cinema, there is little doubt that Egyptian films seemed more familiar to the majority Arab-speaking population than the French and American films dominating the screens.[10]

Songs, popularized by records and radio, played a fundamental role in the appeal of these films, as did the presence of stars with an international aura. The aesthetic value of these productions, however, was denied by the colonial administration, that strived to explain the infatuation of the colonized audiences in purely political terms. Indeed, these films combined Arab-Muslim culture and modernity, thereby contradicting colonial topoi on the alleged immobility of Muslim societies. Most of them gave a prosperous image of independent

Egypt, which particularly annoyed French authorities.[11] The Maghrebi filmgoers certainly favoured a cinema that provided a sense of pride for Arab people. These films could also convey nationalist and pan-Arab demands and the screenings were occasionally the scene of political demonstrations.[12] But, the major appeal of these films was, first and foremost, the use of Arabic, which was largely absent from the media in the early 1930s. Although the spoken Egyptian was far from familiar to the first viewers, it nonetheless elicited a unifying feeling among the public as Arabic suffered the blows of the colonial power – to different degrees, whether in the Algerian departments or the protectorates of Morocco and Tunisia.[13]

The love of Maghrebi audiences for Egyptian cinema fuelled the anxieties of French authorities. Before the Second World War, these mainly focused on the presence of Italian or German investors and technicians, reactivating the classic fear of foreign agitators – another way of denying political autonomy to the colonized.[14] The issue at stake was actually the appropriation of the camera by Arab directors and the feeling of a loss of control. We thus note the concomitance between the development of Egyptian cinema and the rising power of a colonial discourse on the 'native' public and its alleged characteristics.[15] The concern of the colonial administration fed on the demographics of Egyptian cinema's audiences, described as exclusively indigenous. Although the law imposed on Egyptian films to be subtitled in French, disdain largely seemed to prevail among European viewers. This rejection should undoubtedly be qualified, but the fact remains that the enthusiasm of North Africans for Egyptian films had been categorized by the authorities as a communal passion, excluding Europeans. The outraged reactions of colonial officials hid in the most hackneyed way a denial of universality towards non-Western cinemas. Some audiences clearly favoured Egyptian cinema. This was particularly the case in areas where locals had little exposure to French, the language in which most films were shown in the Maghreb. The same applied to Muslim women, who were more restricted in their movements, and therefore in their cinema attendance.[16] But the opposition between a conservative and/or poorly educated public, avid for Egyptian films, and a modern and literate public that preferred American and European films proves to be largely false.[17] The film consumption of North African viewers actually appeared more diversified than that of European viewers.

While the authorities viewed the enthusiastic reception of Egyptian cinema as a symbol of backwardness and an act of mistrust towards the culture of the colonizer, testimonies indicate that the response to these films was more complex and varied than what French observers suggested: entertainment, Arab pride, opposition to colonialism, but also the dream of 'Arab Western-ness' in the words of Massoud Hayoun were all opposed and mixed at the same time. The latter reports the comments of his grandmother, a Jewish Tunisian, born in 1929: 'An Arabic film was good, Daida explained, if it could situate itself between Arabness and Western-ness. A good Arabic film was in Arabic, introduced new Arabic-language songs, and mimicked what Daida described as the class and delicacy of a European film. Deference to Arabic social mores – particularly sexual prudence – were non-negotiables [sic] that faded too as time went on.'[18] Many Egyptian films de facto replicated the pattern of Hollywood musicals and could thus appear as both a gateway to a Western way of life and the catalyst for a pan-Arab identity.

The rarity of these films immediately transformed the screenings into events that won new audiences, especially a family audience.[19] But the distinctive feature of Egyptian cinema also lies in the outreach beyond its viewers. There was, indeed, a broader interest in the cultural dynamism in Egypt. Without even knowing whether the films were to be screened in *Afrique française du Nord* (AFN, French North Africa, the official name of the region during colonization), people closely scrutinized the news of shooting and releases in the press. Fashion was also inspired by the outfits of Egyptian stars. More importantly, songs, popularized by records, radio and printed lyrics,[20] helped bring Egyptian cinema beyond the closed circle of filmgoers. Thus, Egyptian films reached female and rural audiences who had little access to theatres. Undoubtedly, these significant intermedial practices contributed to the moral panic of the French authorities, who felt all the more a loss of control. This prompted a multitude of reports and projects on French Arabic-language production, which continued to multiply after the war, without much success.

The one-sided representation of Egyptian cinema audiences as a dissenting public accounted for the specific regulation of these films. The Blum-Byrnes agreements (28 May 1946) had established screen quota. These were quickly implemented in AFN, but instead of targeting Hollywood films they were distorted to counter the Egyptian film industry.[21] The status of the protectorates that allowed for relative local autonomy preserved the use of Arabic in Morocco and Tunisia and forced the authorities to grant more space to foreign films than in Algeria, considered as an integral part of France, where the Blum-Byrnes agreements were stringently applied. Yet, the obligation to subtitle or dub films in French particularly made an impression in Tunisia where the subtitling of films in Arabic was not mandatory.[22] With the *arrêté résidentiel* of 31 December 1946, the French authorities explicitly chose to treat Arabic as a foreign language. The aim here was to weaken the already poor position of Arabic on screens and to prevent cinemas from specializing in Egyptian films.[23] The colonial administration was thus trying to protect French cinema, which, in many ways, seemed more foreign to Arab audiences than films from Egypt.[24]

Imposing quota proved to be extremely difficult, if not impossible, to enforce and theatres specializing in Egyptian cinema soon expanded.[25] Distributors played an indirect role in the specialization of cinemas, by displaying a reluctance to rent out the French or American box-office hits to theatres showing Egyptian films, on the pretence that this would devalue their products.[26] Cinemas specializing in Egyptian films suffered from the overall stigmatization of indigenous audiences and their behaviour, deemed irrational and violent. Elizabeth Thompson has shown how hygienist rationales have been widely used to control public space in Morocco. In the European neighbourhoods of Meknes, petitioners criticized the screening of Egyptian films on the grounds that their neighbourhood was 'transformed into a veritable garbage dump'.[27] These pressures actually aimed at restricting the circulation of Moroccan filmgoers in the city, a practice favoured by the development of cinema attendance.

The exhibition of Egyptian cinema was also regulated by censorship. The issue of film control will only be briefly mentioned here, as several studies have already addressed the subject. Control appeared to be more severe in North Africa than in French West Africa, where the censors lacked arguments for banning Egyptian films and struggled with the language barrier.[28] Scenes calling for Arab union, attacks against the West and references to King Faruq or the Egyptian army were systematically cut out.[29] But the censorship of Egyptian films, like the whole process of film control, proved to be versatile and often counterproductive. In this respect, the famous *Gharam wa Intiqam* (*Love and Revenge*, 1944) by Yusuf Wahbi proves characteristic. The film was first authorized in Tunisia in 1946 and was enthusiastically applauded by nationalists.[30] It reappeared on screens a year later, this time with cuts, which infuriated the audience.[31] More than often, the censor had to conclude that films were 'subject to interpretation by whoever wanted to interpret them' and that the demonstrations were 'determined more by the local atmosphere, the theatre, the region and its political climate than by the film itself'.[32] This, however, did not prevent Egyptian cinema from replacing the arch-enemy of French cinema, Hollywood, in colonial obsessions.[33]

The colonial economics of distribution

Distribution channels were established in a constrained political context, further complicated by the precariousness of the film industry in AFN. While foreign films almost systematically transited through metropolitan France, the increasing influx of Egyptian films raised the question of the cinematic independence of the Maghreb.

The scarcity of the product, which was far from being sufficient to supply the Egyptian domestic market, must be emphasized.[34] Distributors also had to adapt to the weakness of film exhibition in the Maghreb, particularly in rural areas. Films Régence, for instance, supplied 16 mm films to the smallest exhibitors. The market itself was closely linked to religious festivities. Concerns about the shortage of Arabic films regularly arose at the time of Ramadan, with 'id al-fitr (the religious holiday after Ramadan) a crucial period for business.[35] Foreign films usually arrived to AFN from France, through Algiers. The historical experience of metropolitan distribution companies obviously contributed to imposing this Parisian stage, but the main motive was financial. By trading with metropolitan retailers, North African distributors avoided the cumbersome import-licensing process and the change of currency. Goods coming from French territory (here Algeria) benefited from reduced customs duties when entering the protectorates and, in the case of films, were even admitted duty-free.[36] The currency issue was especially acute at the end of the Second World War, at a time when the French economy was in a very difficult position. Distributor Jacques Haïk, for instance, had to cancel a contract in 1945 because the Alexandria-based Brothers Behna production and distribution company refused to be paid in francs. He then organized a system of barter of French and Egyptian reels.[37]

After the war, more distributors started to venture into the business. In the confusion that followed the liberation of Tunisia, Egyptian films were even smuggled in on military aircraft.[38] The automobile journey of the young law student Hamouda Chaabini through Libya and Lower Egypt at the beginning of the 1950s is just one illustration of the small-scale nature of this trade.[39] In Alexandria, the law student and his father, owner of the Ciné-Soir in Tunis, made contact with Behna Films, thanks to a middleman from the city of Sfax. The prices turned out to be too high, so they settled on a smaller producer and acquired the rights to three films for all of North Africa, together with the Agence tunisienne de films (Tunisian Film Agency).[40] Such examples demonstrate that exchanges could occur at a very small level (three films in this case). Friends and family networks served to build bridges between Egypt and the Maghreb. For even the most ambitious distributors, such as Edmond and Édouard Khayat, Greek-Orthodox Lebanese established in Tunisia, Egyptian films remained a rare commodity. In absolute figures, these were probably more present on French screens than on Tunisian screens.[41] An anecdote testifies to this shortage: with only two prints, the Khayat brothers managed to screen a film in six Tunis cinemas, with each screening giving rise to frantic reel races between the theatres.[42]

Yet, direct exchanges were far from being encouraged: Egyptian producers were discouraged from travelling to North Africa by the French embassy in Cairo,[43] and the allocation of foreign currency depended on the political approval of the colonial administration.[44] In spite of the geographical proximity, France remained the main gateway for Egyptian productions. Some technical arguments supported a financial reasoning: the North African studios did not have the necessary means to subtitle in French the reels coming from Egypt. Thus, the Parisian firm Francorexfilms, owned by the brothers André and Pierre Bensimon, imported and subtitled films to be distributed in AFN by Mabrouka Films, a company born in Algiers in 1950, in which they also had interests.[45] Obviously, these obstacles concealed evident political interests.

The Egyptian film trade depended heavily on political fluctuations. The correspondence of Films Régence bears witness to the difficult conditions in which distributors operated, in constant battle with the French administration. Following the banning of French films in Egypt and in a context of exacerbated tensions around the Suez Canal, the importation of Egyptian films was prohibited from October 1956.[46] The restrictions eased somewhat at the end of 1959 and films purchased just before the Suez crisis were screened in metropolitan cinemas attended by North African workers. In Algeria, however, the Délégation générale stubbornly tried and multiplied the administrative quibbles in order to slow down the distribution of Egyptian films. Films Régence, on the verge of bankruptcy, protested against the irrationality of this type of backdoor censorship while phonograph records spread the voices banned on screens and the *Sections administratives spécialisées* (SAS), a civil and military programme operating in rural areas, exhibited Egyptian films in the countryside.[47] The Algerian cinema bureau could hardly speak of economic retaliation, since the restrictions also concerned films already paid to Egypt and involved the non-renewal of screen certificates for old films.[48] The actual purpose of the blockade was rather to reduce the circulation of Egyptian films, which now only served as bait for French propaganda in the SAS.

While Egyptian films were often traded in precarious conditions and sometimes on a very small scale, the distribution was not limited to minor companies. The state-controlled Actualités Françaises itself distributed Egyptian films, which did not prevent the company from dealing with censors.[49] A few large firms expanded, as shown by the example of Films Régence, owned by Jacques Haïk (1893–1950).[50] This Tunisian Jew had become a famous producer, distributor and exhibitor in interwar Paris. Placed in forced residence by Vichy, he was allowed to leave for Tunisia in 1941.[51] In July 1943, just a few weeks after the liberation of Tunis, he set up a joint venture company to distribute Egyptian films prevented from being released in the Maghreb because of the war. Was this merely a stopgap solution, at a time when his cinematic empire had been lost to 'aryanization' and France was still occupied? In any case, the former mogul dealt with the biggest production companies: Misr, Nahas, Behna and so on. As early as 1944, he began to covet the sub-Saharan market. Although he invested in Spanish Morocco and Libya, his activity remained essentially limited to the French colonial sphere.

A 1953 contract provides an overview of the expected distribution of profits: 30 per cent for Algeria, 30 per cent for Morocco, 25 per cent for Tunisia, 7.5 per cent for French West Africa and French Equatorial Africa and 7.5 per cent for

Figure 1.1 Promotional material for the films *Mughamarat 'Antar wa-'Abla* (Salah Abu Seif, 1948), *Zuhur al-Islam* (Ibrahim 'Izz al-Din, 1951) and *Lahn al-Khulud* (Henry Barakat, 1952) in a cinema (Centre des archives diplomatiques de Nantes, Protectorat Maroc, série C: section d'iconographie, n° 5602, 1952).

metropolitan France.⁵² As the business grew, Haïk launched three companies in 1947: Régence-Tunisie, Régence-Maroc and Régence-Algérie. Algiers remained, however, the bridgehead of Egyptian cinema in the Maghreb. It was registered as a *société anonyme* (public limited company), while Régence-Tunisie and Régence-Maroc held the lower status of a *société anonyme à responsabilité limitée* (limited liability company). This structure ensured local anchorage, but the Maghrebi intermediaries seemed relatively few in number. The majority of the shareholders remained French, and decision-making still took place at the Parisian headquarters⁵³ (Figure 1.1).

The irresponsible businessmen⁵⁴

The latter point raises questions about the sociology of the Maghrebi networks of distributors and investors, as the various obstacles to the Egyptian film trade raised awareness about the limited role left to Muslims in the film industry, especially in post-war Morocco where the nationalist bourgeoisie launched campaigns to take over theatres.⁵⁵

The Egyptian film trade in AFN was dominated before the war by a Greek-Orthodox Lebanese based in Casablanca, Théodore Khayat (born in 1905), nephew of the Baida brothers and concessionaire of the famous Baidaphon label.⁵⁶ For these newcomers, the record business constituted a gateway to film distribution as Egyptian cinema maintained close ties with the music industry. Distributors often negotiated the release of songs together with the film rights. As new companies emerged after the war, the distributors of Egyptian films remained Arab-speaking minorities, Lebanese Christians and North African Jews. Neither colonizer nor colonized, 'more or less hoodwinked, more or less beneficiaries', these characters embody the '*métis* of colonization' as defined by Albert Memmi and, as such, often acted as cultural intermediaries between the Muslims and the French.⁵⁷ More and more Muslims were nonetheless getting involved in distribution in the years leading up to independence, like Abderrazak Slouma, head of Tunisia-Film, or Benzakour, manager of SEAM-Films in Morocco. Obviously, Egyptian cinema opened a breach in a business where Muslims were hitherto very little involved. Still, nationalist distributors as Benzakour, a supporter of the Istiqlal Party, had to deal with the constant interference by colonial officials.⁵⁸

Aside from the distributors themselves, the financing of these companies needs to be examined more closely. We then note that Muslim investors were present at a very early stage. The first joint venture company created in 1943 by Jacques Haïk brought together a Tunisian Muslim, 'Abd al-Rahman al-Luz, an industrialist from Sfax, co-owner of the Majestic cinema in the same city, and a Tunisian Jew, Joseph Smadja, a businessman in Tunis.[59] This association contradicts the image of a segregated society but was not exceptional in the film industry. Diversity prevailed in the exhibition sector, and during the interwar period we find several examples of partnerships between Tunisian Jews and Italians, some of them even known for their fascist sympathies.[60] The participation of a Muslim, however, was less common. The distribution of Egyptian cinema only attracted French settlers at a later stage: in 1944, several prominent figures joined Haïk's company. Among these new members, we also note the presence of a Muslim dignitary, and no less than the minister of *hubus*,[61] Mohamed Salah Mzali.[62] The presence of these personalities attests to the legitimacy that the Egyptian film trade was gradually gaining.

The issue of legitimacy is no small matter when one recalls the sarcasm that Egyptian cinema used to elicit in the cinephile community. Tahar Cheriaa, director of cinema at the Tunisian Ministry of Cultural Affairs between 1962 and 1969, has described the reservations raised by these films in post-war film clubs.[63] Jean-Marc Leveratto has strongly criticized the 'cultural disqualification' of the distributor, commonly opposed in French scholarship to the figure of the auteur, whose occupation is solely considered in economic terms and, rarely, in terms of expertise. Yet, the 'emergence of a skill' is also at stake, as distributors must establish tools to measure film quality.[64] These distributors had chosen to specialize in the cinema of one country, Egypt, conceived as a genre in itself. According to Leveratto, genre is 'certainly a vague reality. But it is an effective tool to objectify the viewer's judgement, by identifying objects likely to attract him, by comparison with spectacular objects authenticated by experience'.[65] The example of Films Régence appears all the more singular as the company did not hesitate to invest directly in the production of Egyptian films from 1952 onwards, thanks to the close and friendly ties that the company had established with the Cairo-based actor, musician and producer Farid al-Atrash.[66] Films Régence's contract with the star demonstrates a clear will to reproduce its most popular films: 'The titles of the films have not yet been decided, but they will, in any case, be interpreted by Farid El Atrash and will have at least the same quality as all his previous films (*Akhir Kidba* [*The Last Lie*, 1950], *Afrita Hanim* [*Little Miss Devil 1949*] etc.)'; that is his enormous successes with the dancer Samia Gamal, flamboyant musicals spiced up with belly dancing.[67]

How exactly did these distributors view their audiences and their films? This point is difficult to assess because the traces left by distributors in the administrative archives stem mostly from negotiations with the colonial power.

The distributors constantly tried to justify the need to screen films in Arabic, which was far from self-evident: 'Algerian Muslims, with rare exceptions, are not capable of appreciating purely European cinema and their tastes, habits and morals lead them to a show combining song and dance, supporting a sentimental storyline', states a report on 'The problem of Arab film in Algeria' around 1960.[68] They thus attempted to define a specific audience by adopting the colonial stereotypes of the 'native' public. 'This liberal measure [the end of the blockade of Egyptian films] will not undermine the presence of France in Algeria, nor its culture, quite the contrary. It will bring to the cinema a clientele too primitive to value European films, which they will no doubt come to appreciate by virtue of a foreseeable evolution', wrote Pierre Vercel,[69] the head of distribution at Films Régence. Vercel subscribed to a developmentalist vision then in vogue – one thinks of Daniel Lerner's famous survey:[70] the love of Egyptian cinema was just a stage in a process of necessary modernization. Above all, distributors must reassure the colonial authorities. Vercel insists on the 'purely entertaining' character of Egyptian films[71] and is quick to ensure that the films he distributes 'never have a subversive or political nature'.[72] To what extent did these discourses reflect their own categories or those best able to engage the colonial administration?

In a note written around 1954, distributors were described as mere businessmen unaware of the 'insidious propaganda' of their films.[73] Yet, Films Régence, which distributed *Gharam wa Intiqam* (*Love and Revenge*, 1944), could not pretend to ignore the demonstrations to which some films gave rise, leading to screening bans. It is actually difficult to decide on the naivety or cunning of these distributors. Régence pursued a pro-French line before independence. Asking for the support of the Syndicat des distributeurs indépendants in its negotiations with the colonial administration, Pierre Vercel recalled that the bankruptcy of Régence would leave 'the field clear for nationalist traders in Cairo, Beirut or Casablanca who are waiting for the impending collapse of our company and a possible change in the status of Algeria to take over the important Arab film market in North Africa'.[74] In an interview conducted by Nidam Abdi in 2003, Vercel stated that he was supportive of independence. The firm would even pay the revolutionary taxes in metropolitan France, under pressure from the National Liberation Front.[75] With independence achieved, the firm played the Algerian card in order to preserve its interests in the country, while pressure was strong to make the business fall into Algerian hands and Régence-Algérie was being blackmailed with screen certificates. Now, Vercel emphasized the struggle against the French administration to screen Egyptian films between 1956 and 1960 and, in a desperate letter alerting Ahmed Ben Bella

Figure 1.2 The Donyazad Cinema in Algiers, postcard.

about the situation, promised, once again, that none of his films was 'of a political or tendentious nature'.[76]

Defending an Arab-speaking public sphere in the Maghreb

The Maghrebi film market was characterized by a rather open model in comparison to the rest of the French colonial empire – Indochina or West Africa in particular. The distribution business was nevertheless a major site of interference by the colonial state. During the 1930s, France watched helplessly as Egyptian films arrived on screens, a business then monopolized by the Baida family, which operated on a pan-Arab scale. The post-war period witnessed the economic and political strategies of France to regain control of the Egyptian film trade, and reconfigure its circulation within a colonial framework. In this context, the economy of distribution appeared to be more dependent on political meddling than the exhibition sector.

As this chapter has shown, the political positioning of the distributors themselves often proved ambiguous, hovering as it did between a prudent neutrality beneficial for business and a more or less asserted nationalist commitment in a context of colonial repression. These distributors were not defending the right to see films in Arabic any less. In 1960, Films Régence thus pointed out the injustice suffered by North African spectators deprived of entertainment in their own language and denounced discrimination, referring to the 'considerable mass of French-Muslim citizens who consider themselves unjustly disadvantaged compared to French citizens of European descent who, for their part, can see films of their choice without any limitation of origin'.[77]

In spite of political constraints, a few large firms managed to impose themselves, such as Régence, which established close ties with Egyptian studios. Haïk used his prestige and skills as a major Parisian producer and distributor of Hollywood films to promote Egyptian cinema internationally. The firm also distributed the neorealist films of Salah Abu Seif and the 1958 *Bab al-Hadid* (*Cairo Station*) by Youssef Chahine.[78] While these films have been fervently analysed at the Carthage Film Festival or in film clubs, and praised by local cinephiles as a model for the Maghrebi cinema to be, the intermediaries that were the distributors have been completely forgotten: they symbolize the industrial and commercial side of the seventh art. Yet, those businessmen were able to cross with ease, and intelligence indeed, the barriers too easily and falsely erected between '*Afrita Hanim* (*Litte Miss Devil*) and *Bab al-Hadid*, between scorned belly dances and an esteemed neorealist cinema.

For Ramon Lobato, there is no doubt that distribution is the branch of the film industry that has been least theorized in cinema scholarship. He calls for moving beyond 'familiar narratives of cinematic hegemony and resistance', which have influenced many studies on distribution.[79] The case of Egyptian cinema allows us to challenge overly simplistic dichotomies. A real thorn in the side of colonial authorities, the Egyptian film trade participated in the expansion of an Arab-speaking public sphere at a time when language was under attack from the French occupying forces. The role of Jewish and Lebanese traders also demonstrates the importance of pre-colonial economic structures. Yet, in the Maghreb, Egyptian cinema became part of a colonial economy, with Paris as its hub.

Notes

1 See, for example, Kristin Thompson, *Exporting Entertainment: America in the World Film Market, 1907–1934* (London: British Film Institute, 1985) or Kerry Segrave, *American Films Abroad: Hollywood's Domination of the World's Movie Screens from the 1890's to the Present* (London: McFarland, 1997).

2 See among other references, John Fiske, *Understanding Popular Culture* (London: Routledge, 1989); Richard Maltby and Melvyn Stokes (eds), *Hollywood Abroad:*

Audiences and Cultural Exchange (London: BFI Publishing, 2004); Richard Maltby, Melvyn Stokes and Robert C. Allen (eds), *Going to the Movies: Hollywood and the Social Experience of Cinema* (Exeter: University of Exeter Press, 2007); Daniel Biltereyst, Richard Maltby, and Philippe Meers (eds), *The Routledge Companion to New Cinema History* (London; New York: Routledge, 2019).

3 Sébastien Denis, 'Cinéma et panarabisme en Algérie entre 1945 et 1962', *Guerres mondiales et conflits contemporains* 226 (2007): 37–51; Morgan Corriou, 'Un nouveau loisir en situation coloniale : le cinéma dans la Tunisie du protectorat', PhD Diss., Université Paris Diderot-Paris 7, Paris, 2011; Odile Goerg, 'Les films arabes, une menace pour l'Empire ? La politique des films arabes à la veille des indépendances en Afrique Occidentale française', *Outre-mers* 100, no. 380–381 (2013): 287–312.

4 'Néo-colonialisme occidental', 'impérialisme du fric international'. Tahar Cheriaa, 'Inventaire du cinéma en Tunisie en 1970', Tunis, 1970, fol. 18. Rapport pour le premier séminaire sur l'inventaire du cinéma dans les pays francophones, organisé du 20 au 24 novembre 1970 par l'Agence de coopération culturelle et technique à Dakar.

5 I wish to express my gratitude to Jean-Marie Bonnafous, who granted me access to the precious archives of Films Régence. I also extend my warmest thanks to Nolwenn Mingant, who kindly shared with me copies of the archives she consulted at the National Archives and Records Administration (NARA), and to Mohamed Bennani for introducing me to his printed lyrics collection (Beit el Bennani, Tunis). Finally, I would like to thank the organizers and participants of the conferences *Distribution, diffusion et réception des cinémas d'Afrique et du Levant* (Montréal, 20–22 April 2018), *Cinema-Going in the Arab World: Exhibition, Distribution, and Audiences* (Cairo, 14–15 September 2018) and the panel 'Industrial, Institutional, and Ideological: Cinema Histories in the Middle East/North Africa' (Middle East Studies Association Annual Meeting, New Orleans, 14–17 November 2019) for their informed comments on various drafts of this work.

6 Jean-Marc Leveratto, 'Histoire du cinéma et expertise culturelle', *Politix* 16, no. 61 (2003): 18.

7 Arthur Asseraf, *Electric News in Colonial Algeria* (Oxford: Oxford University Press, 2019), 142.

8 Centre des Archives diplomatiques de Nantes (CADN), 1TU/1V/1890, fol. 700: le directeur de la Sûreté publique au directeur général de l'Intérieur, Tunis, 15 juillet 1932.

9 Mary Dewhurst Lewis, *Divided Rule: Sovereignty and Empire in French Tunisia, 1881–1938* (Berkeley, CA: University of California Press, 2013); M'hamed Oualdi and Noureddine Amara (ed.), 'La nationalité dans le monde arabe des années 1830 aux années 1960. Négocier les appartenances et le droit', *Revue des mondes musulmans et de la Méditerranée* 137 (2015): 13–172.

10 Ahmet Gürata, 'Tears of Love: Egyptian Cinema in Turkey (1938–1950)', *New Perspectives on Turkey* 30 (2004): 74, has shown how 'while Turkish films were non-existent, [Egyptian] films were presented as local products', most notably through dubbing by Turkish singing stars.

11 For the head of the *Centre cinématographique tunisien*, Egyptian cinema was 'false propaganda as the audience is led to believe that all Egyptians have achieved the same level of education and lifestyle as suggested by the scenes seen on screen' (CADN, 1TU/1V/2394(2), fol. 108–109: Tunis, 13 août 1947).

12 The colonial archives record a few such incidents, although the interpretation of the demonstrations is often debated by the authorities. See, for instance, CADN, 1MA/200/187.

13 'Especially in North Africa, where the language is less pure, the expansion of the teaching of literary Arabic through the action of the Ulema and the campaign speeches, has helped to strengthen the popularity of Egyptian films', wrote the rapporteurs of the Haut Comité méditerranéen (Fondation nationale des sciences politiques, Archives d'histoire contemporaine, fonds Charles-André Julien, JU 12: rapport n° 3, 'Le cinéma en pays musulman et en Afrique du Nord', session de mars 1939). Sheikh Mohammed El-Fadhel Ben Achour, *Le mouvement littéraire et intellectuel en Tunisie* (Tunis: Alif, 1998), 177–8, insisted on the role of the Egyptian radio, even if it remained difficult to receive.

14 See Martin Thomas, *Empires of Intelligence: Security Services and Colonial Disorder after 1914* (Berkeley, CA: University of California Press, 2008).

15 See Morgan Corriou, 'La France coloniale et le spectateur "indigène": histoire d'une incompétence cinématographique', *MEI – Médiation et information* 49 (2020): 63–77.

16 See, for instance, Fatima Mernissi, *Dreams of Trespass: Tales of a Harem Girlhood* (Cambridge: Perseus Books, 1995).

17 See Morgan Corriou, '"Le choix entre l'Orient et l'Occident?" Les Tunisiens et le cinéma dans les dernières années du protectorat français (1946–1956)', in *Cultures d'Empires. Échanges et affrontements culturels en situation coloniale*, ed. Romain Bertrand, Hélène Blais and Emmanuelle Sibeud (Paris: Karthala, 2015).

18 Massoud Hayoun, *When We Were Arabs: A Jewish Family's Forgotten History* (New York: The New Press, 2019), 130.

19 In 1939, Khelil Mamlouk rejoiced in the Tunisian magazine *Leïla* that the development of the Egyptian film industry brought to the theatres alongside 'Si Ali, the average Tunisian', 'Mrs Si Ali' and 'Miss Si Ali' ('À bâtons rompus...', March 1939, 10).

20 The al-Manar bookstore in the medina of Tunis, for instance, used to publish the lyrics of Egyptian film songs.

21 In French West Africa, the decree of 5 October 1954 establishing a quota of French films also explicitly targeted Egyptian cinema (Goerg, 'Les films arabes, une menace pour l'Empire?', 298).

22 In 1951, the US Embassy reported to the Department of State that 'some patrons object to superimposed titles' (National Archives and Records Administration [NARA], Department of State Records, RG 59, box 5361: Proposal for Arabic-dubbed 16 mm motion pictures, 21 February 1951).

23 CADN, 1TU/1V/2183, fol. 332: circulaire aux exploitants de salles de spectacles cinématographiques et de circuits cinématographiques itinérants, Tunis, 23 août 1947.

24 In 1947 and 1948, American films accounted for 60 per cent of the market share, compared to 17 per cent for France and 13 per cent for Egypt ('En Tunisie, chaque année 10 millions de spectateurs vont au cinéma', *Le Cinéma nord-africain*, January 1950, no 1).

25 CADN, 1TU/1V/2394(2), fol. 108: le directeur du CCT au chef du cabinet du résident général, Tunis, 13 août 1947.

26 CADN, 1TU/1V/1799, fol. 231: plan triennal de l'industrie cinématographique en Tunisie.

27 Quoted by Elizabeth Thompson, 'Boycott d'un cinéma à Fès en 1948', in *Publics et spectacle cinématographique en situation coloniale*, ed. Morgan Corriou (Tunis: IRMC, CERES, 2012), 187.

28 Goerg, 'Les films arabes, une menace pour l'Empire?'.

29 In Morocco, unlike Algeria and Tunisia, censorship of Egyptian films was both political and moral.

30 CADN, 1TU/2V/885, dossier 'Cinéma'; 1TU/1V/2898: note du 30 janvier 1947.

31 This second censorship file has unfortunately been lost, but the archives preserve a note from the security services (CADN, 1TU/1V/2898: 18 février 1947). The report of the policeman on duty in the theatre suggests that the musical number *Mawakib al-'Izz*, the most obviously political as it is a tribute to the founders of modern Egypt, was left untouched. We formulate the hypothesis that the editing of musical numbers was made impossible by the extent of intermedial practices. Thus, the lyrics of *Mawakib al-'Izz* appear in their entirety in the booklet *Aghana film Gharam wa-intiqam* published by the Tunis Al-Manar bookstore (undated).

32 Note anonyme, 'Le film arabe', vers 1954. Quoted by Denis, 'Cinéma et panarabisme', 44–5.

33 Hollywood even came to be considered an objective ally in the colonial empire. 'The American cinema itself constitutes an element of national propaganda, as, more often than not, the Natives believe the films to be French, and, as they enjoy them, they are grateful to us', wrote Charles Noguès, Résident Général of France in Morocco. Quoted by Nolwenn Mingant, 'When the *Thief of Bagdad* tried to steal the show. The short-lived dubbing of Hollywood films into Arabic in the 1940s', in *Reassessing Dubbing: Historical Approaches and Current Trends*, ed. Irene Ranzato and Serenella Zanotti (Amsterdam: John Benjamins, 2019), 47.

34 Robert Vitalis, 'American Ambassador in Technicolor and Cinemascope: Hollywood and Revolution on the Nile', in *Mass Mediations: New Approaches to*

Popular Culture in the Middle East and Beyond, ed. Walter Armbrust (Berkeley, CA: University of California Press, 2000), 269–91.

35 In 'small towns [. . .] many people only go to the cinema with their families once a year at the end of Ramadan'. Films Régent Archives Jacques Haïk (Régent): Pierre Vercel à Jacques Coup de Fréjac, directeur de l'information à la Délégation générale du gouvernement en Algérie, Paris, 18 février 1961.

36 NARA, Department of State Records, RG 59, box 5361: the US Embassy in Tunisia to the Department of State, 1 September 1951.

37 Régent: Jacques Haïk à Abderrahman Ellouze, Paris, 25 août 1945.

38 1TU/1V/2394(2), fol. 107: le directeur du CCT au chef du cabinet du résident général, Tunis, 13 août 1947.

39 Interview with Hamouda Chaabini, La Marsa, 21 May 2005.

40 L'*Agence tunisienne de films* of Jack Baranès represented Mabrouka Films in Tunis.

41 In 1958, 208 Egyptian films were being screened in France (Fabrice Montebello, 'Films égyptiens et ouvriers algériens dans la Lorraine industrielle. Analyse d'un cas de "diaspora des publics"', in *Publics et spectacle cinématographique en situation coloniale*, ed. Morgan Corriou (Tunis: IRMC, CERES, 2012) 301) compared to 56 at the same date in Tunisia (*Annuaire statistique de la Tunisie 1957–1958*, 1958, 171).

42 Interview with Hamouda Chaabini.

43 CADN, 353/PO/2/101: le directeur d'Afrique-Levant à l'ambassadeur de France au Caire, Paris, 20 août 1946.

44 CADN, 1TU/2V/885, dossier 'Cinéma': 'Les importations de films impressionnés'; 1MA/200/187, dossier 'Importation de films égyptiens'.

45 *Le Cinéma nord-africain*, January 1951, no. 1. 'Francorexfilms a réalisé une double organisation en France et en Égypte', *La Cinématographie française*, 1952, no. 1453, 7.

46 Denis, 'Cinéma et panarabisme', 45.

47 Régent: Pierre Vercel à Nafissa Sid Cara, secrétaire d'État chargée des Affaires sociales algériennes, Paris, 23 mars 1960.

48 Denis, 'Cinéma et panarabisme', 45–6.

49 CADN, 1TU/2V/885, dossier 'Cinéma': compte rendu de vision cinématographique du film *La Chanteuse du fleuve*, 11 janvier 1950.

50 See Chapter 2 in this volume: Eric Smoodin, 'Le Roi du Cinéma: Joseph Seiberras and North African Film Exhibition, 1925–1945'.

51 CADN, 1TU/701/2/133, dossier 'Jacques Haïk'.

52 Régent: convention du 14 septembre 1953 entre Farid al-Atrash et Régence-Algérie.

53 Régent: Pierre Vercel à Ali Khiar, directeur de Régence-Algérie, Paris, 30 décembre 1962.

54 Around 1954, a colonial official signalled a propaganda for which 'the distributor – who is a trader – cannot be held responsible' (note anonyme, 'Le film arabe'). Quoted by Denis, 'Cinéma et panarabisme', 44.

55 CADN, 1MA/200/190.
56 CADN, 1TU/701/2/148, dossier 'Théodore Khayat'.
57 'Plus ou moins mystifiés, plus ou moins bénéficiaires', 'métis de la colonisation'. Albert Memmi, *Portrait du colonisé; précédé de Portrait du colonisateur* (Paris: Gallimard, 2002), 19 and 41. The Crémieux decree gave French nationality to all the Jews of Algeria, but for a long time they remained second-class citizens, plagued by the anti-Semitism of the colonists. There was no such decree in Morocco and Tunisia, which were Protectorates, but many Jews obtained French nationality and/or were educated in French in the schools of the Alliance Israélite Universelle, which put them in an ambiguous position perfectly described by Albert Memmi.
58 CADN, 1MA/200/190.
59 Régent.
60 Corriou, 'Un nouveau loisir en situation coloniale', 129–30.
61 A *hubus* is an inalienable endowment dedicated to charitable purposes.
62 After a PhD in France, Mohamed Salah Mzali (1896–1984) made his career in the Beylical administration. He was briefly prime minister in 1954. See his autobiography *Au fil de ma vie: souvenirs d'un Tunisien* (Tunis: H. Mzali, 1972).
63 Morgan Corriou, 'Des ciné-clubs aux Journées Cinématographiques de Carthage. Entretien avec Tahar Cheriaa', *Maghreb et Sciences Sociales 2009–2010* (2010): 168.
64 Leveratto, 'Histoire du cinéma et expertise culturelle', 27 and 17.
65 Leveratto, 'Histoire du cinéma et expertise culturelle', 38.
66 Régent: convention du 14 septembre 1953 entre Farid al-Atrash et Régence-Algérie.
67 '*Afrita Hanim (Litte Miss Devil)* by Henry Barakat, 1949; *Akhar Kadba* by Ahmed Badrakhan, 1950.
68 Régent. This is probably the report, or draft report, sent by the Gaullist Senator of Oran-Tlemcen, Sliman Belhabich, to the Délégué général Paul Delouvrier on 6 October 1960. Films Régence initiated the report and seems to have written all or part of it (the arguments presented in the document were used as early as spring in the correspondence of the company with the administration).
69 Régent: Pierre Vercel à Nafissa Sid Cara, Paris, 23 mars 1960.
70 Daniel Lerner, *The Passing of Traditional Society, Modernizing the Middle East* (Glencoe: Free Press, 1958).
71 Régent: Pierre Vercel au président du Syndicat des distributeurs indépendants, Paris, 27 décembre 1960.
72 Régent: Pierre Vercel à Nafissa Sid Cara, Paris, 23 mars 1960.
73 Quoted by Denis, 'Cinéma et panarabisme', 44.
74 Régent: Pierre Vercel au président du Syndicat des distributeurs indépendants, Paris, 27 décembre 1960.

75 Nidam Abdi, MA. Diss., Université Paris 8 Vincennes – Saint-Denis, 2003.
76 Régent: Pierre Vercel au président du Conseil Ahmed Ben Bella, Paris, 25 janvier 1963.
77 Régent: Pierre Vercel à Nafissa Sid Cara, Paris, 23 mars 1960.
78 Abdi, MA Diss.
79 Ramon Lobato, *Shadow Economies of Cinema. Mapping Informal Film Distribution* (London: Palgrave Macmillan, BFI, 2012), 3.

2

'Le Roi du Cinéma'

Joseph Seibarras and North African film exhibition, 1925–45

Eric Smoodin

One North African source from the late 1920s called him '*le grand animateur du cinéma*' (the great mover and shaker of cinema) in the region. Another insisted that he was, simply, '*le roi du cinéma*' (the king of cinema).[1] Such was the reputation of the movie entrepreneur Joseph Seibarras, who was, nevertheless, little known outside of North Africa. For contemporary film scholars unable either to read or access materials in Arabic or Berber, the dominant languages of Algeria along with some dialects that long predated the colonial-era imposition of French, the only way to find out about Seibarras is to look to the region's francophone sources from the 1920s, 1930s and 1940s. These include the period's newspapers and journals, like *L'Echo d'Alger*, *Oran Spectacles* and *L'Afrique du Nord illustrée*. Only occasionally will there be evidence from France, for instance, the issue of the film journal *Hebdo* from 9 April 1932, making a brief mention of Seibarras moving into film exhibition in Tunis.[2] His relative invisibility today says something about the difficulties of uncovering much about colonial film history. But his career brings into historical focus the systems of film exhibition that extended well beyond the Parisian epicentre while depending on French colonial authority. Seibarras also demonstrates the significance, in North Africa, of a man who could be considered the ideal colonial subject while nevertheless representing the possibilities for Arab financial and cultural self-determination during the last few decades of French control.

Film scholars have long known about another significant North African film impresario, Jacques Haïk, a Tunisian who came to Paris and had one of the great boom and bust careers in a national film industry famous for them. In the years just before 1920, when he was still in his early twenties, Haïk was among the most significant film distributors in France, handling films from Keystone, Kay-Bee, Majestic and other early studios, while also being one of the first to bring Charlie Chaplin's films to the French public. He parlayed that success into the most lucrative aspect of the movie industry, film exhibition. At the height of his career in the early 1930s – before his business became overextended and then eventually was confiscated by the Nazis during the occupation – Haïk owned his own production company as well as a chain of cinemas including the spectacular Grand Rex in Paris' second arrondissement, which is still in operation today. There is at least some measure of research about Haïk.[3] But what about the case of a major distributor and exhibitor like Seibarras, who chose to stay in North Africa, and who, as a result, has had no place in contemporary scholarship from the United States and Europe?

Seibarras seems to have been born in Algeria, although even this is unclear, and none of the available French sources provides his age. An appreciative retrospective in the weekly journal *Annales Africaines* from 1925 reported that Seibarras had been a 'simple bar owner', who, tired of serving *apéros* to his clients, rented a shed in the Plateau-Saulière section of Algiers, and installed a makeshift cinema there.[4] An article in *L'Afrique du Nord illustrée* from 1929 provides 1912 as the date of that first cinema, 'a small, modest place ... that, through judiciously chosen programs ... attracted an enthusiastic and lively audience'.[5]

The ex-bar owner then devoted himself to creating 'a vast North African cinematic movement', as that story in *L'Afrique du Nord illustrée* put it, and opened other exhibition sites in Algiers. By the late 1920s he could best be described as an 'indefatigable worker, an amazing leader, a well-informed businessman', and, perhaps most importantly in terms of his relationship with Europe, 'one of the most characteristic figures of French cinema'.[6] This set the template for discussions about Seibarras, at least in North African francophone sources: a man of superb taste, devoted to his public and creating an empire of cinemas showing the best films, committed to France while not fully dependent on that country for his success, a cosmopolitan at home in Berlin or Paris and also a proud Algerian (Figure 2.1).

At the end of the 1920s, Seibarras owned cinemas throughout Algeria, Morocco and Tunisia.[7] By the early 1930s he had around two dozen establishments, most of them cinemas, some of them casinos and music halls, a few combining movies with gambling and live performances.[8] Even while expanding his business throughout North Africa, the centre for Seibarras remained Algiers, which was, along with Casablanca, Cairo and a few other large urban areas, the most important location for cinema in the region, usually the first stop there for the best films that came from France or the United States.

Figure 2.1 Joseph Seibarras, 'le grand animateur du cinéma'. From L'Afrique du Nord illustrée, 13 July 1929. Bibliothèque nationale de France.

Algeria's special status among France's North African colonies assured the particular importance of the country's capital, Algiers, to France broadly and to the extension of French film culture in particular. France had invaded Algeria in 1830 and annexed it shortly thereafter, but in 1870 civil authorities replaced the French military government there, and, as Clifford Rosenberg has pointed out, 'the minister of the interior in Paris rather than the minister of colonies appointed [Algeria's] governor-general', establishing what might be called 'quasi-colonial status' (Algeria was never a protectorate, in the manner of Tunisia and Morocco).[9] This contributed to Algiers becoming home to 'the largest French population living outside France' for the first half of the twentieth century, with the *pieds noirs*, those Algerians of European descent, making up about one-third of the population.[10]

During the interwar period there was a significant film scene in Algiers, particularly for French and American movies. By the time the Second World War began there were around twenty cinemas in the sections of the city populated mostly by the *pieds noirs*. While Arabs and other 'non-Europeans' lived throughout Algiers, the centre for them was the Casbah, the old walled citadel of the city.[11] This was the site of numerous cultural activities and organizations, but it is difficult, from existing francophone sources, to get a sense of the place there, if any, of motion pictures.[12] Those French-language materials, the newspapers from the city, inform us that the films shown in the European sections typically would be the same ones that played in Paris and elsewhere in France.[13]

It was not even unusual for a film to open in Algiers before it had made its way to all of the major French cities. Almost certainly, for example, the most anticipated French film of 1930 was René Clair's *Sous les toits de Paris*. For French intellectuals and artists at the time, and even the general public, any new

Clair film was a very big deal, and many understood this film to demonstrate the possibilities of a French sound cinema equal to the country's silent film heritage.[14] As was the case with most movies, Clair's opened in Paris, in April 1930 at the Moulin Rouge cinema, a major site for important films, playing there for several months. But even as it made its way through the rest of France, *Sous les toits de Paris* appeared in Algiers in late September 1930 at the Régent (a Seibarras cinema), two weeks before showing in Nantes and three months before beginning its run in Lille in January 1931.[15]

Exhibition and colonial cinema

Dating from the beginning of their occupation, the French systematically destroyed the vast Ottoman architectural spaces of Algiers, transforming much of the city into one that seemed European, with street names and buildings that could pass for Parisian. In the twentieth century, even with our modest bar owner-turned-film-exhibitor, the film culture of Algiers reflected the same colonial impulse. The cinemas there, including Seibarras's, had names echoing those in Paris: Palace, Empire, Olympia and Colisée. Significantly, they served a European community. The major cinemas in the city, for instance Seibarras's Majestic on rue Borély-la-Sapie or his Régent cinema on rue d'Isly, were located in the European section of Algiers. The French left the Casbah more or less alone, architecturally, concentrating instead on other parts of Algiers, developing certain spaces as French zones and leaving the Casbah for those residents considered 'non-European'. Seibarras's exhibition empire extended throughout North Africa, but only partially throughout Algiers.[16]

Seibarras owned at least four cinemas in Algiers by the early 1930s: the Moderne and the Alhambra in addition to the Majestic and the Régent, with French-language newspapers from the city providing some of the details of going to the movies there. The Seibarras cinemas were all *cinémas d'exclusivité*, showing movies in their first appearances in the city.[17] These spaces also showcased various kinds of performance, and the range crossed the cultural spectrum. In November 1930, Seibarras brought the religious theatrical piece *La Passion de Nancy* to the Majestic, with sixteen acts and twenty-two *tableaux vivants*, all accompanied by the music of Bach and Mendelssohn. For those, perhaps, with less classical tastes, just a few months later, in May 1931, there would be a boxing programme, featuring France's middleweight champion.[18]

This fluidity of the exhibition space, from movies to live performances to sports, was particularly marked in Seibarras's sites because of the way they presented the most significant cultural events to audiences in Algiers. Those events often came directly from Paris, or directly evoked the French capital, making Seibarras a conduit between European authority and the colonies. In 1930, Seibarras signed an agreement with Parisian theatrical impresarios to bring the finest acts to his own Majestic, acts that would move from Paris to London to Berlin and then to Algiers. These included the famous music hall performer Lyna Tyber, the renowned female impersonator Barbette, and, 'in the great event of the season' for 1931, Josephine Baker.[19] The most celebrated chanteuse of them all, Mistinguett, also played the Majestic, and her act showed the connection between two cities, as well as between France and the Europeans in Algiers and the importance of bringing Paris to them. In her December 1930 appearance, she sang one song greeting her audience, *Bonjour Alger*, but then began her revue, *C'est Paris*. She returned to the Majestic in 1932, in *Voilà Paris*.[20] Just as the locations of the Majestic and other Seibarras sites underscored the ethnic and racialized demarcations of the city, so too did the performances assure audiences that they were more firmly linked to France and to Paris than to North Africa. ·

Mostly, there were movies. All the important films from Hollywood, France, Germany and the UK came to Algiers and circulated through North Africa, of course, but Seibarras's exhibition sites were known to show the very best. In 1934, the entrepreneur announced that he had contracted to present forty of the most important French films throughout his cinemas, including *Les Misérables* (1934) with the great star Harry Baur, director Marc Allégret's *Lac aux dames* (1934), Anatole Litvak's *Cette vieille canaille* (1933, once again with Baur), *Tartarin de Tarascon* (1934), starring Raimu, who probably surpassed even Baur in popularity, *Sidonie Panache* (1934), with Antonin Artaud making one of his last film appearances, and Julien Duvivier's *Le Petit Roi* (1933). Most of these films, alone or in combination, were either adaptations of major French literary works, featured the most important French stars, or were directed by some of France's most respected filmmakers. More importantly, Paris had already passed judgement on them. Announcing Seibarras's coup, *L'Afrique du Nord illustrée* alerted readers that 'metropolitan' audiences, those in Paris, previously had given these films a 'warm and spontaneous welcome'.[21]

A single Hollywood movie from the 1930s provides yet another indication of the significance of Seibarras's exhibition sites and their status as practically the equal of the most important cinemas in Paris. For his entire chain of cinemas, Seibarras booked the film that was probably the greatest international hit of the decade and certainly the most critically acclaimed, *Blanche-Neige et les sept nains* (*Snow White and the Seven Dwarfs* [1937]). When Walt Disney's first feature-length animated film arrived in Algiers in the fall of 1938, it was major news. *Blanche-Neige* had already been a sensation in Paris and elsewhere in Europe and the United States, and *L'Echo d'Alger* began running advertisements a full week in advance of the opening at Seibarras's Régent cinema, an extraordinary publicity campaign at the time.[22] When *Blanche-Neige* opened, the newspaper ran the story not just on the movie page but also in the column *La Vie artistique*, with news of other significant cultural events in Algiers, such as a concert devoted to the works of Mozart and Bach.[23]

Seibarras's empire

Even more than the films, the cinemas themselves marked Seibarras as a visionary of modern North African culture, indebted to, while also asserting some independence from, French colonial authority. A Seibarras cinema stood out as an aesthetic accomplishment, but, of course, despite praise from the local press, architectural achievements in colonial locations are usually fraught, and this was particularly true in North Africa. In Algeria, French builders began changing the city from the moment France claimed the country in 1830. Architects designed the Place d'Armes in Algiers as a site for military manoeuvres as well as control of the residents of the city, and the location itself served to block any view of the headquarters of the previous ruling power, the Ottoman governor.[24] Over the course of the nineteenth century, in Algiers, Casablanca and elsewhere in the region, the French engaged in 'improvement' efforts, building Parisian-style streets to serve both commerce and the military. In the process, French architects also worked to 'Arabize' new buildings, to produce a brand of authentic experience for locals and tourists even as they Europeanized North African cities.[25] This kind of *Arabisance*, a French 'reinterpretation of the forms of ... local architecture', met with significant criticism throughout North Africa as a sort of literal window-dressing, typically limited to the details of the facades of new buildings.[26]

A Seibarras cinema, however, either new or renovated, was understood as a significant architectural event. The cinema that attracted the most attention, the Empire, in Fez, Morocco, opened in 1931, and even the name of the cinema, as well as its location on the avenue de France, invoked the vast range of French colonial authority in the region. Nevertheless, while the cinemas in North Africa might stand as monuments celebrating allegiance to France, they could

Figure 2.2 The Empire cinema in Fez, Morocco. From *Les Chantiers nord-africains*, January 1932. Bibliothèque nationale de France.

also indicate the possibility for some aesthetic independence. We can know the details about the Empire because of an extraordinary francophone architectural journal from the 1930s, *Les Chantiers nord-africains* (*North African Building Sites*), which covered the region's new commercial spaces, gardens and much more. *Les Chantiers* particularly celebrated streamlined Arab modernism, and it was precisely the new cinemas, built for sophisticated, usually European audiences, that typified the journal's taste. Seibarras built more of those cinemas than anyone else, and *Les Chantiers* devoted an extended article to the triumph of the Empire in its issue from January 1932[27] (Figure 2.2).

The 2,000-seat Empire served as a cinema and casino, not altogether uncommon at the time, especially for the very best sites which typically belonged to Seibarras. Entering the Empire, moviegoers walked by arcades with a shop in each one: a brasserie, a tobacconist and a patisserie, among others. The large lobby space, decorated with Moroccan terra cotta tiles, allowed filmgoers to walk easily without disturbing those in line at the ticket booths, which were also inside, with the magnitude of the interior and the ease of movement in marked contrast to the more typical and cramped 'provincial cinemas'. A 'monumental staircase' made of Moroccan marble fanned out in the centre of the lobby, providing access to the balcony, with the entire interior space coloured in shades of what *Les Chantiers* called 'Berber yellow and black'.[28]

This seems, then, like the perfect 1930s ultra-modern space, a mix of European and North African aesthetics as well as a flâneur's dream, given the possibility of walking idly from shop to shop, going into the orchestra section, strolling up the staircase to the balcony or wandering into the casino that stood adjacent to the cinema. We have no other description in any francophone source as thorough of a Seibarras cinema, nor so full an assertion of how such a venue might signify North African capabilities and self-reliance. *Les Chantiers*, in fact, ended its discussion of the Empire with just such a claim. This newest Seibarras cinema was 'one of the most beautiful jewels in Fez', perfectly capturing Morocco's tradition as a 'pioneer . . . in progress, comfort, and good taste'.[29]

Along with showing films, Seibarras's cinemas also served their communities, with the exhibition sites emerging as multi-purpose locations for commercial and non-commercial activities. There was the benefit in Algiers, at the Régent, for the *Societé des Ingénieurs Civils de France*, and the medical conference hosted at the Modern in Mostaganem, and the masked ball at the same cinema. But most often, Seibarras lent his cinemas to causes for children. There were special screenings for kids, for instance, and a benefit for school cafeterias in Algiers, and, in 1940, for those children whose fathers were prisoners of war.[30] There are ample other examples that show Seibarras donating the use of his cinemas in the manner of many urban film impresarios, probably in other locations in North Africa and certainly in France.[31] Seibarras here typifies, then, the exhibitor with significant links to the community, who understood the cinema, broadly, as a public good, and the space of cinema as serving the public, in this case primarily European, in a variety of ways. These events were communal and charitable, but just as often, Seibarras assumed the position of colonial authority, bringing the alleged benefits of Europe to the remotest parts of Algiers, using the space of the cinema as the space of French cultural control.

The colonial project

In 1932, the French press took one of its rare notices of Seibarras. The Algerian showman had gone to Berlin for the International Congress of Educational Cinema conference to offer a demonstration of Pathé-Rural. That was the mobile system, launched in 1927 by the film company Pathé, to take cinema where it had yet to go, in rural France and also in the colonies, all of which was made possible by the development of Pathé's small gauge, 17.5 mm format.[32] Reporting on the conference, the French film magazine *Hebdo* celebrated Seibarras as the 'energetic champion' of Pathé-Rural who had brought this 'admirable invention' to 'the remotest villages in the desert', so that people there would now 'be able to enjoy all the instructive and spectacular benefits that the cinema brings with it'. Largely through Seibarras's efforts, Pathé-Rural had achieved 'considerable success' in Algeria, and as a result would extend its reach to Morocco and Tunisia.

Comœdia, a daily Parisian review of cultural events, ran the same report as did *Hebdo*, and appropriately enough headlined the story, 'Pathé-Rural Conquers Algeria'.[33] French-language North African sources also applauded Seibarras's efforts in the same terms as the French articles, for bringing all the parts of Algeria together through the miracle of cinema, even those farthest from the Algiers metropolis. In April 1933, *L'Afrique du Nord illustrée* wrote that, through the 'magnificent task' assumed by Seibarras and the 'marvelous instrument' of Pathé-Rural, the northernmost sections of Algeria would become one with those of the interior.[34] Seibarras would unify Algeria and use the French cinema to do it, the Algerian businessman working in the service of empire, using the technologies that empire had given him.

This was also the case in 1930, the centennial of French control of Algeria. Seibarras opened his 4,000-seat, appropriately named Majestic cinema in Algiers that same year, in April, and made this crowning contribution to the urban landscape a means of celebrating 100 years of France's colonial control. The centennial has been well documented, taking up, as it did, so much of Algerian civic life and particularly for the first six months of 1930, serving as an overture to the International Colonial Exhibition of 1931 in Paris.[35] The festivities in Algeria promoted a view of a benevolent French military occupation, with colonial dignitaries counting on friendly Algerian officials to praise the progress of the preceding century.[36] Some Algerians, of course, resisted these efforts, but there would be less of this in 1930 than in the period just before the Second World War, around Bastille Day events in particular, in large part because of the gradual development of the Algerian Communist party over the decade.[37]

The opening of the Majestic left no doubt of Seibarras's dedication to France. At least according to *L'Afrique du Nord illustrée*, by the late 1920s Seibarras had decided to build the Majestic precisely 'for the occasion of the Centenary'.[38] While this may have been a little journalistic over-excitement, the first screening at the new cinema linked the businessman and his exhibition site directly to French colonialism and occupation. Seibarras opened the Majestic with Jean Renoir's newest film, *Le Bled* (1929), the director's apologia for French authority in Algeria, with the title referencing the country's sparsely inhabited interior.

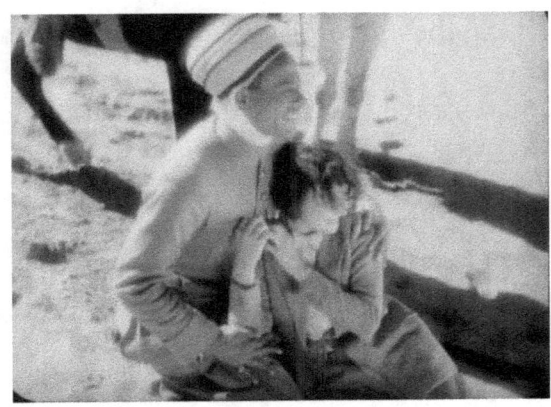

Figure 2.3 An Algerian helps the French heroine in Jean Renoir's *Le Bled* (1929).

Renoir made *Le Bled* to honour the centennial, and the French-language Algerian press considered this *Film du Centenaire* an honour bestowed upon the region because so much of it was made on location, in Algeria.[39] *Le Bled* had opened in Paris not quite a year before, so anticipation had been building for a long time in Algiers and throughout North Africa.[40] Renoir's son claimed that filming in Algeria had completely changed his father's mind about colonialism, but the movie leaves little doubt about its political position. Renoir's last silent film, *Le Bled* is a love story about two French expatriates caught up in the disputed inheritance of an Algerian farm. Extolling France's 'modernizing' and 'improvement' efforts, the film contrasts French superiority to an Orientalized Arab culture. Renoir included an extended fantasy sequence of the 1830 landing of French troops at Sidi Ferruch, the beginning of the European invasion but here the justification of a young Frenchman's continued cultivation of his ancestral Algerian farm[41] (Figure 2.3).

Seibarras screened *Le Bled* for an invitation-only first-night audience of local dignitaries from government and business, including the vice president of the city's chamber of congress, the director of the Crédit Lyonnais in Algeria and the mayor of Algiers. Linking the evening firmly to the anniversary of French control, another official in the audience that night was the Commissaire Général du Centenaire, the director of all centennial events in Algiers.[42] There were dozens of other events related to the centennial around the same time as the opening of the Majestic; *L'Echo d'Alger* ran a regular *Manifestations du Centenaire* column so readers could keep track of all the festivals, meetings, concerts and lectures. The screening of *Le Bled* at the Majestic seemed designed to coincide with *La revue du Centenaire* held the same day, with many officials undoubtedly at both events, reviewing the parading French and Algerian troops in the afternoon and then watching Renoir's movie in the evening.[43]

Attacking the emperor

Seibarras was not without detractors, sometimes in print and sometimes much more dangerously, and his cinematic empire might not simply be seen as a benefit to the region. At the end of 1932 and the beginning of 1933, for instance, *La Tranchée*, a periodical for Algerian veterans (the name of the newspaper translates, in English, to *The Trench*), attacked Seibarras for several months, directly referencing his status as an emperor of sorts. In this case, the businessman seemingly refused to help the community enough and, at least to *La Tranchée*, denied the history of Algerian sacrifice during the Great War.

'Napoléon Seibarras, Emperor of Cinemas', *La Tranchée* headlined on the front page on 1 October 1932, and the comparison to the former French leader was not meant to be a kind one. Seibarras, apparently, had booked the Amar circus, a troupe of four French brothers, all of whom were veterans. They had requested that Seibarras donate some of the proceeds to veterans' groups, and for reasons *La Tranchée* could not imagine, except for wanting to keep the money from the circus to himself, Seibarras refused.[44] *La Tranchée* maintained the attack. Two weeks later, and again on its front page, the newspaper noted that the 1932 French film *Les Croix de Bois* directed by Raymond Bernard played at Seibarras's Alhambra cinema in Algiers. *Les Croix de Bois* was something of a French version of *All Quiet on the Western Front*, Lewis Milestone's 1930 antiwar film, made in Hollywood, that was one of the great international sensations of the early sound era. This was, then, an ideal film for *La Tranchée* to champion, and one that might directly benefit the newspaper's readership. When Seibarras apparently refused to donate any of the box office to Algeria's veterans, *La Tranchée* dismissed the showman as someone who only engaged in 'philanthropy when the gesture makes him rich'.[45]

Seibarras had other enemies who created damage more tangible than critical editorial comments. Early in the morning on 8 October 1935, Seibarras's Alhambra, where *Les Croix de Bois* had appeared a few years earlier, was burned down. For the fall 1935 season, Seibarras had converted the Alhambra from a cinema to a legitimate theatre to bring significant live performances to Algiers and also, importantly in the events leading up to the fire, to bring them a new casino as well.[46] Just after the fire, a man was arrested as he tried to leave Algiers for Marseille, picked up by the notoriously tenacious port police who kept close track of those leaving North Africa for France or trying to come back.[47] Moïse Lebrati was about twenty-five years old and worked at the Alhambra, selling candy there.

He claimed at first that he had merely opened the theatre doors for the arsonists, but then admitted that he set the fire. He also named an accomplice whom the police soon arrested: Georges Hanoune, the owner of the Splendid Cinema in Algiers, one of the leading *cinémas d'exclusivité* in the city, although Hanoune would not have been in Seibarras's class as a businessman. Hanoune seems to have been upset that Seibarras was granted a casino licence for the Alhambra, perhaps instead of his own establishment, and he would soon be imprisoned.[48] Seibarras rebuilt the Alhambra quickly, and by early 1936 the theatre began a full schedule of performances.[49] But the fire there was the sign of significant local conflicts in North African film exhibition, with Seibarras, the cultivated man-of-the-world, also very much involved in the rough and tumble of Algiers' entertainment industry, where rivals might burn your business to the ground.

Joseph Seibarras died on 13 November 1942. *L'Echo d'Alger* reported the 'sad news', adding that the businessman 'had succumbed . . . after a short illness'.[50] Just weeks before, the same newspaper announced the 'liquidation' of Seibarras's *Societé des cinématographes*, and added that creditors might now stake claims to the money they were owed.[51] Before this, there had been no reporting about any financial difficulties facing Seibarras. For at least the next few years, his cinemas continued, although francophone newspapers in Algiers no longer identified them as Seibarras sites, which might indicate some changes in ownership or simply a shift in journalistic policy. The last mention of Seibarras in the available materials comes not from Algiers but from Casablanca, in December 1946. *Le Petit Marocain* informed readers of the 'generous gesture' of a Seibarras cinema in the city, donating box office proceeds to an orphans' association.[52]

There is little evidence to go on, in French-language sources, regarding the decline of Seibarras's empire. Of course, many film careers from the period, in North Africa, France and elsewhere, faced the unpredictability of a difficult industry. Seibarras's death came towards the end of Operation Torch, the successful Anglo-American invasion of North Africa in November 1942 that liberated the area from Vichy control. It is certainly possible that the hardship of the war contributed to problems in the national film industry, although the greatest victims of fascism in Algeria were Jews and Muslim nationalists rather than successful businessmen like Seibarras.[53]

Algeria and the rest of North Africa were never quite under the same forms of fascist control as France broadly and the French occupied space – including Paris – in particular. American films continued to play in Algiers throughout the war, when they had been banned in the Occupied Zone in 1940 and in Vichy in 1942. There were fewer of those movies, and all of them seem to have been reissues rather than new, but nevertheless they played.[54] The war, however, did disrupt the typical colonial relationships between France and North Africa. France itself became something of a colony, either controlled by German forces or by governmental authorities enthusiastically on the side of Germany, as was the case in Vichy. As they did with other French industries, the Nazis took over the French cinema. There is an extensive bibliography on the subject, dealing mostly, however, with issues of representation. That is, the question preoccupying Western film scholars has been what happened to French films, narratively, visually and politically, when they were made under German jurisdiction. These scholars have less frequently addressed shifts in the film industry and only in the French national context.[55] But these industrial concerns need to be extended to those areas that had been dependent on French cinema, in Southeast Asia, for instance, and also in North Africa.

For cinema historians, a career like Seibarras's highlights the networks and pressures of how films moved through cities and were screened there. Examining exhibition quickly leads to intensely local issues, as with the conflict between Seibarras and Georges Hanoune. But, this kind of study also requires an understanding of film distribution and exhibition as a function of colonial authority. Seibarras built cinemas that were understood in Algiers, at least in a range of journalistic sources, as quintessentially North African, but he was also doing the work of the empire when he brought Pathé-Rural to the Algerian desert or screened *Le Bled* at the centennial, and he was dependent on France as the central colonial source that facilitated his own expansion through Algeria and the rest of the region. The decline and apparent end of Seibarras's empire certainly had at least something to do with the decline, for the duration of the war, of France's colonial power and the abruptly implemented German control of France's film exhibition sites and film studios. Joseph Seibarras, *le roi du cinéma* in North Africa and also the loyal colonial subject, died before having the chance to be restored to the position that might have followed the Allied victory, a victim, of course, not only of his illness but also of the dramatic industrial shifts brought on by the fascist takeover of France.

Notes

1 André Sarrouy, 'Un grand animateur: M.J. Seibarras', *L'Afrique du Nord illustrée*, 13 July 1929, 12. Ernest Mallebay, 'Un Trusteur', *Annales Africaines*, 27 November 1925, 753; 'L'Exploitation en Afrique du Nord', *L'Afrique du Nord illustrée*, 15 April 1933, 6.

2 'Ciné-Finances', *Hebdo*, 9 April 1932, 17.
3 Colin Crisp, in one example among many, writes extensively about Haïk in *The Classic French Cinema, 1930–1960* (Bloomington, IN: Indiana University Press), 1997.
4 Ernest Mallebay, 'Un Trusteur', *Annales Africaines*, 27 November 1925, 753.
5 André Sarrouy, 'Un Grand animateur', 12.
6 André Sarrouy, 'Un Grand animateur', 12.
7 For Seibarras's cinemas, 'Cinématographes J. Seibarass, Afrique du Nord, les plus beaux films dans les plus belles salles', *Notre Rive*, 27 October, 10.
8 'À bien noter', *L'Echo du Tiaret*, 21 February 1931, 2.
9 Clifford Rosenberg, 'The International Politics of Vaccine Testing in Interwar Algiers', *The American Historical Review* 11, no. 3 (2012): 672.
10 Henry S. Grabar, 'Reclaiming the City: Changing Urban Meaning in Algiers after 1962', *Cultural Geographies* 21, no. 3 (2014): 389–90.
11 Around this time, French authorities understood these 'non-Europeans' as comprised of seven 'races': Moors, Jews, Arabs, Berbers, Negroes, Turks and Kulughlis, the latter a term to designate 'the offspring of unions between Algerian Muslim Arab women and Turkish soldiers'. See Julia Clancy-Smith, 'Exoticism, Erasures, and Absence: The Peopling of Algiers, 1830–1900', in *Walls of Algiers: Narratives of the City Through Text and Image*, ed. Zeynep Çelik, Julia Clancy-Smith, and Frances Terpak (Los Angeles: The Getty Research Institute; Seattle, WA: University of Washington Press, 2009), 23.
12 Omar Carlier, 'Medina and Modernity: The Emergence of Muslim Civil Society in Algiers between the Two World Wars', in *Walls of Algiers*, 62–84.
13 Estimates for cinemas in Algiers come from movie advertisements in *L'Echo d'Alger*, for instance 12 February 1939, 6.
14 Complicating this sense of the importance of the film to French film history, *Sous les toits de Paris* was produced and distributed by Tobis-Klangfilm, a German company that had built a studio in Epinay, France, to make movies in French, and Clair's would be among the first.
15 For *Sous les toits de Paris* in Algiers, see *L'Echo d'Alger*, 28 September 1930, 5.
16 For discussion of the architectural realignment of Algiers, see Afaf Zekkour, 'Les lieux de sociabilité islahistes et leurs usages: la ville d'Alger (1931–1940)', *Le Mouvement social* 236 (2011): 23–34.
17 'Les Spectacles', *Annales Africaines*, 1 December 1928, 463.
18 'Spectacles', *L'Africain*, 4 November 1930, 4; 'Les Sports', *L'Africain*, 4 November 1930, 4.
19 André Sarrouy, 'Le 'Majestic' d'Alger', *L'Afrique du Nord illustrée*, 10 October 1930, 14; 'Joséphine Baker', *Les Spectacles d'Alger*, 2 December 1931, 2.
20 'Mistinguett dans *C'est Paris*', *Les Spectacles d'Alger*, 24 December 1930, 2; 'Mistinguett', *Les Spectacles d'Alger*, 28 December 1932, 2.

21 'En Afrique du Nord', *L'Afrique du Nord illustrée*, 8 September 1934, 16.
22 *L'Echo d'Alger*, 26 October 1938, 6.
23 F. Herlin, 'La Vie artistique: À L'Écran, au Régent, *Blanche-Neige et les sept nains*', *L'Echo d'Alger*, 1 November 1938, 2.
24 Zeynep Çelik, 'Colonial/Postcolonial Intersections: *Lieux de mémoire* in Algiers', *Historical Reflections/Réflexions Historiques* 28, no. 2 (2002): 144.
25 Jean-Louis Cohen, 'Architectural History and the Colonial Question: Casablanca, Algiers, and Beyond', *Architectural History* 49 (2006): 349–72.
26 Seth Graebner, 'Contains Preservatives: Architecture and Memory in Colonial Algiers', *Historical Reflections/Réflexions Historiques* 33, no. 2 (2007): 257–76. For *Arabisance* defined, see Hiba Barbara and Tamás Molnár, 'Towards Understanding the Colonial Heritage in Algeria: The Case of the Sheridan Villa', *Pollack Periodica: An International Journal for Engineering and Information Sciences* 14 (2019): 226.
27 De Chabot, 'Un casino-cinéma à Fez', *Les Chantiers nord-africains*, January 1932, 55–8.
28 De Chabot, 'Un casino-cinéma', 55, 57.
29 De Chabot, 'Un casino-cinéma', 59. The article referred to Morocco as a 'pays d'avant-garde en matière de progrès dans le bien-être et le bon gout'.
30 Fred Bédeil, 'Vulgarisation des Sciences', *L'Afrique du Nord Illustrée*, 16 December 1933, 5; 'Conférence du Médecin Capitaine Daigre', *La Gazette de Mostaganem*, 21 February 1932, 2; 'Les Petits Mostaganémois', *La Gazette de Mostaganem*, 20 December 1931, 1; 'Fête scolaire au profit des cantines scolaires', *L'Echo d'Alger*, 21 March 1941, 2; 'Pour les enfants des démobilisés et des prisonniers de guerre', *L'Echo d'Alger*, 25 December 1940, 2.
31 For rallies in cinemas in and around Paris, see Eric Smoodin, *Paris in the Dark: Going to the Movies in the City of Light, 1930–1950* (Durham, NC: Duke University Press, 2020), 92–7.
32 'Pathé-Rural sonore en Afrique du Nord', *Hebdo*, 29 October 1932, 7.
33 'Pathé-Rural fait la conquête de l'Algérie', *Comoedia*, 4 November 1932, 6.
34 'Le cinéma partout et pour tous', *L'Afrique du Nord illustrée*, 15 April 1933, 16.
35 Jan C. Jansen, 'Fête et ordre colonial: Centenaires et résistance anticolonialiste en Algérie. Pendant les années 1930', *Vingtième Siècle: Revue d'histoire* 121 (2014): 61.
36 Jansen, 'Fête et ordre colonial', 65.
37 Jan C. Jansen, 'Celebrating the "Nation" in a Colonial Context: "Bastille Day" and the Contested Public Space in Algeria, 1880–1939', *The Journal of Modern History* 85, no. 1 (2013): 55.
38 Sarrouy, 'Un grand animateur', 12.
39 'Le Film du Centenaire', *L'Afrique du Nord illustrée*, 29 December 1928, 14.
40 *La Semaine à Paris*, 10 May 1929, 89.
41 For production of *Le Bled*, see Pascal Mérigeau's *Jean Renoir: A Biography*, trans. Bruce Benderson, Chapter Six (Philadelphia, PA: Ratpac Press; Running Press,

2017). For Alain Renoir's comments about his father's changing attitudes towards colonialism, see 350.
42 F.G., 'La soirée d'inauguration du "Majestic"', *L'Echo d'Alger*, 12 April 1930, 3.
43 'La revue du Centenaire fut une magnifique et glorieuse évocation de cent ans d'histoire', *L'Echo d'Alger*, 13 April 1930, 2.
44 'Napoléon Seibarras, Empereur des Cinémas', *La Tranchée*, 1 October 1932, 1.
45 Kerdavid, '*Les Croix de Bois* à Alger', *La Tranchée*, 16 October 1932, 1.
46 'Le théâtre de l'Alhambra est complètement détruit par un violent incendie', *L'Echo d'Alger*, 10 October 1935, 1.
47 For the arrest, A. Souquet, 'Une main criminelle a mis le feu au théâtre de l'Alhambra', *L'Echo d'Alger*, 17 October 1935, 1; A. Souquet, 'Moïse Lebrati est-il vraiment l'incendiaire du théâtre de l'Alhambra?', *L'Echo d'Alger*, 18 October 1935, 4. Kathleen Keller discusses Algerian port police in *Colonial Suspects: Suspicion, Imperial Rule, and Colonial Society in Interwar French West Africa* (Lincoln, NE: University of Nebraska Press, 2018), 53–85.
48 The suggestion Hanoune sought a gambling licence and was upset that Seibarras received one instead comes from 'Le Juif tabou', *L'Action Française*, 22 September 1936, 4. As a fascist, anti-Semitic newspaper, *L'Action Française* assumed the guilt of both Lebrati and Hanoune because both men were Jewish.
49 André Sarrouy, 'L'Information', *L'Afrique du Nord illustrée*, Winter 1936, 40.
50 'Mort de M. Joseph Seibarras', *L'Echo d'Alger*, 14 November 1942, 1.
51 'Liquidation judiciaire Seibarras', *L'Echo d'Alger*, 18 October 1942, 3.
52 'La Bataille du rail', *Le Petit Marocain*, 21 December 1946, 2.
53 James McDougall, *A History of Algeria* (Cambridge: Oxford University Press, 2017), 178.
54 For Hollywood films playing in Algiers, see, *L'Echo d'Alger*, 8 October 1942, 2; 25 December 1941, 2.
55 Work on the wartime French film industry includes Evelyn Ehrlich, *Cinema of Paradox: French Filmmaking under the German Occupation* (New York: Columbia University Press, 1985) and Sylvie Lindeperg, *Les écrans de l'ombre: La Seconde Guerre mondiale dans le cinéma français, 1944–1969* (Paris: Éditions Points, 1997).

3

Access for the Axis

The battle for ideological supremacy on Middle Eastern, North African and Turkish cinema screens between 1933 and 1945

Kajsa Philippa Niehusen and Ross Melnick

In recent years, scholars have paid increasing attention to the Nazi effort to globalize its cinematic propaganda infrastructure beyond Germany's borders. In addition to Roel Vande Winkel and David Welch's canonical edited collection, *Cinema and the Swastika: The International Expansion of Third Reich Cinema*, historians are continuing to excavate the history of Nazi film distribution and exhibition around the world from Los Angeles to Johannesburg to Buenos Aires.[1] 'Access for the Axis' continues this research in a new direction by examining how the ideological battle lines drawn between the Allies and the Axis played out on Middle Eastern, North African and Turkish cinema screens, exposing the ways in which the United States and Britain as well as Nazi Germany and Fascist Italy saw the Middle East and North Africa (MENA) as well as Turkey as an all-encompassing region, a fertile site for ideological expansion and cinematic propaganda through the distribution and exhibition of motion pictures.

The contours of the Allied and Axis approach did not always target their cinematic propaganda campaigns ethnically or linguistically, however, but instead drew up and managed these cinematic strategies through a much larger regional lens. For example, the Nazi-controlled Ufa (Universum Film AG), Germany's most prolific production and distribution company during the 1930s and until the end of the Second World War, divided up the world by region and targeted MENA as a whole. Colonial legacies between Europe and MENA, of course, created immediate cinema territories for German and Italian propaganda and orientation. France's colonial order over Lebanon, Syria and much of North Africa provided a number of tentacles throughout the region for the growing Nazi octopus of occupation and subjugation, all under the political supervision of Vichy France, the authoritarian French state under Marshal Pétain that was set up after the German invasion of France in June 1940. Vichy France, as a collaborator with Nazi Germany, enforced a pro-Nazi slate of motion pictures in the bustling cinemas of Vichy-controlled Syria and Lebanon until 1941 and in the cinemas of French colonial Morocco and Algeria from 1940 to 1942, before all of these territories were captured by the Allies and those screens were subsequently refreshed with a very different slate of films. In Libya, alongside the Nazis, Fascist Italy spread its own colonial wings in cities like Benghazi where cinemas were taken over and converted into either Nazi-managed *Deutsche Soldatenkinos* (German Soldier Cinemas) or Italian-run *Cinema di Partito Nazionale Fascista* (Cinema for the National Fascist Party). The Nazis as well as Britain and the United States also focused their attention on MENA's most important market – Egypt – with the largest number of cinemas and highest economic viability of any other.

Much further east, during negotiations with West-Osteuropäische Warenaustausch Aktiengesellschaft (WOSTWAG), a trading company registered in Berlin but run by the Soviet secret service, Ufa proposed three combinations of Muslim-majority countries as potential regions for building an exhibition monopoly and for the export of German films. These 'monopoly regions' focused on Egypt, Saudi Arabia, Sudan, Iraq, Syria, Palestine, Iran, Afghanistan and Turkey.[2] Rather than paying attention to linguistic, cultural and/or historical differences, the Nazi focus on MENA grouped Turkey (as well as Iraq, Iran and Afghanistan) in with these Arabic-speaking territories, considering the Turkish market, for example, to be closer affiliated with those nations than with Europe. According to manuscripts consulted at the German Federal Archives in Berlin, which house the majority of internal Ufa documents that survived the war, Ufa's expansion into the Turkish market was perhaps the most successful out of this region of opportunity. Unfortunately, there is a distinct dearth of archival sources documenting Ufa's forays into these significant (mostly) Arabic-speaking markets. From the American and German trade press, we can gather limited but important information on films being screened or produced in countries like Egypt, but the only extensive collection of internal Ufa documents on Nazi film activities in MENA pertains to the Turkish market. This is probably less due to the fact that the Nazi film industry refrained from engaging in other markets in MENA and other surrounding nations but, instead, is likely a result of Ufa documents being lost in the chaos of the last days of the war, which saw the bombing of the Ufa complex in Babelsberg outside of Berlin. Another reason why Turkey presents a crucial case study here – beyond the comparative richness of internal Ufa files documenting the German film industry's approach to this market – lies in the fact that Turkey remained a neutral nation throughout most of the war, allowing both Allied and Axis countries to conduct business and political suasion there. On the other hand, many MENA countries were controlled by Britain and its Allies before the war or as a result of the conflict, making the large-scale distribution of German films significantly harder in these territories.

MENA at war and at the movies

During the 1930s, Nazi Germany and Fascist Italy sought to expand their film distribution and exhibition in MENA, moves which corresponded with infrastructural and cinematic propaganda efforts by private American and British film companies. Cairo, for example, became a key battle zone for cinematic ideology in the 1930s. A local Jewish boycott had reduced the appeal for local exhibitors to book Ufa and other German films being produced under the aegis of Nazi control and racial politics. By contrast, the appeal for Hollywood films only grew during this period in major cities such as Alexandria and Port Said as Egypt had produced few talkies in the early 1930s, allowing the appetite for sound films to be largely sated by British, French and American films. The ongoing cosmopolitanism of Cairo also made these films key attractions for the city's multitudes of both foreign and local cinemagoers.

The Nazis were resolute, however, about the need to distribute their films in the key Egyptian market. The local boycott against German cinema was solved, in part, by Ufa both drastically reducing rental prices for Egyptian exhibitors to book German films and by the company's efforts to lease its own 'second-class' movie house in Alexandria charging around six pennies per ticket as opposed to the more typical one or two shillings for comparative cinemas.[3] In the years that followed, Ufa films began cropping up in other Egyptian cinemas, despite the boycott, including at the Ramsis and Fouad movie houses, as well as at the 3,000-seat Wahbi Cinema in Cairo, owned by one of Egypt's best-known cinematic figures, actor-director-producer Yusuf Wahbi.[4] Understanding that newsreels, even more than feature films, could sway public opinion, Ufa also struck a deal with the ascendant Studio Misr, one of the leading producers of Egyptian cinema, for an exchange of newsreels 'of common interest' in which Ufa Wochenschau footage would reportedly be screened in Egyptian cinemas while the Misr (Egypt) Newsreel would be sent to Germany.[5] Studio Misr also became the site of German-Egyptian co-productions in the form of two feature films directed by Fritz Kramp, *Widad* (in

1936) and *Lashin* (in 1938). In her recent publication on the transnational history of early sound filmmaking in Egypt, Henriette Bornkamm writes that both films enjoyed popularity with Egyptian and Arab audiences, with *Lashin* successfully running for three weeks at Cairo cinemas despite the simultaneous runs of large Hollywood productions.[6] Local Nazi agents also worked to pressure Egyptian exhibitors not to screen anti-Nazi films such as Warner Bros.' *Confessions of a Nazi Spy* (1939). However, after *Lashin*, no other Egyptian-German co-productions were completed as German filmmakers were forced to leave at the outbreak of the war in order to avoid internment.[7] Nazi newsreels and other short and feature films, regardless of their content, were also banned.

Hollywood was similarly focused on Egypt and had also eyeballed the growing importance of the 'Arabic-speaking world' as part of its efforts to replace lost wartime European revenues by expanding its foreign distribution operations and infrastructure in MENA (as well as in Latin America, Australia and South Africa). At the outbreak of the Second World War, there were only 500 cinemas in MENA from French colonial Morocco to newly independent Iraq where German forces had just helped overthrow British colonial rule, softening up Iraq for Ufa, not Hollywood, films. As Elizabeth Thompson writes, Egypt's economic prowess and cinematic infrastructure and importance outshone all others with 118 cinemas in the country compared to only a *combined* 103 in Iraq, Lebanon, Palestine, Syria and Transjordan. The remainder of those 500 cinemas could be found in North Africa, where, Thompson notes, 'European colonial elites' – not local moviegoers – 'dominated the urban audiences'.[8] Although as Morgan Corriou's chapter in this volume shows, Arabic-speaking audiences in North Africa did also make up a significant percentage of audiences at certain cinemas (see Chapter 1).

British colonial power, linguistic and cultural affinities, and Jewish-led boycotts of Ufa films all made Ufa's impact in Egypt pale by comparison to the ongoing *urban* popularity of Hollywood films. Literacy in Egypt had risen during the 1930s but less than 20 per cent of the total population could read subtitles by 1937, numbers that were far higher in major cities like Cairo, Alexandria and Port Said.[9] Owing to that reality and the lack of dubbing in this market, films screened in smaller villages were often Egyptian, not American, British or German. (Post-war efforts to dub Hollywood films into Egyptian Arabic were met with deep hostility by actor-director-producer Yusuf Wahbi, who lobbied the Egyptian government against allowing dubbed films to be exhibited, which would have made them accessible to all Egyptians regardless of education or class, threatening Egypt's national cinema industry.[10]) 'A mix of Arabic-speaking elites and Levantines (of Italian, Greek, and Jewish descent) dominated the best theaters', Thompson writes of Egypt's cinemas in the early 1940s, as 'side screens with text in French, Greek, Italian, and Arabic provided translation of Hollywood films, which were only rarely dubbed into Arabic before 1945'.[11] 'Half the entertainment in seeing a picture here', *Variety*'s George Lait observed in 1943, 'is to watch how the translators have wrestled with, and ultimately mangled, some nifty [gag] which took the Marx Bros. months to sweat . . . over'.[12]

As the Egyptian, largely urban, demand for Hollywood films continued to grow, Loew's International built their own 'shop window' theatre, the Cinema Metro in Cairo, for the premiere presentation of MGM short and feature-length films and as a home for MGM's foreign newsreel. The Cinema Metro opened at the end of January 1940, just months before fighting in North Africa began between Allied and Axis armies which threatened not only to upend all of Egyptian cinema-going but the nation's sovereignty as well.[13] The following year, German planes bombed Alexandria, causing the deaths of hundreds of Egyptians.[14] The Nazi effort to win many remaining hearts and minds was buried in that rubble. Egypt also became the MENA base for British forces fighting German and Italian troops, flooding Cairo's cinemas with British soldiers anxious for both British and Hollywood feature films and newsreels. They were not alone. United Artists executive Al Lowe wrote that following the outbreak of the Second World War, 'thousands of natives who never could visit the cinema before, are [also] becoming regular customers'.[15]

After Egypt, Palestine was the second most important English-speaking market for Hollywood and the British film industry during the 1930s and 1940s in MENA. (Lebanon's overall ticket sales outpaced Palestine's, but many of those screens were dedicated to Egyptian, French and other films.) Due to the growing influx of Jews to this British Mandate, German films had also been largely kept off local screens due to an ongoing Jewish-led boycott of German products – especially highly visible exports such as motion pictures – by the mid-1930s.[16] In addition to the Egyptian and other films playing in cinemas, such as the Alhambra in Jaffa that catered to Palestine's Arabic-speaking population, Hollywood and British films flowed in during the 1930s and during the Second World War as pro-Nazi films remained prohibited and Vichy-era French cinema was similarly despised (Figure 3.1). Motion pictures, like all things in Palestine, remained under the watchful eye of the British, which ruled this increasingly fractious and geographically important territory. While the Mandate was British, many of the films imported into Palestine were from the United States where, thousands of miles away, an anxious Hollywood worked to promote the Allied war effort through both fiction and nonfiction

Figure 3.1 The luxurious Alhambra Cinema towers over the Jaffa, Palestine streetscape in 1937. Courtesy of G. Eric and Edith Matson Photograph Collection, US Library of Congress.

films for receptive markets such as this. A. P. Waxman wrote in *Variety* that 'There's nothing the Nazis can do in the way of propaganda that we can't do better, once the High Command in Washington really realizes that movies are weapons'. After all, he added, 'The movies have sold American ideas to the whole world for years. The movies can also sell the whole world the idea that "The Yanks Are Coming" and Uncle Sam ain't clowning!'[17]

As the war expanded globally in 1941, especially after the United States' entrance following the Japanese attack on Pearl Harbor, Thompson notes that 'Arabic-speaking countries in the Middle East were a vital, early front in World War II'.[18] In addition to the installation of Nazi films in Vichy France's colonial possessions, foreign affiliations and control also provided the Axis with ideological authority over Libyan screens, a vestige of Italy's colonization of lands to its south. Allied intervention in MENA had also profited from its own colonial ties, as Egypt remained wedded to the Anglo-Egyptian treaty of 1936, which continued British military control over the Suez Canal and in support

Figure 3.2 A box containing a presentation print of the British Ministry of Information-produced *Desert Victory* (1943) sent from Prime Minister Winston Churchill to 'The Spartan General', Field Marshall Bernard Law Montgomery, who commanded the Allied troops to victory over German General Erwin Rommel in North Africa. Crown Copyright.

of the country's monarchical, Wafd-era politics.[19] Control over Palestine and relations with Saudi Arabia and Transjordan were part of that colonial legacy.

Colonial authority regulated screen content, blocked enemy films from importation and curated the set of newsreels, shorts and feature films that were screened around the country. During a battle for MENA hearts and minds, the inclusion or exclusion of Nazi-, Fascist-, British- or Hollywood-produced newsreels and feature films had the great potential of swaying *local* moviegoers who flocked to urban and village cinemas for entertainment and wartime information. The Deutsche Wochenschau, the renamed wartime Nazi newsreel, was adapted linguistically and politically for distribution to each receptive overseas market. Hollywood distributed its own adapted newsreels abroad, as did the US Office of War Information. Italy, too, sent its Giornale Luce newsreel into its own colonial outposts in Libya and Ethiopia. (In addition to its colonial occupation of Libya, Italy had invaded Ethiopia in October 1935 and remained in control of the territory until May 1941, when British troops gained control and deposed Ethiopian Emperor Haile Selassie was able to return. Libya, however, remained under both Italian and German control until the Allies forced both armies out in February 1943.) (See Figure 3.2.)

Both the Allies and the Axis understood that military control over a given territory also meant ideological control through each nation's most popular form of public amusement: motion pictures and the venues that housed them. Radio waves carrying propagandistic messaging could be easily transmitted across political and geographical borders; film, however, required the physical infrastructure of state-regulated distribution and exhibition. Nazi propaganda broadcasts to the 'Near East' were indeed finding some traction by 1941, according to a top commissioner at the US Federal Communications Commission, and the Nazis' use of Arabic-language broadcasts in fomenting anti-Semitism and anti-Allied sentiment has been discussed at length by Jeffrey Herf, who points to the way the medium was used in order to assert the idea of an 'elective affinity between Nazism and what the Nazis claimed Islam to be'.[20] David Motadel notes that while the use of Arabic-language radio programmes in MENA was considered to be of great importance by German authorities, the Nazis also used broadcasts in Turkish to try and spread their propaganda there.[21] All of these transnational radio broadcasts could easily permeate physical borders; control over movie screens, by contrast, required a local mandate. French and Italian colonialism in MENA enforced the early but fleeting control over local screens.

The Axis' early domination of much of North Africa (and its cinemas) was directly challenged during the shifts of power between 1941 and 1943 when, after a series of military battles, the Allies retook much of the region and in 1943 fully routed and expelled both Nazi and Italian forces, setting the stage for the Allies' eventual invasion of Italy through Sicily. The loss of North Africa was a key military defeat for the Axis and it also brought a swift end to pro-Nazi ideology in and control of cinema screens from Morocco to Libya.

In November 1942, as the Allied effort was turning the tide in North Africa, Robert Riskin, head of the United States' Office of War Information (OWI) Overseas Film Division, cited 'the importance of motion pictures in the propaganda battle against the Axis' in the OWI's shipment of prints to territories newly taken by the Allies as they routed Axis armies. Hollywood films, which had been banned under Vichy orders in favour of Nazi propaganda, were now being screened across the region. Riskin told *Motion Picture Daily* that the presentation of Hollywood films and the US government's OWI newsreel there included 'President Roosevelt's delivery of his speech to the people of France and North Africa [which] had been cheered'.[22] *Motion Picture Herald* argued that 'the North African campaign has demonstrated that wherever the United States and her Allies strike a blow at the Axis, American motion pictures follow quickly upon the heels of the successful troops'.[23] OWI's mass distribution of fiction and nonfiction films – in addition to pro-American newspaper advertising in Turkey, Egypt, Sudan and throughout North Africa – as well as in the rest of the now-Allied controlled MENA, became a blueprint for the military-to-movies changeovers to come in Europe and Asia.[24]

German films in Turkey during the Second World War

Nazi efforts in MENA diminished heavily between 1940 and 1943 as Allied control meant the removal of Nazi and Fascist cinema in favour of British, American and other films. A more successful and lasting campaign for Nazi cinema infiltration took place in Turkey, instead, and provides a granular model (and case study) for the Nazis' initial and more hopeful designs for cinematic expansion in MENA. Unlike many other countries in the region – including ongoing post-Ottoman British authority or protectorate status in Iraq, Transjordan and Kuwait – Turkey was one of the few nations of MENA not directly or indirectly controlled by an outside power. It was, therefore, able to choose sides as it pleased.

After the Nazis invaded Greece in May 1941, adding 175 movie houses to the increasingly global Nazi cinema circuit, the *Motion Picture Herald* lamented that Greece was now the '15th country lost by Hollywood to Nazis'.[25] By that time, a total of 11,184 cinemas in Europe were under Nazi influence and film distribution. Losses in market presence and sales revenue had become synonymous with concerns over the weakening of American cultural and political influence as the war continued, still tilting in the Axis' direction half a year before the bombing of Pearl Harbor and the entrance of the United States into the global conflict.

Throughout the 1930s and into the 1940s, Ufa had already pursued an expansion of their business in Turkey. At the time, domestic Turkish film production remained low as most films screened in Turkey were of American, British, German and French origin. Ufa's decision to strengthen their position in the Turkish market was logical both from an economic standpoint and in the interest of disseminating Nazi film propaganda. In the following section, we will trace the efforts made by Ufa, which sought, in cooperation with the Reich Film Chamber, the Ministry of Enlightenment and Propaganda, and the German Ambassador to Turkey, to strengthen their position in the Turkish market, and discuss how Ufa attempted to establish a productive relationship with local distributors and exhibitors to increase German influence and push Allied film propaganda off Turkish screens.

Turkey, the Allies and the Axis

When the Republic of Turkey was founded in 1923, the abolishment of the sultanate brought an end to over 600 years of monarchical Ottoman rule. While Turkey officially became a secular parliamentary republic, it would be controlled by one party, the Republican People's Party, until 1945, even leading the Nazis to consider Turkey as among the Fascist states next to Italy and Germany.[26] During the Second World War, it was the main directive of German Ambassador to Ankara, Franz von Papen, to keep Turkey neutral and unaligned with the Allies.

The Turkish government had the same goals, hoping to stay out of the armed conflict with a great deal of diplomatic manoeuvring while the Allied and Axis powers tried to win over Turkey to their respective side. Diplomacy and various types of propaganda, from radio broadcasts to the dissemination of fake stories in newspapers to film exhibition, were all part of this ultimately unsuccessful effort.[27]

In October 1939, Turkey, Britain and France signed a treaty under which Turkey guaranteed that it would not close the Dardanelles against Allied warships should they need to pass through in the event of a war between the Allied powers and Russia – at the time allied with the Germans – while not guaranteeing that Turkey would take up arms against Russia. Another provision of this treaty was that Turkey would enter the war on the side of the Allies should Italy enter the war on the side of Germany. This was considered a crucial victory for the Allies; after all, Turkey and Germany had been staunch allies in the First World War.[28]

In May 1941, Germany occupied Greece, Turkey's neighbour to the west. On 18 June 1941, Turkey and Germany signed a non-aggression pact, negotiated by Ambassador Franz von Papen, which included stipulations preventing Turkey from entering the war on the side of the Allies. Turkey ultimately played both sides during the war as it retained not only diplomatic ties with the Allies but also served as one of the main suppliers of chromium ore to the Third Reich, a resource needed for building weapons. By the time Turkey officially joined the Allies in February 1945, the war was almost over, and no Turkish soldiers saw combat.

Ufa's distribution partners in Turkey

In 1923, when the Republic of Turkey was founded, there were only about 30 cinemas in the country; ten years later, that number had more than doubled to around 80,[29] and by 1939, it quickly rose to about 130. Istanbul was the centre of film exhibition with more than a dozen cinemas.[30] In 1934, Radio Pictures (RKO) local chief Harry Leasim, described the Turkish market as an 'overexpanded' film business with 'too many theaters'.[31] But the lack of Turkish production coupled with the rising number of cinemas wired for sound made for an attractive export market for nations with strong film industries, such as the United States and Germany.

Despite the popularity of certain German stars with young Turkish audiences, the number of German films screened in Turkey during the 1930s had not been able to reach a market share close to that of Hollywood. As internal documents of Germany's largest film studio, Ufa, show, the perceived failure of German films to hold a strong place on the Turkish film market was attributed to two factors: the supposedly 'primitive taste' of Turkish audiences that was satisfied by American and French productions and the fact that a majority of Turkish exhibitors were Jewish. Unhappy with the strength of the American market position in Turkey, Ufa began planning a reorganization of their Turkish distribution business in 1937.

Istanbul, with around sixteen cinemas, was considered the most promising city for the exhibition of German film. The district of Pera, located on the European side of the city, was especially attractive due to its cosmopolitan flair and its diverse residents, which included immigrants from various Mediterranean and West European countries. Beyond the large cities of Istanbul and Ankara, rural areas were also considered to have a decent market potential.[32] According to an internal Ufa report written in 1937 by Hermann Hersch, an employee stationed in Istanbul, there were few entertainment options for Turkish audiences with expandable time and income. Cinema was deemed to be the only form of entertainment enjoyed regularly by all Turks, irrespective of class, making it a crucial area for the distribution of Nazi propaganda and cultural affinity. However, a concern remained regarding the Turkish preference for fast-paced, action-oriented American films, as opposed to German films, which Ufa considered more tasteful, complex and serious. Hersch was confident that, over time, Turkish audiences would learn to appreciate Germanic-style films that, Ufa argued, displayed more 'depth and dignity'. Hersch also pointed out that, due to the brotherhood in arms forged between the Ottoman Empire and the German Kaiserreich during the First World War, the Turks felt generally sympathetic towards Germans and German culture.[33] This feeling was confirmed when the Ufa office in Berlin took note of an article in the Istanbul-based French-language newspaper *La République*, which called the 'Americanization of Turkish youth' a 'national danger' and proposed that cinemas should be dedicated to the showing of historical and educational films 'like in certain European countries', perceived by Ufa as a nod to their own productions.[34]

In his report, Hersch proposed a new distribution and exhibition partner for Ufa: Fernando Franko. Franko owned and operated the Saray cinema, which was deemed to be the largest movie house not just in Turkey but in the entire Balkan region. Hersch described Franko as trustworthy, reputable and well connected to all players in the Turkish film industry, with many years of experience. Hersch posited that 'no other film distribution company here is as well, let alone better, organized', and pointed to the firm's successful partnership with United Artists. Concluding his report, Hersch stressed: 'I believe that we have found in the company Franko the most suitable connection, one we can trust and one which promises to yield the best chances for business.'³⁵ However, an unidentified individual reviewing Hersch's report added a handwritten note stating, 'Franko is Jewish' to the document. Ufa's foreign department ultimately declined this potential collaboration, likely in an effort to keep its foreign film arrangements entirely *judenrein* (free of Jews).³⁶

Interestingly, though, it appears that members of Ufa were not especially keen on having to follow these kinds of anti-Semitic and racist policies in their dealings with Turkish exhibitors. In a confidential August 1939 memo written by Fritz Tietz and addressed to directors Meydam, von Theobald and Thorhauer, Tietz, who had travelled to Turkey to study the situation of the film market in the summer of 1939, happily noted that in his consultation with a representative of the Ministry of Propaganda he learned that the Turkish market was, for the time being, 'completely free' for the German film industry, meaning that Ufa would be able to 'begin constructing relationships with Turkish *Dönme*, half-Jewish and Jewish distributors and cinema owners without having to fear that any German authority would hinder or disturb such work based on racist principles or personal interests'.³⁷ (The *Dönme* [Turkish for 'converts'] are a small, originally Jewish sect which officially converted to Islam in the seventeenth century and have remained the subject of conspiracy theories ever since.³⁸)

Nonetheless, Ufa's relationship with one of the main exhibitors of German films in the late 1930s, Boman Sinema Filmleri, ended because Dr Schwarz of the Reich Film Chamber announced that business with the Boman group was no longer acceptable for cultural-political reasons precisely because the company was owned and operated by individuals belonging to the *Dönme*. This was unwelcome news to Ufa's foreign department, which was worried that 'with the termination of relationships with our previous client [Boman group], it is likely that we will lose the [Turkish] market for a long time'.³⁹

Ufa finally did find an 'acceptable' partner in Turkish distributor/exhibitor Necip Erses. In December 1939, Erses had contacted the Reich Film Chamber to share his observations that German films had in recent years largely disappeared from the local market, and had been replaced instead by other foreign films, mainly from Hollywood: 'Assuming that you are interested in distributing films in the Turkish market not only for economic, but also for cultural reasons, I would like to ask if you may have interest in establishing a business relationship with me in order to supply me with films directly or via Italy.'⁴⁰ Ufa initially declined, based on their belief that Erses did not have any cinemas in the district of Pera, and was thus unsuitable.⁴¹

Looking to find a new partner for the distribution and exhibition of German films in the Turkish market while visiting Turkey in 1940, Dr Schwarz of the Reich Film Chamber contacted Erses to start negotiations. Ideologically, Erses was a perfect match for the Nazis, being of 'Aryan Turkish' descent, and having lived, worked and studied in Germany for ten years.[42] He operated and co-owned the Sakarya cinema and later, in 1943, gained part ownership of a 650-seat cinema called Cemberli-tasch. Additionally, his company Ses-Film leased another cinema, the Sark. Negotiations initiated by Reich Film Chamber representative Dr Schwarz in September of 1940 established Necip Erses as the main exhibitor of German feature films, cultural films and newsreels. The initial contract with Erses included a minimum import of ten German films per year.[43] The distribution and exhibition of German films became far more successful once Erses officially became Ufa's middleman. By 1942, Erses was distributing two dozen German films in Turkey, more than twice as many as the previous year. In fact, the business relationship with Erses was such that Dr Schultz, another representative of the Reich Film Chamber, projected that Erses' company, Ses-Film, could eventually be developed into an exclusive distribution outlet for Ufa.[44]

Out of the hundreds of feature films produced in Germany every year, Ufa's foreign department compiled lists of films for the Turkish market from which Necip Erses and the other distributors could choose. These included wartime films made by the other German production companies Bavaria, D.F.E., Terra, Tobis, Continental and A.C.E., the latter of which produced films in France. Thus, some of the feature films that Ufa brought into Turkey were screened under cover of appearing to be French films, rather than obviously German. In fact, Necip Erses had specifically requested these non-German language productions from Ufa after he had encountered unspecified 'resistance' to his exclusive exhibition of German films, which led to him being considered a German propagandist by some.[45] Likewise, many of the German films were dubbed into Turkish. Most of the films cleared for the Turkish market fell into the genres of musicals and romantic dramas, which had been most successful with Turkish audiences. Generally, the films that had proven most popular in Germany and that could be considered flagship productions were also considered for export. Among the films Necip Erses accepted in 1942/1943, for example, were *Wiener Blut* (*Vienna Blood*), an operetta film directed by Willi Forst and starring Willy Fritsch, one of Germany's most popular actors. The film was one of the most financially profitable productions during the Nazi regime. Likewise, *The Great Love*, directed by Rolf Hansen, made it unto Turkish screens. The film cleverly combined Zarah Leander's star appeal, a love story, and *Durchhaltepropaganda* (perseverance propaganda), reminding German audiences that they were expected to make sacrifices for their fatherland. Ufa also offered Erses the pictures *D III 38*, a war story glorifying German fighter pilots, directed by Herbert Maisch in 1939, and even the infamous anti-Semitic hate propaganda film *Jud Süß* (1940), directed by one of Nazi Germany's most prominent directors, Veit Harlan, but, notably, neither of these films were accepted by Erses for distribution. In July 1936, Turkish censors had stipulated that permits would be refused for films which were propagandizing a particular country, were demeaning of any race or nation, showed people of the Orient and the colonies as wild or half-wild creatures and propagandized against them or that included religious propaganda.[46] Necip Erses's reluctance to accept highly militaristic and anti-Semitic films was likely informed by these regulations. The censorship laws in Turkey also banned the showing of political figures and scenes from the current war, which posed a problem for German newsreel exhibitions in the country. Fritz Tietz, second manager of the *Deutsche Wochenschau* (German Weekly Newsreel), in his frustration over the Turkish censorship rules, opined that the principle followed was one under which any instances of 'German strength, German order, German discipline, great German achievements' were 'eradicated', not leaving much worth showing.[47]

On the other hand, some of the German entertainment feature films that were screened, like Gustav Ucicky's 1940 drama *Der Postmeister*, *Madame Bovary*, a historical drama based on the popular novel by Gustave Flaubert and directed by Gerhard Lamprecht in 1937, and the operetta *Der Unsterbliche Walzer* (E. W. Emo, 1939) proved such a success in the Turkish market that several Syrian distributors who were staying in Istanbul at the time of their exhibition contacted Necip Erses through the German embassy in order to discuss licence agreements for German films for the Syrian market. Unfortunately, there is no paper trail documenting the outcome of these discussions, but the interest demonstrates the usefulness of the Turkish cinema market domestically and perhaps as a model for other MENA exhibitors. What this episode shows is that beyond guaranteeing regular exhibition of German films in Turkey, Erses also became an important part of Ufa's efforts to distribute its films throughout other Middle Eastern markets.[48]

By June 1942, *Variety* observed that the 'Nazis are willing to subsidize all of their film product to get their screen propaganda across in Finland and Turkey, rated on-the-fence nations presently. Influx of Nazi product at outlandishly low film rentals thus far has prevented US film companies from getting their normal bookings'.[49] Ufa's reorganization of their film distribution in Turkey (and beyond) and their policies of subsidizing film screenings seemed to be paying off. In Necip Erses, Ufa had found a reliable exhibition partner with an astute knowledge of the Turkish market. Through Erses and his dubbing studio and cinemas, Ufa was able to centralize their film distribution and do so under the aegis of a local exhibitor which could guarantee that the German films chosen would appeal to Turkish audiences. In addition, Germany's now state-regulated and state-sponsored film industry, unlike Hollywood's free-market film companies that required inflows of capital, was not deterred by unprofitable film rental agreements. Spreading German films in neutral territories and pushing Allied product off Turkish screens was a stronger motivation than any economic considerations. The flood of Nazi film propaganda was now a chief concern for the Allied forces (and their respective film industries) with regard to 'on-the-fence nations' like Turkey.[50] To make matters worse for the Allies, the dubbing of German films into Turkish was also ramped up, making German films amenable to local audiences, regardless of literacy. Indeed, the Germans had expanded their partnership with Erses to include the synchronization of German films into the Turkish language. For each German film, Erses would pay the costs associated with synchronization and then deduct those costs from the film rental, meaning that, essentially, Ufa paid for the dubbing. Dubbing was, once again, a crucial element in making foreign films attractive to local audiences, especially in rural areas where literacy was lower.[51] Cut rate prices and Turkish dubbing thus facilitated the growth of Nazi cinema. Britain's Ministry of Information attempted to counteract the Nazi-Erses alliance by distributing ever more British and American films in Turkey it deemed to be uncontroversial.[52] As *Variety* put it in early 1943, the neutral country had now become a 'pawn on the international chess table in the diplomatic game being played by the Axis and the United Nations' and 'a center of competition in the motion picture trade with control of the propaganda at stake'.[53]

While German films mostly came to cinemas operated by Necip Erses, the Ufa, as well as the Reich Film Chamber and Ambassador von Papen, were hoping to ultimately find a 'more worthy premiere theatre' for German film product. In 1943, Dr Schultz of the Reich Film Chamber received authorization by Ufa's foreign office to initiate the acquisition of a newly built cinema in Istanbul's Pera district. The 600-seat cinema, Ar-Sinemasi, had originally been constructed by an Armenian exhibitor, encouraged by the Italian embassy, and was supposed to serve as a first-run outlet for Italian films. In October 1943, however, a lease agreement for five years was signed, and German films finally had their own cinema 'at the eleventh hour', according to von Theobald and Dr Schultz. The Reich Ministry of Economics supported Ufa in the lease financially. Ufa, with increasing control, even began considering ending its business with Erses, hoping to no longer rely on him as a distributor and exhibitor for German films in Turkey.[54]

Ultimately, though, Ufa lost its cinematic influence there as the country ceased diplomatic and economic relations with Germany in August 1944, after the Soviet Army invaded Bulgaria. On 23 February 1945, Turkey declared war on Germany. By April, days before the end of the war, Ufa's foreign office noted that they had not been informed about the status of their German first-run cinema in Istanbul for over a year.[55] Ufa certainly had larger concerns by then.

Conclusion

Despite all of their efforts in Turkey, Ufa was never fully able to overcome the allure and infrastructure of Hollywood. And with the nation's late turn against the Nazis, Ufa and German cinema vanished altogether. As always, Nazi and Fascist Italian cinema could only dominate markets fully controlled *militarily* by the Axis. Even in neutral nations in MENA and other surrounding territories, Hollywood's cross-class appeals and widely liked narratives tended to sell better, helped by a vast prewar marketing and distribution infrastructure.[56] British colonial control certainly aided and abetted that absorption and the inevitable American and British fiction and nonfiction films that flowed with it. As Nezih Erdogan argues, American films still dominated the Turkish film market after the war broke out in 1939, and by the mid-1940s, American cinema had fully (re-)established its hegemony in Turkey.[57]

As for the MENA, Elizabeth Thompson reminds us that during the war far more was at stake than cinematic control. 'Arab peoples', she writes, 'were concerned about surviving wartime food shortages and ousting European armies from their soil'.[58] As an industry forged by immigrants and outsiders, Hollywood had purposely developed a global menu of films that spoke to the multiple heritages outside and within its own borders – including the many Egyptian, Lebanese, Syrian and other immigrants that now called the United States home. The Nazis' own desire for racial purity, and the covert and overt messaging of their films, required an appreciation for German supremacy and wartime 'kultur', a less desirable quality for those viewing these films under Nazi control or in countries where the Nazis certainly meant to.

Turkey, therefore, represents the Axis' most successful efforts in and around MENA and certainly its longest lasting. While Vichy's control over Moroccan and Algerian screens was all-encompassing, it was also short-lived. As those and other countries like Libya fell to the Allies, Turkey remained the region's only viable hub for ongoing Nazi suasion. The battle for control over Turkish screens demonstrates once more the importance of MENA, Turkey and other nearby countries as sites of wartime conflict, both militarily and cinematically, and how fiction and nonfiction films and the venues that exhibited them were an essential part of that struggle.

The interest in controlling MENA screens and the ideologies projected onto them did not end in 1945. As the Cold War quickly heated up after the Second World War, the Soviet Union on one side and the United States and Great Britain on the other side battled for hearts and minds in Palestine and throughout the region. The Soviet Union even planned a new global exhibition empire for its own communist films, a plan that included financing the construction of cinemas throughout the region in exchange for guaranteed playing time for its ideologically oriented motion pictures.[59]

The endless desire to carve up MENA for cinematic and ideological control is a reminder that this expansive region has been a perennial target for economic, military, mineral and political exploitation and that cinema has played an important role in that effort, from oil company promotional films to clandestinely produced foreign newsreels (such as those produced by the United States Information Agency) for local, domestic consumption. Before, during and after the Second World War, MENA remained subject to outside forces seeking to use both cinematic entertainment and information for political and strategic ends.[60] MENA's wartime cinemas and the struggle to control the content on their screens are a reminder that this history remains a generative source to see more clearly the persistent consistency of these efforts and their varying degrees of efficacy and influence.

Notes

1 Roel Vande Winkel and David Welch (eds), *Cinema and the Swastika: The International Expansion of Third Reich Cinema* (New York: Palgrave Macmillan, 2007). Among other works, see Kajsa Philippa Niehusen. "Naziganda in the United States: Third Reich films in American Cities." Ph.D. Dissertation, University of California, Santa Barbara, 2022.

2 'Memorandum for the negotiations with WOSTWAG', 3 June 1937. BArch, R/109/I – 2556. [BArch stands for Bundesarchiv or German Federal Archives. The Ufa documents are located at the film archives of the German Federal Archives in Lichterfelde, outside of Berlin].

3 'Ufa Out to Spike Boycott in Egypt', *Jewish Daily Bulletin*, 11 December 1934, 6.
4 Mohannad Ghawanmeh, 'Entrepreneurship in a State of Flux: Egypt's Silent Cinema and Its Transition to Synchronized Sound, 1896–1934' (PhD Dissertation, Los Angeles: UCLA, 2020), 60–3; Edward Asswad, 'Chatter: Egypt', *Variety*, 6 June 1933, 61.
5 'Reich, Egypt in Deal', *Motion Picture Daily*, 1 December 1936, 13.
6 Henriette Bornkamm, *Orientalische Bilder und Klänge: Eine transnationale Geschichte des frühen ägyptischen Tonfilms* (Marburg: Schüren Verlag, 2021), 146.
7 Bornkamm, *Orientalische Bilder und Klänge*, 201.
8 Elizabeth F. Thompson, 'Scarlett O'Hara in Damascus: Hollywood, Colonial Politics, and Arab Spectatorship during World War II', in *Globalizing American Studies*, ed. Brian T. Edwards and Gaonkar Dilip Parameshwar (Chicago: University of Chicago Press, 2010), 187–8.
9 Israel Gershoni and James P. Jankowski, *Redefining the Egyptian Nation, 1930–1945* (Cambridge: Cambridge University Press, 2002), 12.
10 Michael Hollingsworth, 'Education in Egypt's Development: The Need for a Wider System of Appraisal', *Project Appraisal* 1, no. 4 (1986): 247; Jacques Pascal, 'Egypt', *Motion Picture Herald*, 22 February 1947, 50; Robert Vitalis, 'American Ambassador in Technicolor and Cinemascope: Hollywood and Revolution on the Nile', in *Mass Mediations: New Approaches to Popular Culture in the Middle East and Beyond*, ed. Walter Armbrust (Berkeley, CA: University of California Press, 2000), 269–91.
11 Thompson, 'Scarlett O'Hara in Damascus', 188.
12 George Lait, 'Vaude Troupe Under Fire on Sahara; Show Biz Hot, Too; No Africa Closeup', *Variety*, 20 January 1943, 2.
13 Cinema Metro Advertisement, *Egyptian Gazette*, 31 January 1940.
14 '200 More Killed in Alexandria Raid: German Planes Smash Block of Apartments – British Bomb Foes in North Africa', *The New York Times*, 9 June 1941, 1.
15 A. A. Lowe, 'Egypt', 10 June 1944, 99AN/1F, Box 7, Folder 1, United Artists Corporation Records, 1918–1969, Wisconsin Historical Society.
16 'Palestine Would Bar Nazi Picts', *Variety*, 15 April 1936, 13; 'U.S. Pictures Have Head Start in Favor With Palestine Public', *Motion Picture Herald*, 20 February 1937, 70.
17 A. P. Waxman, 'Movies Are Weapons', *Variety*, 27 January 1943, 14.
18 Thompson, 'Scarlett O'Hara in Damascus', 187.
19 Thompson, 'Scarlett O'Hara in Damascus', 184.
20 'Effect Of Nazi Propaganda', *Broadcasting*, 2 June 1941, 24; Jeffrey Herf, *Nazi Propaganda for the Arab World* (New Haven, CT: Yale University Press, 2009), x.
21 David Motadel, *Islam and Nazi Germany's War* (Cambridge: Belknap Press of Harvard University Press, 2014), 103.
22 'Cites Films as Key Propaganda Force', *Motion Picture Daily*, 20 November 1942, 4.
23 'Majors Plan Recapture of Foreign Markets', *Motion Picture Herald*, 16 January1943, 17.

24 'OWI Acts as International Ad Agency', *The Billboard*, 9 October 1943, 3, 12.
25 '15th Country Lost by Hollywood to Nazis', *Motion Picture Herald*, 10 May 1941, 54.
26 'As the Nazis see it, Europe now counts three "Simon pure" Fascist states: Italy, Germany and Turkey'. Quoted in 'Nazis to Campaign Outside Germany', *The New York Times*, 9 July 1933, 3.
27 'Nazi "Party Line"', *National Association of Broadcasters Report*, 13 February 1942, 84.
28 Edwin L. James, 'Allied-Turkish Treaty Has Large Importance', *The New York Times*, 22 October 1939, 67.
29 *Film Daily Yearbook, 1933* (New York: J.W. Alicoate, 1933), 1013.
30 'US Films Hold Lead in Eastern Europe', *Motion Picture Herald*, 11 March 1939.
31 'Modernization of Turkey a Break For Yanks; Fezzes Out and Jazz In', *Variety*, 25 December 1934, 11.
32 The feasibility of course would need to be examined against the backdrop of Turkey's expanding transport network system. This is beyond the scope of this chapter, but for more information, see Nevin Coşar and Sevtap Demirci, 'Incorporation into the World Economy: From Railways to Highways (1850–1950)', *Middle Eastern Studies* 45, no. 1 (2009): 19–31.
33 Hermann Hersch, 'Report About the Introduction of Ufa, Universum Film AG, Berlin, into Turkey/Bericht über Einführung der Ufa, Universum-Film A.G., Berlin nach Türkei', 5 June 1937, 21. BArch, R/109/I – 2556.
34 File Memo, Ufa, Berlin, 3 March 1943. BArch, R/109/I – 2556.
35 Hersch, 'Report About the Introduction of Ufa', 21.
36 Hersch, 'Report About the Introduction of Ufa', 21.
37 Fritz Tietz, Confidential memo addressed to Director Meydam, Director von Theobald, Thorhauer, 30 August 1939. BArch, R/109/I – 2556.
38 Adam Kirsch, 'The Other Secret Jews', *The New Republic*, 14 February 2010, https://newrepublic.com/article/73081/the-other-secret-jews
39 Notes to the protocol of the thirtieth meeting of the panel for film export of the Reich Film Chamber and the state-mediated film companies, 3 June 1939. BArch, R/109/I – 2556.
40 Letter from Necip Eres to the Reich Film Chamber, 13 December 1939. BArch, R/109/I – 2556.
41 'Türkei', *Licht-Bild-Bühne*, 6 May 1939.
42 Von Theobald of Ufa's foreign department writing to Ufa's board of directors, 5 November 1940. BArch, R/109/I – 2556.
43 Protocol about the negotiations in Turkey, signed Necip Erses, 6 September 1940. BArch, R/109/I – 2556.
44 Excerpt from the protocol of the meeting of the board of directors, assembled for the Ufa foreign department by von Theobald and Dr Schultz, 15 September 1942. BArch, R/109/I – 2556.

45 Letter printed on the letterhead of the president of the Reich Film Chamber addressed to all members of the central committee of the Reich Film Chamber, 28 March 1941. BArch, R/109/I – 2556.
46 Memo from the Reich Ministry for Enlightenment and Propaganda addressed to Deutsche Wochenschau GmbH, 24 September 1941. BArch, R/109/I – 2556.
47 Confidential file note from Fritz Tietz to Dr Fried (Reich Ministry of Enlightenment and Propaganda), Dr Schwarz (Reich Film Chamber), and the Ufa board of directors, 25 August 1939. BArch, R/109/I – 2556.
48 Letter from Necip Erses, Ses-Film Istanbul to Ufa Berlin, 14 February 1941. BArch, R/109/I – 2556.
49 'Nazis Push Their Pix in Finland, Turkey', *Variety*, 24 June 1942, 16.
50 'Nazi War Films Widely Shown', *Motion Picture Herald*, 14 February 1942, 16.
51 'Axis Threatens U.S. Market in Turkey', *Motion Picture Herald*, 6 February 1943, 28.
52 'British Navy, RAF Deliver Own, U.S. Films to World', *Motion Picture Herald*, 14 February 1942.
53 'Allies and Axis Wooing Turkey's Film Interest', *Variety*, 20 January 1943, 20.
54 Report about the acquisition of a first-run theatre in Istanbul, compiled by von Theobald and Dr Schultz, 1943. BArch, R/109/I – 2556.
55 'On the state of our foreign branches that are threatened or already in enemy hands', internal Ufa memo, 12 April 1945. BArch, R/109/I – 2556.
56 John Trumpbour, *Selling Hollywood to the World: U.S. and European Struggles for Mastery of the Global Film Industry, 1920–1950*, Cambridge Studies in the History of Mass Communications (Cambridge: University Press, 2002).
57 Nezih Erdogan, 'The Making of Our America: Hollywood in a Turkish Context', in *Hollywood Abroad: Audiences and Cultural Exchange*, ed. Melvyn Stokes and Richard Maltby (London: BFI, 2007), 123.
58 Thompson, 'Scarlett O'Hara in Damascus', 188.
59 Thomas M. Pryor, 'All New U. S. Films Barred by France', *The New York Times*, 5 December 1945, 29.
60 Ross Melnick, 'A Long Ride on the Metro: Metro News, Hearst Metrotone Inc., and U.S. Studio-Government Relations', in *Rediscovering U.S. Newsfilm: Cinema, Television, and the Archive*, ed. Mark Cooper, Sara Levavy, Ross Melnick, and Mark Williams (New York: AFI Film Readers/Routledge, 2018), 195–7.

4

Egyptian women's empowerment and early cinema-going

Mohannad Ghawanmeh

The theatre of Egypt – its venues, texts, practices, practitioners, poetics and appeal – contributed to the early cinema more than the latter did the former, for two reasons. First, theatre predated cinema as a cultural form in Egypt as it did in many regions of the world. In the case of Egypt the theatre developed over a quarter-century, institutionalized as it was in the Azbakiya Theatre, inaugurated in 1868, and the khedival Opera House, founded in 1869. Second, cinema borrowed much from theatre, including the latter's practitioners, directors, writers and especially actors, who were discussed in the Egyptian press and in modern histories of the country since. Scholarship on these practitioners' lives and careers has helped us better understand the relationship between Egypt's theatre and its cinema, of how the country's Arabic playhouses fostered the careers of many who then figured prominently in film production. For example, Fawzi al-Jazayirli, comedic actor and troupe leader, along with his troupe Dar al-Salam featured in one of Egypt's first narrative (short) domestic film productions *Madam Loretta* (1919), which was based on a theatrical sketch of al-Jazayirli's.[1]

It is not surprising that studies centred on audiences of the Egyptian cinema in its early decades are rare.[2] The prolific press of the era scantly discussed the experience of Egyptian women attending theatres and cinemas. Egyptian periodicals instead covered actions taken by activist women, led by Huda Sha'rawi, an influential organizer and vociferous public figure, and their male allies, affirming women's role in their country's development, women who had sought greater participation in public life and national affairs. In this chapter, I sketch the experience of women's attendance of film exhibitions in Egypt during what I term the 'early industrial era' – spanning the introduction of film screenings in 1896 to the founding of Studio Misr in 1935, the Middle East's first full-fledged, industrial capacity film production studio – to demonstrate their gradual empowerment as audience members. Moreover, I offer that the legendary Ramsis Theatre, under the ownership and leadership of actor, playwright and director Yusuf Wahbi, helped legitimate and promote domestic narrative film production and women's patronage of the cinema concurrently so that both practices linked to the modernization of the nation.

Egyptian playhouses exhibited movies to countless Egyptians in the first decade of the twentieth century and continued to do so at least through the early industrial cinema era in Egypt. The Egyptian theatre was relatively young and considerably undercapitalized when the cinema was introduced to Egyptians in 1896, which, as I elaborate partly, explains convergence in their presentation for the next quarter-century or so. However, by the early 1920s Egyptian theatres had gained enough practitioners and audience patronage to permit it to do away with film screenings. One theatre, however, the Ramsis, continued to screen movies made by its own troupe for promotional and presentational purposes.

Founded by Yusuf Wahbi as director and lead actor, the Ramsis served not only the Egyptian cinema, it turns out, but also Egyptian women as practitioners and members of the audience. As an impassioned letter to *al-Kashkul* magazine in 1925 observes:

> You have created a field of criticism not perfectly known, and you have presented the actor before the people as better than a mendicant or 'tramp' as the people had known him, and have shown the actress as better than a 'harlot,' as she had been known. You have transformed theatres into honorable fora for families and thoughtful women, after they had been pits of corruption that righteous women were not permitted to frequent. And you transformed the people's view of art and its beauty, so that it was desired by young men and women after they had long avoided it. And you presented stars that were it not for your theatre would have still suffered the dark of night and the distress of approaching dark clouds.[3]

In what follows I trace the origins of film exhibition in Egypt's theatres and sketch out Egyptian women's introduction to these venues as audiences, leading up to the founding of the Ramsis Theatre in 1923. As it turned out, 1923 was a momentous year that also witnessed the promulgation of the country's constitution on the heels of Britain's unilateral declaration of Egypt's (nominal) independence the year prior. Adding to the significance of 1923 for the purposes of this study is it also saw the establishment of the first Arabic-language film magazine *Motion Pictures* (al-Suwar al-Mutaharrika, 1923–5), a publication proffering a few, rare references to women as audience members. To these references I add findings drawn from two later Egyptian Arabic-language film magazines, *Fan al-Sinima* (*Screen Art*, 1933–4) and *Cinema Planets* (*Kawakib al-Sinima*, 1934), as well as from popular Egyptian and industry American periodicals from the era, so that such scant references taken together and put into conversation with the limited relevant literature may signify an evident, if under-documented, experience of gradual empowerment on the part of Egyptian women who ventured out to playhouses and movie houses seeking entertainment, enculturation and social engagement.

Audience persuasion and education before Ramsis

The first films in Egypt were screened not in designated spaces but in clubs, cafes, casinos, hotels and especially playhouses. The first person to screen motion pictures was likely legendary singer turned actor Salama Hijazi. Possibly to compete with his former employer Iskandar Farah's Egyptian Theatre's (*al-Tiyatru al-Misri*) regular exhibition of motion pictures, Hijazi founded his Arabic Acting House in Cairo (*Dar al-Tamthil al-'Arabi*) in 1906, a theatre that concluded its opening ceremony with a presentation of colour motion pictures. Coupling variety performances and motion pictures became common practice in Egyptian theatres, beginning in the late 1800s, particularly in Cairo and Alexandria. Film historian Mahmud 'Ali has it that the 'Abdalla 'Ukasha and Brothers troupe was the last to take up cinematographic presentations in 1914, leaving George Abyad's as the lone troupe not to do so.[4]

Women attended film screenings in either designated spaces or dedicated timeslots. In the former, such spaces took the form of women-only boxes – referred to as loges. By 1914, a correspondent for *The Moving Picture World* in Cairo reported that cinemas in the capital had finally enabled women's attendance of all screenings 'by building special boxes for women, which they call harem boxes'.[5] The correspondent described them thus: 'These have fine blinds drawn over them through which the occupants can see, but which shield them from the crude, staring men in the pit below.'[6] The correspondent's account is credible, not that of the behaviour of the lascivious men in the pit, but in terms of exhibition practice relating to such women's loges and in terms descriptive of such boxes' architectural design. The Olympia Cinema offered as advertised *Loges spéciales Harem* seating for forty piasters and *Fauteuils de Loge Harem* for ten, the first being the entire loge and the latter merely a seat in it.[7] A description of the women's box, including its blinds, is offered by Rawiya Rashid of the Ramsis Theatre in her biography of Yusuf Wahbi.

Ramsis Theatre was among the houses[8] that offered women's loges, either originally or after refurbishing. I have not encountered a list of these, nor have I come across an explanation in primary or secondary sources of the conditions that led to such an architectural augmentation, but I believe that they were typically venues that could attract audiences at the premium ticket prices assigned to such seating. In the case of the American Cosmograph, the cinema named by the *Moving Picture World* correspondent, a newspaper advertisement listed, in French and in English, balcony seats for seven piasters and orchestra seats for three. The advert listed *galerie* (balcony) seats for two piasters, but in French, not in the English listing.[9] At the Olympia, balcony women's box seats sold for ten piasters and similar seats in the non-gendered loge, effectively the men's loge, were five piasters. *Troisièmes* (third-rate) seats were listed at one piaster, a tenth of the cost of the least expensive seat for women.[10] Seat pricing thus accounted for class and gender considerations. Including loges into a newly constructed cinema or refurbishing existing ones came at a substantial cost. Offering relatively expensive balcony seating, especially for women, signalled opulence that appealed to members of the middle and upper classes. It was these classes that establishments wished to attract, such as was the case with Ramsis Theatre.

Far more common than designating women's only seating sections in theatres and cinemas was that of dedicating performances or screenings, often matinees, to women only. This practice must have been current during the first quarter-century or so of the theatre in Egypt, because it was applied to the first film screenings in Cairo, in Schneider Hammam in January of 1896, *al-Mu'ayad* newspaper printed a notice of screenings for 'national and foreign mesdames'.[11] The *Pathé Cinématographe*, founded in 1906 as the first place to screen films exclusively in Cairo, designated a women's session on Thursday afternoons.[12] One of the most telling reports relating to such a practice was in the Arabic-language *al-Express* in early 1918. The newspaper noted that Egyptian women in Cairo were attending theatres regularly, 'neither veiled nor disappeared, in the best attire and the most splendorous, beautiful appearance . . . especially on Tuesdays when special performances are held for them in theatres that are not attended by men. And cinemas crowd with women on Thursday afternoons, and they occupy all of its seats and loges'.[13] For the first time since its launch in 1869, the Sultanic Opera began offering performances exclusively for women in 1917, instead of its long-standing gender-mixed but separate audiences, suggesting that the Opera was keen on attracting a female patronage it had deemed lucrative.[14] Before the end of the Great War women were, therefore, attending theatres and cinemas with vigour and sitting according to at least two arrangements – separate seating in a mixed audience or in exclusive women's sessions.

Ramsis sets a standard

The 'dean of the Arab Theatre' (*'amid al-masrah al-'arabi*) Yusuf Wahbi has been written about widely, but seldom at length.[15] His role in reviving theatre in Egypt is acknowledged as resulting from his troupe's appeal to audiences through an active catering to their tastes, as the Ramsis exceeded Egyptian theatre-goers' expectations of the theatrical experience, in both staging and environment.[16] Launched in 1923, the Ramsis attracted dignitaries and upper-class Egyptians from the outset.[17] By 1931, the Arabic theatre had garnered sufficient esteem as to attract government dignitaries, including the head of the leading political party of the interwar period the Wafd, several ministers, and even the prime minister himself. Among the Arabic theatres in the capital city, the Ramsis was one that the country's ruling elite attended, conveying unprecedented approval in their patronage of a native Arabic theatre.[18]

Ramsis's success conditioned Egyptian audiences to experience the cinema as a serious and generative art form in its own right. Ramsis was the theatre that instated the three-season regular performance schedule, excepting summer: a schedule other troupes followed and which then became the standard annual exhibition season for the country's cinemas.[19] Ramsis Theatre also set the stage for Egyptian audiences' support of and enthusiasm for the cinema, beginning in its year of foundation of 1923, by projecting magic lantern images of troupe performers in the theatre's entrance, screening footage of upcoming plays onto a stage screen during intermissions,[20] and by coupling projected filmic segments with theatrical performances.[21]

Contrary to the Opera's shift towards women-only sessions, during the First World War, Yusuf Wahbi's Ramsis moved towards gender-mixed sessions. Wahbi was no altruist, but he did lionize the theatre and did demand respect for it as he pursued glory for himself. He also realized that by 1923 women were attending entertainment houses prolifically, and consequently he sought them out as customers. Further, Wahbi may have determined that the customer base for the playhouse's performances would grow overall if audiences were gender integrated. According to Rawiya Rashid's most expansive biography of Wahbi, Ramsis first welcomed women to two performances on Sunday afternoons, but attendance was lacklustre, until Wahbi invited one of the most powerful Egyptian woman of the era, predominant Wafd party member and feminist Huda Sha'rawi, to attend an exclusive performance with her companions. The promotional move paid off, as over time women attended evening performances with their spouses,[22] and sat in designated loges with net-like coverings, as the previously noted report in the *Moving Picture World* describes of the Cairene American Cosmograph cinema nearly a decade earlier.

Wahbi did not care for exclusive spaces in his gender-mixed venues. Self-serving and intemperate as he may have been, Wahbi believed in the power of the theatre to move audiences and as such aimed to optimize the connection between audience and performers. It is for this reason that he preferred the theatre to the cinema. As Rawiya Rashid relates, Wahbi slyly got what he wanted by replacing the netted loge covering with a velvet one, so that women in attendance could hardly see the stage and consequently complained. Responding to audience complaints, Wahbi had the curtains removed completely so as to usher in a new standard of public audience configuration whereby women's sections in venues were no longer covered in any way.[23] Rashid's account of Wahbi needs to be taken with a pinch of salt since it was already the case not later than the year of the Popular Revolution of 1919 that women could attend Arabic troupe performances offered to mixed-gender audiences in Cairo and Alexandria, and their spouses and children could join them in theatre balconies.[24] Documentation does exist of mixed seating for non-relatives from 1923, as may be deduced from the pages of *Motion Pictures*, the first of Egypt's Arabic-language cinema magazines.

Egypt's early cinema magazines on women as audience

The three cinema magazines published in Egypt during the early industrial era scarcely commented on women's attendance of the cinema, although the first of these, *Motion Pictures* (*al-Suwar al-Mutaharrika*, 1923–5), allotted considerable space to a discussion among its readers about the propriety and value in Egyptian women's taking to the stage as performers. One such reader wrote in to admonish against such a practice on religious grounds. To support his argument, he cites a scandal at the Ramsis: 'Have we not heard of "N" who one member of the Ramsis troupe wanted to tempt to fall into the epicentre of corruption. This is the state of actors with audience members.'[25] Implicit in this reader's reference to the Ramsis Theatre is that if women were imperilled therein, at the most prestigious of the

Egyptian theatres, then it could be assumed that impropriety thrived at other, lesser, houses of entertainment.

Remarks about women's attendance in reader letters, presumably authored by men where unidentified, intimated that the cinema was not a place for women. A reader wrote in to complain about women's chewing of gum in the cinema, as indicated by the title of his note: 'The woman who attends the cinema to listen to music only, not to watch the narrative film (riwaya) has no place there and she must not be among the fans of cinema.'[26] Another reader from Alexandria, where theatres offered mixed seating for non-family members from at least 1919, wrote in to poetically relate his experience of being asked at the cinema by a portly woman behind him who Charlie Chaplin was, underscoring her ignorance of the cinema.[27] These men wrote to complain about undeserving women invading their exclusive cinema spaces at such proximity as to interfere with their viewing experience. It is unclear if this practice of non-familial, gender-mixed seating had spread to other parts of the country until nearing the end of the noted early industrial era, as soon discussed.

Men also voiced concern about the impact certain film content would have on women's morals and virtue. One person wrote in to denounce the screening of the controversially prurient *La garçonne* (Armand Du Plessy, 1923) for reasons including the film's 'interest in inciting a girl's degeneracy'.[28] He also called for banning the film 'to save the dignity of our women and morals'.[29] The magazine's resident film critic Questions Man (*Rajul al-As'ila*) in reviewing *La garçonne* joined the insistent reader's call for its ban on the grounds that it imperilled Egyptian women's virtue:

> Why do we permit these shameful narrative films the opportunity to appear before the eyes of our women when the vast majority of them are ignorant, tricked by the ways of corrupt European modernity to think that it is better than what they enjoy in their current lives? It is a duty of government to protect members of its populace, especially the weak among them and is there weaker than our women?[30]

The Question Man's concern for women as audiences was born out of a dismissive paternalism, that men must protect women from corruption, because women are incapable of protecting themselves, even intellectually.

Whereas the subject of women as cinema patrons was touched on a few times over the twenty-seven issues of *Motion Pictures* magazine, it is telling that I have not encountered even a passing reference to women as audience members in the tens of issues of culture magazines I have reviewed dating from the 1920s to first-half of the 1930s, publications such as *al-Musawwar*, *al-Sabah* and *al-Kashkul* except for that quoted earlier in this chapter. The subject was, however, broached once by each of the shorter-lived cinema magazines – *Screen Art* (*Fan al-Sinima*, eighteen issues, 1933–4) and *Cinema Planets* (*Kawakib al-Sinima* three issues, 1934). The passing mentions in these magazines are significantly indicative of women's cinema-going experience. The first such mention appears in a regular feature concerning cinema news in *Screen Art* titled 'The Cinema in Egypt and Abroad', which upon the release of the highly anticipated Egyptian film *The White Rose* (*al-Warda al-Bayda'*, Muhammad Karim, 1933) related, 'It has been evidently apparent that the smashing majority of women in morning screenings that may be attributed to the rough sex's [men] being busy during these times.'[31] That women and men attended the same screenings in Cairo's Royal Cinema, site of *The White Rose*'s premiere, was not new. However, what had developed was a steady, if relatively scant, Egyptian narrative film production, an industry whose success depended on the patronage of all patriotic Egyptians, including women. That the unparalleled success of *The White Rose* was boosted by women's prolific attendance was not lost on *Screen Art* or likely on other cultural observers.

A year after the release of *The White Rose* a film magazine appeared that proffered a final and significant observation about Egyptian women's cinema-going. In *Planets*' first issue, the editor in the publication's introductory statement banters about women's cinema-going: 'The most repugnant thing to me is to accompany a woman to one of the cinemas.' He goes on to explain: 'Not that I am that backward . . . only that no sooner is the light turned off than hot kisses are launched from every point and in every direction and in their wake "soft" laughs take off that "electrify" "yours truly".'[32] Considering that *Planets* was published in Cairo,[33] the cinema the editor attended was likely there, suggesting that the practice of non-familial, gender-mixed cinema attendance was happening in Cairo too. Equally important is the boldness, the defiant pluck that women were willing to exhibit in public, if not to be seen, then at least to be heard. Egyptian women by the mid-1930s had broadly made their voices heard, including when at the movies, and become important consumers of an increasingly popular leisure activity.

Notes

1 See Ahmad al-Hadari, *Tarikh al-Sinima fi Misr, al-Juz' al-Awwal min Bidayat 1896 ila Akhir 1930* [*History of the Cinema in Egypt, Part I from the Beginning of 1896 to the End of 1930*] (Cairo: The Cinema Club, 1987), 145–6.

2   For discussions of early cinema audiences, see Mahmud 'Ali, *Fajr al-Sinima fi Misr* [*Dawn of the Cinema in Egypt*] (Cairo: Egypt Ministry of Culture, Cultural Development Fund, 2008).
3   M. Shawkat al-Tuni, 'Wada'an ya ibn Wahbi' [Farewell, Oh Son of Wahbi], *al-Kashkul*, 15 April 1927, 7.
4   Mahmud 'Ali, *Fajr al-Sinima fi Misr* [*Dawn of the Cinema in Egypt*] (Cairo: Egypt Ministry of Culture, Cultural Development Fund, 2008), 87–8.
5   Homer Croy is exculpated from misappropriation here because indeed *harem* does appear in venue promotional materials in French and English that he would have been able to read. The word '*Harim*' meaning women appears in Arabic promotional materials from the same era. An advert in al-Sinima al-Sharqi (Eastern Cinema) from late 1912 states, 'and as it matters to management to please the honorable national element, it shall hold screenings at three of every Friday, designated especially for *harim*, whose service will be overseen by women'. See Ali, *Fajr al-Sinima fi Misr*, 63. However, Croy does later in his piece state, 'All their lives they have been shut up and now for the first time they are having a chance to see what is going on outside the doors of their harems', which definitely presents harem as a location. See 'Just Think of That', 26 December 1914, 1831. https://archive.org/stream/movingpicturewor22newy#page/1830/mode/2up
6   Homer Croy, 'Just Think of That'.
7   The advert is in French. 'Ali, *Fajr al-Sinima fi Misr*, 70.
8   Plays and films were not presented only in theatres and cinemas respectively but also in clubs, restaurants and bars among a variety of public venues. See 'Ali, *Fajr al-Sinima fi Misr*, 63–7. Also note a reader's question about moving images screening in Cairene venues (nawadi) in 1905.
9   The advert is in two parts, the French above the English. See Mahmoud 'Ali, *Fajr al-Sinima fi Misr*, 64.
10 The advert is in French. 'Ali, *Fajr al-Sinima fi Misr*, 70.
11 The advert is in French. 'Ali, *Fajr al-Sinima fi Misr*, 28.
12 'Ali, *Fajr al-Sinima fi Misr*, 83.
13 As quoted in 'Ali, *Fajr al-Sinima fi Misr*, 20–1.
14 Lutfi 'Abd al-Wahab, *al-Masrah al-Misri: al-Mawsim al-Masrahi, 1917–1918* [*The Egyptian Theatre: 1917–1918 Season*] (Cairo: National Center for Theater, Music & Folklore, 2001), 123.
15 An exception is Rawiya Rashid's *Yusuf Wahbi: Sanawat al-Majd wa al-Dumu'* [*Yusuf Wahbi: Years of Glory and Tears*] (Cairo: Dar El Shuruq, 2016). Otherwise, Jacob Landau discusses Wahbi's contribution to the Arab theatre in *Studies in the Arab Theater and Cinema* (Philadelphia, PA: University of Pennsylvania Press, 1958), 81–6.
16 Several years after the launch of the Ramsis Theatre, it was praised, for some of what had won it plaudits early in its activity, when art critic in *al-Jadid*, a publication with differing ownership and writing staff from the earlier cited

al-Ahram reporting on the troupe, characterized the Ramsis among Cairo's four Arabic theatres as having 'the most sophisticated audience and the quietest seating', in 'Theatres and Amusements: Preface' (al-Masarih wa al-malahi), 25 March 1929, 2692.

17 Rashid, *Yusuf Wahbi*, 105.
18 Suhayl, 'Alam al-Tamthil: al-Mawsim al-Tamthili al-Munsarim' [Acting World: The Previous Acting Season], *al-Musawwar*, 19 June 1931, 16.
19 A brief discussion of the theatrical season is offered in Suheil, 'Acting World: The Previous Acting Season'.
20 Rashid, *Yusuf Wahbi*, 101.
21 See Hadari, *Tarikh al-Sinima fi Misr*, 26–7. 'Alam al-tamthil: al-'Adala 'ala Masrah Ramsis [Acting World: Justice on the Ramsis Stage], *al-Musawwar*, 1 May 1931, 16.
22 Rashid, *Yusuf Wahbi*, 99.
23 Rashid, *Yusuf Wahbi*, 15, 99–100. Wahbi's memoirs in three volumes 'Ishtu alf 'aam [I lived a Thousand Years] is best avoided to my mind, because Wahbi, as Rawiya Rashid herself has observed, wrote them as if they were 'a play he wrote hurriedly'. Rashid's own biography is the most detailed I have encountered of the celebrated figure, and is sourced by several memoirs, multiple interviews, and a host of contemporary periodical press. The biography is not annotated, however, a condition of many Egyptian history books I have encountered.
24 'Hadith al-Tamthil wal- Mumathilin' [Discussion of Acting and Actors], *Alexandria Express*, 10 August 1919, 2–3, reprinted in *The Egyptian Theatre: 1919–1920 Season*, 138–40.
25 H. M., 'Barlaman al-Suwar al-Mutaharrika: Rad 'ala I'tiradat' [Motion Pictures Parliament: A Response to Objections], *al-Suwar al-Mutaharrika* [Motion Pictures] 25 October 1923, 9.
26 M. 'B., 'Barlaman Al-Suwar Al-Mutaharrika: Madgh al-liban' [Motion Pictures Parliament: Gum Chewing], *al-Suwar al-Mutaharrika* [Motion Pictures], 31 May 1923, 21.
27 Muhammad 'Abd al-Karim, 'Barlaman al-Suwar al-Mutaharrika: Zajal' [Motion Pictures Parliament: Poetry] *al-Suwar al-Mutaharrika*, 8 November 1923, 11.
28 Muhammad Hijazi, 'Barlaman al-Suwar al-Mutaharrika: al-Mar'a al-Mutarajjila' [Motion Pictures Parliament: La Garçonne] *al-Suwar al-Mutaharrika* [Motion Pictures], 20 March 1924, 2.
29 Muhammad Hijazi, 'Barlaman al-Suwar al-Mutaharrika: al-Mar'a al-Mutarajjila aydan' [Motion Pictures Parliament: La Garçonne Also], *al-Suwar al-Mutaharrika* [Motion Pictures], 17 April 1924, 7.
30 Questions Man, 'Isti'rad al-Riwayat: al-Mar'a al-Mutarajjila [Review of Narrative Films: La garçonne] *al-Suwar al-Mutaharrika* [Motion Pictures], 29 May 1924, 15.
31 'al-Sinima fi Misr wa al-Kharij: al-Warda al-Bayda' [The Cinema in Egypt and Abroad: The White Rose], *Fan al-Sinima* [Screen Art], 9 December 1933, 4.

32 See Muda'abat [Quips], *Kawakib al-Sinima* [Cinema Planets], 22 September 1934, 4.
33 See Farida Mar'i and May al-Tilmisani, 'Majallat Kawakib al-Sinima' [*Cinema Planets* Magazine] in Sahafat al-Sinima fi Misr: al-Nisf al-Awwal min al-Qarn al-'Ishrin [*Cinema Press in Egypt: The First Half of the Twentieth Century*] ed. Farida Mar'i (Cairo: Egyptian Film Center, 1996), 249.

5

Anti-colonial masculinity, the Catholic Film Center and the screening of religious difference in 1950s Egypt

The multiple lives of Husayn Sidqi's *Night of Power*

Rahma Bavelaar

On the 13th of March 1952, *Laylat al-Qadr* (*Night of Power*), a feature film produced by actor and producer Husayn Sidqi (1917–76), was launched in cinemas in Cairo, Alexandria and Port Said.[1] The romantic melodrama chronicled the interfaith romance between Shaykh Hasan, a pious Azhar student and imam in a popular neighbourhood, and Louisa, the beautiful daughter of a wealthy Christian businessman of European origin. The release followed on the heels of what is today remembered as 'the Cairo Fire', when rioting crowds tore through Cairo's commercial district, burning down businesses and leisure spots associated with European domination and privilege. One of the immediate causes of the riots was the massacre of fifty Egyptian policemen at the hands of the British military in Ismailia; an attempt by the remaining colonial troops to root out persistent guerrilla warfare in the Canal region. Oft historicized as a foreshadowing of the Free Officers' coup that occurred just months later, the events laid bare the profound social discontent caused by the continuing British military presence and control over the economy, by deepening social inequality and by the eroding popular legitimacy of parliament and palace.[2] The political upheaval also unsettled intercommunal relations. When a church was burned to the ground in Suez and a number of Coptic Christians were murdered in January 1952, Coptic writers and activists publicly questioned what had become of the promise of religious equality that had been nurtured by the 1919 revolution.

Night of Power, with its unusually blunt discussion of Christian-Muslim differences, became deeply implicated in the political fallout from the violence.

After screening for a mere three days, it was pulled from all cinemas by direct orders from the National Security Agency. This decision followed reports of arson and clashes at one of the cinemas where the movie had been screened. These incidents were followed by appeals for a ban on the film by a group of Catholic professionals and clergy, spearheaded by the then newly founded Catholic Film Center (CFC). Negotiations over the film were reinitiated several times in the months and years that followed, until the Free Officers dusted off and reframed the film for their own political purposes one more time, before deciding to uphold the ban.[3]

In my examination of *Night of Power*, I draw on ethnographic approaches to cinema in anthropology and cultural studies as well as on the previously unexamined archival sources of the CFC. I approach the debates and censorship practices around the film as a case study in the social life of cinema. My point of departure is the insight that 'interpretations are profoundly influenced by the broader social discourses [primarily those on gender and nationalism] in which they are interpellated; they are shaped by events in the viewers' lives and by the relationships in which those viewers define themselves'.[4] In keeping with the approaches of other chapters in this volume, I will go beyond a 'textual' analysis of the script by approaching the film's content and meaning as negotiated between different producers, censors and audiences. I will show that these various actors – by virtue of their social and institutional locations and aspirations, their attitudes towards the social and ethical role of film and their differing perspectives on Egyptian nationalism – took very different views of the meaning and potential impact of *Night of Power*, and hence of the type of censorious interventions that were required (or not).

The debate and censorship practices around *Night of Power* centred on the gendered representation of religious difference and its connections to national identity and decolonization. Sidqi, like many filmmakers and novelists of his time, approached the theme of marriage as a microcosm of the nation and a vehicle for the representation and cultivation of modern, patriotic and morally virtuous men and women. Recent scholarship has shown that representations of ideal masculinities in Egyptian film and literature during the first half of the twentieth century were in perennial conversation with colonial and orientalist tropes that depicted Arab men as predatory and licentious.[5] Like much literary fiction produced during this period, Sidqi's plot dramatized an 'interracial' marriage between an Egyptian man and a woman of European origin in order to explore the nature and impact of colonial domination, to negotiate a space between modernity and authenticity and to articulate an aspirational anti-colonial masculinity.[6] Little scholarly attention has been paid, however, to how religious difference *within* the nation informed representations of gender during this period, in contrast with work on more recent cinematic production (since the late 1990s). In this work the intersections between gender, nationalism and religion have been analysed in relation to national security, censorship, cultural politics and the relationship between the state and the Coptic Orthodox Church.[7] I extend the questions raised in this literature about the cultural politics of religious difference to explore how representations of masculinity and gender relations in mid-century Egyptian cinema were negotiated in the censorship and debates that troubled the screening of *Night of Power*.

The 'cinema's preacher' or 'the people's artist'?

Few stars of Egypt's often nostalgically recalled 'golden age of cinema' are as contested as Husayn Sidqi. Although he was a wildly popular actor and producer during his lifetime – and arguably the first heartthrob of the Egyptian 'star system' – millennial film critics tend to assess his legacy in polarized terms. Some dismiss him as an insufferable demagogue who perverted the purpose and aesthetics of cinematic art by using it as a pulpit for his conservative morality. Others laud him as an artist who was committed to social and political reform and gave voice to the values and aspirations of Egyptians of all walks of life, posing a successful challenge to the frivolity and 'westernization' of commercial cinema.[8] In recent years, Sidqi has been claimed by a range of cultural commentators, from representatives of the Muslim Brotherhood, who link him to Sayyid Qutb's support for 'purposeful art' (*al-fann al-hadif*), to nationalist chauvinists, who draw on ambiguous statements by the star to anachronistically pigeonhole him in an anti-Islamist camp.[9] In academic histories and anthologies of early Egyptian cinema his work is often ignored altogether, considered, in retrospect, too 'middle brow' and didactical to merit serious attention.

These conflicting public memories are more revealing of current political fault lines than of Sidqi's historical context and cinematic project. A careful review of Sidqi's biography and filmography suggests that he successfully navigated and drew creative inspiration from the prevailing political, nationalist and religious movements of his time, in step with the broader objectives and themes of cinematic realism in the 1940s. Like other prominent actors and directors who made a name for themselves during this period, he benefited from the post–Second World War boom in private investment in cinema to project a vision on decolonization and national identity that resonated widely with Egyptian audiences.

Sidqi was brought up by his widowed Turkish mother in the well-to-do neighbourhood of Hilmiyya al-Jadida, an area popular with Turkish aristocrats in the early twentieth century. His mother took a keen interest in his religious formation, alongside his private schooling. In interviews, he frequently recalled his early attendance of religious lessons and Sufi gatherings. As a high school student he trained as an actor with the most popular theatre troupes of the 1930s, including companies directed by Fatima Rushdi and Yusuf Wahbi, who went on to become founding figures and prolific directors in Egypt's early film industry. After having been launched as a leading man by the theatre actress and director Amina Muhammad (in the romantic drama *Tita Wong*, 1937) and having built an audience for himself, Sidqi founded his own private production company, New Egypt (*Misr al-Haditha*), for which he produced sixteen films, often taking on writing, directing and acting roles.[10]

Sidqi's work was profoundly shaped by the nationalist and anti-colonial struggles of the 1930s and 1940s. With other pioneers in social realist film, he was in the vanguard of a growing push for an independent national cinema, which aspired to represent the everyday experiences and concerns of Egyptians of all class backgrounds. His passionate advocacy for films that engaged with popular concerns – but were in practice primarily focused on the lives of the educated middle class – fit into a broader trend towards 'Egyptianization' and criticisms of the supposed commercialism, frivolity and European cultural influence on interwar Egyptian cinema.[11] His early output as an actor and producer included a number of movies that addressed social and political ills, including the 1939 *al-'Azima* (*Resolution*), which is often cited as the first social realist film. The plot was concerned with the formation of the educated middle-class 'efendi' and his romantic and financial struggles.[12] The film's director, Kamal Salim, is often celebrated as a founder of the genre, unlike Sidqi, who took on the lead role and adopted many of the same social concerns and narrative conventions in his own work, albeit not with the same level of technical innovation and skill.

Themes covered in Sidqi's films include labour activism for equal pay and equitable working conditions (*al-'Amil, The Worker*, 1943), the challenges faced by street children (*al-Abriya', The Innocent*, 1944), depression and suicide (*Ghadr wa 'Adhab, Treachery and Misery*, 1947) and drug addiction (*Tariq al-Shawwak, Path of Thorns*, 1950). All these works eclectically incorporated the concerns of socialist, nationalist, Islamic revivalist and anti-monarchical political currents of his day. Like other anti-colonial realist movies of the time, as well as the emergent nationalist cinemas in the wider region, the films Sidqi wrote and directed in the 1940s were at once commercially driven and deeply invested in nationalist and anti-colonial narratives. His films challenged social injustices in a melodramatic mode and narrative structure and were explicit in their moral messaging. Scripts in this genre were often structured around binary oppositions between foreign/indigenous, moral/immoral, authentic/imported that served to convey and inculcate a 'national consciousness disassociated from the West'.[13] Sidqi's film *Yasqut al-Isti'mar* (Down with Colonialism) was one of the earliest Egyptian movies in this genre. Its blunt treatment of the 'faulty weapons' debacle of the 1948 Arab-Israeli war raised the ire of King Faruq and landed Sidqi in prison. Together with *Night of Power*, which was completed around the same time, the film was banned and released to the public only after the Free Officers' coup, when popular media received both films as revolutionary statements against the vanquished monarchy and its moral corruption.

Several months before *Night of Power* was to be first released, in October 1951, the popular entertainment magazine *al-Kawakib* featured a portrait of Sidqi on the cover, clad in the garb of an Azhar scholar.[14] The issue included a two-page spread discussing his cinematic output as well as a profile that listed his 'core values'. The content offers an impression of what viewers who were enthusiastic about his work found fresh and exciting about it in that moment of intense political struggle, and of how he conceived of the purpose and potential impact of 'socially committed cinema' and his role in it.

In the spread, titled 'Ten Years in the Service of Cinema and Society', Sidqi, 'the socially conscious artist' (*al-fannan al-ijtima'i*), is described as a pioneer of 'a sorely needed new direction in cinema' concerned with contemporary social problems and addressing 'all social classes'. Sidqi's explicit moralizing treatment of these problems was precisely the quality the reviewer found appealing. Sidqi's films, he gushed, 'diagnose social problems . . . and offer a remedy . . . by presenting the most virtuous examples' and so inculcate in viewers how to 'work towards their own uplift and that of the nation'.[15] He praised the two films that were soon to be re-released, *Night of Power* and *Down with Colonialism*, as a 'new kind of nationalist and anti-colonial cinema . . . the cinema we have all been waiting for'. These films, the author argued, not only reflected the aspirations of the Egyptian people towards national liberation but would also 'spark fire in the hearts and awaken the passions to strive towards liberation from colonial tyranny . . . and cultivate in all citizens strength and unity of purpose in the service of the Egyptian cause'.[16] (Figure 5.1).

Sidqi shared this reviewer's high-minded idealism about the ability of film to cultivate a virtuous and unified national public, to appeal to potential foreign

Figure 5.1 Husayn Sidqi/Shaykh Hasan in *azhari* garb, featured on the cover of *al-Kawakib* Magazine (October 1951). The caption states: 'Husayn Sidqi as he will soon appear in the role of Shaykh Hasan in his new film *Laylat al-Qadr*.'

audiences and impart a positive image of Egypt. Islam-inspired ethics played an important role in this project, but these were firmly hitched and subservient to the nationalist objectives he shared with other realist filmmakers: 'I believe', Sidqi said to the author of the column titled 'My Principles',

> that film is Egypt's finest ambassador to the world. Egypt can present itself through it . . . and erase the distorted image projected by some opportunists. I believe that art was created to serve humanity and that all artists should orient their work towards serving this goal. . . . I believe artists must transcend selfishness and purify themselves and others from it . . . I believe cinema sustains the people; like the sun, the air and freedom.

Sidqi's stories about 'ordinary Egyptians' and his discussions of poverty, unemployment, love and generational tensions – related in a moralistic mould inspired by Islamic ethics – were hardly unique in mid-century Egypt. What distinguished him, particularly in retrospective accounts of his career, is the way he publicly cultivated his personal commitment to religious practice as a condition for making good films.[17] *Al-Kawakib*'s article concludes the list of Sidqi's 'key beliefs' with the following citation from the 'committed artist': 'Artists bear responsibility for modeling virtue and good repute in their private lives.'[18]

A carefully cultivated public piety was certainly an important element in Sidqi's cinematic project and popular appeal. He was proud of his friendships with prominent representatives of 'official Islam', most notably three Grand Shaykhs of al-Azhar: Shaykh Mahmud Shaltut, who frequented *dhikr* gatherings at Sidqi's home, Shaykh Mustafa al-Maraghi and Shaykh 'Abd al-Halim Mahmud, who attended to him on his deathbed.[19] Much is made of his avoidance of spaces of leisure and the company of celebrities in more recent 'Shaykh of the cinema' narratives of Sidqi's career. He nonetheless worked with all the great male and female stars of his day and gained significant personal wealth from his political networking skills. He befriended several prominent generals of the Free Officer regime and represented the Maadi constituency in parliament in 1961, inspired, he stated after he retired, by the example of Mustafa Kamil.[20] When he opened a mosque on the ground floor of his home – a fourteen-storey apartment building facing the Nile in Maadi – in April 1954, President Muhammad Naguib, Gamal Abdel Nasser and Anwar Sadat prayed in the front row, alongside the Shaykh al-Azhar and the Minister of Religious Endowments.[21]

The coloniality of *Night of Power*

Night of Power was marketed as a 'religious film' (*film dini*); a new genre descriptor that had thus far been used primarily to describe a very small number of epic films with plots situated in a reimagined Islamic past. Sidqi was first to use this label to describe a plot located in the present and concerned with the everyday lives of the middle- and working-class Egyptians. The promotional campaign that preceded the film's release played with the similarities between Sidqi, the pious director, and the character of Shaykh Hasan he took on in the film. In October 1951, *al-Kawakib* featured a coloured-in portrait of Sidqi/Shaykh Hasan donning a fez and the dark woollen cloak of an Azhar scholar.[22] *Al-Kawakib*'s cover art throughout the same year – which featured a succession of scantily clad foreign and national divas – aptly illustrates the idiosyncrasy of a clergyman lead character. On the day of the premiere in Cairo, Alexandria and Suez, a promotional image on the front page of *al-Ahram* depicted Sidqi/Shaykh Hasan sermonizing from the pulpit of a mosque.[23] The newspaper reader views him from the perspective of the congregants, seated on the carpet below the pulpit. The accompanying text reads: 'Today, Husayn Sidqi will deliver the Friday sermon.' The location of the Cairo premiere, Cinema Royale, appears beneath the image, playfully blurring religious sermon and film screening, mosque and cinema. Yet another advertisement for the film, featured in *al-Ahram* the next day, describes Sidqi as 'the believing artist' (*al-fannan al-mu'min*).[24]

Although Sidqi made pious claims for the film, it was also a calculated commercial risk that rode the wave of the religiously inspired cinematic and literary work that was gaining in popularity in the late 1940s. Accessible and modernized literary treatments of early Islamic historical themes (*islamiyyat*) proliferated and enjoyed a wide readership among Egypt's literate class from the 1930s. These narratives played an important role in the contested articulations of Egyptian nationalism more firmly in an Islamic past; reimagined in a pan-Arab, nationalist and positivist historical mould.[25] Novelistic biographies of the Prophet Muhammad, his companions and other historical Islamic figures eschewed the specialized language of religious scholarship, elided miraculous and mystical elements in the Prophet's life and laid claim to scientific historical method. Alongside literature, theatre performances inspired by Islamic and Arab historical themes flourished and were performed by major theatre troupes, including numerous grass-roots companies founded across the country by the Muslim Brotherhood.[26]

Night of Power was released mere months after the two first two historical dramatizations of early Islamic history were brought to Egyptian cinemas. In 1951, Ibrahim 'Izz al-Din, a lawyer turned Hollywood-trained director, released the first feature film depicting the emergence of Islam, *Zuhur al-Islam* (*The Rise of Islam*), with a screenplay by Taha Husayn which was based on the latter's literary biography of the Prophet.[27] 'Izz al-Din trained with the American master of blockbuster religious epics, Cecil Blount DeMille, and was eager to bring the commercially successful formula of romantic melodrama, visual spectacle and religious messaging to themes in Islamic history. *Rise of Islam* drew large crowds all over the country, generated unprecedented profits and drew crowds in the wider Muslim world.[28] The second film on early Islamic history, *Intisar al-Islam* (*Victory of Islam*), directed by Ahmad al-Tukhi, came out in early 1952.[29] By marketing *Night of Power* as a 'religious film', Sidqi sought to capitalize on this emerging and commercially viable international cinematic register of religiously themed drama. Applying its melodramatic rendering of religious themes to modern Egyptian life, he tried to carve out a space for the explicit discussion of Islamic norms in films set in the present; moving beyond stock images of clergymen and religious ritual as mere 'authentic' local colour, to make cinema a viable site for the discussion of religious identity and practice in a postcolonial Egypt. *Night of Power* draws heavily on another genre of popular Islamic writing that circulated in the newspapers and journals of the 1930s and 1940s: popular apologetic texts and polemics in response to orientalist and missionary (mis)representations of Islam.[30] Louisa questions Hasan – her younger brother's Arabic-language tutor – about Islam throughout the film. Her critical comments and questions echo colonial representations of practices such as polygamy, the spread of Islam 'by the sword', women's dress and the presumed incompatibility of Islam with modernity. Shaykh Hasan, ever the patient instructor, addresses each question in extended monologues, filmed in close-up shots. Like popular apologetic texts, Hasan's answers are informed by a mixture of Hadith, Qur'anic exegesis, Islamic law, history and sociological argument. The overall message is that Islam is a comprehensive way of life; perfectly compatible with modern life and a wellspring of superior solutions for its moral quandaries. As Shaykh Hasan puts it in his explanation of *zakat*: 'Were Muslims to practice Islam correctly, there would be no poverty.' When Louisa retorts: 'Is it like socialism?', he answers, 'the principles of Islam are superior to socialism.'

Shaykh Hasan, an Azhar student of Islamic law from a popular neighbourhood, stands out among contemporary popular cultural representations of religious scholars who vacillated between the satirical, comfortingly rustic and stubbornly backward.[31] On closer inspection, however, he does not stray terribly far from the middle-class masculinity that was most celebrated in the cinema of the late 1940s; he merely integrates its qualities with explicit religious commitment and an outspoken Islamic identity. In many ways, Shaykh Hasan embodies the virtues of what Hoda Elsadda has coined the '*nahda* hero', supplemented with the Islamic learning and personal piety of the religious scholar.[32] In Elsadda's analysis, the '*nahda* hero' represents the dominant yet contested ideal of masculinity of the first half of the twentieth century:

> invariably middle class (or espouses middle-class mores and values), literate, modern (having received a modern Western education and aspiring to a Western way of life), and ambivalent about his relationship with women (aspiring to a more egalitarian relationship with women that does not, however, compromise male dominance and control). This *nahda* hero is equally ambivalent about his relationship with the colonial West and is pithily described as having a love-hate relationship.

Like many film heroes of the time, Hasan 'mitigates [the excesses of the rich] through the development of a sophisticated and responsible middle class which can partake of the best Europe offers without losing its authenticity'.[33] He shares with many of the '*nahda* heroes' of the literary field a commitment to upward mobility and 'modernization' through formal education and the professions (he joins the Shari'a bar after graduation), respect for the rule of law, and the pursuit of romantic love and companionate marriage with the preservation of spousal and paternal authority. His familiarity with upper-class 'western' tastes (knowledge of French, piano skills, the bespoke suit and fez) does not, however, diminish his rootedness in the '*hara*', the alley of the popular neighbourhood where he continues to reside after ascending to the professional class. He masters what Lucie Ryzova describes as an effective performance of modern manhood through the ability to 'code-switch' between *azhari* embodiments of piety and an urbane 'efendi masculinity'.[34]

Shaykh Hasan, however, goes beyond 'switching into' a pious mode when he is among his kin in the popular neighbourhood. In *Night of Power* the *Azhari* may occasionally exhibit 'upper-class' tastes in music and dress but these never vanquish the body language and spoken register of the Islamic scholar. In Sidqi's vision, the turbaned shaykh does not provide a mere touch of traditional authenticity: he should enjoy pride of place in the moral education of both the poor and the well-to-do.

Attitudes towards marriage in early- to mid-twentieth-century films and novels 'entailed a visioning of new masculinities needed for the new nation',[35] representations that 'invariably engage with, contest, or reproduce colonial discourses'.[36] Interracial marriage frequently featured as a narrative trope through which masculinity was negotiated and discussed. The wildly popular film – and first Egyptian talkie – *Awlad al-Dhawat* (*Sons of Aristocrats* 1932), with a screenplay by theatre veteran Yusuf Wahbi and director Muhammad Karim, was one of the most popular early iterations of the interracial love theme. The plot inverts the colonial stereotype of the predatory and licentious Arab who poses a threat to white womanhood. Wahbi casted French actress Colette Darfeuil in the role of white femme fatale; one of the 'vipers in the bed of our nation's sons', as he put it in his memoir.[37] The emasculation visited upon Egyptian men by British rule – embodied in the 'westernized' upper class – is played out on an intimate level in Darfeuil's corruption of her weak and effeminate Egyptian lover. This depiction echoed debates in newspapers and magazines in the 1920s and 1930s, in which men and women debated the risks of marriages between Egyptian men and European women. Many authors and letter-writers were concerned that the offspring from such relationships would not be sufficiently loyal to the national cause, yet they sometimes called on Egyptian women to emulate the pedagogical and housekeeping skills of European women.[38] In her analysis of *Sons of Aristocrats*, Ifdal Elsaket argues that the film's inversion of male colonial violence 'reordered the gendered dynamics of colonial violence, providing in turn anti-colonial ideas of marriage, relationships and love'. Although the film was intended to resist the insult and humiliation of colonial representations, its conception of ideal masculinity mirrored white colonial ideas about manhood in its affirmation of male authority over Egyptian women, constraining the role of the latter to that of loyal and asexual mother/wife.[39]

By 1951, when Sidqi started making *Night of Power*, Egypt was formally independent and radical movements that demanded full military and economic sovereignty were taking to the streets. The trope of the white femme fatale had lost some of its parabolic appeal. For Sidqi, imbued with the insurgent spirit of 1940s activism, the white seductress or foreign wife was no longer a mortal threat to Egyptian masculinity. With some gentle persuasion by an upstanding Muslim man, she might even willingly assimilate. *Night of Power* does not transfer the colonial gaze from Arab men onto a scheming white woman, but rather presents its male hero as a model of Islamic civility so appealing that his lover is persuaded to join his camp. The compulsive, colonized desire of Wahbi's character in *Sons of Aristocrats* makes way in Sidqi's film for a Muslim identity and ethic that aspires to global appeal.

Critical viewers of *Night of Power*, however, did not focus on Sidqi's vision of an Islamic modernity, nor did they read Louisa as a European woman. Instead, the lengthy controversy that haunted the film centred on what critics perceived to be an unfair and bigoted comparison between Christianity and Islam, a comparison embodied by Hasan and Louisa. From the critic's perspective, the film's comparative discussion of religious doctrine was an inappropriate trespass of the domain of film into the realm of specialized religious learning. Critics did not see in Louisa and her family the cinematic stock image of a morally corrupted, Westernized aristocracy, drinking and dancing their time away – a reading that Sidqi encouraged in his defence of the film. Instead, they read in the plot's conflation of an (ambiguous) ethnicity, religion and class privilege a direct attack on Egyptian Christians. From this perspective, Louisa did not appear as a novel iteration of the white femme fatale but as a Christian of ambiguous ethnic origin that could be far too easily mapped onto arabophone Christians.

Conflicting readings of Louisa and her family's belonging were a result of their non-specific and pastiche-like depiction as both generically 'Christian' (*masihi*) and ambiguously 'foreign' (*khawaja*). The semantic range of these two terms was often muddled by the blurry boundaries of national and communal belonging within wider public discourse. Readings of the film's meaning and intent were read through the lens of contemporary debates over the national belonging of both immigrant and Christian communities; categories that were not always seen as distinct.

The term of address used for Louisa's father, '*khawaja*', was frequently used to denote European origin, but could, depending on context, also include arabophone Levantines or even Coptic Christians. The character of Louisa's father was performed by the Italian-Austrian film and theatre actor Istifan Rusti, who embellished his character with an undefined European accent that was experienced by audiences as highly comedic. The role of Louisa's uncle was taken on by Mansi Fahmi, an Upper Egyptian actor with Coptic Orthodox roots. In the film he plays a priest whose black clerical garb could pass for both Greek Orthodox or Melkite Catholic. Both denominations were prevalent in the urban centres of Egypt. Members of the Melkite Catholic Church (*Rum Katolik*) were mostly of Levantine origin while the former (*Rum Orthodox*) included migrants from former Ottoman lands, including Levantines and communities from southeastern Europe, particularly Greeks. Unlike the European femme fatale in *Awlad al-Dhawat* (Sons of Aristocrats), the actress who played Louisa was not of European origin but the Turkish-Egyptian former Miss Egypt, Layla Fawzi. The role of her mother was played by Dawlat Abyad, the daughter of a Coptic Orthodox father from Asyut and a Russian mother. The performances and mixed religious and ethnic backgrounds of the cast opened up the identity of the characters to multiple readings, producing a slippage between European foreign minorities, Levantines and indigenous Christians – categories that were already subject to indeterminate yet highly politicized boundaries in public discourse.[40]

The association between Christian mission and imperial power was well established in popular Egyptian perception in the late 1940s, when the dovetailing of anti-colonial and anti-missionary sentiment resulted in the government's legal curtailment of missionary education.[41] Accounts of violence directed at Coptic Christians and churches became more numerous in the Coptic press and in the advocacy of new Coptic associations. Egyptian Christians of various denominations were active participants in the anti-colonial movement. Some participated in missionary projects as translators and missionaries. In the heat of popular mobilizations against the remaining colonial presence, the distinction between foreign occupiers and indigenous Christians was not always clearly maintained. The depiction and reception of Louisa and her family as extravagantly rich, foreign-accented and undifferentiated 'Christians' must be considered in this volatile political climate.

'Rate movies like a concerned father': The moral mission of the CFC

The CFC, which spearheaded the campaign against *Night of Power*, pursued a vision of film remarkably similar to Sidqi's 'purposeful of cinema': its founders saw film as a key pedagogical tool for the cultivation of ethical, patriotic and religious subjects. The Center was founded in 1949, when the Vatican encouraged film critic Farid al-Mazawi (1913–88) and the Franciscan monk Boutros Faranzidis[42] to combine their separate efforts to produce film ratings under the auspices of the Office Catholique International du Cinéma (OCIC). The OCIC, which had been founded in the Netherlands in 1928, marked the institutionalization of a shift in Catholic attitudes to film in the course of the first-half of the twentieth century. Lay Catholics founded Catholic Film centers all over the world from the 1920s onwards, with the Vatican gradually and reluctantly taking their lead in moving from a primarily censorious to a more optimistic and instrumental approach to cinema.[43] The Egyptian CFC's pedagogical mission was directly inspired by a psychology of viewership that was described in the Papal encyclical *Vigilanti Cura* (Painstaking Vigilance), issued by Pope Pius XI in 1936. In this document, the pontiff describes film as a means more potent than any other for influencing the masses. The material context of film-viewing (darkened cinemas), he stated, facilitated a direct and pleasurable impact on the sensorium: 'taken in by the mind with enjoyment and without fatigue'.[44] The pontiff not only emphasized the need to protect the malleable minds of the young from becoming imbued with commercially driven projections of immorality and atheism, but he also ratified lay projects to rate films and offer viewers education that had been ongoing for several decades in local Catholic communities. Commending the efforts and successes of the Legion of Decency in negotiating Catholic influence on censorship guidelines for cinema in the United States, the pope called on bishops all over the world to oversee and centralize initiatives to rate movies for the benefit of their flock. Film, when deployed correctly, could be 'a true gift of God, [which] may be ordained to His glory and to the salvation of souls'.[45]

The founders of the CFC embraced the generative potential in this cautious endorsement, and in their own publications and institutional narrative stressed the more optimistic and universalistic passages in the encyclical, such as the power of film to

> arouse noble ideals of life, to communicate valuable conceptions, to impart a better knowledge of the history and the beauties of the Fatherland and of other

countries, to present truth and virtue under attractive forms, to create or at least to favour understanding among nations, social classes and races, to champion the cause of justice, to give new life to the claims of virtue, and to contribute positively to the genesis of a just social order in the world'.[46]

They also drew loosely on contemporary sociological and psychological theorizations of the social and cognitive impact of film on cinema audiences, particularly on children and youth.

The universal formulation of Catholic ethics in the encyclical and its presumption of a nation-state framework worked well for the founders of the CFC in the context of Egyptian decolonization. It permitted their alignment with the broader nationalist discourse of the late 1940s and a framing of their mission as an inclusive moral pedagogy aimed at all citizens, whether Christians or not. Like other foreign Christian missions that remained in Egypt after 1952, the small Franciscan community adjusted its work to the new legal restrictions on Christian education, cultivating new forms of cultural and developmental work that emphasized Christian 'witness' through practice and good works, rather than direct proselytization and the tallying of converts.[47]

Under the leadership of al-Mazawi,[48] who was an active member of the Melkite Greek Catholic Church and its mostly Levantine community,[49] the CFC started producing weekly ratings of foreign and Egyptian films for distribution in Christian schools, churches of various denominations and the military. The aim was to help families and servicemen avoid films 'unsuited to their moral abilities' and to select ones that would assist their ethical formation as moral guardians of the nation.[13] With support from the Franciscan Canadian Sacred Land Foundation the published ratings were soon supplemented with a range of activities, including seminars, film screenings, workshops for industry professionals, clergy and the public. Soon after opening its doors, the Center laid the foundation of what would soon become the largest and most up-to-date film archive in the country. The CFC's film festival, the first in Egypt when launched in 1952, continues to be one of the most important annual cultural events in the country in the early 2020s. When *Night of Power* was released, the CFC was growing into a key institution in the Egyptian cultural landscape with a wide network among filmmakers and state bureaucrats, including in the censorship office.

The CFC's rating criteria partly overlapped with categories applied in the Ministry of Interior in the late 1940s, particularly in terms of their targeting of the depiction of social vices and sexual immorality, as well as pointed concern with Egypt's image abroad.[50] In 1948, the censorship office was moved from the Ministry of Social Affairs to the Ministry of Interior in an effort to integrate censorship practices more tightly with security policies that were meant to contain brewing social unrest around domestic politics and neighbouring Palestine. The depiction of religious conflict and official religious authorities – or anything that could disturb 'national unity' – were grounds for censorship. However, records from the censorship office and the CFC archive on censorship discussions around *Night of Power* demonstrate that everyday censorship practices were flexible and negotiated between a number of actors and agencies, including filmmakers, al-Azhar and representatives of Christian communities, the National Security Agency, the executive, as well as, from 1952, the CFC.[51]

Al-Mazawi described the CFC's moral responsibility in explicitly paternalistic terms: 'Films that the head of a respectable family, aware of his sacred duty, would rather not show to his family, should not be shown to the public.'[52] The negotiations between the Ministry of Interior and the CFC over *Night of Power* shed light on the convergences and, more markedly, the tensions between the security-driven 'national unity' calculus of the Ministry and the CFC's concern with the precarious national inclusion of Christians in the context of surging anti-colonial nationalism. The encounter of these conflicting concerns with Sidqi's own particularly gendered project for a moral cinema and national awakening in *Night of Power* delineated both the limits and possibilities for popular representations of religious difference.

Religion for God and marriage for all?

Upon his arrival at the Cairo premier of *Night of Power* at Cinema Royale on the night of 13 March 1952, Farid al-Mazawi was handed a glossy booklet that featured a synopsis of the film and a series of attractive publicity stills. The dissemination of this material, handed out in all cinemas where the film was screened, was the outcome of a review process that included bureaucrats in the Ministry of Interior's censorship office, a viewing committee at al-Azhar and a final vetting in the National Security Agency.

Several reviewers in the censorship office referenced the volatile political circumstances in the country and expressed concern that 'despite the sterile way in which the idea is presented', the film might 'stir up communal discontent and cause division between the segments of the nation. A matter that must be avoided at all costs under present circumstances, which demand unity and calm.'[53] After negotiations with Sidqi and a renewed round of reviews by the head of the censorship office, Shaykh Mahmud Shaltut (who later became Shaykh al-Azhar), and a national security officer, some of Louisa's scene lines were removed, including 'do not baptize her [Louisa's newborn], do not Christianize her, hand my corpse [to Hasan], bury me in the graveyard of the Muslims'. The censor who signed off on the internal report confidently stated that 'despite the delicacy of the subject matter in our present moment, the film depicts Christianity with all due veneration and respect. The film ends with a return to mutual understanding and an end to intolerance'. To resolve the tension between the potentially divisive elements in the film and security imperatives, the Ministry decided to actively pre-frame the viewing experience as an ode to national unity, per the advice of one reviewer to 'provide a written introduction in Arabic before the screenings to emphasize that the movie does not promote religious bigotry but is a love story' (Figure 5.2).

One of the movie stills in the leaflet scrutinized by al-Mazawi as he took his seat depicts the character of Louisa's uncle – in priestly garb – and Shaykh Hasan amiably shaking hands under the slogan 'Islam is the religion of peace . . . and Christianity is the religion of love and brotherhood' (a newspaper announcement that featured the same image has the byline 'the cross and the crescent meet'). The handshake, pictured under a calligraphic image of the divine name 'Allah',

Figure 5.2 Newspaper advertisements for *Laylat al-Qadr* (1952) on the left, and *Shaykh Hasan* (1954) on the right.

did not appear in that form in the film. It was staged in a way that called to mind the visual aesthetics of state-managed interfaith unity. This and other images and slogans in the booklet communicated patriotic associations with the cross and crescent banners of the 1919 revolution, frequently reproduced in nationalist imagery of the time. Elsewhere in the booklet, similar fraternal images appear with the byline 'Religion is for God, and the nation for all', the official slogan of mid-century Egyptian secularism.[54]

The report al-Mazawi penned after viewing the film leaves no doubt that the tension between Sidqi's message and the PR campaign was neither lost on his trained critical sensibilities nor on the predominantly Muslim audience with whom he shared his viewing experience.[55] Interspersed with his detailed summary of the plot are several critical 'asides' that reflect on the interaction between dialogue, audience response and the politics of representation. Al-Mazawi's most vehement objections centred on the contrast between Hasan's virtuous character and the 'lack of morals' of the Christian family, embodied in Louisa's rude and frivolous comportment and the tyrannical behaviour of her male kin.

In one of several scenes described by al-Mazawi in detail, Hasan scolds Louisa for wearing a short tennis skirt. When she retorts that 'your religion restricts women', Hasan explains the social purpose behind modest dress (the veil is never included in the conversation) with his characteristic air of rational scholarly authority: modest dress protects women's dignity by ensuring that sexual desire is safely channelled within the marital relation. Al-Mazawi's irritation is palpable when he comments:

> With this discussion . . . the scenarist tries to demonstrate that the words, character and style of dress of Louisa and her parents – and even vices and habits associated with a particular social class – are part of the essence of Christianity and permitted by its teachings. He compares [this behaviour] with the character, personality and virtue of Shaykh Hasan, even though these virtues are neither uniquely Islamic nor practiced by the majority of Muslims. Yet the scenarist presents them as uniquely associated with Islam; the exemplary religion that orders all things.

Another critical comment follows al-Mazawi's description of a scene in which Louisa's parents barge into Hasan's home to reclaim their daughter, a policeman in tow. The father shouts and gesticulates wildly in response to Hasan's calm assertion that he and Louisa are legally married and have committed no wrong. Al-Mazawi denounces the 'tyrannical' comportment and 'idiotic' behaviour of Louisa's father and observes that 'the ridiculous imitation of the Greco-Arabic accent – which is habitually imitated in this country to provoke malicious laughter – made the spectators cackle uproariously [. . .] at the two imbecilic Christians whose daughter was successfully seduced and taken away from them by this Muslim, despite their protestations'. Al-Mazawi repeatedly gauged the impact of the film's characterizations from audience responses: 'Numerous conversations can be heard among the audience, most of whom treat this Mr. George [Louisa's father] as a narrow-minded foreigner (*khawaja*).' Further on, he comments on a scene in which Louisa's mother finds her daughter engrossed in a book and whispers to her husband, 'she's reading an Arabic book'. The camera zooms in on the cover, which reveals that the book is a Qur'an, provoking, al-Mazawi notes, 'frenetic applause from the audience'.

The Interior Ministry had clearly failed to persuade al-Mazawi of the benevolent coexistence lens through which it not so gently coaxed the audience to consider the story. Commenting on an apparently serene promotional still of the priest/uncle sitting next to Louisa's bedside, crucifix in hand, al-Mazawi notes with unconcealed irony: 'The booklet features a still of the scene in which the priest sits at Louisa's bedside. The scene it depicts was in fact cut from the film by the censor. In it, Louisa defiantly pushes the crucifix away and declares she has converted to Islam.' 'This depiction', al-Mazawi concludes about the film in general, 'will make Muslims hate Christians'.

Al-Mazawi immediately petitioned the Ministry of Interior, demanding the withdrawal of the film from all theatres. His letter was co-signed by a number of clerical authorities in the Roman Catholic and Uniate Coptic-rite churches, such as the Coptic Catholic Patriarch of Alexandria and the Syrian Jesuit Father Ayrout, who was the head of the Association of Catholic Schools – attesting to the possibly unprecedented flurry of ecumenical activities between the Latin, Coptic and Melkite Catholic leadership from the late 1940s.[56] The National Security Directorate, fearing social unrest and bypassing the national censorship office, immediately issued an order to end all screenings.

Retrospective coverage of the *Night of Power* debacle in the Egyptian entertainment press from the early 2000s frequently frames the controversy as a clash between an undifferentiated 'Church', on one side, and Sidqi, as either a 'religious bigot' or a besieged artist robbed of his freedom of expression, on the other. This account flattens important historical and theological differences between Egypt's Christian churches, collapsing all Egyptian Christians into the Coptic Orthodox Church. It also anachronistically accounts for mid-twentieth-century Muslim-Christian difference from the perspective of twenty-first-century tensions between the state and the Coptic Orthodox Church over Coptic personal status law, and from the perspective of conflict between the state and militant Islamist movements. These factors deeply inform more recent censorship practices.[57] Yet, as I have shown, the mid-century debate over the representation of Christians – foreign and 'local' – in *Night of Power* must be understood in its particular political and institutional context; one in which armed nationalist struggle, discussions around the future of Christian missions, debate around the identity and national inclusion of Levantines and Christian Egyptians and the film's potential effect on national security, deeply informed the censorship of religion in film. Meanwhile, Catholic institution building in the field of film criticism and pedagogy simultaneously created new opportunities for Egyptian Christians to engage with and affect the cultural representation of Christians and Christianity in Egyptian film.

What emerges from the CFC archive is that its founders mostly shared Sidqi's vision in *Night of Power* of the ideal modern Egyptian man, as well as his conviction that cinema should occupy a privileged didactical role in the cultivation of modern and morally sound Egyptian men and women: Western and upper-class tastes and sensibilities could be adopted with careful moral discernment, spousal and paternal authority should not be undone but reconstituted in light of modern norms around companionate marriage and romantic attachment, and religious teachings and practices should be defended through enlightened rational argument, and not imposed through force. Al-Mazawi's main grievance was not the thematization of interfaith marriage as such, but what he saw as the depiction of Muslims as more enlightened, rational and morally virtuous in their *response* to the marriage – as well as the way the representation of the 'mixed' marriage was instrumentalized by Sidqi to demonstrate the superiority of Islam. These points are borne out by a list of suggested edits to the script submitted to the censorship office by an anonymous 'Christian director' in late 1952, when Sidqi was contesting the ban of his film in court.[58]

The reviewer argued that Louisa, as a representative of Christian womanhood, should be a moral exemplar rather than an 'ill-mannered' and 'morally corrupted' girl. Her dress must be modest. She should not make rude remarks about Islam and Hasan's piety. She should not be associated with lewd practices such as alcohol consumption and dancing and, most importantly, rather than converting to Islam, she should express the deathbed wish of reunion with her husband in heaven rather than in this world. Other suggested changes addressed what the critic considered to be Louisa and her male kin's bigoted and 'foreign' behaviour. They must speak 'proper Egyptian dialect', should exhibit tolerance and constraint towards Louisa when she elopes with Hasan and must convince her to return to the fold through rational arguments about the virtues of Christianity, rather than by enticing her with 'foreign' and 'upper-class' vices such as dancing and alcohol. Louisa's uncle, the Greek Orthodox priest, should stand up to Louisa's conversion to Islam and denial of the divinity of Christ with a thoughtful defence of the faith, rather than by meekly giving in to her deathbed wishes.

To restore the dignity of Egyptian Christians and represent Christianity objectively, the director argued, the Christian characters should be depicted as no less modern, benevolently (rather than aggressively) patriarchal, rational and steadfast in their faith than Shaykh Hasan. The Greek characters should be 'Egyptianized' by fixing their broken vernacular. In sum, Egyptian Christians and Christianity had to be extracted from the inverted East versus West binary on which Sidqi's anti-colonial plot hinged.

Sidqi persisted in his rejection of these demands, which were channelled by the CFC through the state censor. In his perspective, 'Western' Christian bias towards Islam and colonial power were indeed inextricably linked, but this tension, he maintained, did not implicate Egyptian Christians. This was a distinction the CFC did not believe the film audience capable of making, since their views were already influenced by journalistic and political discourses that questioned the national loyalty of Copts. As the anonymous reviewer put it: 'In reality, no single change would make this film acceptable to Christian viewers.'

Paternal and spousal authority over women, even if ideally exercised through affection and rational persuasion, was assumed to be normative by all parties to the dispute. For the CFC, it was also a condition for the full equality of Egyptian men, regardless of religious status. Thus, a representation of a Christian-Muslim marriage in which the Christian wife is 'assimilated' to Islam as an allegory for national unity, or as a demonstration of the efficacy of Islamic norms and an ideal Muslim masculinity, could not but chafe against the claims of a male Coptic elite to inclusion, dignity and equality. Like the filmmakers of *Sons of Aristocrats* analysed by Elsaket, the CFC, in its resistance to what they perceived an emasculation of Coptic men by a domestic hegemon, insisted on cinematic representations that would do justice to their guardianship over Christian women, even if Muslim personal status law denied them this prerogative.[59]

Cinema in the service of Islam and regional politics

After the initial ban of *Night of Power* in March 1952, the matter was not indefinitely settled in the CFC's favour. Sidqi embraced the Free Officers' coup and made use of the possibilities it offered to return his banned films to the screen. In September 1952, he was among the first in the film industry to publish a passionate endorsement of the revolution/coup, aligning his 'socially conscious cinema' and demands for 'Egyptianization' of the industry with the Officers' call for a 'purification' of the film industry from commercial and foreign influence. He resubmitted his film to the state censor once again.

Al-Mazawi quickly pre-empted the possibility of a renewed screening with a petition to President Muhammad Naguib, this time with support from an expanded Christian coalition, including not only Catholic and Uniate leaders but also Armenian Orthodox clergy and the Coptic Orthodox Patriarch Yusab II, a notable alliance at a time when ecumenical cooperation was limited and, more often than not, constrained by cultural and theological differences as well as divergent approaches to mission.[60] The framing of demands was adjusted for the revolutionary context and Naguib's avowed commitment to religious inclusion. The petition stressed that the film would 'cause immediate social strife (*fitna*) between communities' and present 'the most potent weapon [...] for the enemies of Egypt'. A response by Naguib's secretary stated that Naguib viewed the film in person and decided to prohibit its return to the cinema. Days later, the Coptic Catholic Patriarch, Markos II Khouzam, wrote to Naguib to express gratitude for his intervention and to urge him to make the ban 'unequivocal and final'.

Night of Power became subject to public consideration one more time in 1954 when Anwar Sadat, with whom Sidqi was on friendly terms, became the general secretary of the newly founded Organization of the Islamic Conference, which was to convene its first meeting in Saudi Arabia that year; an early effort by the Free Officer regime, now led by Nasser, to forge an, ultimately unsuccessful, political alliance with the Gulf monarchies. The state censor urged that the movie be renamed *Shaykh Hasan* to avoid associations with the previous conflict. The proceeds of the film were to boost Islamic Conference funds. The revamped film posters that accompanied the promotional campaign for the film featured a message very different from the one that had been orchestrated by the state censor in 1952. This time, Shaykh Hasan's Islam-inflected nationalism was underlined rather than elided; a message appropriate to the pan-Islamic rhetoric of the Islamic Conference. In the newspapers, Shaykh Hasan's image was signed: 'Today, art and the nation are placed at the service of Islam' and 'Today, Egyptian cinema takes pride in its Islamic production'. The CFC was not fooled by the name change and successfully appealed to the authorities once more. *Night of Power/Shaykh Hasan* never returned to Egyptian cinemas nor was it ever broadcast on public television.

Coptic-Muslim romance continues to be an appealing theme for film and television producers in the new millennium – sometimes with explicit support from the state – to project a nostalgic and aspirational image of national solidarity against an amorphous 'religious extremism'. Since 1952, the representation of such cinematic love affairs has continued to be subject to close scrutiny from the state censor and, increasingly since the late 1990s, from the Coptic Orthodox Church and its allies (incl. Muslim intellectuals and filmmakers), who have succeeded on several occasions to prevent the release of offending productions, or to push through changes to a plot. Unlike the CFC in the early 1950s, critics today often invoke a human rights frame. They point out that producers are happy to 'use' the Coptic wife married to a Muslim to promote 'national unity', but would not dare attempt an on-screen love affair between a Muslim woman and a Coptic man. The colonial hauntings that bedevilled *Night of Power* have shape-shifted with transformations in the social and political landscape but continue to trouble cinematic representations of interfaith love. Muslim-Christian romance is put to work to imagine a more inclusive past in the service of a united future, or to juxtapose a love free from political attachments that transcend the nation, but these love affairs are rarely permitted to survive tragedy or regret.[61]

However social changes may shape censorship policy and debates about cinematic representations of interfaith relationships in the future, what is clear is that an examination of the *Night of Power* within its specific historical context reveals the networks of censorship, industry and the role of religious institutions in shaping cinema programming in Egypt. In general, the historical and ethnographic approach I have employed in this chapter shows that simple textual film analysis is unsatisfactory in revealing the multiple strands of ideology and industry that underpinned cinematic production.

Research for this chapter was conducted as part of the ERC advanced grant 'Problematizing "Muslim Marriages": Ambiguities and Contestations'. I am grateful for valuable feedback from Ifdal Elsaket, Mina Ibrahim, Hanan Kholoussy, Annelies Moors, Julie McBrian and Gaétan du Roy.

Notes

1 *The Night of Power* is described in the Qur'an as 'better than a thousand months' and refers to the night when the Qur'an was revealed. The title suggests the providential nature of the events that occur in the film.

2 For the disputed historiography of the Cairo Fire, see the introduction in Nancy Reynolds, *A City Consumed: Urban Commerce, the Cairo Fire and the Politics of Decolonization in Egypt* (Stanford, CA: Stanford University Press, 2012).
3 The 1954 version of the film, renamed *Shaykh Hasan*, is available on YouTube: https://m.youtube.com/watch?v=Qj0dtPcLf3g (accessed 12 January 2021).
4 Purnima Mankekar, 'National Texts and Gendered Lives: An Ethnography of Television Viewers in a North Indian City', *American Ethnologist* 20, no. 3 (1993): 543–63. Mandekar's claim refers to television, but is equally applicable to cinema production. I'm using the citation of the text in Laila Abu Lughod, 'The Interpretation of Culture(s) After Television', *Representations* 59 (1997): 109–34.
5 Seminal texts on the construction of (anti-colonial) masculinities in Egyptian novels and film of the 1930s and 1940s include Hoda Elsadda, *Gender, Nation and the Arabic Novel in Egypt: 1892–2008* (Edinburgh: Edinburgh University Press, 2012); Lucie Ryzova, *The Age of the Efendiyya: Passages to Modernity in National-Colonial Egypt* (Oxford: Oxford University Press 2014); and Ifdal Elsaket, 'Sound and Desire: Race, Gender, and Insult in Egypt's First Talkie', *International Journal of Middle East studies* 51, no. 2 (2019): 203–32.
6 For a thorough discussion of this literature, see the introduction to Elsadda, *Gender, Nation*. For an overview of key texts on gender, nationalism and religious difference in Arabic novels, see Sarah Irving, 'Gender, Conflict, and Muslim-Jewish Romance: Reading 'Ali Al-Muqri's The Handsome Jew and Mahmoud Saeed's The World through the Eyes of Angels', *Journal of Middle East Women's Studies* 12, no. 3 (2016): 343–62.
7 For analyses of gender, religion and nationalism that touch on interfaith marriage as a trope in contemporary Egyptian cinema and television, see Lila Abu Lughod, *Dramas of Nationhood: The Politics of Television in Egypt* (Chicago: University of Chicago Press, 2005), 163–91; Viola Shafik, *Popular Egyptian Cinema: Gender, Class and Nation* (Cairo: The American University in Cairo Press, 2006), 23–51; Samia Mehrez, *Egypt's Culture Wars: Politics and Practice* (London: Routledge, 2008), 171–88; Karima Laachir, 'Sectarian Strife and "National Unity" in Egyptian Films: A Case Study of Hassan and Morqos', *Comparative Studies of South Asia, Africa and the Middle East* 31, no. 1 (2011): 217–26; Lina Khatib, 'The Orient and its Others: Women as Tools of Nationalism in Egyptian Political Cinema', in *Women and Media in the Middle East: Power Through Self-expression*, ed. Naomi Sakr (London: Bloomsbury, 2004); Gaétan du Roy, 'Union des Corps et Civilités Urbaines: Shubrā ou le Cosmopolitisme au Petit écran', in *Culture Pop en Egypte: Entre Mainstream Commercial et Contestation*, ed. Frédéric Lagrange and Richard Jacquemond (Paris: Riveneuve, 2020).
8 For a recent example of the first assessment, see Mahmud Qasim, 'Yasqut al-Isti'mar', *al-Shuruq*, 15 June 2018, https://www.shorouknews.com/mobile/columns/view.aspx?cdate=15062018&id=fcf91079-b505-40fe-8fc3-e29a1b0e4ec0 (accessed 23 April 2021) and Ashraf Al-Sharif, 'An Husayn Sidqi wa Sinima al-Tayar

al-Ra'isi fi Misr', *Mada Masr*, 8 October 2014, https://www.madamasr.com/ar/2014/10/08/opinion/u/م-في-الرئيسي-التيار-وسينما-صدقي-حسين-عن/ (accessed 3 April 2021). Jubilant reviews of the film's depiction of Islam prevail in the comments section on YouTube (see fn. 4). Some effort has been made recently to place Sidqi's work within the broader context of 1940s and 1950s cinema. See Usama Saffar, *al-Jazeera*, *Al-Jazeera al-Watha'iqiyya*, 21 May 2019, https://doc.aljazeera.net/portrait/-حسين-صدقي-عقل-في-الأستديو-وقلب-في-المس/ (accessed 20 April 2021), and Nahed Salah, *Husayn Sidqi al-Multazim* (Cairo: Mahragan al-Qahira al-Sinima'iyya, 2014).

9 Unsupported claims about Sidqi's alleged MB sympathies are replicated in some scholarly literature, e.g. Walter Armbrust, 'Political Film in Egypt', in *Film in the Middle East and North Africa*, ed. Josef Gugler (Austin, TX: University of Texas Press, 2011), 249.

10 Sidqi discussed his early career at length in an interview recorded after his retirement from cinema and shortly before his death: Muhammad al-Susha, *Ruwwad wa Ra'idat al-Sinima al-Misriyya* (Cairo: Mu'assasa Ruz al-Yusuf, 1993), 112–13.

11 Armbrust has complicated the historiographical assessment of pre-1950s cinema as mere mimicry of Western narratives and styles, and argues that the celebration of middle class 'effendi' values continued through the first half of the twentieth century. Walter Armbrust, 'The Golden Age Before the Golden Age: Commercial Egyptian Cinema Before the 1960s', in *Mass Mediations: New Approaches to Popular Culture in the Middle East and Beyond*, ed. Walter Armbrust (Berkeley, CA: University of California Press, 2000), 292–329.

12 Armbrust shows that *Resolution* contrasts middle-class aspirations with both a 'westernized' and effeminate aristocracy, and with a 'popular class' in need of social reform: Walter Armbrust, *Mass Culture and Modernism in Egypt* (Cambridge: Cambridge University Press, 1996), 94–5, 102, 111–15.

13 Viola Shafik, *Arab Cinema: History and Cultural Identity* (Cairo: AUC Press, 1998): 211.

14 *Al-Kawakib*, October 1951.

15 All translations from Arabic and French are mine.

16 *Al-Kawakib*, October 1951, 43.

17 See Ryzova's characterization of Yusuf Wahbi's cinematic and theatric language as 'consistently moralistic': Ryzova, *The Age of the Efendiyya*, 76, n.66.

18 *Al-Kawakib*, October 1951, 94.

19 The latter two also supported Sidqi in his plan to make a film about the Prophet Yusuf, which was nipped in the bud by the state censor. See the entry on Sidqi in the *Encyclopedia of Modern Egyptian Culture*, an online resource curated by the Library of Alexandria. http://modernegypt.bibalex.org/TxtViewer/TextViewer.aspx?ID=1136&type=Article (accessed 20 April 2020).

20 Al-Susha, *Ruwwad wa Ra'idat al-Sinima al-Misriyya*, 112–13.

21 The mosque's website proudly narrates the revolutionary atmosphere of its inauguration. https://masjidhusseinsidky.com/about (accessed 2 December 2020).
22 *Al-Kawakib*, October 1951.
23 *Al-Ahram*, 13 March 1952.
24 Ibid., 14 March 1952.
25 For a discussion of *islamiyyat* literature, see Israel Gershoni, 'The Reader: "Another Production": The Reception of Haykal's Biography of Muhammad and the Shift of Egyptian Intellectuals to Islamic Subjects in the 1930s,' *Poetics Today* 15, no. 2 (1994): 241–77.
26 Essam Tallima, *Hasan Al-Banna wa Tajrubat al-Fann* (Cairo: Maktaba Wahba, 2008); Hussam Tamam, *Tahawwulat al-Ikhwan al-Muslimin: Tafakkuk al-Idiyuluji wa Nihayat al-Tanzim* (Cairo: Maktaba Madbouli, 2010), 87–9.
27 Another noteworthy film from this period that positively portrays an Azhar law student, by director Ahmad Kamal Mursi (who was a close friend of Sidqi's) is *The Public Prosecutor* (*Al-Na'ib al-'Amm*). The plot contrasts the arbitrariness of 'European' codified law in Egypt's modern courts with the mercy and holism of Islamic legal ethics as taught by Islamic scholars.
28 'Izz al-Din's brother, a Wafdist minister of foreign affairs, facilitated generous public and private assistance for the film. Some actors participated for free, Studio Misr made studios and technology available and the military offered its cavalry. Film critic Muhammad Salah al-Din notes that delighted audiences loudly proclaimed 'Allahu akbar' in the cinema when Islamic heroes appeared on screen. See Muhammad Salah al-Din, *Al-Din wa-l-'Aqida fi al-Sinima al-Misriyya* (Cairo: Maktaba Madbouli, 1998), 13–28.
29 Under Nasser's presidency, Sidqi contributed to a minor trend in grand historical epics in the service of nationalist and pan-Arab narratives; e.g. his government-sponsored production *Khalid Ibn al-Walid*. See Shafik, *Arab Cinema*, 165–74.
30 For a close reading of anti-missionary and apologetic writing in the early twentieth century, see Umar Ryad, *Islamic Reformism and Christianity: A Critical Reading of the Works of Muhammad Rashid Rida and His Associates (1898–1935)* (Leiden: Brill, 2009).
31 Cinematic parodies of clergymen echoed anti-clerical satire in colloquial literature where Azhar students and their style of dress frequently figured as negative foils for a 'correct modernity' and 'good religion'. See Ryzova, *The Age of the Efendiyya*, 56–8, 61–2; Armbrust, *Mass Culture*, 56–7.
32 Elsadda, *Gender, Nation*, xxxi.
33 Armbrust, *Mass Culture*, 95–6.
34 Ryzova, *The Age of the Efendiyya*, 61.
35 Elsadda, *Gender, Nation*, 94.
36 Ibid., xxxvii.

37 Ifdal Elsaket cites this line from Yusuf Wahbi's memoir to illustrate how the film 'upended the normative imperial narrative by positioning the Egyptian male as the victim of the European female': Elsaket, 'Sound and Desire', 215.
38 See Hanan Kholoussy, 'Stolen Husbands, Foreign Wives: Mixed Marriage, Identity Formation and Gender in Colonial Egypt', *Hawwa* 1, no. 2 (2003): 206–40.
These press debates were more concerned with national loyalty than with religious identity. However, interfaith marriage contracts issued by Shari'a courts during the same period suggest that lawmakers were concerned that Muslim husbands would be unable to exercise authority over European wives and the religious education of their offspring. See Hanan Kholoussy, 'Interfaith Unions and Non-Muslim Wives In Early Twentieth-Century Alexandrian Islamic Courts', in *Untold Histories of the Middle East: Recovering Voices From the 19th and 20th Centuries*, ed. Amy Singer, Christoph K. Neumann and Selçuk Aksin Somel (Oxon: Routledge, 2011), 54–70.
39 Ibid.
40 On nationalist mobilizations against Levantines, see Rim Naguib, 'The Ideological Deportation of Foreigners and "Local Subjects of Foreign Extraction" in Interwar Egypt', *Arab Studies Journal* 28, no. 2 (2020): 6–44.
41 Heather Sharkey, *American Evangelicals in Egypt: Missionary Encounters in an Age of Empire* (Princeton, NJ: Princeton University Press, 2008), 183.
42 I have not found any reference to Al-Faranzids other than in the publications of the CFC. The Arabic transcription of his name may be misspelled there.
43 For the activities of Catholics in establishing censorship and pedagogical initiatives in various national contexts in the first half of the twentieth century, see Daniel Biltereyst and Daniela Treveri Gennari, *Moralizing Cinema: Film, Catholicism, and Power* (London: Taylor and Francis, 2014).
44 The full text of the *Vigilanti Cura* can be found on the Vatican's official website: http://www.vatican.va/content/pius-xi/en/encyclicals/documents/hf_p-xi_enc _29061936_vigilanti-cura.html (accessed 12 December 2020).
45 Ibid.
46 This passage from the *Vigilanti Cura* and other papal sources pertaining to cinema are cited extensively in the introduction to the CFC's self-published history: Naji Fawzi, *Al-Markaz al-Kathuliki al-Masri lil-Sinima wa Khamsun 'Aman min al-Thaqafa al-Sinima'iyya* (Cairo: al-Markaz al-Kathuliki, 1999).
47 Sharkey, *American Evangelicals*, 193.
48 Farid al-Mazawi (1913–88) was trained in law and worked for the Mixed Courts and the Ministry of culture before getting involved in filmmaking, film criticism, archiving, translation and film education. He also authored several technical textbooks on various aspects of filmmaking. During his tenure at the Director of the CFC he became a central figure in the world of Egyptian cinema, attending countless foreign festivals as an Egyptian delegate and serving on the board of the

first filmmakers' union. For an extensive discussion of his activities, see Fawzi, *Al-Markaz al-Kathuliki*.

49 Greek Melkite Catholics in Egypt numbered around 7,000 in the 1940s. The majority were Levantine migrants who settled in Egypt in the late nineteenth and early twentieth centuries. By the mid-twentieth century they made up only fraction – albeit wealthy and influential – of the 1.3 million Catholics in Egypt. Being arabophone, unlike most Franciscan monks, Melkites were often 'translators' of Latin Catholicism within broader Egyptian Catholic circles. See Catherine Mayeur-Jaouen, 'Le Vatican II des Catholiques Égyptiens: Au temps de Nasser, l'Espoir d'un Monde Meilleur', *Archives de Sciences Sociales des Religions* 175 (2016): 361–86.

50 For an overview of the expansive censorship criteria established through internal ministerial regulations in 1948, see Mustafa Darwish, 'al-Riqaba wa al-Sinima al-'Ukhra: Shahada Raqib', *Alif: Journal of Comparative Poetics* 15 (1995): 91–8.

51 The negotiated nature of the everyday practice of film censorship is stressed in recent scholarship on film censorship in Egypt since the Jan 25 revolution, in contrast with theorizations of censorship that exclusively focus on its authoritarian and unidirectional nature. See Mehrez, *Culture Wars*, 7. The case of *Night of Power* demonstrates that censorship was highly negotiated and decentralized in the early 1950s. See Walters, Meir L., 'Censorship as a Populist Project: The Politics of Managing Culture in Egypt', (PhD diss., Graduate School of Arts and Sciences, Georgetown University, Washington DC, 2016).

52 Fawzi, *Al-Markaz al-Kathuliki*, 91.

53 A comprehensive overview of discussions of *Night of Power* in the Ministry of Interior censorship office, based on records in the Ministerial archive, is provided in Mahmud 'Ali, 'al-Shaykh Hasan: Awal Azma Fanniyya Tuwajih Thawrat Yuliu', *Shari'a al-Fann*, 28 October 2003.

54 The promotional booklet, al-Mazawi's reviews of the film in French and Arabic and his correspondence with the censorship office and President Muhammad Nagib are located in the 'Shaykh Hasan' file in the archive of the Catholic Film Center.

55 The CFC archives contain individual files on all foreign and Egyptian movies that were screened in Egypt since the early twentieth century. Each report features a synopsis of the plot, an assessment based on the CFC's rating criteria and additional comments on plot, cinematography and ethical content. The report on *Night of Power* contains more commentary than any other rating by the CFC's reviewers I viewed.

56 Another prominent Melkite Catholic, Boutros Kassab, founded the Catholic Youth Association in 1947, which brought together Catholic and other Christian students across public schools: Catherine Mayeur-Jaouen, *Voyage en Haute-Egypte. Prêtres, Coptes et Catholiques* (Paris: CNRS Éditions, 2019).

57 See, for example, discussions of debates and censorship around the soap series *Time of Roses* (*Awan al-Ward*, 2000) in Abu Lughod, *Dramas of Nationhood*, 176–9, and Mehrez, *Egypt's Culture Wars*, 192–3. State sponsorship of this series was part of its 'war on terror' agenda and sought to challenge sectarian violence against Copts, as well as appeals to American protection by some (mostly diasporic) Copts. Under pressure from the Coptic Church, changes were made to some of the final episodes: the female Coptic lead character's views were adjusted to express regret for marrying a Muslim man. Objections from lay Copts and clergy ranged from opposition to Muslim-Christian marriage in and of itself on the basis of theology and canon law, as well as human rights concerns, such as legal impediments on marriages between Coptic men and Muslim women – concerns that did not come up in the discussions about *Night of Power*. Since the early 2000s the Coptic Orthodox Church has designated a department for the assessment of films that touch on Christianity and Christian life.

58 The report reiterates nearly all the points brought up by al-Mazawi in his review and was submitted in the context of renewed advocacy by the CFC. He most likely authored it himself.

59 The incommensurability of Muslim and Christian personal status laws (PSL) on this point is an unspoken but important point of tension underlying the discussion of the film. Muslim PSL permits marriages between Christian women and Muslim men, but not between Muslim women and Christian men. Most Christian PSL's do not permit marriages to non-Christians, but these laws have no jurisdiction in the national courts.

60 Sharkey, *American Evangelicals*, 30, 147.

61 In 1979, the CFC gave its annual award for films that promote moral virtue and coexistence in an artful way to *Liqa' Hunak* (*A Meeting There*). The plot, which defends belief in God against scientific positivism, stars Nur al-Sharif as a young science student in love with his Coptic neighbour; framed as a symptom of his crisis of faith. Appropriate boundaries are re-established in the end: he marries his pious Muslim cousin and regains his faith. His former Coptic lover enters a monastery. Muslim-Christian romance may bolster a shared civil religion under the canopy of the nation, as long as 'intimate' boundaries remain in place.

6

Bollywood film traffic

Shaping routes for Hindi films in the Arab world, 1954–2014

Némésis Srour

By the 1950s the Hindi film industry became increasingly aware of the popularity of its productions in the Middle East.[1] Hindi films appeared on Egyptian and Lebanese screens in two successive waves, in the 1950s to the 1960s and then in the 1970s to the 1980s. From *Aan* (*Pride*, Mehboob Khan, 1954), *Sangam* (*Confluence*, Raj Kapoor, 1964), *Suraj* (*Sun*, T. Prakashrao, 1966), *Haathi Mere Saathi* (*Elephants Are My Companions*, M. A. Thirumugham, 1971) to *Mard* (*Man*, Manmohan Desai, 1985), popular Hindi films attracted a wide audience in the Middle East. As the popularity of Hindi films waned in Egypt and Lebanon in the 2000s, the Gulf emerged as a central market for Bollywood.[2]

The purpose of this chapter is not to offer an argument of cultural exchange between Indian films and Arab countries[3] but to document the circulation of films and contribute to a global history of South-South cinematographic circuits.[4] This chapter will focus on three modes of circulation of Hindi films in the Middle East. First, it will focus on the role of the Egyptian state in the rise and fall of Hindi films, showing how it played a crucial role in both bringing Hindi films to the market and stifling their circulation later on. Second, this chapter focuses on the merchants' circuits, both informal and formal, that connected Beirut and the Gulf through Iran. Finally, it analyses how a Bombay film company implemented a distribution strategy in Dubai in order to consolidate its presence in the Middle East market. One of the unique aspects of this chapter is that I use interviews with industry insiders to better understand the circulation of Hindi films in the Middle East.

Examining the Middle East from the perspective of the Indian film industry provides an alternative vision of the region's film cultures. It shows how different cinema markets adapted and responded to the influx of Hindi films. This chapter aims to lay out Indian film circuits over a long period, from 1954 to 2014, in order to historicize cinematographic exchanges and see broader shifts and changes. The approach, based on a transnational ethnography of circulation networks in Beirut, Cairo and Dubai, contributes to tracing the urban history of film distribution and exhibition.

The rise and fall of Hindi films in Egypt

The rise and fall of Hindi films in Egypt was highly regulated, linked to government policies and a strong local film industry that ensured its share of the market was never threatened. The entrance of Hindi films into Egypt needs to be seen in a context of a larger political relationship between India and Egypt,[5] and India's recognition of the lucrativeness of its export. At the Film Industry Seminar of 1955, established by the Indian government to facilitate national unity through the arts, a spokesman for cinema halls operators highlighted the links between cinema and foreign policy in a speech about the distribution and exhibition of Indian films abroad:

> Indian films enjoy increasing popularity in the Far East and Middle East countries. [. . .] But I believe that if both government and the industry set themselves fully to the task of expanding the foreign market, it will not only help the industry but also help to foster friendly international relations for us.[6]

The first screenings of Indian films in Egypt in the 1950s were embedded in the context of the Non-Aligned Movement. India and Egypt formalized their trade relationship in a 1953 'Trade and Payments Agreement'. The agreement aimed to bring the two countries, which had 'trade contacts since the time of the Pharaohs', closer together.[7] A special Indian Trade Exhibition was also organized in Cairo in 1954. As far as Egypt was concerned, the exhibition was 'a memorable step in the promotion of trade between the two countries'.[8] This Trade Agreement went hand in hand with the establishment a year prior in 1953 of an India-Egypt Association that aimed to further strengthen 'the bonds of brotherhood between two great sister nations' in the words of General Muhammad Naguib, president of Egypt.[9] At its head was the illustrious Nabab of Palanpur, popularly known as the 'Muslim Maharajah' who was based in Cairo. The Indian Ambassador to Egypt and the Egyptian Ambassador to New Delhi were the Association's honorary presidents. The Association's work focused mainly on cultural exchange:

> It is to strengthen friendly, cultural and social relations that this association was founded, and its members include eminent Egyptian intellectuals. India-Egypt's activities will include translations of selected Indian literary works into Arabic and vice versa, the publication of these works and their sale at popular prices. The association will also sponsor goodwill missions, exchanges of professors and students, presentations in Egypt of selected Indian films and vice versa, cultural events, exhibitions in both Egypt and India.[10]

These economic and cultural agreements paved the way for Hindi films to take their first steps into first-class Egyptian theatres. This happened on 4 January 1954. The release of the 1952 *Aan* by the famous director Mehboob Khan was first screened in Alexandria at the Strand Cinema under the patronage of the Liberation Committee headed by then deputy prime minister Gamal Abdel Nasser.[11] Publicized as the 'first Indian film to be shown in Cairo' it premiered in Cairo on 7 January 1954 at Miami Cinema.[12] Members of the Revolutionary Command Council and the Indian Ambassador in Cairo attended the screening, with the show's proceeds going to the Liberation Rally health scheme fund. Although the film ran for six weeks in Cairo, it must have garnered the attention of only local elites as it was subtitled in French.[13]

According to *Film Trade*, the outbreak of the Arab-Israeli conflict in 1967 turned Egypt into 'a major export market for Indian films'.[14] It argued that 'as far as the film industry is concerned, at least the step taken by the Government of India to uphold the cause of Arabs has become a boon to the industry', as the Indian 'Information and Broadcasting Ministry has been requested by some of the West Asian countries for a supply of 200 Indian films'. The political decision of the Egyptian government to embargo some British and American films after 1967 enabled the first major wave of Hindi films in Egypt. As shown by Ifdal Elsaket's interviewees for her chapter in this volume, these films were popular in the 1960s. The real turning point for Hindi films in Egypt was in 1970 when they were increasingly shown in first-class cinemas and prioritized in advertisements.

From 1970 onwards, a clear break occurred as a record number of Hindi films flooded the market, and exhibitors consistently offered them in their programmes with a choice of about two different Hindi films per week, an unprecedented programming configuration.[15] As audiences flocked to see these films, the government tried to curb the phenomenon. Herein lays a paradox.

Increasing popularity of Hindi films did not take place at the time the two countries were strengthening ties in the 1950s but occurred at the time when government regulation of their circulation was at its peak.

In 1973, the Egyptian government took two major steps to hinder the popularity of Hindi films in the country. The Egyptian Chamber of Cinema placed quick and severe sanctions against Indian and martial arts films from Hong Kong.[16] An official decree stipulated that all importation to Egypt of films from India or Hong Kong required the reciprocal exportation of Egyptian films to these two countries. Thus, Indian and Hong Kong films could only be released in an Egyptian theatre if the Official Board of Cinema received a confirmation note from a bank, attesting that the Egyptian distributor had collected at least 2,000 sterling pounds in exchange of a film exported to India.[17] This strict reciprocity clause was only meant for Asian films and not for European or American productions. Cinemas were also asked to give national preference to Egyptian films and, whenever possible, to reserve Muslim holidays for the exhibition of national productions only. Hindi films were believed to harm national film production and faced the aggressive lobby of the Egyptian cinema industry.[18] While Hindi films returned to Egyptian screens later on, they faced another political deadlock.

In contrast with the first wave, the second wave of Hindi films in the 1980s was confined to popular and second-rate cinema halls such as Cinema Modern, downtown Cinema Karim and the most famous Shubra Palace Cinema.[19] The latter cinema was owned by the well-known Egyptian distributor of Hindi films Badiʿ Subhi and located in the popular neighbourhood of Shubra in Cairo. The success of these films was dazzling and spanned a short period from 1986 to 1991. Even though the films featured in mainly cheaper second-rate cinemas, this era was considered the Golden Age of Hindi cinema in Egypt. The films that ensured the success of Subhi's new venture was the 1985 film *Mard (Man)* by Manmohan Desai, staring the iconic Amitabh Bachchan. Hurriya ʿAbdin, Subhi's sales manager, argued that the release of *Mard* was like a 'revolution in the Egyptian market'.[20] Amitabh Bachchan became a major star in Egypt and the film's 'astounding success completely wiped out its main competition at the box office, a film starring Egyptian superstar actor Adil Imam'.[21]

The government of Hosni Mubarak, in view of the exponential popularity of Indian films in Egypt during this time, and the complaints of the local cinema industry, feared that Hindi films would destabilize domestic production. In 1987, the government therefore issued a decree limiting the number of Indian films and their screen time.[22]

Circulations in the Gulf: Merchants' circuits and 'shadow economies of cinema'

While in Egypt the circulation of Hindi films was heavily regulated, the same cannot be said for Gulf countries. The circulation of Hindi films in the Gulf followed the routes of merchants and traders[23] in a less formal economy[24] and highlighted the flow of films through Beirut and Tehran in a way that expands the map of distribution in the region. As the historian Claude Markovits puts it, 'while the study of diasporas is an expanding field in South Asian studies, little attention is being paid to the history of merchant networks', which is not a story of migration but a story of circulation.[25] This history of merchant networks helps us understand the circuits of Hindi films in the Gulf.[26] It is a history that makes visible those 'shadow economies of cinema'.[27]

Rather than established distribution companies, old trade networks linked the Bombay film industry to the Gulf. Chor Bazaar in Bombay, one of India's biggest flea markets, was one of the main points of exchange of films. There, in a shop of old cinema posters, a former Indian film merchant remembers selling film reels to the 'Arabs' after 1964. These circulations happened through informal merchants' networks. T. N.,[28] one of the merchants in the flea market claimed:

> Actually, all the distribution was illegal, it was not legal. [...] There were no laws at that time, nowadays we can't distribute anything except if we've got written permission. At that time, you could do anything. After the TV, it [became] totally different.

Arab merchants from the Gulf were buying film reels, sometimes even only the cabaret song and dance sequences reels. Selling to Arab merchants was a profitable trade for T. N. But the products would then have their own circulation after the initial selling. Merchants from Dubai, who would buy the films illegally in Bombay, would then resell the film to exhibitors in Sharjah, who would then sell them to exhibitors in Syria.

> And we are also selling them for a good profit. If it's worth 100, for the Arabs we charged 700. So we were making seven times more. Arabs are paying this because they think this is cheap. [...] And then they buy it from us, ... they show it in Dubai and then they sell it to Sharjah people. Sharjah people finish their thing, then they sell it to people in Syria. So that is also good business for them also.[29]

B. J.,[30] an Iranian emigrant,[31] regularly brought films from India. Between 1964 and 1971, B. J. acquired Indian films through the gold merchants' networks between India and the Gulf. He bought old films such as the 1957 film *Ganga Jamuna* (*Mother India*), and even older black-and-white Raj Kapoor films. During one of his trips to Bombay he tried to acquire the 1970 film *Mera Naam Joker* (*My Name Is Joker*) directly from Raj Kapoor. While he could usually buy old worn films for 50, 100, 300 or 400 US dollars, Raj Kapoor asked for US$5,000. B. J. remembers telling the Indian filmmaker, 'there's no market here in Dubai, I can't pay that much'. He tried to negotiate, but since it was a big production, Raj Kapoor was not willing to let his film go for a small amount. Somebody pirated it and tried to sell it for US$500. B. J. adds, 'In fact, there were always stories about pirated copies. . . . We did not know there was theft by projectionists at Indian screenings. After the screening, they made copies that they resold in Africa, Bahrain and Oman.'[32]

If Arab merchants were regularly travelling to Bombay for trade, the reverse was also true. The Hinduja family, a merchant Sindhi family, played a pivotal role in bringing Raj Kapoor's movies to the Middle East.[33] The Hinduja family established its first trading relationship with Iran. The most prominent merchant in the region Sri Hinduja began trading in 1919. A textile merchant in Shikarpur, he traded a variety of products in Iran: spices, fruits and vegetables and cutlery. He made a fortune and invested largely in real estate, laying the foundation for one of the largest Indian commercial companies of the twentieth century, although the trade of the Hinduja family really took off in the 1960s. The family moved the headquarters of the company from Iran to London in 1979, where it operated in a number of sectors: banking, finance, media, energy, health and real estate. Founders of what is today an international empire, members of the Hinduja family are among the richest people in the UK. While marketing materials from the 1964 Cannes festival described Deepchand Hinduja as the world distributor for Raj Kapoor's film *Sangam*, no scholar has yet examined the way he circulated the film in the Middle East. A local Indian distributor of Raj Kapoor's films filled in some of the gaps:

> At the time, the Hinduja were a small trading company in Iran. Very small. But one of the family members loved cinema. So he met Raj Kapoor during a shooting in Europe and bought the international rights. Then Hinduja learned that the Shah of Iran had loved *Sangam*, so he installed a projector in the palace of the Shah, offered him a copy of the film and said: 'Now you can look at it as many times as you like.' The Shah loved this movie so much that he granted them business privileges for trading in Iran.[34]

After their success in securing Raj Kapoor films, the Hinduja family contributed to the production of Amitabh Bachchan films and distributed them in the Middle East through their own merchant networks. Two central cities that emerged as significant places of funding and production at this time were Tehran and Beirut. S. L.,[35] the nephew of the Hinduja merchants, at first based in Tehran, worked jointly with the family on film distribution. S. L. himself says, 'Tehran was a stopover point for filmmakers before going to shoot elsewhere. Directors such as Shakti Samanta who directed the 1967 *Paris Ki Ek Shaam* (*An Evening in Paris*) made a stop in Tehran to raise money for the film, and then shot the film in Beirut.'[36] S. L. would meet with Lebanese and Jordanian distributors in Tehran. In this configuration, Tehran became an essential nodal point for meetings with other distributors in the Arab region.

Although some Hollywood studios had local offices in the Iranian capital until the 1970s, the Iranian film market was also supervised by regional offices based in Beirut.[37] Studio representatives based in Beirut therefore travelled to Tehran to distribute the American films they were mandated to distribute. S. L. discovered through this means the lucrative potential of the Lebanese market as a key site for production, distribution and exhibition. This period of the 1960s indeed corresponded to the Golden Age of Lebanese cinema industry, as the effects of the nationalization of Egyptian cinema in 1961 pushed many filmmakers to Lebanon. S. L. even opened an office in Beirut in the late 1960s, but left at the time of the Civil War. The Egyptian nationalization of cinema and the Lebanese Civil war disrupted the circulation of Hindi films in the region.[38] While Hindi films continued to circulate, it was not until the early 2000s that they saw a resurgence. This time the distribution networks were absorbed by the emergence of Dubai's media industry.

A changing Arab market and Dubai's new monopoly

As part of a general strategy of preparation for the post-oil period, the Emirate of Dubai sought to position itself as the centre of a media and film industry. With the creation in January 2001 of Dubai Media City (DMC), established in a free zone, it sought to attract investors to make Dubai a 'strategic economic centre' and create a sustainable film industry there.[39] The creation of the Dubai International Festival (DIFF) in 2004 also aimed to assert Dubai's key role on both the regional and international level in the media industry.[40] In terms of infrastructure, the UAE quickly gained pace, attaining the highest number of screens in the region, 374 screens in 2014, and presenting one of the higher ratios of screens to population, forty-one screens for 100,000 inhabitants.

With the establishment of this infrastructure in the early 2000s, Indian company Yash Raj Films quickly saw Dubai as an attractive market. Yash Raj Films (YRF) is a landmark company, which has brought to the screen some of the greatest commercial and popular films of the last forty years. Closely associated with the trajectory of the man who founded it, the director Yash Chopra, YRF was founded in 1971. In 1997, the company started to develop its market abroad by establishing its first office outside India, in London. It then extended to New York and Los Angeles. In 2004, the company opened a branch in the booming Dubai film market, where its films were already distributed, but in a random manner. Their aim was to regain control over the distribution of their films and organize screenings on a regular basis in Dubai cinemas.

Even though not everyone in India speaks Hindi, Hindi films still managed to dominate screens there overall, especially in the North of India. The situation, however, is different in the Gulf. Hindi films face competition from Tamil or Malayalam films from South India as the significant migrant worker population in the Gulf is predominantly from Kerala, a Malayalam-speaking southern Indian state.[41] In this case, the development of a distribution plan for the whole Middle East region seemed all the more essential for YRF. The United Arab Emirates has the advantage of political stability, allowing for coordination across the region. Since the 1990s, and because of the Indian government's pro-diaspora policy, the Bombay film industry perceives its international market in terms of diaspora presence.[42] It distinguishes between 'traditional markets', which are the regions where there is an Indian population, and 'non-traditional markets', which do not have Indian populations. It is the non-traditional markets that YRF tried to develop, thus switching its distribution strategy from a diaspora-oriented one to a non-diaspora one.

With the 2013 film *Dhoom 3*, YRF attempted to open a new market beyond the Gulf. On 26 December 2013, the film was screened in Beirut and Amman, on 1 January 2014 in Cairo and the next day in Erbil in Iraq. To appeal to the Arabic-speaking audience, the title song of the film was even recorded by the Lebanese singer Naya. Empire Entertainment, a major distributing company based in Beirut and Dubai, coordinated with the Yash Raj office to release the film in Lebanon and in Empire's new cinema complex in Erbil. Yet, the film ran into problems from the start. The United Motion Pictures company, which took charge of distribution in Egypt, struggled to find multiplexes to screen the film.[43] While the film was a huge box-office success in India, running for eleven weeks, it ran for only one week in Lebanon and three weeks in Egypt.[44] The very limited success outside the Gulf illustrates the difficulties of bringing Arab-speaking audiences back to cinemas to watch Hindi films[45] and the limits of an expansion strategy outside the diaspora market in the Gulf.

In addition to the already discussed economic and structural aspects, not to mention the war in Syria and the current political and economic crisis in Lebanon, the industry also has to deal with a tendency to view Hindi films as low-class melodramas.[46] These stereotypes associated with Bollywood productions do not encourage regional distributors to take the risk of distributing Indian films. A wide gap has grown, therefore, between the first Indian successes in the 1950s, their exponential popularity in Egypt in the 1980s, and the contemporary era, where Hindi films cannot shake off their bad reputation. The failure of Yash Raj's transnational release of *Dhoom 3* in the Middle East signalled a change in audience composition. The multiplex culture marked the advent of a different type of audience, which did not warm up to Hindi films.[47] While Hindi films did not do well at the cinemas outside the Gulf, television remains the heart of Indian film distribution in the Middle East, especially in countries where films are not distributed to cinemas anymore.

Conclusion

Examining a broad history of Hindi film circulation in the Middle East can give us some insight into the channels they flowed through since the 1950s. It is clear that the circulation of Hindi films was different in each country depending on how regulated the local film industry was and moved alongside already established trade lines, whether formally or informally produced. Whereas scholars have been aware of the distribution lines of Hindi films, there has been little information on how they circulated and how certain political and commercial contexts facilitated their movement. The circulation of Hindi films in Cairo, Beirut and Dubai points to two types of media circuits and of their evolution over time. First, the Egyptian case highlights the state's role in facilitating the rise and fall of Hindi films in the country. While the state facilitated the distribution of Hindi films in the context of the Non-Aligned Movement, in the 1970s and 1980s it imposed laws controlling the import of Hindi films to protect the local industry. In the case of Dubai, informal merchant circulation between the Gulf and Bombay centred on flea markets and pirated tapes, morphed into an organized distribution system fully integrated into the global film industry.[48] With the booming media industry of the Emirates in the 2000s, the Gulf emerged as an attractive media market for the Indian film industry. Hindi film circulation in the Arab region, therefore, draws lines of cultural and political borders. It shows how the 'global' aim of Bollywood can shift in various localities in the Arabic-speaking region and is shaped by how regulated or not distribution channels are.

Notes

1 S. K. Patil, 'The Year in Retrospect: An Annual Survey of the Film Industry by Leading Spokesmen', *Filmfare*, 16 March 1956.
2 For more on how Dubai replaced Lebanon in many sectors, see Joseph Bahout, 'Dubaï-Beyrouth: l'ombre et son double', *Esprit* 11 (2006): 76–85.
3 The argument of cultural proximity has been long used, in particular by French film historian Georges Sadoul. He formulated the reasons for Hindi films' success in the Arab-speaking countries in an essentialist way, as 'a kind of innate spontaneity'. See Centre Interarabe du Cinéma et de la Télévision, *Cinéma et Cultures Arabes. IVème Conférence de La Table Ronde Organisée Avec l'aide Technique de l'UNESCO* (Beirut: n/a, 1965).
4 For more on the historiography of Indian Cinema transnational exchanges, see Dimitris Eleftheriotis and Dina Iordanova, 'Indian Cinema Abroad: Historiography of Transnational Cinematic Exchanges', *South Asian Popular Culture* 4, no. 2 (2006): 1–183.
5 For more on the political relationships between Indian and the Middle East, see Sushil J. Aaron, *Straddling Faultlines: India's Foreign Policy toward the Greater Middle East* (New Delhi: Centre de Sciences Humaines, 2003).
6 Patil, 'The Year in Retrospect'.
7 *Egyptian Gazette*, 23 April 1954.
8 *Egyptian Gazette*, 23 April 1954.
9 'Une belle manifestation d'amitié indo-égyptienne', *Le Progrès égyptien*, 17 March 1953, 3.
10 'Une belle manifestation d'amitié indo-égyptienne', *Le Progrès égyptien*, 17 March 1953, 3.
11 *Le Progrès égyptien*, 1 January 1954.
12 *Le Progrès égyptien*, 5 and 7 January 1954.
13 For more on Cinema culture in Egypt, see Marie-Claude Bénard, *La sortie au cinéma : palaces et ciné-jardins d'Égypte (1930–1980)* (Marseille: Éditions Parenthèses MMSH, 2016).
14 'Big Demand for Indian Films in Arab Countries', *Film Trade*, 26 July 1975.

15 This is based on an analysis of the film schedules published in the Egyptian newspapers *Egyptian Gazette* and *Le Progrès égyptien*, from 1954 until the 1970s. For a comparative review of Indian film exhibition in Egypt in 1955 and 1970, see Némésis Srour, *Bollywood Film Traffic: Circulations des films hindis au Moyen-Orient: 1954–2014* (Ecole des Hautes Etudes en Sciences Sociales (EHESS), 2018), 283–93.

16 Unesco, 'Importation of Films for Cinema and Television in Egypt: A Study', Communication and Society (Paris: Unesco, 1981), 7, 23.

17 Cited by Viola Shafik in Dina Iordanova with contributions from Juan Goytisolo, Ambassador K. Gàjendra Singh, Rada [Sbreve]e[sbreve]ić, Asuman, Suner, Viola Shafik and P. A. Skantze, 'Indian Cinema's Global Reach', *South Asian Popular Culture* 4, no. 2 (2006): 132. She is referring to the following source: Ahmad Sayyid al-Najar, 'Sina'at al-Sinima fi Misr', in *al-'Ittijahat al-'Iqtisadiyya al-'Istratijiyya*, ed. Ahmad Sayyid al-Najar (Cairo: al-Ahram Center for Political and Strategic Studies), 301–33.

18 It traces back to an ambivalent relationship as demonstrated by Walter Armbrust, 'The Ubiquitous Nonpresence of India: Peripheral Visions from Egyptian Popular Culture', in *Global Bollywood: Travels of Hindi Song and Dance*, ed. Sangita Gopal and Sujata Moorti, NED-New edition (University of Minnesota Press, 2008), 200–20.

19 Aly Abou Shadi, Fadel el-Aswad and Marie-Claude Bénard, *Le Caire et le Cinéma égyptien des Années 80*, (Le Caire: CEDEJ, 1990).

20 Interview with Hurriya 'Abdine, 3 May 2014, Cairo.

21 Interview with Hurriya 'Abdine, 3 May 2014, Cairo.

22 This restriction was then lifted by Ministerial Decree (No. 388) in 1994.

23 For more about the historical exchanges between India and the Arabian Peninsula, see Khaliq Ahmad Nizami, 'Early Arab Contact with South Asia', *Journal of Islamic Studies* 5, no. 1 (1994): 52–69 and Patricia Risso, 'India and the Gulf: Encounters from the Mid-Sixteenth to the Mid-Twentieth Centuries', in *The Persian Gulf in History*, ed. Lawrence G. Potter (New York: Palgrave Macmillan, 2009), 189–206.

24 For more on audiovisual piracy and its link to cultural globalization, see Tristan Mattelart, ed. *Piratages Audiovisuels : les Voies Souterraines de la Mondialisation Culturelle* (Bruxelles, Belgique, France: De Boeck, 2011).

25 Claude Markovits, *The Global World of Indian Merchants (1750–1947): Traders of Sind from Bukhara to Panama* (Cambridge; New York: Cambridge University Press, 2000), 4–5.

26 For more on a history focused on the diaspora, see Rachel Dwyer, 'Bollywood's Empire: Indian cinema and the diaspora', in *Routledge Handbook of the South Asian Diaspora*, ed. Joya Chatterji and David A. Washbrook (London: Routledge, 2013), 407–16.

27 Ramon Lobato, *Shadow Economies of Cinema: Mapping Informal Film Distribution* (London: Palgrave Macmillan BFI, 2012).
28 Name and initials were modified in order to preserve confidentiality.
29 Interview with T. N., 5 October 2013, Bombay.
30 Name and initials were modified in order to preserve confidentiality.
31 For more on migrations routes in Dubai, see Alain Battegay, 'Dubaï : Économie Marchande et Carrefour Migratoire. Étude de Mise En Dispositif', in *Mondes En Mouvements: Migrants et Migrations Au Moyen-Orient Au Tournant Du XXIe Siècle*, ed. Françoise Métral and Hana Jaber (Beyrouth: IFPO, 2005), 271–91.
32 Interview with B. J., 14 December 2014, Dubai.
33 On the commercial role of this family, see Claude François Markovits, *The Global World of Indian Merchants, 1750–1947: Traders of Sind From Bukhara to Panama* (Cambridge; New York: Cambridge University Press, 2000).
34 Interview with R. K. Choukse, December 2014, Indore, Madhya Pradesh.
35 Name and initials were modified in order to preserve confidentiality.
36 Interview with S. L., 14 May 2018, Cannes.
37 For more about the distribution sector in Lebanon, see Georges Sadoul (ed.), *Les Cinémas des Pays Arabes* (Beyrouth: Centre Interarabe du Cinéma et de la Télévision, 1966).
38 More information about the contemporary situation of the cinema industry in Egypt and Lebanon, see Sahar Ali, 'Projects of Statistical Data Collection on Film and Audio-Visual Markets in 9 Mediterranean Countries, Country Profile, 1. Egypt'. Euromed Audiovisuel / Observatoire Européen de l'Audiovisuel, 2012; Sahar Ali, 'Projects of Statistical Data Collection on Film and Audiovisual Markets in 9 Mediterranean Countries, Country Profile, 2. Lebanon'. Euromed Audiovisuel / Observatoire Européen de l'Audiovisuel, 2012.
39 Muhammad Abdullah, CEO of TECOM Media Cluster, on Dubai Media City official website.
40 For more about Dubai's global role, see Roland Marchal, Fariba Adelkhah and Sari Hanafi, *Dubaï: cité globale. Espaces et milieux* (Paris: CNRS, 2001).
41 For more on South Asian Migrations, see Tristan Bruslé and Aurélie Varrel, 'Introduction. Places on the Move: South Asian Migrations through a Spatial Lens', *South Asia Multidisciplinary Academic Journal* 6 (28 December 2012): 1–12.
42 Interview at Yash Raj Films, 7 October 2013, Bombay.
43 Interview with Antoine Zeind, April 2014, Cairo.
44 Analysis of film releases in India, Egypt and Lebanon based on UNESCO Institute for Statistics (UIS) http://data.uis.unesco.org and boxofficemojo.com
45 For more about the changes in cinema culture and consumption in Egypt, see Mona Abaza, *Changing Consumer Cultures of Modern Egypt: Cairo's Urban Reshaping* (Leiden/Boston: Brill, 2006).

46 Muhammad Suwayd, *Ya Fu'adi: Sirah Sinima'iyah 'an Salat Bayrut al-Rahilah* (Beyrouth: Dar al-Nahar, 1996), 72–3.
47 About the multiplex culture in India, see Adrian Athique and Douglas Hill, *The Multiplex in India: A Cultural Economy of Urban Leisure* (New York: Routledge, 2010).
48 For more on piracy and films, see Kerry Segrave, *Piracy in the Motion Picture Industry* (Jefferson, NC: McFarland and Co, 2003).

7

The business of cinemas in Ismailia with a case study of Ghweba Cinema
An interview with Abbas Ghweba and Tareq Ghweba

Asmaa Gharib

The Ghweba family is one of the most important cinema families in the Egyptian city of Ismailia. Since the 1950s the family, under the leadership of Hasan Ghweba, has operated six major cinemas across the city. Although many of their cinemas have closed down, they still rent and operate two out of the three cinemas that exist in the city today.

The Ghwebas hailed from the coastal and fishing town of Matariya, moving to Ismailia in the early twentieth century as merchants.[1] Founded in 1862, Ismailia owes its existence to the Suez Canal project and its company.[2] As a newly established city, it attracted many people from different origins, social classes, nationalities and professions. Soon it boasted leisure spaces, including a number of cinemas, the history of which the Ghwebas came to play a key role.

Tracing the Ghweba's family history and its relationship to cinemas can help shed light on the history of cinemas in Ismailia, especially from the perspective of exhibitors. Histories of exhibition have been much neglected in Egyptian cinema history, and the following interview with two prominent members of the family is a step towards filling the wide gap in the literature. The Ghwebas saw many political changes and power shifts, including under the colonial period before 1952, nationalism in Nasser's era, the involvement of the city in two wars with only six years in between (1967 and 1973), the forced displacement of inhabitants for seven years and their return in 1974, and an Islamist wave in the 1980s and 1990s. Listening to the Ghwebas speak of their cinemas can also reveal how changing political contexts and shifting populations impacted the business of cinemas in the city.

The following interviews, conducted in Arabic between 2017 and 2022, illuminate the relationship between the city and cinemas, and point to interesting historical changes in audience composition. The interviews also shed light on how nationalism post-1952, when the monarchy was deposed and the military took over, impacted cinema exhibition practices. For example, in the years after 1952, Ghweba Cinema changed the rules of the cinemas' class division in the city. For the first time in the city's history, one of the best cinemas in the city was located in the middle of a majority Egyptian and working-class neighbourhood – known as the Arab neighbourhood, instead of just existing in the foreigners' upper-class neighbourhood, what was known as al-Afrang (or foreigners) neighbourhood. Also, as a city in a constant state of construction, at one point in its history the cinema cultivated a relationship with male labourers, who in the 1970s became the primary audience.

Before 1952, Ismailia was a starkly segregated city – with two distinct urban districts, one for wealthy foreigners and the other for workers and Egyptians. Al-Afrang had been designed in the style of modern European cities with wide streets, villas, water supply, a robust sanitation network, gaslighting and gardens all over the district. Al-Afrang was mainly inhabited by French citizens and foreign employees working at the Suez Canal Company.[3] Exhibitors built their theatres and cinemas in the al-Afrang district especially on the main street (al-Sultan Husayn Street) and seemed to exclusively cater to European audiences. Thus, it is not a coincidence that the establishment of the first cinema (Cinema Al-Ta'awun) for Arabs (Egyptian residents) in the city in 1935 was motivated by a need to preserve a sense of national dignity. The Arab neighbourhood had different aesthetic features than al-Afrang. The dwellings of this neighbourhood were initially nests, then the pattern of the houses developed to become buildings of stone with wooden balconies.[4] The Arab neighbourhood was also subdivided based on class, and also included poorer and lower-middle-class foreigners such as Greeks and Armenians. For example, from 1900 to 1930, about 130 Greek families lived in the Arab neighbourhood, working as owners of cafes, grocery stores and hotels.[5]

In the following interviews we can get a sense of those who attended cinemas and the class and racial differences that split the city. As the interviews highlight, class divisions and stereotypes played a key role in determining audience makeup, as well as business decisions. Throughout the history of cinemas in Ismailia, this class and racial segregation seemed very prominent and shaped experiences of the cinema in the city.

The interviews also shed light on the changes and investments cinema exhibitors were willing to make in tandem with changes in film production and star appeal, as well as changes in attitudes towards certain films. The interviews reveal how cinema exhibitors were very much in tune with wider community discourse about the morality of films – especially after 2000 with the advent of 'clean cinema' – a type of film considered morally superior and family-friendly.

Cinema exhibition, audience, war and displacement: An interview with Abbas Ghweba

The first interview was conducted with Mr Abbas Ghweba, a cousin of Hasan Ghweba. Born in 1944, he was not directly involved in the cinema business but nonetheless witnessed the family relationship with the cinema since its start in the 1950s.

Asmaa Gharib (AG): What are your memories of cinemas of the city in general, and Ghweba Cinema in particular?

Abbas Ghweba (AGhweba): There were a lot of cinemas in the city, some of them were for Arabs such as Faruq Cinema, which was in front of al-Fanfar Club (Suez Canal Company social club). After 1952, Faruq Cinema, owned by Ibrahim Ayub, changed its name to Misr (Egypt) Cinema (as King Faruq had just been deposed). Another cinema was Al-Ta'awun Cinema (The Co-operative Cinema) which has been demolished and replaced by the Agricultural Development Bank (Figure 7.1). There was al-Ta'awun Garden Cinema (The Co-operative Garden

Figure 7.1 The entrance of Cinema Al-Ta'awun in Ismailia (image from the Ismailia House Goods Cooperative Association's book that was issued in 1949 to celebrate its Silver Jubilee).

Cinema) which was renewed and reopened at the end of the 1990's and its name changed to Renaissance Cinema. Both of them (al-Ta'awun and Al-Ta'awun Garden Cinema) were owned by the Home Cooperative Association, which means that they were supposedly owned by the people of Ismailia. Also, there was al-Ahli Cinema which had been demolished and replaced by the central bus station. Its owner was a Greek man and it was a summer cinema (open-air) like al-Ta'awun Garden Cinema. Both the al-Ta'awun Cinema and Misr Cinema were the preferable destination for families, while the rest of the cinemas were attended mostly by young people.

Ghweba Cinema was built in the second half of the 1950s (1958 or 1959), it was not the first cinema in the Arab district, but with its modern equipment and furniture, it was the most famous and contemporary cinema in the city at that time. It had an unusual turnout rate, especially that the cinema did something that was not usual in the city. In this period romance films were popular, specifically 'Abd al-Halim (Hafiz) and Farid (al-Atrash) films, and the cinema administration always tried to bring one of the film stars to attend the premier for publicity purposes. One time they brought the famous belly dancer Nagwa Fu'ad, which was good publicity for the cinema. Also, they used to advertise films with a microphone and sometimes the film posters were held on a car, this car would usually go to all the city's neighbourhoods.

Ghweba Cinema attracted audiences from all over the city and it was a convenient destination for families and women. This was different from al-Ahli Cinema, for example. Al-Ahli cinema was also situated in the Arab part of the city, and its owner used to sit directly in front of the cinema door. The cinema ticket price was 9 millimes. We would give the owner 10 millimes, and the owner would give us a ticket and with the remaining 1 millime, he usually gave us one candy. It was the most popular cinema in the city; its programme was mostly Tarzan film series or a similar genre, and Arabic films. The cinema location was in the Arabic side of the city opposite Ismailia Train Station. I went to this cinema once only because there was a lot of violence as its audiences were train station workers and other workers from the area. It was a popular (*sha'bi*) cinema and its audience didn't inspire a sense of safety.

For the foreign communities, they enjoyed refined cinema theatres such as the Broadway Cinema, which had two halls; one for winter and the other (an open-air screen) for summer. There was also Royal Cinema and in front of it there was the Hollywood Cinema which after 1952 changed its name to al-Hurriya (Liberty) Cinema. There was also the Summer (open-air) Rio Cinema, and it was in front of the al-Muthalath (Triangle) Café. Most of these cinemas targeted foreign audiences. For example, Hollywood Cinema only screened foreign films and as I remember its owners were *Shwam* (Levantine people). The other cinemas' owners were Italians and Greeks. Ismailia was full of foreigners from different nationalities, French, Greek, Italians and also *Shwam* and it was they who established the cinemas in the city.

After 1952 we could attend films there if we wanted. However, when we were young, it was rare for us to go to al-Afrang or al-Sultan Husayn Street. On our way to our schools we avoided passing through these streets, we took another road instead. I can still remember the British soldiers sitting next to the Alio Building (a famous building in the city). We were shy, truly, it was our town but we were shy. This district was full of foreigners, not only shop owners but also workers in the Suez Canal Company, so it made sense to build these cinemas for entertaining them.

AG: You mentioned that some cinemas changed their names. For example, you said that Hollywood Cinema became al-Hurriya Cinema (Liberty). Why do you think this happened?

AGhweba: All the al-Afrang Cinemas had foreign names. After the 1952 revolution, some of these names changed to sound more Arabic to suit the post-1952 era. For example, Faruq Cinema which had been named after former King Faruq became Cinema Misr (Egypt Cinema). Noticeably, after the revolution, cinemas, restaurants, streets and anything named after the king had been changed. Hollywood Cinema was rented by Hasan Ghweba in the fifties so he wanted to give it Arabic characteristics; therefore, he changed its name to al-Hurriya (Liberty). However, there are also cinemas that did not change their names such as Broadway Cinema, Royal Cinema and Rio Cinema. Well, Broadway Cinema changed its name to Dunya but this was after 2000.

AG: Do you know why Hasan Ghweba chose an Arab neighbourhood (al-Mahatta al-Jadida) to build Ghweba Cinema. Why not in the foreign district, especially, as you said good cinemas and good facilities existed there?

AGhweba: I do not know why he chose to build the Ghweba Cinema in this place, maybe it was a coincidence or it was the available place at this time. Maybe also because it was the best place to attract audiences from the Arab district. Good comfortable cinemas only existed in the al-Afrang neighbourhood, so building a modern cinema in the Arab district would have been profitable because it would attract audiences from the entire Arab district which at this time included three main neighbourhoods (Al-Mahatta al-Jadida, 'Arayshiyat Misr, Manshiyat al-Shuhada').

AG: There was also a third cinema in the Arab neighbourhood of Manshiyat al-Shuhada', called al-Jumhuriyya Cinema (the Republic Cinema, which opened in the mid-1950s and closed in 1965). What are your memories about this cinema?

AGhweba: Yes, this cinema was not very popular. It was located in a poor neighbourhood and I do not think a lot of people liked to go to it because there were no seats or good facilities. The audience used to sit on the ground. Besides, its audience would not go to watch films. For example, lots of fights took place there. Therefore, people would prefer to go to the other side of the city, to al-Afrang, if they wanted to go to the cinema.

AG: Why was this cinema in this condition? Do you have any explanation?

AGhweba: Look, this neighbourhood's old name was 'Arayshiyat al-'Abid (roughly translated to 'slave quarters').[6] Manshiyat al-Shuhada' (Martyrs) was its new name after 1974, when the displaced residents returned. The main residents of this neighbourhood were working-class people who worked at the British Troops camp, which was nearby. It was densely populated and at the same time deprived of proper housing and basic services such as water and sewage systems. This neighbourhood did not have any kind of progress or enlightenment, and therefore it was not a coincidence that some fights, harassment or similar things occurred at the film screenings. So I believe this cinema was primarily established to attract audiences from this neighbourhood.

AG: Do you have any other particular memories about cinemas, especially before the 1967 war?

AGhweba: Before the 1967 war, there were many cinemas in the city. The summer, open-air cinemas were large. al-Ta'awun Garden Cinema was a very big cinema theatre. Its screening usually started after sunset, and its programme consisted of two or three foreign films. Young people usually had a fun time at this cinema. Also, I remember that Broadway's summer and winter theatres were big. Actually, audience attendance was high and all the cinemas were working very well. Also there was this remarkable thing where one film would be screened across multiple locations. Sometimes it was a problem though because there was only one roll of the film. So, as a solution, the cinema's administrators exchanged the film roll with each other on the same night, and transported it to each other by bicycles. In this way, different audiences got the opportunity to see the film in the cinema they prefer. Also, in this way, the film does not cost the cinema a lot of money which fits with the ticket prices.

AG: Do you remember the average price of the tickets at this time?

AGhweba: I think it ranged from 3 to 7.5 piasters. It was not a lot of money at this time compared to the economic value of the Egyptian pound and the sometimes expensive cost of making films – considering the film production costs and the film star's high salaries. However, videotapes did not exist yet, nor did film pirating, and television programmes were very limited. Therefore, the cinema was the only open path for entertainment. But back then most of the films were suited to the community's ethics and values. In fact, films provided entertainment and at the same time preserved the community's values which is much different from films today.

AG: In your opinion did cinema audiences change over time?

AGhweba: Yes, I believe so. Today families do not go to the cinemas as they did in the past. In the past, cinemas were the best destination to go out (as a family). Nowadays, the cinema is a place for the youth; it is rare to find a family who wants to spend their spare time in the cinema. Maybe they would like to attend foreign films and I think this also happens more in Cairo, but I think Egyptian films do not attract families anymore. Of course, television is a reason for this but also the ticket price is not affordable for a lot of them; in the past the ticket price was more affordable.

AG: Do you think the cinema audiences changed during the forced displacement which lasted from 1967 to 1974? What were the main changes in audiences after the 1973 war and during the 1970s?

AGhweba: By the time people returned to the city, video players and renting tapes to watch at home became very popular. Most of the city's cinemas, therefore, did not do very well because audiences preferred to watch films in their homes instead of going to cinemas. However, a new type of audience emerged: the (male) workers who played a role in the reconstruction of the city. Their numbers were large. They worked in establishing the Shaykh Zayid neighbourhood, repairing the facilities in the city and purifying the Suez Canal.[7] Some of the city's affordable cinemas or clubs that owned film screening machines, such as the *al-Taʿmir* (Construction) Club Cinema – which later became the National Party Club in the city then Metro Super Market – accommodated workers.[8] The Construction Club Cinema used to receive those workers, and the tickets were, I think, a small sum, like what it was before the 1967 war, around 3 piasters.

The second cinema that accommodated workers was the Egyptian Railway Company Cinema, which was sometimes run by the railway company itself or was operated by a renter. Of course, as the audience became mostly workers, families abstained from attending this cinema. In the past, there were specific spots and cinemas for families and other spots for youth like the summer cinemas. These distinctions guaranteed a safe space for families where they can avoid the vulgar and inappropriate comments from younger audiences.

Cinemas started to come back at the end of the 1990s and early 2000s. People started to enter cinemas again. That is why al-Taʿawun Garden Cinema was renovated and its name changed to Renaissance. But Ghweba Cinema was already closed down.

Cinema, stars and challenges: Interview with Tareq Ghweba

Mr Tareq Ghweba is the youngest son of Hasan Ghweba; he was born in October 1959 and spent his early youth in Cairo until 1994, when he returned to the city to work with his father and help run the family-owned and -operated cinemas. Currently he is responsible for running two of the three cinemas still operating in the city. These are the last two cinemas operated by the Ghwebas. The only one they owned, Gweba Cinema, was closed down.

AG: Where is the family originally from?

Tareq Ghweba (TQ): Originally our great grandfather was from Matariya in the Dakahlia governorate. My grandfather was a Bey. He owned real estate, an ice factory, and he built a mosque. He was working in the construction sector and other businesses too. Also, he was renting Timsah Lake for his fishing business.

AG: Your father, Hasan Ghweba, had an interesting relationship to the history of the cinema theatres in the city; can you tell me more about this relationship?

TQ: My father's passion for the cinema started when he decided to rent two cinemas from their original foreigner owners (Hollywood Cinema and Royal

Cinema). Two Levantine brothers owned Hollywood (which was later renamed al-Hurriya (Liberty) Cinema) and an Italian man owned the Royal. He was in love with the cinemas to the extent that directly before his death (in 2009) he renovated and rented the Railway Company Cinema. When he died, we let it go. In the late 1950s, his passion motivated him to invest further in cinema exhibitions. He chose an old pasta factory land that his family owned and built Ghweba Cinema in its place. The cinema was located in the heart of al-Mahhta al- Jadida neighbourhood, and was the first cinema established there. After a short time, he rented another three cinemas (Broadway Cinema, al-Ta'awun (Co-operative) Cinema and al-Nasr (Victory) Cinema). Al-Nasr Cinema was originally the Royal Cinema's winter (indoor) theatre. Royal's two screens were separated in the 1950s into two cinemas: (Royal and Al-Nasr). So, before 1976, he was responsible for six cinemas in the city, including the cinema he built and owned (Ghweba Cinema).

AG: When did you start to work with your father?

TQ: The Hajj (an honorary title given to older men or those who have performed the pilgrimage to Mecca) was running everything, he was administering Ghweba, al-Hurriya, Royal and al-Ta'awun Cinemas. I entered the faculty of engineering and after graduation, I worked in the construction field. I lived in Cairo until 1994 then I returned to Ismailia and started to work with him. I was responsible for al-Hurriya and Royal Cinemas.

AG: Between the 1967 war and the 1973 war, the city had to be evacuated due to the war. After the return of residents in 1974, the city's cinemas started to close or were demolished one by one. There seem to be only three cinema theatres remaining. I would like to know more about the Hajj's relationship to cinema during this period of decline and also, in your opinion, what are the reasons behind the closure of cinemas?

TQ: Yes, after the 1967 war all the cinemas closed due to the mass evacuation of the city. After 'the return' (*al-'awda*) of 1974 Hajj Hasan controlled most of the cinemas in the city. He also rented al-Ta'awun Garden Cinema, which was the summer (open-air) screen of al- Ta'awun cinema, al- Hurriya Cinema and Royal Cinema. He was very interested in forging a relationship with artists (actors and actresses). Once, in al-Hurriya Cinema he invited the actors Su'ad Husni, Kamal al-Shinawi and Nur al-Sharif to attend their film's opening and greet the audience.[9] The cinema was his life. He always wanted to expand and control all cinemas in Ismailia. He always knew how to get films, his mind was always busy in this field of work. He was really good at it to the extent that he established a film distribution company in the 1970s, naming it Bahia. He distributed foreign films and controlled the distribution market in Ismailia.

Regarding the closure of cinemas, if you offer 500.000 pounds to someone to leave his apartment, he would take the money and leave it. This is exactly what happened with the cinemas. al-Ta'awun Cinema was demolished and replaced with a bank, Cinema Misr became part of a schoolyard and so on. Currently, the Cinema Renaissance is being demolished and they will build a tower in its place or something similar.

AG: Isn't there a Sadat-era law stating that if a cinema is demolished, the new building in its place should also be a cinema? According to that law, they should have built a cinema in the place of the Renaissance.

TQ: Actually this law was repealed during former president Hosni Mubarak's era. I do not remember which year exactly. Before that (there were loopholes). For example, when Cinema Broadway was demolished, the land's owner built a very small hall inside a mall just to secure the building permits. That small hall was then taken by Dollar Film Production Company and prepared to be a cinema hall with around 150 seats and named it Cinema Dunya.

AG: How would you characterize cinema audiences after the 1973 war and 'the return' of displaced inhabitants?

TQ: In 1974, after the population returned after being displaced for seven years, the city went through a reconstruction period. Therefore, most of the audience were labourers. During screenings these labourers would make inappropriate comments when a kiss or hug or something similar appeared on the screen. They caused some bother for families. But when everything settled down and those workers left the city, families came back to the cinema. Also, do not forget that ticket prices became a bit expensive. It was not possible anymore to enter a cinema with a pound like you could in the 1970s. So only respectable people were able to go to cinemas.

AG: Yet it remained that people still shied away from attending cinemas. Audiences changed, video tapes meant people stayed at home to watch films. Do you think film content also played a role in keeping people away?

TQ: In a way, this is true. During this period, most films did not suit families. They had very audacious scenes, included to attract a young audience, such as in the (1973) film *Hammam al-Malatili* (*The Bathhouse of Malatili*) and films of a similar genre.[10] Of course, no one would take his wife and his sons/daughters to watch such films; therefore, it was not the best period for cinema theatres. However, there are always some good films that attract audiences of all types, including families. Many came even if they heard something inappropriate about the films. The cinema hall was divided into sections: the loge and balcony. The balcony was for families and the loge was for young people. Nowadays, films are very different, they are 'clean cinema', so no kisses or bold scenes. Good stories too. Karim Abd al-Aziz's films are respectful films, same for Ahmed al-Saqqa and Ahmad Helmy films.[11]

AG: Do you select the films that you will screen in your cinemas with this in mind?

TQ: No, you usually work with a distribution company. The company gives you the film which you have to screen. It is not an option to choose a film by yourself. Even if the distributor gives me a bad film and I know that this film will not attract audiences, I still have to screen it. As a cinema owner, you should deal with the distributor's good films and also bad films. If all the cinemas refused to screen this company's films, it would lose its money; therefore, sometimes we had to do this as a favour to the distribution company. There are three big distribution companies in this field: Synergy, United Brothers and Dollar film. Synergy does not own cinemas so it usually distributes its films in United Brothers and Dollar film cinemas. Also, there is Oscar Company which distributes films only in Cairo. Oscar's company owns cinemas, around four or five halls. These big companies work with each other.

Currently, as a cinema theatre owner you have to be connected to a distribution company to receive films. Sometimes you can be connected by a contract in which the company takes 5 per cent of the film profit in the cinema to secure the film. Other times, if your cinema is old and you have a well-established reputation then the distribution company will give you the film without contracts.

AG: Can you please explain how this film distribution process works?

TQ: Currently, the production company is also a distribution company; every producer has his/her distribution company except El Sobky Company. Synergy

Company distributes their own films, the same for al-Arabia Cinema Company. This was a little bit different during Hajj Hasan's time when the distribution companies were separated from the production companies and were more independent. Consequently, the cinema theatre owners were able to select a film to screen exclusively in their cinemas. Now, the distribution company can screen the same films in all the cinemas at the same time if they want. This combination between both production and distribution at the same company makes these companies monopolize the cinema theatre sector.

AG: Your cinemas are well established, so does this make a difference when you order a film?

TQ: Actually, the most important thing is the cinema's income; if the cinema can secure good box-office returns. That will force the company to deal with you. If the cinema can gain the company 3 million pounds, no one will refuse such profit.

AG: The production/distributor company percentage of the ticket is 50 per cent and the cinema has the other 50 per cent. Do you think it is a fair share?

TQ: Yes. Producing a film costs millions of pounds. It is true that cinema theatres need to pay their workers and have other costs. However, production companies pay millions in salaries for actors and other giant costs. Therefore the producer has to earn more than the cinema owner. After the governmental tax deduction, the ticket earnings are divided 50/50. It is fair so the producer can produce more films; if they lose money they will not make any more films. If their films fail at cinemas they will definitely lose more than the cinema theatre owners.

AG: Do you think that operating a cinema is more profitable nowadays or in the past?

TQ: In the past the cinema business was not very profitable. However, compared to today, the currency rate was more valuable. In other words, the profit was not very high but compared to the currency rate, it was very reasonable.

For example, nowadays in Cairo the ticket price in some cinemas reaches 100 pounds which is very expensive. The cinema's profit can sometimes reach 5 or 6 million pounds in a year. However, (the value of the pound has decreased significantly) so that profits are more like 5,000 or 6,000 pounds. In the past, you could buy a car for 100 pounds, currently, a car can cost 1, 2 or even 3 million pounds. Therefore, maybe now it is more profitable (on paper) but compared to the currency value, the situation was better in the past.

AG: Let's look at your direct experience. You started managing a cinema in 1994. When was the most profitable time for you?

TQ: After the release of the 1997 film *Ismailia Rayih Gay* (*Round Trip to Ismailia*). After that film, there was a sequence of films starring Muhammad Hinaydi and Muhammad Sa'ad.[12] The stars in these films made cinemas gain a lot of money. So, the era between 1998 and 2010 was very profitable. Even after this era the cinemas worked well but with new stars such as Karim 'Abd al-Aziz, Ahmad al-Saqqa and Ahmad 'Izz.

AG: And superstar Muhammad Ramadan?[13]

TQ: Yes, him too, but actually Karim 'Abd al-Aziz and Ahmad al-Saqqa's fan bases are larger than Muhammad Ramadan's. Ramadan's audience is mostly young people who come out mostly during the holiday season. Ramadan's draw decreases after that. Karim 'Abd al-Aziz or Ahmad al-Saqqa's audiences are more permanent, like the TV series, the (overall) watching rates are more in favour of these stars than Muhammad Ramadan.

AG: You mentioned the film *Ismailia Rayih Gay* and how it changed the film industry and cinema theatre sector, can you please tell me more about this film's influence?

TQ: *Ismailia Rayih Gay* changed cinema-going because with this film, big audiences started coming back to cinemas. Before this film, films would usually stay at a cinema for one week or a maximum of two weeks. This film stayed for three/four months and the audience turnout was unprecedented. The cinemas were very crowded. This period was a transitional period. (It also pushed many cinemas) to renovate to receive audiences.

You know, the cinematic season was usually winter, not summer. People used to go to cinemas in the winter. In the summer most cinemas were too hot and hard to bear. In the past, many theatres were usually divided into two parts (summer and winter) (an indoor and open-air screen). As cinema audiences became few in number and most of these cinemas were demolished, the remaining (indoor) cinemas were not prepared for summer screenings. Until the screening of the *Ismailia Rayih Gay*. It broke these scales. Thanks to this film the cinematic season all over Egypt became the summer season, and it led to revitalizing cinema theatres. It made owners renovate their cinemas ... to fit the summer season.

AG: Did you also renovate your cinemas?

TQ: After *Ismailia Rayih Gay*, I started with small renovations. The Royal Cinema was fully renovated in 2006 to be a first-class cinema as you can see now. Same with al-Hurriya Cinema, which I fully renovated four years ago. Renovating a cinema costs a lot of money. For example, a new air conditioner costs 1 million pounds and one seat costs 2,000 pounds. Cinemas like Royal, with a 400-seat capacity, can cost almost 800,000 pounds to renovate, and that's besides the decorations and installing sound insulation.

AG: On a different note, do you think cinema stars participating in television series would affect the cinema industry?

TQ: No, I do not think so. The cinema audience is different from the TV audiences. There are people who would like to go to the cinema, even every day. If there is a good film, it would bring in the audience. There is no doubt that a good film attracts audiences. A good film playing at the cinema in good condition: the audiences will definitely come.

However, the coronavirus pandemic changed everything for the worse. When it first hit, the cinema attendance percentage had to sit at 25 per cent. Of course, that's very low. Producers have not released any films; no one has the courage to release films in cinemas these days. Now the percentage has increased to 50 per cent. Hopefully, it will increase during the upcoming holiday season because producers will not make new films until they distribute the old ones first.

AG: Do you think online platforms such as Netflix and Shahid.net are taking audiences away from cinema theatres?

TQ: No, I do not believe so. Netflix screens old films and Shahid mostly takes the films after their cinema screening. Also, Netflix shows unpopular films. Blockbuster films have to be screened in film theatres to cover production expenses. Screening films at cinema theatres is the only way to cover production costs. If the film is a good one, of course, it will cover its cost; people will come to watch it and it will be booked out completely. It won't matter if it is a film season or not.

AG: What do you mean by a 'good film', do you mean an Arabic film with a popular star?

TQ: Yes. Only Dunya cinema screens foreign films, and of course, these are not as popular as Arabic films. Also, the tax percentage on the tickets for foreign films is more than that on Arabic films, so the cinema's profit from screening foreign films is less than screening Arabic films. Although we are studying the idea of specifying one of our cinema halls for foreign films. Yet we will also wait until everything becomes clearer concerning corona.

AG: During your long experience in the cinema field, did you feel at any moment that cinema theatres would become extinct?

TQ: No, absolutely not. On the contrary, cinema theatres are doing great. As I said before, as long as there are good films, audiences will come. Currently, the situation is not good due to corona. For example, we can only fill theatres to 50 per cent capacity, which means half of the seats will be empty, even though it will also cover the cinema operation's expenses.

AG: Around ten years ago you decided to demolish Cinema Ghweba. Why did you do this?

TQ: We demolished it because the surrounding area is not a cinema area (popular neighbourhood). It was not working well and we had to close it many times. It was not successful like the other cinemas. The two other cinemas we run are still gaining profit, so I like to preserve them. However, you cannot guarantee the future.

AG: Do you still rent the cinemas you run from their foreign owners, and why do you keep them?

TQ: Yes, until this moment their owners still take rent. These two cinemas are profitable and part of al-Hajj's Legacy. Also, I like to administer them and I look for ways to develop and organize them in order to preserve them. Besides, their rent contracts are old, so the rent is not much.[14] If I left them, the government would take them. They actually work well and cover their expenses and make a profit too. Besides these cinemas, I am still working in the construction sector. Like I said, you cannot guarantee the future.

Notes

1 Rajiya Isma'il Abu Zayd, *Tarikh Madinat al-Isma'iliya: Min al-Nash'a ila Muntasaf al-Qarn al-'Ishrin* (al-Qahirah: Maktabat al-Adab, 2012), 17.

2   Ahmad al-Sayyid Abd al-Fattah, 'al-Tabi 'al-'Imrani li-Mudun al-Qana: Dirasa li Madinat al-Isma'illiya fi Qarn al-'Ishrin', *Alexandria University, Faculty of Fine Arts* (2010): 118.
3   Abu Zayd, *Tarikh Madinat al-Isma'iliya*, 211.
4   Abu Zayd, *Tarikh Madinat al-Isma'iliya*, 261.
5   Abu Zayd, *Tarikh Madinat al-Isma'iliya*, 212.
6   'Arayshiyat al-'Abid neighbourhood is located in the northwestern part of the city. It was the closest neighbourhood to the British camp. The first residents of this area were poor labourers and families from Upper Egypt and Black families from Nubia and Sudan who came to work digging the canal and serving its workers. This is why it is called 'Arayshiyat al-'Abid to distinguish it from other 'Arayshiyat Misr neighbourhoods. It is clear that because of its poverty and the existence of poor Black families, this district was neglected by the Suez Canal Company. It was also not included in infrastructure reforms that happened after the Suez Canal opening to the other Arab neighbourhoods. It continues to be the poorest and least organized neighbourhood in the old Arab district.
7   The United Arab Emirates funded the construction of the Shaykh Zayid's neighbourhood, hence the name.
8   The interviewee refers to the National Democratic Party, the ruling party in Egypt from 1978 until the revolution of 2011.
9   Su'ad Husni, Kamal al-Shinawi and Nur al-Sharif were popular cinema stars in the 1970s. Here he might have been referring to the premiere of the 1975 film al-Karnak, which they all starred in.
10 *Hammam al-Malatili* (*The Bathhouse of Malatili*) is a 1973 Egyptian film directed by Salah Abu Seif. The film tells the story of Ahmad, a young man who comes to Cairo from Ismailia looking for work. Ahmad falls in love with Na'ima, a prostitute, while Ra'uf Bey a gay man, falls in love with him. This film is considered one of the first films in Egyptian cinema to tackle and represent issues of homosexuality which until this moment is a taboo.
11 Karim Abd al-Aziz, Ahmed al-Saqqa and Ahmad Hilmi are contemporary movie stars who rose to fame in the 1990s and 2000s.
12 *al-Limbi* is the name of a comedy film produced in 2002, this film achieved huge audience turnout. Muhammad Hinaydi is a comedy actor whose 1998 film *Sa'idi Fil Gama'a al-Amrikiya* (An Upper Egyptian at the American University) is considered the first film to inaugurate a comedy-film wave that lasted ten years.
13 Muhammad Ramadan is an Egyptian actor, who rose to fame around 2011.
14 The contract is referred to as 'old rent'. This means that the rent remains the same as when the first contract was signed by Hasan Ghweba. Under the 'old rent' law, the rent cannot be increased significantly.

8

Cinema-going in Egypt in the long 1960s
Oral histories of pleasure and leisure

Ifdal Elsaket

In his memoir *The Cinema and I*, the Egyptian novelist and social commentator Mahmud 'Abd al-Magid wrote that

> the cinema is not simply a film that I watched, then went home. It was a marvelous *mishwar*, a long outing with friends that I have lost; marvelous in the paths and streets that have since lost their luster and beauty, and in cities that have mostly disappeared, although they still bear their [former] names. The cinema as I knew it was a nation's history, and a manifestation of the nation's soul.¹

Similarly, Mahmud 'Abd al-Shukur, an Egyptian art and cinema critic, described going to the cinema, in his memoir *I Was a Boy in the 1970s*, as 'not simply watching [a film] then leaving, but a complete and organized ritual'.²

'Abd al-Magid and 'Abd al-Shukur's cinema-going memories provide useful launch pads for exploring a much-neglected topic in Egyptian cinema history: the experience and memories of audiences. For decades studies of the cinema in Egypt have focused on a handful of films or the lives of celebrities. High levels of attention have been particularly paid to canonized – often public-sector and highly stylized – films from the Nasser or Sadat period. Recently newer anthropologies,³ of filmmaking, focusing on labour, contracts, censorship and festivals have infused the field with fresh perspective.⁴ Yet, the audience, the motley crowd upon whom the box-office success or failure of a film depended and whose very existence the cinema owed its sustainability, has largely been ignored.

In French, Marie-Claude Bénard has done important work on the atmosphere and memories of going to the cinema.⁵ In English, the last time audiences featured as a primary focus of academic study was almost twenty-five years ago in a study by the anthropologist Walter Armbrust.[6] Based on fieldwork in the late 1990s, Armbrust describes cinema-going as 'secular ritual' analysing class distinctions, gender dynamics and ambiguity of subversion in downtown cinemas he attended. He particularly focuses on the cinema as a semipublic space that cultivated an environment in which young male students – those in a 'liminal position' – experimented with the boundaries of social acceptability and pushed against elite fantasies about the ostensibly educational role of cinema. But as Armbrust himself has noted, little attention has been paid to a historical study of audiences, and so questions of change and continuity in terms of cinema-going practices remain unanswered.[7]

From at least the 1910s, as silent films from Hollywood and Europe streamed into Egypt, movie-going formed an integral part of social life. Post–First World War saw the rapid expansion of movie-going as cinema theatres multiplied across major cities. Within a decade from the mid-1940s, the number of movie theatres in Egypt almost tripled, from 121 theatres in 1944,[8] to 358 in 1955.[9] By the time the 1960s swung around, cinemas were ubiquitous features of Egypt's urban landscapes.

No doubt, the cinema's ubiquity in the 1960s concealed a slow decline. From the late 1950s, partly due to increased television set ownership in middle-class homes, and changing economic fortunes, movie theatres slowly shuttered up: their status as reputable places of leisure disintegrating in an ever-changing social milieu.[10] The change, however, happened gradually. Despite declining fortunes, movie-going continued to be a widely popular leisure activity across classes and generations. The 1960s, then, straddled two eras in the history of cinema-going, its rise and fall to use the cliché. Ultimately, the long-1960s represented the last hurrah of a widespread movie-going culture in Egypt, a time when cinemas were still reputable places of socialization across all classes.

To gain a better understanding of movie-going cultures in Egypt, I examine the oral histories of ten people, four women and six men who lived in Cairo and Alexandria around the 1960s.[11] Most participants are of middle class and upper class, and so they present us with cinematic experiences very specific to a particular segment of the population. While limited in scope, the oral histories are a step towards opening up an entirely new vista of cinema studies, animating the experience of the audience and broadening our understanding of the role of cinema in society and in the lives of ordinary people.[12]

During interviews, participants cast themselves as enthralled children or teens, out for fun with siblings, cousins or friends, and remembered the cinema space as a key site of leisure, a conduit through which they nurtured bonds of family, cultivated friendship and experienced coming of age. Put together their oral histories and memories recreated the sounds and rhythms of the cinema theatre; the hustling of the food vendors selling simits, seeds and drinks; and the audience eating, laughing, talking and shuffling in their seats, contracting and blooming as the day wore on. In the memories of these participants, films were only part of the experience, with interviewees regularly admitting to having forgotten the titles of films they saw. As such, cinemas emerge as far more than a collection of films. They become sites of intimate history-making and key spaces of socialization.

The stories participants shared were by no means straight-lined or identical. Cinemagoers drew divergent meanings to their movie-going experiences, and programmes differed throughout the city as proprietors targeted diverse audiences with their programmes.[13] Open-air cinemas offered a different atmosphere to indoor cinemas, and each session of the day attracted a certain target group. Even during the same session, different sections of the cinema enabled specific experiences and expectations. In this way, the atmosphere in the cinema was constantly shifting. Yet combined, the narratives, punctuated by giggles and laughs, orbited around key motifs and emotions: fun and mischief, socializing and key seasonal memories; of balmy, casual summer nights in the open-air cinemas. Specifically, the cinema emerges both as a local site of family gathering – providing fun and games to children in their local areas – and a place in which social conventions were challenged – giving dark cover to canoodling teenage lovers or school-boy truants.

The gathering of these memories – which often began in the 1950s and spilled into the early 1970s – tempers the dominant narratives associated with Nasserist Egypt which centre around trauma, the *Naksa* (the loss of the six-day war in 1967), and the failure of the Nasser system.[14] Oral histories of cinema-going offer new ways of thinking about the 1960s, one associated not only with wars and the rhetoric of 'permanent revolution' but with the intimate, the personal and the pleasurable. I bounce off Omnia El Shakry's entreaty to denaturalize 'the dystopic narratives of Middle Eastern social and cultural history'.[15] In this way, I hope to render palpable the pleasures of cinema-going. The oral histories raise new questions about how the cinema cultivated sensibilities of leisure and frivolity and became committed spaces of entertainment against an intellectual backdrop that insisted on cinema's educational or uplifting role.[16]

In short, this chapter is an invitation to shift our gaze away from the screen and onto the audiences, huddled together in dark spaces of the cinema, splayed out on the balcony seats, crunching on their chips or nibbling on their pumpkin seeds and enjoying the summer breeze in the now-extinct open-air cinema. The main aim of this chapter is to reanimate some of the experiences of 1960s cinema-going in a way that can lead us to explore cinema's larger social role. Recurrent themes and narratives during interviews cast cinemas as transient local playgrounds, at once family spaces and emancipatory adolescent haunts. This chapter demonstrates that cinemas were sociocultural spaces committed to entertainment and pleasure, in which Egyptians of all classes could find time to socialize, relax and play. They were also sites that cultivated neighbourhood dynamics of leisure in which home and the cinema were intimately linked.[17]

The main attraction

In Egypt, like in many parts of the world, middle-class childhood beaconed a world of cinema and stars. For many 1960s movie-going children, cinemas were prominent features in their leisure infrastructure, key nodes in their memories of the city. Farida M. (b.1943) an interviewee from Cairo, conjured a sprawling geography of celluloid options, recalling that cinemas were 'everywhere'. Naguib K. (b.1941), another interviewee from the sea-side city of Alexandria, likewise, remembers the cinema as the 'main attraction, with the exception of the beach' where one would spend at least one night a week:

> Naguib K: What was the movies to us? Back then, entertainment was very limited. In other words, it was only the movies. So our outing was basically to go have dinner or just a few sandwiches, and then go to the movies.

Not only were cinemas an integral part of the physical landscape. Cinemas animated children's imaginations of leisure before they even stepped foot into a movie theatre. News of films and movie stars filled magazines, radios played film songs and the plots of films were told and retold in family settings. For the most part, therefore, children came to the cinema with a developed cinematic literacy, holding cinematic expectations in a way their grandparent's generation perhaps did not. Magazines and film posters flooded the market, and the ubiquity of cinema-going cultivated a certain understanding of what cinema-going meant. By the 1960s, the cinema didn't constitute a wondrous discovery except for a few:

> Nabila S: My generation and my mother's generation went to the cinema as children. Not so with my grandmother's generation. We in fact took her to

her first cinema when she was a grandmother. During the screening, the film showed a car driving forward towards the audience. Of course she was shocked and scared, rising from her chair, thinking that the car would come out of the screen and run her over.[18] This made us laugh and we always brought it up. After that experience, she decided never to go to the cinema again.

It's not surprising that for 1960s children the cinema constituted a permanent fixture in their experiences and also imaginations of leisure. By this period, hundreds of cinemas dotted urban landscapes, saturating social and public life with film celebrities splattered across magazines, advertisements and street posters. Children collected celebrity posters, and photos of stars wrapped in confectionery were a common treat.[19] In some cities, like Naga Hamadi in Qena, children 'clapped with happiness' at the human billboard's dramatic entreaties to attend the cinema.[20] Mahmud 'Abd al-Shakur recalls a scene of two men in the 1970s, one beating on a drum and the other holding up posters of the newest films showing at the nearby cinema, calling out:

> Come closer, come closer, come closer! Two films in one program at the Nile Cinema! A story of a girl called Mirmir, a story of a girl called Mirmir. A film of beauty and youth. Mirmir, the beautiful girl, and a story as strange as fantasy. The great foreign film: *Superman Saves the World*. The man who flies through the sky will save humanity.[21]

Cinema as a playground

Childhood memories of cinema-going, therefore, did not, for the most part, revolve around wonder. Instead, they orbited around family and feelings of fun and familiarity. Reaching as far back to when they were five or six years old, interviewees painted light-hearted scenes of trips to the cinema, describing 'the joy'[22] of dressing up and trickling into matinee, afternoon or evening sessions, meeting friends and cousins, watching films, snacking and enjoying live performances and games. In the memories of these 1960s kids, the cinema morphed into a fun-filled playground, replete with amusements of which films only formed a part. Often children were chaperoned by teenagers – forming a 'cinematic convoy' – in the words of Mahmud 'Abd al-Shakur – that streamed into local cinemas as their parents socialized at home.[23] In one sense, the cinema hovered in the space between home and public life, a sort of backyard where people felt a sense of comfort and also could have fun. Religious festivities,

Figure 8.1 Advertisement for a children's 'cinema show' at the Rivoli Cinema. The event was at 9am and promised 'gifts and prizes and surprises'. *al-Musawwar*, 9 January 1959, 27.

weekends or school excursions often framed the memories of children's visits to the cinema (Figure 8.1):

> Nabila S: It was a must, for us kids, during the *Eid*,[24] to get together and go to the cinema. We would take our *'idiya* – which is the monetary gift given to us by our parents – or part of our *'idiya*, and go to the cinema... On Fridays – the day off school, and on Sunday during the morning session, Metro Cinema would put on children's shows and movies. Schools would take children on excursions to the Metro Cinema.

Children constituted a significant bulk of the cinema audience, and proprietors especially catered to their tastes. Cinemas frequently screened Disney and other cartoons, which provided children an occasion to dress up and socialize. Hossam A. (b. 1952) recalls that the Maadi Club screened cartoons in an open-air cinema every Thursday. 'I remember vividly Snow White, Sleeping Beauty, and the fairies changing the colours of sleeping beauty.'

Metro cinema, considered in those days an upper-market cinema, not only screened cartoons but organized kids raffles and live entertainment. Madiha S. (b.1952) remembers that Metro's children's sessions were 'like a party':

> Madiha S: Disney was a big thing. We would get dressed up like it was Eid. It was a big party. You would sit down with your parents or relatives and get excited

for the performance about to commence. Disney characters would come to the podium before the screening. The celebration and rituals around the screening were very important – the dressing-up, the performance before the film. It was a very exciting trip to go with my cousins and my uncle to the cinema as a child. It was very exciting to see the performance. It was not just about the cartoon, it was about the whole event. It was an important event to do.

Cinema for families

Participants in the interviews spoke of the cinema as a site of family leisure and family activity. Sayyid I., who in the early 1970s worked at the Rio, an open-air cinema in the Cairene neighbourhood of *Bab al-Luq*, affirmed that cinemas were family spaces, affordable enough to take several children along. Cinemas offered multiple sessions during the day, with families attending the 10 am or 6 pm sessions.

> *Farida M*: They'd put on a screening at 10, a screening at 1, a screening at 3, a screening at 6, and screening at 9. The screening at 10 would be attended by parents, who'd take their children who like cartoons. The 10 am session was mainly children's cartoons. The *shabab*, the older kids, would attend either the 1 pm or 3 pm sessions. Groups of friends and Egyptian families attended the screenings at 6 pm to 9 pm. The upper classes would go to the 9 pm session. The 9 pm session was distinct because it was when the elite, the literati, the thinkers, the artists, would go. They'd wear formal clothes to this session. Or this would be the first screening, and people go because there would be celebrities and they'd dress up. You couldn't go to these premieres unless you had an invitation.

It is not surprising that children often discovered the city and its leisure spaces within the confines of family life. Adult family members not only accompanied children to the cinema (sometimes napping as the films reeled on, as one interviewee fondly remembers) but introduced children to films and cinema life. One interviewee, Mona S. (b.1945) remembers that on Friday mornings, her mother would regale her family with the stories of the films she'd watched the night before. On weekends, going to the cinema was a family trip:

> *Mona S*: When I was a bit older, our weekly *fusha* [outing] was that on Friday morning from 11-1. . . . baba would take us all, including mama, to the cinema in downtown – not the open-air cinema (but the cinema) that screened the new films. Every Friday, he would pile us up in the car, with mama, and we would go to the cinema. And then as part of the *fusha*, we would go out to have lunch.

Cinemas also created spaces for entire families to sit together. Madiha recalls that the family would often hire out special compartments at the cinema:

> *Madiha S:* You would have what we called a 'loge' whereby a family would sit together-like you would have in the theatres – and you could buy a box, I remember my uncle would buy a box and my family would sit together with a small table and you would get food and drink and what have you. We would be quite well served.

Food consumption

The programmes at these cinemas often lasted for hours, with at least three films screened consecutively. Most interviewees said they would sit for the whole three screenings, which meant they would be at the cinema for five to six hours at a time. The long programme, therefore, necessitated the consumption of food at the cinema, and participants remembered having dinner and snacking throughout the night. The continuous snacking, and availability of meals, which patrons sometimes brought from home, further demonstrates that people saw cinemas as casual local spaces, akin to parks or picnic gardens. The practice of bringing dinner to the cinemas, especially to open-air cinemas, had a long tradition. One respondent remembers that in the 1940s people would bring plates of cheese and bread. Sometimes interviewees remembered the food and snacks (and other aspects of the experience of movie-going) more than the name of the movie being shown:

> *Madiha S:* I remember going to an open-air cinema with my uncle in Bab al-Luq/ Lazughly. There was an open-air cinema there. I don't remember any particular movie, but I remember where we used to sit, and I remember we used to eat and drink . . . you would have food coming, nibble on pumpkin seeds, and have a coke, ice cream.

In all cases, the consumption of food at the cinema or as part of the cinema outing contributed to the social atmosphere inside the cinema. Other than drinks and ice cream and the popular bags of pumpkin seeds, people ate sandwiches, and dinner. Mona S. recalls having hearty dinners at the local open-air cinema:

> *Mona S:* Sometimes, mama would come during the program for one of the films, and bring us dinner. Or our nanny would bring us dinner, and we would have our food while watching. You will laugh at this, but one time, mama sent everyone a packet of rice, *mulukhiyya* (a traditional Egyptian jute-leaf dish) and chicken.

Mahmud 'Abd al-Shakur fondly remembers the 'tastiest falafel sandwiches' he would purchase before entering the cinema.[25] Hossam A. also recalls fondly the freshly baked potato chips sold at the cinema: 'I remember vividly that I used to love the chips or crisps, and it was fabulous. . . . That was a feature of the whole thing.' The selling of food in the cinema, usually at the interval, but sometimes throughout the film, usually added an additional layer of noise to the outing. Madiha S. recalls cinemas getting 'quite noisy' as food sellers walked up and down the aisle selling a variety of food. Hossam remembers food sellers 'would say "simit, simit" [a circular piece of bread]. So you say OK and you buy them, or you buy seeds and you keep eating it'. Naguib K. remembers the food consumed inside the cinema:

> *Naguib K:* The thing that really stuck in my mind is how much seed was consumed in the cinema. Before you go to the cinema you buy seeds and peanuts. The sound of clicking is still in my ears. The whole cinema was eating seeds . . . You're lucky if someone doesn't spit (the shell) in your back.

Cinema for women

A key motif of cinema memories is the image of mothers taking children to the cinema and the sound of crying babies. In his poem 'Cinema Audiences', the popular poet Bayram al-Tunisi snarky described a mother whose son 'screams and barks because he sees shadows in the dark'.[26] The writer and cinema critic Mahmud 'Abd al-Shakur, in his cultural and social memoir, *I Was a Boy in the 1970s*, writes that as a toddler he screamed and wailed when his family took him to the cinema.[27]

Many of the interviewees mentioned going to the cinema for the first time with their mothers. Mona links her experiences in the cinema to her mother, who was 'passionate' about the cinema. 'My love of cinema came from mama. My mother loved it so much, she couldn't do without it.' For Mona's mother, not a week went by without a trip to the cinema, either with her children or with her husband on a Thursday date night: 'When it came to the cinema, mama had the ultimate power. Mama would make the decision and baba would comply.'

> *Mona S:* I remember that if I got good grades at school – in Arabic or Maths, or anything, mama would ask me: 'So! Should I buy you a dolly or would you like to come with me to the cinema?' And I would reply, 'I want to go with you to the cinema!' So I never had dolls. My sister had dolls and I would play with them with her. But me, I'd go to the cinema with mama.

Madiha S. remembers her first cinema experience was also with her mother and auntie. Naguib N. also recalls that he attended a 1970 film with his mother and aunt, and Naguib K. remembers that his mother was fond of going to films:

> *Naguib K*: My father never liked the movies ... he didn't enjoy it ... when he sees people crying, he considered that an emotional thing, [he'd say] '... this is stupid, it's just a story' ... he was very not emotional. My mother was the opposite and liked films.

Mona S. continued to go to the cinema with relative ease as she got older. For other women of the same generation, cinema-going began to be fraught with parental disapproval. For Madiha S., cinemas diminished in importance as she became a teenager.

> *Madiha S*: As I got older, I didn't go to the movies as much as Hossam [her husband] because my father was a bit. ... As a child you get more allowances than a teenager. Once I became a teenager, my father was very reluctant to allow me to go to the movies.

Madiha admitted that her father 'was conservative ... originally from the village'. And that before him her grandfather, although urban, 'was also conservative':

> *Madiha S*: My father was not a great believer in this type of art – he would let us read ... but not go out to watch films. He did not go out himself to watch films. And especially, we had a television at home from 62. So, he thought, what's the point, why do you need to go out to watch anything when you've got everything on the TV.

The coming of the television was a game changer for leisure experiences of the middle and upper-middle class. Madiha's family was among the first families in the country to embrace the television set, and she remembers that she, along with her siblings, hurray-ed their father when they finally convinced him to buy one.

There were exceptions for Madiha though. When in high school, her father made an exception once when a friend from school invited her to come along to a screening at the Cinema Radio in downtown Cairo, a ten-minute bus trip from her family home.

> *Madiha S:* I also remembered that it was a bit of independence to go on my own, get there, get the bus, and meet my friend outside, then go together to watch a film. I don't remember what the movie was but I remember the feeling of independence and going in. She bought the tickets, she invited me ... she had

to come home and get permission from my father. He had to see who she was. Then she said 'we will just go . . .' I can't remember what movie was playing, an Arabic movie. She said 'I'm inviting her to come with me to a movie. Is that OK?' And he allowed it, and I went and met her. I travelled by bus.

Going to the cinema was, for Madiha's father, an activity tolerated in childhood, but not to be continued in teenage life. Madiha's story is duplicated among other teenage girls. Farida M. remembers that while she was allowed to go to the cinema with her sister, she had to be chaperoned by an older neighbour: 'I didn't have any male siblings, and my father had passed away. . . . My sister was three years older than me, and my mum would be worried for us to go on our own. So the neighbor's daughter who was older than us both, needed to accompany us to the cinema – for safety reasons.'

Hossam A. remembers that throughout the 1960s 'cinema remained the domain of boys more than girls because you can go out more than girls'. Unlike the girls, who needed permission or a chaperone, he admitted to attending the cinema 'with my parents' knowledge or without'. 'Abd al-Magid also remembers that certain cinemas, such as Alhambra in Alexandria, were filled with 'single men. It was rare if a guy came in with a girl'.[28]

Open-air cinemas and geographical memory

Most interviewees located their memories of going to the cinema in the balmy atmosphere of an Egyptian summer in Cairo and Alexandria's famous but now-extinct open-air cinemas. Open-air cinemas were considered second-rate cinemas, playing second-rate films or films that had already premiered in more luxurious first-class cinemas in the city's centre. Interviews confirmed the ubiquity of summer cinemas in people's memories, and it is clear that they constituted the main feature of a city's cinematic landscape. Interviewees spoke of open-air cinemas as casual spaces, often close to home or close to extended family homes.

Memories of attending these open-air cinemas were structured around not only seasonality, therefore, but also geography. Usually these summer leisure spaces were chosen for the proximity to people's homes or close to family homes. Participants spoke of attending these summer cinemas as casual affairs, bundled together with other family outings and activities.

Farida M: I became acquainted with the cinema when [I was] little. We had an aunt who lived in an area called Imbaba. We would spend our summer vacations there. I was around five. In this house in Imbaba, she lived on the top floor. Near her was the Imbaba Cinema – an open-air cinema. I would sit on the balcony, and watch the film. So, in the summer, we would watch films while at home.

Mona S: We were lucky that near our house – in the street near our house – was a cinema called Cinema al-Hadaiq. This was a summer cinema – it didn't have a roof. My father didn't like us going to the local social and sporting club, no one knows why. He didn't like the club, so Cinema al-Hadaiq became for us like a club. We were there almost every day . . . and mama would come in the evenings and would watch with us for a bit – just like a club, exactly.

Mona's mention of a club is in reference to the exclusive sporting and social clubs available to Egypt's middle- and upper-class families. The clubs acted, and continue to act, as spaces of socialization, where families with membership meet throughout the day. People drop in and greet friends and families or have a bite to eat. For Mona and her family, the cinema duplicated the social function of 'the club', as a place to linger for many hours and to come and go as one pleased.

Open-air cinemas also gave an opportunity for non-ticket holders to watch from nearby balconies surrounding the cinema venue. The well-known practice expanded the parameters of the cinema space to include the surrounding neighbourhood, and further situated the cinematic experience within the sphere of family life. People fortunate enough to live in one of these buildings, or know someone with a balcony, flanking the open-air cinema, relished at the opportunity to spend summer nights on the roof or balconies:

Nabila S: There was a cinema in front of our two-story house: It was Miami Cinema. Every day we would ascend to the roof of our house, take our dinner and watch the film. The sound of the film would be loud enough because there were not that many cars in the street. It was very calm at night with not that many houses and the trams would have ceased operating.

Madiha S: There were tall buildings around the open-air cinema whereby people would come out and watch the movie for free. We would talk about them and say, we pay, and these people get out on their balconies (to watch the film with us).

Open-air cinemas and class

By offering much cheaper tickets, open-air cinemas were, according to Hossam A., 'more open', allowing access to a variety of classes.[29] Although various classes could attend the same cinema, seating prices meant they remained divided in the auditorium. 'There was class division in where you sit at the cinema', recalled Madiha S: 'the ticket prices were different depending on if you sit really at the front – which is the worst seats, they called them the *terso*, which means the worst seats. Then you have the balcony then the loge . . . where the families will be.'

Although socially stratified, open-air cinemas cultivated a more relaxed atmosphere among audiences, with active participation a feature of the programme. The audience in the *terso* section, who according to Hossam A. were younger and poorer, would often actively participate in the action on the screen. Love scenes would prompt whistling, and the appearance of certain actresses would trigger some to rush the screen and kiss it. Hossam remembers that films starring Farid Shawqi – popular tough-guy films known for including fist fights and action – were a hit among the *terso* audience:

> **Hossam A:** The audience would get up and clap for him and so on. They would go onto the podium, and they'd run, and they'd hit, they'd shout and they'd clap . . . if someone would be coming behind Farid Shawqi, people [would yell] 'be careful, he's coming from behind you' [*khud balak, huwa gayy min warak*]. People interact. . . . He was so popular, he was known as '*batal al-tirso*' the hero of the *terso*.[30]

According to Hossam, the active participation of the audience was most prevalent in the open-air cinemas, and would not have been seen in the upper-market cinemas such as Metro. He did admit that you might have seen audience participation at Cinema Miami, Cinema Diana and Cinema Rivoli where they showed Egyptian films.

The antics and playfulness of the audiences in the terso section, who became known as *gamahir al-tirsu* [the terso audience], horrified many conservative film critics and filmmakers at the time. They believed this segment of the audience did not appreciate cinematic art and often attacked directors for bending to the tastes of this crowd. Yet, despite the jeremiads of critics, local open-air cinemas allowed for a mixing of classes in a way that was not duplicated elsewhere. Cinemas cultivated a sense of community and neighbourhood across class lines that later disappeared as middle-class Egyptians abandoned those spaces.[31]

Shrine for school-boy truants

While much of the interviewees recollected family occasions of cinema-going, they did point to other instances, often in earlier sessions, usually the 10 am or 1 pm sessions where the cinema became a place of subversion and skipping school. When the 1 pm session rolled around, the city's school truants, most often teenage boys, replaced the cartoon-loving toddlers and their mothers.

Interviewees corroborated the transformation that at particular times of the day cinema theatres across Cairo and Alexandria turned into a 'domain of boys' or, in the words of 'Abd al-Magid in his description of the Alexandrian Cinema Alhambra, 'a shrine of school escapees . . . and single men'. During these times, the atmosphere in the movie theatre shifted. Rowdy boys replaced excited children and juvenile boisterousness filled the movie theatre. Farida M. disapprovingly remembered that

> [during the time these young men attended], the cinema was filled with noise (*malyana dawsha*). There would be fights, and the cinema security guards had to throw people out. During screenings, the audience would poke fun at the film. When there was a comedic or intimate/emotional scene, they would make such a commotion that the security guards had to intervene and kick them out.

Sometimes students concocted a clever scheme to get from home to the cinema instead of school:

> *Hossam A:* Those who skipped school to attend the cinema would usually go to the 10–1 pm session. I skipped school to go to the cinema sparingly during high school. But my brother, he would skip school literally the whole week to go to the cinema. There was a bus that passed through al-Giza Street, where we lived. It would stop by his school, near the Misr al-Dawli hospital, and then carry on to Emad al-Din street, where he would get off to go to the cinema.

Romance and sex at the cinema

In the 1959 film *Hikayat Hubb*, the supporting character, played by 'Abd al-Salam al-Nabulsi, gives dating advice to 'Abd al-Halim Hafiz, who is struggling to get a woman's attention. To win the woman's affections, al-Nabulsi advises a smile, an admission of sleepless-ness nights and then, matter of frankly, an invitation 'to the cinema from 3 to 4:30'. Interviewees confirmed that at certain sessions during the day and at certain cinemas, young lovers found a refuge for romance and intimacy, and that some cinemas were known as perfect dating spots.[32]

> *Nabila S:* During the daytime sessions, the balcony section of the cinema is often reserved by lovers [*al-habiba*]. Guys with their fiancés or whoever, would book

seats in the balcony section. It's a way to keep away from the rest of the audience, so they can exchange caresses and kisses and that sort of thing.

Naguib K: If the film's really sentimental, you would take your girlfriend. So you'd see 'Abd al-Halim Hafiz with a girlfriend. . . . Back in the 60s, social interaction between girls and boys was much more difficult than it is now. . . it was difficult for example for one to have his girlfriend at home to visit him, so we go to the movies, so we can at least sit in the movies and hold hands, and maybe a kiss or something. So the cinema was also a place for young people to interact.

Hossam A. also confirms that the 'movies were a place you can take your girlfriend and kiss her . . . especially [at] Cinema Odeon'. When asked why Cinema Odeon was the best place to make-out, Hossam responded matter-of-factly: 'because it used to have Russian films'. His wife Madiha S. completed his sentence, 'and nobody would go to them'. Hossam A. continued: 'So you would have couples of all social classes actually. And they scatter themselves in the cinema. They watch half of the film and keep kissing each other in the other half.' Hossam remembers that lovers would attended the 3–6 pm sessions because they would not be busy then.

Although the cinema provided a space for lovers to kiss and hug, they could also attract unwanted attention from other audience members. Naguib K. admits that it was usually accepted for young men to take women to the cinema, but the women would be frowned upon. Hossam also remembers an unpleasant incident when he took a woman to the cinema:

Hossam A: [suddenly remembering] Oh my God! I remember once going with a girl. She was nice and I used to like her. . . . But the guy sitting in the chair in front of me would put his arm . . . to try to go into her underwear . . . he considered her a loose girl to be coming with [me].

The Cinema Club, which met at a downtown cinema in the 1960s, to view and discuss the latest films, also provided ground for romances to blossom. The Cinema Club acted as a place of sociality and meeting for leftist circles, usually including panels and discussions after the film screening. Albert A., one of the interviewees, met his wife at the cinema club during the screening of *Breathless*, and in the early 1970s Madiha S. met Hossam A. at a film screening at the club.

Interviewees also remembered that the cinema provided an avenue through which they could explore narratives of sex and romance on the screen.

Hossam A: Going to the cinema was a way . . . of seeing the naughty films. So if you want to go and see sex and all the sex scenes – just a semi-naked somebody or a swim suit – you would go to the cinema and pretend you were 16 – because those under 16 were not allowed . . . I remember the film *Blow Up*, and I remember going to see that film when I was 14 or 15 and pretending I was 16.

While romance and courting were prevalent at certain cinemas, other cinemas were also known for solicitations of sex work:

Naguib K: There were theatres, very cheap, and sorry for the expression . . . but no respectable girl would go to them. . . . There were two that I can think of, one was called Concordia and the other is Plaza. Cinema Plaza and Cinema Concordia . . . not very respectable. . . . It's almost like a step above brothels. . . . You go there not for the film. You give a tip to the man who seats people, he would put you in a place and not bring anyone near you, so in other words, he'd give you a corner. So it was not a very respectable cinema.

On films

In the 1960s, foreign films accounted for the majority of films screened in Egyptian cinemas. During the second-half of the 1960s, at least 80 per cent of films screened came from abroad.[33] In 1965, Egyptian films represented only 10.3 per cent of screened films. Hollywood films dominated, amounting to, by some estimates, more than 60 per cent of total film projections.[34] Interviewees remember American films and noted the popularity of celebrities such as Audrey Hepburn, Julie Andrews, Kirk Douglas and Elvis Presley (Figure 8.2):

Hossam A: I remember going to Cinema Rivoli where *My Fair Lady* was being shown. Every Thursday for twelve weeks I would go to the cinema to see the film. I remember being absolutely fascinated with the film, and certainly with *The Sound of Music* when that came out after. I honestly saw *The Sound of Music* fifteen times when it came to Egypt, that would have been in late 65.

While American films may have dominated the market, Egyptian films remained what Madiha S. called 'the highlight of the night'. Programmes would often include three films, and according to Madiha: 'The Egyptian film had to come last or else people would have seen it and left.' She remembers that some people even missed parts of the first film, coming into the cinema late. Indian films were also highlighted by Madiha S. as being popular with audiences (Figure 8.3). She remembers the 1964 Hindi film *Sangam* as taking the country by storm and recollects that one of its songs 'Ich Liebe Dich, I Love You' became a hit with people.

Figure 8.2 An article about Hollywood musical films in *al-Kawakib* magazine with a focus on *The Sound of Music*. *Al-Kawakib*, 23 November 1968, 92.

Figure 8.3 A regular feature in Egyptian magazines and newspapers is the 'Where will you go out this week?' section, which features advertisements for screenings of films. This section promotes four Egyptian films and one Indian film showing that week in Cairo, Alexandria and Tanta. *Alwan Jadida* magazine, 23 March 1969, 23.

Throughout the interviews, memories of specific films swung between detailed knowledge of film credits (actors, directors, significance of film) to vague descriptions of scenes and snippets. For the most part, specific films were not spoken of in detail, and most participants struggled to remember the name of the film or the exact date of its release. Often films were remembered by their star: 'the films of 'Abd al-Halim', for example. When providing the overriding plot of one film, Madiha S. also noted that she probably would have seen the film many times on television and therefore could recall the film better. Memories of films were therefore both fragile and layered with multiple viewing experiences (whether multiple times at the cinema, which was a common practice or on television).

If relating one's own experience or memory of a film was slightly less structured, film history provided the focus around which some interviewees could comfortably relate and structure their relationship to the cinema. Egyptian film history is a popular interest in Egypt. Information about directors, writers, actors and the film's themes is commonly circulated in the media. Segments about actor's lives, for example, regularly appear on Egyptian television. A general understanding of the narrative of film history is, therefore, common knowledge in Egypt. Certain interviewees switched from memory making – discussing their own personal experiences – to film analysis and history. One of the interviewees spent a significant portion of the interview listing political films made in the 1960s and discussing their significance. He easily remembered the names of these films, and especially their famous writers, Yusuf Idris and Naguib Mahfouz or Yusuf al-Siba'i. One interviewee, Naguib K., also displayed a high level of knowledge of film history and used the opportunity to also make a comment on today's films:

> *Naguib K*: One of the things I would really emphasize about the films of the 60s and even perhaps the 70s is this: In the 1960s the main thing was the story, the element of the story. I think personally that the element of the story is 90% of the film, even if the acting is really very weak, you at least enjoy the story. Now they produce good actors but not good stories. I think in Egypt today we have a poverty of literature. While in the 1960s we had writers like Naguib Mahfuz, Taha Husayn, Yusuf al-Siba'i. My God! I mean all the wealth of Arabic literature came in the 60s. I think that in the 60s we knew that we had very good writers. I would go and see a film with a story written by Yusuf al-Siba'i because I knew that whatever Yusuf al-Siba'i wrote [will be good]; he is a good writer, he's a good narrator. That was even emphasized in the film [credits], always, 'the story by Yusuf al-Siba'i.' (Figure 8.4).

While Naguib K. focused on the links between literature and film, another interviewee Farida M. spoke of the 1960s as an era of awakening to films as a

Figure 8.4 Advertisement for the film *Bayn al-Atlal*. The film was based on a story written by Yusuf al-Siba'i, who is here given celebrity status with a photo. *al-Musawwar*, 6 February 1959, 43.

didactic medium. She also spoke of the cinema industry's reliance on literary greats and focused primarily on epic films that had political and social impact:

> *Farida M*: I remember the types of films that used to interest me before the 1960s: they were the films of Isma'il Yassin, Marie Munib – comedy films used to interest me, and I would enjoy them very much. When I got older, and entered the 1960s, films started taking a different path. Films began to rely on literary works like those of Ihsan 'Abd al-Quddus, Naguib Mahfuz, and Yusuf Idris. This helped cultivate an awareness that films have a wider message beyond entertainment and laughter. So through the cinema, we began to learn about our history, religion (with the rise of religious films). We also learned about Jamila Bouhid, for example, the Algerian resistance fighter. We didn't know anything about her until we saw Youseff Chahine's film about her. We saw films about Khalid Ibn al-Walid, Antar bin Shadad.... Starting from the 1950s, we also saw films that dealt with women's rights – the idea that women not only had a right to go to university, but also had the right to employment.

Naksa and memories of leisure

At least three of the participants, therefore, framed parts of their cinema memories in political history by speaking about the political significance of films and pointing to a more socially aware literary tradition of filmmaking. At least two of the interviewees also indicated time by referring to 'after the *Naksa*' or 'before the *Naksa*', opening up questions about whether the *Naksa* had any impact on leisure activities in the late 1960s and early 1970s. The *Naksa* refers to Egypt's devastating defeat in the so-called six-day war of 1967. The 1967 war is often remembered as a traumatic shock: when dreams of Egypt's development and progress turned to dust.

While for many the 1967 war framed their memories of the period, asking about cinema-going in the context of the *Naksa* seemed misplaced. While two of the participants made references to the *Naksa* to signal dates, memories of cinema-going in the 1960s were not framed by politically traumatic memories.[35] For ordinary Egyptians, entertainment was enjoyed even in times of political angst. In his memoir, Mahmud 'Abd al-Shukur put it simply: the 1960s and early 1970s was an era 'of war and anxiety. But it was also the era of coloured stars. Indeed, it was an era of colour, an era of change and discovery, on the personal and national level'.[36] Hossam A., one of the interviewees, acknowledged the fraught nature of leisure at times of political instability by admitting that while some 'radicals' were angry that people continued to seek entertainment, at the end of the day, leisure was a part of life:

> Hossam A: After the *Naksa*, going to the cinema continued, and in fact, was somehow unofficially encouraged. Of course, the militants and the radicals of us were saying that the government was not taking war seriously [by] allowing people to go to the cinemas, [and saying that] people should be serious . . . I personally never took that view. . . . My view is that life is for the living and even in fighting the enemy you need to be alive and a full person.

Conclusion

Going to the cinema in Egypt was one of the main leisure activities in 1960s Egypt, a constituent feature of life and love for most middle-class children and adolescents. Yet despite its ubiquity, memories of going to the cinema have been sidelined by scholars, with far more attention paid to film analysis or the processes of filmmaking. By continuing to sideline the audience, we not only lose access to popular and personal histories of leisure in Egypt, as generations get older and pass away. We also miss the broader social role of the cinema in people's lives and how it was linked with family, coming of age, neighbourhoods and romances. We muffle new and fresh studies on cinema as a sociocultural space committed to entertainment and pleasure.

As in other places in the world, cinemas in Egypt were sites of social connection and ritual, messy spaces where bodies and voices intermingled, and people sought not just the latest film but experiences of leisure, pleasure and a location for socializing. Even after fifty years, interviewees recalled in detail the session times, the food served, the seating arrangements and the people with whom they attended. People bundled cinema-going with visits to relatives, having fun with cousins during *Eid* festivities or negotiating the boundaries of parental or school discipline. They located cinemas geographically in family neighbourhoods or close to home and conjured images of child-led convoys streaming through the streets to get to the neighbourhood film screening. Throughout the country, the cinema was a shape-shifting heterotopian space, at once a playground, a respectable space of family leisure, and a darkened haven for lovers and school-boy truants.

Audience memory can also expand our understanding of how people related to films. Films formed only a part of a much wider social experience, yet they were not entirely absent. While interviewees struggled to remember precise film titles, umm-ing and err-ing about the release dates, they could remember actors, directors and screenwriters with relative ease. Many of the interviewees' relationship to Egyptian films were often mediated through years of re-runs and multiple viewings, whether on television, VHS or the internet; and framed at times by an in-depth knowledge of film history. Some interviewees also provided political analysis of, or recommendations for me to watch, significant films of the period.

For the most part, the long-1960s represented the last hurray of movie-going in Egypt as ticket purchases dwindled in the years following, the television expanded, and new technologies such as the VHS became popular. While cinema-going continued well into the 1970s, the 1980s and 1990s heralded the end of the cinema as a space of neighbourhood family outings as most cinemas moved to suburban malls or were taken over by teenage boys. According to Sayyid, who worked at the Cinema Rio, the open-air cinema in *Bab al-Luq*, tickets became too expensive for parents to take their families to the cinema. Prices continued to increase during the Mubarak years, and with stagnant wages, the family unit was pushed out of the cinema. According to another worker, by the 1990s Rio became a refuge for teenage boys to get stoned during screenings, and it quickly morphed into a disreputable place.[37] Rio couldn't regain its audiences. It was closed soon after.

Today, Rio Cinema is abandoned. Its wooden chairs are overrun by weed, its floor a graveyard for street animals and soda cans. The history of Rio and its audiences has been ignored, relegated to the peripheries of Egyptian history, as obscure and faded as its facade is today. This chapter represents a small part of a much larger research project to try to animate some of the experiences of cinemas like Rio. It tells a different story of the history of cinema in Egypt, not from the perspective of directors, producers or film critics but from the perspective of the everyday audience. It is an invitation to take cinemas seriously as sociocultural spaces where people navigated their childhoods, adolescence and leisure time. Ultimately, by casting light on this dormant part of 1960s history, this chapter situates the cinema in not histories of trauma that dominate histories of the Arab world but histories of fun and pleasure. By raising the voice of audiences, it also sees cinemas not merely as spaces committed to national uplift, as the elites wished them to be, but as places of fun and endless entertainment as the public often experienced them.

I wish to thank the participants for their time and generosity in helping me piece together this chapter. Thank you also to Giedre Šabaseviciute and Adel Abdel Moneim for their ideas and comments on this chapter.

Notes

1. Ibrahim 'Abd al-Majid, *Ana wal-Sinima* (Cairo: al-Dar al-Misriya al-Lubnaniya, 2018), 6.
2. Mahmud 'Abd al-Shakur, *Kuntu Sabiyan Fi Al-Sab'iniyat: Sira Thaqafiya Wa-Ijtima'iya* (Cairo: al-Karma lil-Nashr wa-al-Tawzi', 2015), 50.
3. See in particular Walter Armbrust, *Mass Mediations New Approaches to Popular Culture in the Middle East and Beyond* (Berkeley, CA: University of California Press, 2000); Walter Armbrust, *Mass Culture and Modernism in Egypt*, Cambridge Studies in Social and Cultural Anthropology 102 (Cambridge [England]; Cambridge University Press, 1996).
4. For example, see Chihab El Khachab, *Making Film in Egypt: How Labor, Technology, And Mediation Shape The Industry* (Cairo: Amer Univ In Cairo Press, 2021); Alia Ayman, 'The Artist as Bureaucrat: Documentary Filmmaking in Egypt, 1960–1980s', *American Ethnological Society*, August 18, 2019, https://americanethnologist.org/features/reflections/the-artist-as-bureaucrat (accessed 14 May 2021). Also see first three chapters in Terri Ginsberg and Chris Lippard, *Cinema of the Arab World Contemporary Directions in Theory and Practice* (Cham: Springer International Publishing, 2020).

5 Marie-Claude Bénard, *La Sortie au Cinéma: Palaces et Ciné-Jardins d'Égypte, 1930–1980* (Marseille: Éditions Parenthèses, 2016).
6 Walter Armbrust, 'When the Lights Go Down in Cairo: Cinema as Secular Ritual', *Visual Anthropology (Journal)* 10, no. 2–4 (1998): 413–42.
7 The Network of Arab Alternative Screens commissioned a recent study of audiences that also engaged with similar questions: Nour El Safoury, *Mapping Cinema Audiences* (Cairo: Network of Arab Alternative Screens, 2018).
8 'Favor Hollywood Films in Sparse African Market', *Motion Picture Herald*, September–October 1944, 25.
9 Jacques Pascal, 'Egypt', *Motion Picture Herald*, October–December 1955, 14.
10 Andrew J. Flibbert, *Commerce in Culture* (New York: Palgrave Macmillan US, 2007), 78.
11 As a result of the Covid-19 pandemic, face-to-face interviews were rarely conducted. Instead, I used video calls, telephone calls and, in one case, sent a questionnaire to an interviewee who responded to the questions with voice-notes. One interview was conducted face to face before the pandemic and two during the pandemic – one extended and the other shorter conversation – with former workers at the Rio Cinema in Cairo. These conversations took place near the now abandoned Cinema Rio. The interviewees were mainly from middle-class or upper-class background except for two former workers of the cinema. Because I wanted to highlight the voices of my interviewees, and because their words feature prominently throughout, I smoothed out the interviews slightly for readability.
12 My chapter is inspired and benefited greatly from the work of New Cinema Historians, who have for two decades produced works on memory and moviegoing. For examples, see Laura Fair, *Reel Pleasures: Cinema Audiences and Entrepreneurs in Twentieth-Century Urban Tanzania*. New African Histories Series (Athens, OH: Ohio University Press, 2018); Annette Kuhn, *An Everyday Magic: Cinema and Cultural Memory*, Cinema and Society Series (London: I.B. Tauris, 2002); Annette Kuhn, Daniel Biltereyst, and Philippe Meers, 'Memories of Cinemagoing and Film Memory: An Introduction', *Memory Studies* 10, no. 1 (2017): 3–16; Daniël Biltereyst, Richard Maltby, and Philippe Meers, *The Routledge Companion to New Cinema History* (Abingdon, Oxon; Routledge, 2019); Richard Maltby et al., *Going to the Movies: Hollywood and the Social Experience of Cinema*, Exeter Studies in Film History (Exeter: University Press, 2014); Richard Maltby, Daniel Biltereyst, and Philippe Meers, *Explorations in New Cinema History Approaches and Case Studies* (Hoboken, NJ: John Wiley & Sons, 2011).
13 The multiplicity of experiences in the cinema has been theorized in Annette Kuhn, 'Heterotopia, Heterochronia: Place and Time in Cinema Memory', *Screen* 45, no. 2 (June 1, 2004): 106–14.
14 Mona Abaza, *The Changing Consumer Cultures of Modern Egypt: Cairo's Urban Reshaping* (Leiden; BRILL, 2006), 142–163

15 Omnia El Shakry, 'History without Documents', *The American Historical Review* 120, no. 3 (2015): 934.
16 Armbrust, 'When the Lights Go Down in Cairo'.
17 The intimate links between home and cinema have been identified also in South Africa. See Jacqueline Maingard, 'Cinemagoing in District Six, Cape Town, 1920s to 1960s: History, Politics, Memory', *Memory studies* 10, no. 1 (2017): 17–34.
18 A similar memory of being frightened of cars coming out of the screen is also referred to by 'Abd al-Shakur. The memory seems to serve a function of delineating those who have a cinematic language and those who do not: older people and toddlers. There is also something to be said about the prominence of a global memory of audiences afraid of cars and trains hurtling out of the screen, and what role it serves in understanding early cinema audiences. For more on the contested history of panicked audiences during the first film screenings, see Martin Loiperdinger and Bernd Elzer, 'Lumiere's Arrival of the Train: Cinema's Founding Myth', *The Moving Image* 4, no. 1 (2004): 89–118.
19 'Abd al-Shakur, *Kuntu Sabiyan Fi Al-Sab'iniyat*, 55.
20 'Abd al-Shakur, *Kuntu Sabiyan Fi Al-Sab'iniyat*, 54.
21 'Abd al-Shakur, *Kuntu Sabiyan Fi Al-Sab'inayat*, 54.
22 'Abd al-Shakur, *Kuntu Sabiyan Fi Al-Sab'iniyat*, 49.
23 'Abd al-Shakur, *Kuntu Sabiyan Fi Al-Sab'iniyat*, 49–51.
24 This refers to a religious holiday.
25 'Abd al-Shakur, *Kuntu Sabiyan Fi Al-Sab'iniyat*, 50.
26 Mahmud Bayram al-Tunisi, *Bayram al-Tunisi: al-a'mal al-kamila* (al-Qahira: Maktaba Madbuli, 2002), 174.
27 'Abd al-Shakur, *Kuntu Sabiyan Fi Al-Sab'iniyat*, 49.
28 'Abd al-Majid, *Ana wal-Sinima*, 133.
29 This interaction among classes seems consistent with Janet Abu-Lughod's observations of Cairo in the late 1960s. She wrote of Cairo that 'there has been an undeniable leavening from below. Consumption patterns, way of dress, and leisure time activities which were once the prerogative of a somewhat Westernized middle class have been diffusing down the social structure'. Janet L. Abu-Lughod, *Cairo: 1001 Years of the City Victorious*. Princeton Studies on the Near East (Princeton, NJ: Princeton University Press, 1971), 239.
30 For more on Farid Shauqi, see Walter Armbrust, 'Farid Shauqi: Tough Guy, Family Man, Cinema Star', in *Imagined Masculinities: Male Identity and Culture in the Middle East*, ed. M. Ghoussoub and E. Sinclair-Webb (London: Saqi, 2006), 199–216.
31 For a good discussion on more recent urban developments and middle class spaces, see Anouk de Koning, *Global Dreams: Class, Gender, and Public Space in Cosmopolitan Cairo* (Cairo: The American University in Cairo Press, 2009); Diane Singerman and Paul Amar (eds), *Cairo Cosmopolitan: Politics, Culture, and Urban Space in the New Globalized Middle East* (Cairo: American University in Cairo

Press, 2006); Farha Ghannam, *Remaking the Modern Space, Relocation, and the Politics of Identity in a Global Cairo* (Berkeley, CA: University of California Press, 2002).

32 'Abd al-Majid, *Ana wal-Sinima*, 128.
33 Gehan Rachty and Khalil Sabat, *Importation of Films for Cinema and Television in Egypt* (Paris: UNESCO, 1987), 18.
34 'Hollywood Movies Are Top Box-Office in Egypt', *New York Times*, 7 November 1965, 132.
35 This broader issue of pleasure in times of political instability is explored by Laleh Khalili in 'The Politics of Pleasure: Promenading on the Corniche and Beachgoing', *Environment and Planning, Society & Space* 34, no. 4 (2016): 583–600. Although indirectly, my explorations of cinema-going during the Naksa speaks to her argument that 'life is many things: capitulation or struggle, anger or fear or laughter, silence and work and yes capitalist leisure. But it is also the joyous sense of a transitory presence in ever-shrinking public spaces of cities that are torn apart not just by war and violence but by the dull discipline of work. Such pleasure, today, can contrast with pasts of suffering and serve as a memory of future utopias'. 596.
36 'Abd al-Shakur, *Kuntu Sabiyan Fi al-Sab'iniyt*, 57.
37 As described in Armbrust, 'When the Lights Go Down in Cairo'.

Part II

Contemporary issues of circulation, experience and memory

9

Film distribution and exhibition in Tunisia since 2011

Is cinema-going back in style?

Patricia Caillé

At the beginning of 2011, a popular uprising launched earlier in the southern part of the country put Tunisia in the global spotlight. This movement was launched by young people exasperated with corruption and the government's indifference to the crowds of jobless graduates condemned to survive on odd jobs in a rampant informal economy. Economic desperation had led to the spectacular self-immolation of a small produce retailer, Mohamed Bouazizi, harassed by the police. His death was the trigger for a popular explosion of wrath that turned into elation as the crowds succeeded in removing a despotic leader and his rapacious clan. With Zine El Abidine Ben Ali's flight to Saudi Arabia on 14 January 2011, the Arab Spring was underway, raising hopes in other Arab countries as well. History was being written by this small North African country with a population of only 11 million.

A few months later, on 26 June 2011, the Human Rights League organized a screening at a small cinema in downtown Tunis, the AfricArt, of a documentary *Laïcité Inch'Allah* (2012), which Nadia El Fani had shot during the uprising about people who choose not to fast during Ramadan. The cinema was violently attacked by Salafists determined to prevent the show, the manager of the cinema was injured and the lobby of the cinema ransacked, leading to one of the very few sites of the fragile revival of a film culture in Tunis to close down. Nadia El Fani became the target of a fatwa and was compelled to flee to France for having said on television that she was an atheist. She suffered an outpouring of hate and death threats on social media. On 7 October 2011, two weeks before the election of the Constituent National Assembly, the broadcast of *Persepolis* (Marjana Satrapi, 2007) on Nessma, a private television channel, generated large

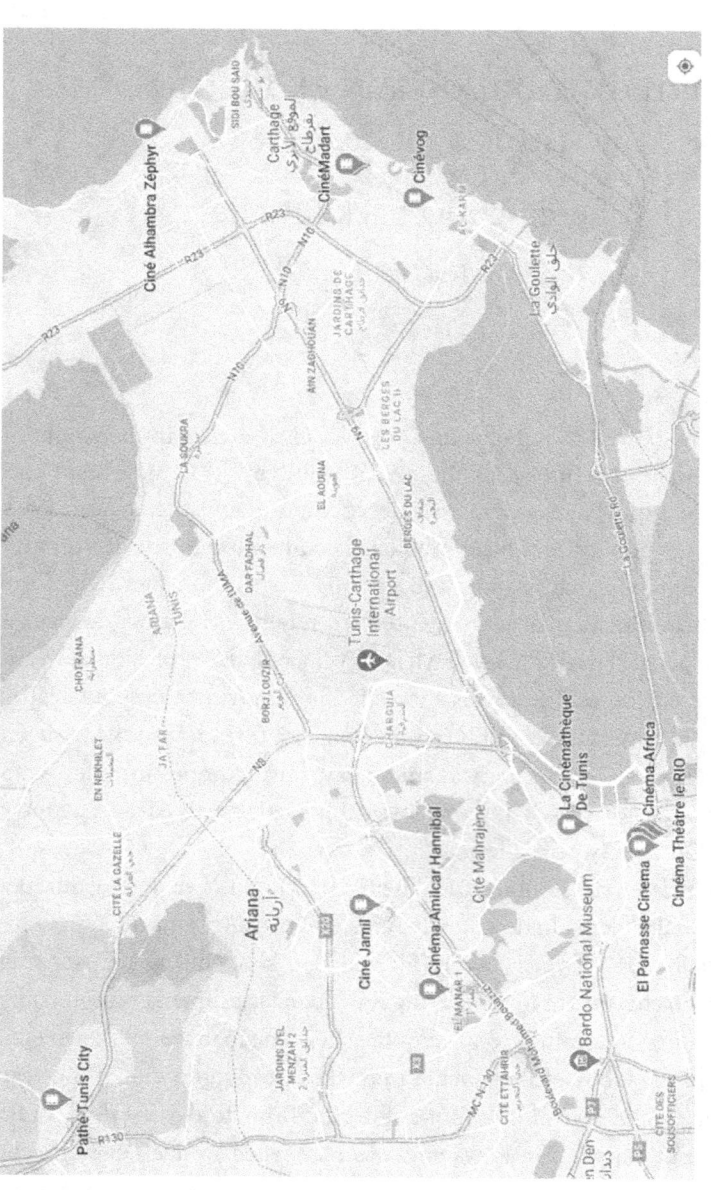

Figure 9.1 Cinemas in the larger Tunis area. Pathé Tunis City, the first multiplex far out in the northwestern suburban part of Tunis. Along the coast, Cinevog refurbished by Moncef Dhouib, a Tunisian filmmaker, and CinéMadart run by Kaïs Zaied (HAKKA Distribution). Both in La Marsa, l'Agora and the Alhambra, a cinema on the side of the Zéphyr shopping centre. Cinéma Amilcar in El Manar (a student area) run by Mohamed Frini (HAKKA Distribution). Much closer to the centre, in the Cité de la culture on the large Avenue Mohamed V, la Cinémathèque and Ciné 350.

demonstrations. Islamists expressed outrage at the representation of God as an old man in the film. Compelled to apologize publicly, the head of Nessma, Nabil Karaoui, was tried and condemned the year after with a small fine. Films had become powerful symbols in claims for identities and exposed the deep political and religious divides in a country that seemed united a few months earlier. Was film on the losing side of Tunisian history?

At the time, there were eleven cinemas left in Tunisia, most of them in downtown Tunis, which mostly showed US and Egyptian genre films, and an odd Tunisian film now and then. The majority of these cinemas were poorly equipped, run down and poorly attended, with chronic security problems and a lack of public transport having chased most cinemagoers away. People watched films on television, and most had a box set up with a satellite dish providing access to a very large variety of television channels. Starting in the early 1990s, media groups from the Gulf states significantly increased the supply of audiovisual productions via thematic film channels broadcasting across North Africa and the Arab world.[1] Numerous video clubs sold cheap VCDs and DVDs for one or two Tunisian dinars and large numbers of movies were available online for young internet users, unconcerned with copyright issues, who could download films using UTorrent or Popcorn time.[2] At the time, everyone agreed that watching films in a cinema was a thing of the past. A few years later, Habib Bel Hédi, a film distributor and former manager of the AfricArt cinema, contended that even though people working in the film sector actively participated in the revolution, 'they were not able to impose a vision for the film sector'.[3] This bleak political and cultural assessment of the outcome of the revolution in relation to Tunisian cinema and film culture is the starting point of a reflection on film distribution and exhibition during the first decade of the twenty-first century (Figures 9.1 and 9.2).

In January 2020, right before the Covid-19 pandemic closed down all these public places, there were nineteen one-screen cinemas and a slew of other non-commercial venues across the country that showed mostly Tunisian films.[4] The opening in 2018 of the *Cité de la culture* in Tunis and that of the first Pathé-Gaumont multiplex in a suburb of Tunis marked steps in opening up new venues for public film screenings. Are these the conflicting signs of a profound reconfiguration of film exhibition and film culture in Tunisia? If so, how? A sharp increase in the production of Tunisian films that audiences have favoured in the wake of the 14 January revolution has boosted cinema admissions. Despite the energy invested by the CNCI together with a few distributors and exhibitors in the late 2010s, there is still no official data collected by the institutions on cinema

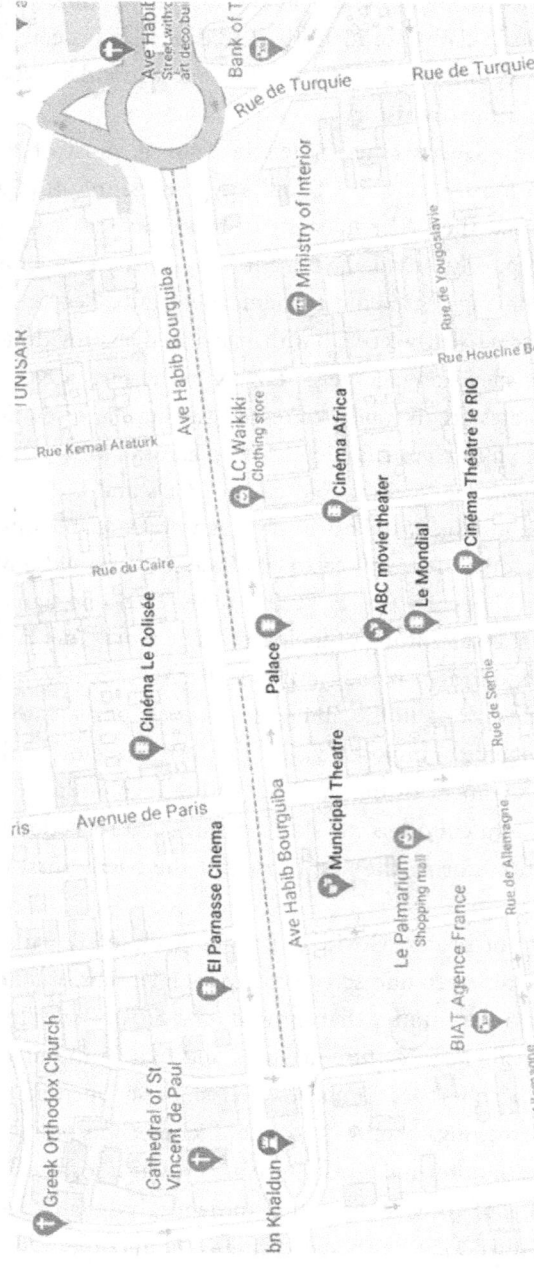

Figure 9.2 Cinemas in downtown Tunis. There has been a concentration of cinemas between the avenue Bourguiba (considered as the City Center in Tunis), the Ministry of the Interior and the French Embassy in Tunis. The cinema AfricArt, which was closed following the Salafist attack on the screening of *Laïcité, Inch'Allah!*, has reopened occasionally for festivals. The Colisée and the Palace belong to Lassaad Goubantini's cinemas, while the others are independent cinemas that survive mostly by showing Tunisian films.

attendance. But rumour has it that admissions for *Chbabek El Janna [Borders of Heaven]* (Fares Naana, 2014) were over 100,000, *Nhebek Hedi [Hedi]* (Mohamed Ben Attia, 2016) around 90,000, *El Jaida* (Selma Baccar, 2017) over 200,000 and *Dachra* (Abdelhamid Bouchnak, 2017), the first Tunisian horror film, over 300,000, the figures are probably much higher especially for the latter.[5]

As argued in the introduction of this volume, despite an early interest in the operation of the film industries,[6] scholarship on national cinemas in the Arab region, and more particularly Tunisian cinema, has focused mainly on political and aesthetic questions raised by the films themselves. Since the seminal contribution of one of the prominent agents in the early development of Tunisian cinema, Tahar Cheriaa's *Écrans d'abondance*,[7] little research has been done on distribution and exhibition,[8] even though going to the cinema in the Maghreb during the colonial period has generated much interest mostly from historians.[9] There has also been an interest in cinema architecture in larger film industries,[10] and a sense that a heritage must be preserved.[11] Festivals have raised a range of issues in relation to the circulation of films,[12] for instance, the ways in which they have contributed to the construction and valorization of a standardized and consensual transnational auteur cinema smoothing over deep political contradictions and unequal relationships of power.[13] But the present reconfiguration of the cinema landscape in Tunisia raises interesting questions that may go against the overall sentiment that cinemas belong to a bygone era.[14] This analysis is based on on-site observations of the operation of the six cinemas in Tunis city centre, those at the Cité de la Culture, and five cinemas in the larger Tunis area together with a survey of the staff (managers, ushers, cashiers, projectionists, etc.) working in those cinemas and present at the time of the visits. This analysis also includes in-depth interviews with the three main film distributors who are also exhibitors in Tunisia, as well as phone interviews with the managers of the cinemas in Bizerte, Monastir and Sousse, as well as a visit of the Majestic in Bizerte. The visit to the first Pathé multiplex included a guided tour with the Cinema Exhibition Manager working at the time but the top management did not return our calls nor replied to email messages.[15] The study was conducted in Tunis in the summer of 2017, the summer and fall of 2018 and a final interview took place in February 2020. The first part of this chapter focuses on the development of film culture and exhibition in Tunisia since independence, the second on film exhibition in Tunisia in the 2010s and the last part will raise the question of film distribution, a venture film exhibitors in need of films have had to experiment with.

Going to the movies since post–Second World War

Morgan Corriou shows that in the period following the Second World War in Tunisia the number of cinemas went up from fifty-four in 1949 to seventy-one in 1956, eleven being equipped with 16-mm projectors, many of them in the suburbs of Tunis or towns outside.[16] Going to the cinema was a very popular and mostly urban leisure activity but the French *Résidence générale*, the administration representing the French state under the protectorate in Tunisia organized a lot of travelling cinemas that attracted larger audiences for shows with educational material in the open air. The circulation of films was controlled by colonial power and ran from Paris via its main hub, Algiers, films being then routed to Tunisia and Morocco, which means that audiences in Tunisia saw the same films as in France after some scenes about miscegenation, anti-colonial values or unrest were cut out. Corriou contends, however, that 'celluloid butchery' was not as fierce as in other African areas. Weekly programmes were a mix of US, French, Italian and other European films, as well as Egyptian films, the latter being imported via more local distributors.

The film circuit from France to North Africa survived after independence because film audiences had been accustomed to French films during colonization and went on watching French films or films dubbed or subtitled in French. Muslim Tunisians entered film distribution in the informal trade of Egyptian films, the Goubantini brothers were the first Tunisian exhibitors, opening the Colisée in Hammam Lif in 1962 and then the El Khadra in Gabès. They also developed various activities around it, film distribution, cinema fittings and projection equipment.

Tunisia became independent in 1956, and the first 'code du cinéma' or film legislation issued in 1960 assigned the supervision and management of film to the Ministry of Information. The 'code' focused primarily on the control of film distribution in Tunisia via a system of visas and on the development of a film fund meant to boost production. The state intended to run the industry via the Tunisian Public Company of Film Production and Expansion (SATPEC, or *Société anonyme tunisienne de production d'expansion du cinéma*) created in 1957 and opened a studio in Gammarth in 1967 to produce newsreels and avoid dependence on foreign laboratories for development. The SATPEC took over film imports in 1969, which led foreign distributors to boycott the Tunisian market.

But Tunisia is renowned for the rise of a strong film culture in the post-independence era that initially developed during the protectorate.[17] In parallel to commercial distribution, the Tunisian Federation of Cine-Clubs (FTCC or *Fédération tunisienne des ciné-clubs*), created in 1949, drew a large number of youth after independence with screenings of international films, Soviet cinema and neorealism and integrated Egyptian films.[18] Debates, often run by teachers and international aid workers (French and other nationalities), shifted progressively from French to Arabic as part of the felt necessity to draw young generations to a nationalist agenda.[19] *Nawadi cinema*, a film journal created in 1958 by the cine-club in Sfax that ran irregularly through the end of the 1960s, and *Goha: Revue de culture par le film,* initiated by the cine-club in Kairouan in 1965 that published issues in fits and starts for a decade, were other outlets for the dissemination of a film culture. The FTCC opened a space for political debates despite the strong surveillance of the growingly authoritarian regime. The Tunisian Federation of amateur filmmakers (FTCA – *Fédération tunisienne des cinéastes amateurs*), created in 1962, which started as a hobby for a group of young men, followed suit. Structured around a federal bureau, local clubs spread out across the country developed regular activities with members gathering nationally once or twice a year for training via the national festival or other events. They saw film as a means of expression with its own logic and language but also as a means to reflect collectively on political, socioeconomic and cultural issues. The FTCA operated as a film school for many first and second-generation Tunisian filmmakers who are still making films today. The activities were also part of the development of an ethos of personal investment in a collective project grounded in rigorous critical training. The activities and debates played an important role in the personal development of the members who could hone strong critical and oral skills, a capacity to support an argument, to stand for one's beliefs, the constructive and reflexive capacity to listen to and learn from criticism. In spite of their limited outreach and repeated periods of agony,[20] these federations contributed to the production of a well-educated elite. Film journal *Adhoua: Lumières du cinéma* was launched at the turn of the 1980s while the Tunisian Association for the Promotion of Film Criticism (ATPCC, or *Association tunisienne pour la promotion de la critique cinématographique*) created in 1986 published *Cinécrits* conceived by Tahar Chikhaoui, and a few issues of a smaller journal, *Le cinéphile*, with the aim of sharpening the analytical skills of budding film critics.

The historical landmarks of Tunisia's promotion of film culture are probably the two well-known film festivals. The first is the annual International Amateur Film Festival in Kelibia (FIFAK, or *Festival international du film amateur de Kélibia*) created in 1964 which is devoted to amateur films and school films.

It has been the showcase for the activities and values of the FTCA, a very open and politically challenging film forum. The second is the Carthage Film Festival (JCC) created in 1966 under the leadership of Tahar Cheriaa who came to film via his influential leadership in the cine-club movement. The JCC's intention has been for Arab and African cinemas against the power of Western entertainment to produce and promote their own images as a means to counter the images of years of propaganda and exoticism. Even though they are very different, one being aimed at young audiences in a resort in the summer, the other being much more international and prestigious but also very popular locally, these festivals have remained loyal to their initial ambition to draw large local audiences to their numerous screenings.

For decades the Tunisian film sector produced a limited number of films (around 2.5 fiction feature films a year between 1970 and 2000, and then about 4 fiction films a year in the 2000s), not enough to sustain a strong film sector. This has led to chronic crises. A sharp rise in the production of feature documentaries followed the 2011 revolution, and since 2014, the number of fiction feature films has been considerably higher. These films have brought Tunisian audiences back to the cinema. Until the Covid-19 pandemic, Tunisian films represented between 60 and 85 per cent of admissions in one-screen cinemas in Tunisia.[21] The number of daily shows has also increased significantly with five shows per day for the Colisée downtown and four at CinéMadart in Carthage, with cinemas being open throughout the summer as well. In a cumulative effect, the increase in film production and the larger number of venues have introduced a larger range of films.

Film exhibition in Tunisia: Three different conceptions of film consumption

After the revolution, the need for culture was very acute and people who participated in the struggle were keen to invest their energies in the development of a new national culture. A large range of associations and cultural cafés sprung up in Tunis and beyond, leading to many run-ins between a defiant civil society and the administration that could close them down arbitrarily without notice. But the Ministry of Cultural Affairs also passed a bylaw in 2015 that provided tax relief to cultural entrepreneurs who wished to open and manage 'private cultural centers' devoted to multiple artistic activities (film, drama, music, visual arts and literature). This led to the opening of new small one-screen cinemas in different areas of Tunis and beyond. As it was retroactive, this bylaw eased some of the financial pressure on cinemas. The Agora opened in 2013 in La Marsa, a small cinema and a very popular café where students and young professionals come to work in the morning in a small garden. An association in Bizerte reopened a cinema, le Majestic, and another one in Monastir, and so on. Many of these new entrepreneurs started screening films using BluRays until they could secure a loan from the bank and a subsidy from the CNCI to invest in a DCP projector.

The shift from celluloid to digital technology also had an impact on cinema management. While projectionists were required to have a certification in order to work, the use of digital equipment has made this unnecessary. Cinema managers now rely on much younger staff with different types of mostly soft skills; project management, motivation, adaptability and flexibility, as well as technical competence to operate a DCP. The switch to digital technology combined with audiences' growing interest in Tunisian films attracting larger audiences encouraged exhibitors to invest in quality equipment with 7.1 Dolby for the sound and 3D technology. Exhibitors feel that the best way to fight film piracy is to provide a real spectacle with new releases coinciding with worldwide film releases. In the 1930s and 1940s, the architecture of the venue and new releases determined ticket prices and selected audiences accordingly, but then as cinema attendance declined, the different categories stopped being a clear class marker in downtown Tunis. A new divide has appeared instead between older and rundown cinemas downtown and new ones in the suburbs or outside Tunis. These categories can be subdivided between cinemas featuring mostly US entertainment films (dubbed or subtitled in French), and those that show mostly independent and auteur films.

There are three competing conceptions of cinema-going as a cultural activity in Tunisia at the turn of the 2020s. The first is characterized by Lassaad Goubantini's management style and approach to film programming. Trained as an agricultural engineer, Goubantini spent his childhood in the cinemas owned by his family and developed a film culture based mostly on American genre films. He took over from his uncle in 2003 – his father died when he was very young – and created a distribution company Ciné7èmeArt in 2007. He owns five cinemas and runs four of them in the Tunis area, among them the beautiful but weathered Art Nouveau Colisée built in 1931 on avenue Bourguiba, as well as one he opened in 2017 in Hammamet after having refurbished it. Film programming for Goubantini consists in bringing Hollywood genre films, mostly dubbed in French, at times subtitled, Tunisian films with a few Egyptian genre films as well, to audiences looking for entertainment.

Table 9.1 List of Cinemas Showing Films at the End of 2019.

Cinemas	Ticket cost[a]	Seating capacity
Downtown Tunis		
Le Colisée (Goubantini)	12 TND	1,650 (before renovation)
Le Rio (stage and cin.)	5 TND	325 (stage and film)
ABC	6 or 8 TND	751
Le Mondial (Goubantini)	6 TND	428
Le Parnasse	6 TND	300
Le Palace (Goubantini)	8 TND	610
Cité de la culture		
Cinémathèque tunisienne	3 TND	150
Ciné 350 (Cité de la Culture)	7 TND	350
Tunis Area		
Multiplex Pathé-Gaumont (8 screens)	16 TND / 10 TND (children)	1,540
Tunis City Mall		
Amilcar (El Manar)	8 TND	211
Ciné Jamil (El Menzah)	From 6 TND (2pm) to 13 TND (3D)	130
CinéVog (Kram)	7 TND	420 (open sporadically)
CinéMadart (Carthage)	7 TND	230
L'Agora (La Marsa)	11 TND	101
Alhambra (La Marsa)	10 TND / 13 TND (3D) (balcony) 12 /15 TND	428
Hammamet		
Ciné-Théâtre Médina (Goubantini)	12 TND / 10 TND	350
Menzel Bourguiba		
Le Métropole	5 TND	
Bizerte		
Le Majestic	6 TND	380
Menzel Temime		
CinéStar	6 TND	100 (closed down in 2020)
Monastir		
Ciné Star	5 TND	400 (closed down in 2020)
Sousse		
Le Palace	8 TND	310
Multiplex Pathé Mall Sousse (6 screens)	16 TND	1250

[a] A lot of these cinemas also offer student discounts that do not appear here.

Note: This list was collected through fieldwork and interviews with film staff from 2017 through 2019.

Downtown cinemas are located in a very busy neighbourhood around the avenue Bourguiba and along the rue Ibn Khaldoun, close to the area where cinema as a leisure activity was born. Most cinemas are run with a minimal and largely male staff except for a few female cashiers, cleaning staff and secretaries, with overall between seven and twelve people working in a cinema (managers, ushers, ticket sales, projectionist and cleaning staff). Goubantini runs film exhibition like a family business relying on supervisors who have been working with him for decades, all agree that it is 'like family', most of them having no initial training in film, marketing or sales. But they share a real interest in US genre films and have developed a knowledge of film programming while reminiscing about the 1980s and 1990s they regard as the heyday of cinemas only to deplore the present lack of interest they see in audiences. Loyalty to Lassaad Goubantini prevails. When staff is asked to name the best film ever, there is only one answer: *Guns of Navarone* (Jack Lee Thompson, 1961). In the day-to-day management of a cinema, working hours in Tunisia are long, with most of the staff having one day off every week, but managers or supervisors coming to work every day is common. In this type of cinemas, cinema-going is an affordable leisure activity that may serve many purposes including that of enjoying privacy for young couples who have nowhere else to go. As a result, ushers regularly tour the cinemas in order to deter any intimacy or disruptive behaviour. Tunisian films may draw larger audiences, but in some of the downtown cinemas the quality of the screenings is not always good, with the credits sometimes cut short in order to maximize the number of shows.

The second conception of cinema at the other end of the spectrum is the outcome of a strong and demanding film culture that has recently marked a shift from political activism wary of commercial cinema to a more cultural and institutionalized approach with the ambition to create a market through commercial distribution. The revolution brought the creation of a national film centre (CNCI or Centre national du cinéma et de l'image) in 2012, the purpose of which has been to regulate, support and manage the film sector. The development and achievements of the CNCI are beyond the scope of this chapter, but its move from La Marsa in the outskirts of Tunis to the imposing Cité de la Culture on the large Mohamed V avenue in Tunis in 2018 is highly symbolic as it gave a stronger institutional presence to cinema. It has made film a more visible and legitimate cultural activity and has added two cinema screens with top-quality projection equipment in Tunis, drawing new audiences to this cultural hub. One of the cinemas, Cine 350, primarily shows Tunisian film releases, the other, Salle Tahar Cheriaa, with 150 seats, added to the Cinémathèque tunisienne created in 2017 started regular programming organized around eclectic thematic weekly cycles in March 2018. The Cinémathèque, funded by the CNCI and the Ministry of Cultural Affairs, headed by Hichem Ben Ammar, a documentary maker who was born in a family of filmmakers and struggled to establish his freedom, has quickly drawn a loyal and multigenerational spectatorship.[22] Since Ben Ammar's resignation in 2020, he has been replaced by Tarek Ben Chaabane. The Cinémathèque fulfilled the need for collective debates around films with the goal of developing an interest in film aesthetics, be it auteur films or genre films. It tapped the audiences of more fragile initiatives, reaping the seeds that had been sown by cine-clubs like Cinefils launched by Kais Zaied between 2007 and 2009 at Al Hamra cinema or the cine-club run by Habib Bel Hédi at AfricArt, as well as other workshops; the purpose of which is to develop an acute understanding of the different ways in which images and films make meaning. The Cité de la Culture's very large and well-equipped 'Salle de l'Opéra' has also become the venue for the opening and closing ceremonies of the Carthage Film Festival, and other prestigious events that have brought larger audiences to the Cité.

Meanwhile, Kais Zaied and Amel Sadallah seeing the deterioration of the cinema landscape decided to step up from running a cine-club to running a cinema, the CinéMadart in La Goulette, a city-owned venue then devoted to the theatre. They started renting the cinema in 2012 in order to promote auteur film in a city with no art cinema and created an attractive space with a recreational area that draws students, and run by a young and motivated staff. They started a partnership with Mohamed Frini, who after studying engineering for a year went on to screenwriting and filmmaking at EDAC, becoming an exhibitor in 2015 at Amilcar, a small cinema in a mall next to a campus in El Manar. Frini also took over Le Métropole in the city of Menzel Bourguiba in 2019, a cinema he had kept an eye on since 2014 while travelling to screen Tunisian films across the country. These initiatives, which aimed to promote independent films as a means to introduce larger audiences to a wider range of films, including shorts, have kept the commitment to developing a cinephile film culture devoted to auteur films. But the agents of this change have opted for a business model based on commercial distribution, veering towards film as an art form, showing films in the original language with subtitles. It means a shift from an activist culture based on volunteering to a market-based approach that is sound enough to create jobs and support film production. Being an exhibitor is a cultural responsibility that involves a range of activities meant to develop film culture, and it is a social responsibility to provide job opportunities for local people. Frini claims that you cannot ask people to volunteer in a state system that does not provide them with anything.[23]

The third and latest development is the recent opening of Pathé-Gaumont multiplexes, the first one opened in 2018 in a shopping mall 20 km north of Tunis with eight screens and over 1,500 seats, the second in Sousse in December

2019 counts six screens and 1,250 seats, a third one is about to open in a southern suburb of Tunis. The Pathé website boasts top-quality projection equipment and the weekly programme includes primarily US genre films (dubbed in French or subtitled), and one or two screens devoted to Tunisian films, with the occasional Egyptian or European film. Even though the management is quite secretive about the business strategy, it is clear that it seeks to lure well-off patrons from the largely middle-class northern areas along the coast by upgrading the spectacle other cinemas in La Marsa, El Manar or downtown can't provide. The multiplex provides a larger choice of films, and young people claim they really enjoy the very large screens and high-quality sound equipment,[24] while parents praise the clean and secure environment where they feel comfortable bringing their children to see a cartoon at the early Saturday or Sunday shows. 'My kid forgot his jacket last Saturday, and when I came back, they had kept it. Unheard of in Tunisia!'[25] With a 16-TND ticket, almost twice as expensive as any other cinema, Pathé-Gaumont has lured young audiences with special deals in the early days of its opening and relied on discounts in partnership with Orange (formerly France Telecom).

The multiplex operates with a business-trained staff at the top and young mostly female receptionists who are recent graduates with language skills (they can speak Arabic, French and some English), with little work experience but strict in-house training in terms of clothing, attitude, language and so on. The atmosphere is that of a company delivering a quality service rather than one actually committed to a specific film culture. In this hierarchical organization ruled by customer satisfaction, everyone working there has to strive to ensure that cinemagoers enjoy the experience. Overall, the development of such multiplexes is mathematically bound to boost the consumption of US genre films, which accounts for the majority of the programming, but there is also room for Tunisian and a few Egyptian films. In the first year, the Pathé-Gaumont in Tunis counted 550,000 admissions, an impressive figure considering the economic recession, but such encouraging results highlight the growing gap between a well-off part of the city that seeks a safe, comfortable, clean and quiet auditorium to experience a top-quality film spectacle, and a larger part of the population that is left struggling behind. The contribution of committed film exhibitors to the promotion of auteur films via commercial distribution has rekindled and bolstered film-going habits around a renewed interest in Tunisian films. At the other end of the spectrum, upgrading cinema-going via spectacles in multiplexes may contribute to the development of a new film market while making up for the lack of cinemas in Tunisia. But doing so, multiplexes relegate the contribution of a dynamic film culture that had traditionally promoted political activism through film and the arts. At this point, it may be too early to say what the future holds for cinemas, all the more so as the impact of Covid-19 restrictions on the economy in general, on the film economy in particular, and on filmgoers' spending is difficult to evaluate. But the shifting landscape in film exhibition may also be affected by the extent of the reconfiguration of film distribution.

Film distribution and the circulation of films today in Tunisia

Film distribution in Tunisia has been the outcome of the necessity felt by exhibitors to find films to programme in their cinemas rather than a real interest in the activity of film distribution itself, even though times may be changing. As there is no training in Tunisia in film distribution, exhibitors have had to rely on in-house training like Lassaad Goubantini, who learned the trade through immersion in the family business, or seek training elsewhere. Kais Zaied, who left fourteen years of studying and working in computing behind,[26] regards his own professional trajectory as being the chance outcome of circumstances. He wanted to become a filmmaker but as there were no venues to show the films, he decided to forego his own calling in order to fill the gap, and becoming an exhibitor pushed him into becoming a distributor. He followed a few courses in business management, and went to Beirut for a training period at Metropolis, the only art cinema in Lebanon, which closed down in January 2020. He also went to work for MK2 Bibliothèque and the Forum des images in Paris to get the experience he lacked and build up a network of professionals he has been able to work with since then.

Since 2013, HAKKA Distribution, run by Kais Zaied, Amal Saadallah and Mohamed Frini, has experimented with film distribution as a means to find an alternative to mass entertainment while deploring the lack of regulation of the sector. They distribute between forty and fifty films a year. Competition between the two main distributors over Tunisian films and the sharp increase in the number of screens contributed to a much more varied supply of films available for cinemagoers. Nevertheless, the recent success of HAKKA Distribution came from a very atypical approach to film distribution tapping the longing for cinephile film culture while bringing these audiences to independent and auteur cinema via a range of events. To get there, HAKKA moved to more spacious offices in Montplaisir and opted for a more open form of business management, quite at odds with that of its competitor. It has created a community of highly motivated young graduates from different disciplines hired for their strong engagement and willingness to contribute ideas. HAKKA's success is also the outcome of more flexible business practices with easier terms of payment than Goubantini's more ruthless approach that exacted exclusive partnerships until mediation through the CNCI helped clarify and put trade relations on a sounder footing. The two exhibitors/distributors refuse to consider the opening of multiplexes as a threat to local Tunis cinemas and prefer to see them as an opportunity for them to expand distribution, and it may be so unless Pathé decides to extend its business to distribution as well.

Conclusion

Analysing the reconfiguration of the cinema landscape in Tunisia during the Covid-19 lockdown is eerie, but Tunisia has been very resilient in its capacity to overcome deep crises, tourism being one of the most salient examples of the ability to deal with adversity. Tunisian film culture has taught its members to find the means to pull themselves up by their bootstraps without expecting any help from the state, which may help the sector to survive.

Whereas in the 1990s and 2000s producers and filmmakers were looking for European releases, which have become few and far between, the surge in nationalist impulse following the revolution combined with the rise in film production have led to a sharp increase in local box-office returns. This in turn created the room and a need for an increase in the range of venues providing access to films. But the sustainability of the sudden reconfiguration of the cinema landscape may be complicated.

Film culture in Tunisia has relied on the investment of a political and cultural activism whose ambition has sought to be more inclusive, albeit catering largely to middle classes, students and a civil society with a longing for cultural engagement. And one of the specificities of Tunisian film festivals has been their capacity to draw large local audiences beyond international guests and the small crowd of regular cinemagoers to a wide range of films for a minimal fee. The institutionalization and growing visibility of Tunisian film and film in Tunisia may succumb to its catering to international norms. Promoting film culture via commercial distribution in order to create a market for film may provide challenging opportunities to develop creative industries: The VOD platform Artify attests to the ways in which access to film can use technological innovations to cater to new tastes and foster new cultural practices (See Anaïs Farine's interview with Jad Abi Khalil in this volume for more on online audiences).[27] But the shift towards expensive film consumption means losing touch with a more popular base and discounting its grass-roots activities; it entails instead a short-term approach to profit making via a reliance on the buying power of small economic elites, while expanding the growing gap between the rich and the poor in Tunisia. Multiplexes can boost box-office returns and temporarily alleviate low admissions covering up the neglect of larger audiences. Morocco's experience with multiplexes shows how raising box-office returns may be a costly plaster on a wooden leg that falls short of developing a film culture in a population three times as large as that of Tunisia. In the same way, funding a much more selective film festival with tuxedo- and bare-foot receptions on the beach for VIPs only may be an attempt to attract the international jet-setting film crowds in order to become more visible and maybe hope for international co-productions. It is bound to cut off Tunisian film culture from its national tradition and to create a deep divide within the film sector between those who are in and those who are left out. At a time of economic constraints, such lavish displays will have to be written off against other probably local investments into production or exhibition. Tunisia traditionally relied on trained intellectual elites whose engagement was with national culture. And the attractiveness of Tunisian films lies in the proximity between people involved in the film sector and the proponents of its film culture. While the national sentiment revived by the 14 January revolution may have boosted film consumption, the need remains to address the conditions of the viability of a film culture via commercial distribution, without severing the tie between audiences and the local figures they admire who had so far always seemed accessible.

Notes

1 Research on the reconfiguration of Arab media has focused mostly on news media and entertainment, leaving film aside as it had traditionally been associated with political and aesthetic issues related with national and regional identities. See for instance Yves Gonzales-Quijano and Guaaybess Tourya, *Les Arabes parlent aux Arabes. La révolution de l'information dans le monde arabe* (Arles: Actes Sud, 2009); Tourya Guaaybess, *Les médias arabes: Confluences médiatiques et dynamique sociale* (Paris: CNRS, 2012).
2 Patricia Caillé and Lamia Guiga, 'Pratiques des films au regard de l'offre et de la demande dans la Tunisie urbaine aujourd'hui', in *Pratiques et usages du film en*

Afriques francophones. Maroc, Tchad, Togo, Tunisie, ed. Patricia Caillé and Claude Forest (Villeneuve d'Ascq: Septentrion, 2019), 33–100; MENA Media Monitoring and Apimed, 'Medbarometer. Final Report', 2017, http://www.gvc-italia.org/images/documenti/2018.04.27%20MedBarometer_final%20report%20with%20annexes.PDF.

3 Habib Bel Hédi, Interview in Tunis with Patricia Caillé, 12 November 2017.

4 Distributors have been organizing screenings in different venues across the country via local partnerships, often with BluRay projectors in order to make Tunisian new releases available to larger audiences. The 2016 CNCI initiative to equip fourteen 'maisons de la culture' with DCP for sporadic screenings has been criticized for its very high cost.

5 Such figures may seem ridiculously low but in relation to the number of cinemas, they mark a steep rise in cinemagoers' interest in Tunisian film.

6 Georges Sadoul (ed.), *Les cinémas des pays arabes* (Beyrouth: Centre interarabe du cinéma et de la télévision, 1966).

7 Tahar Cheriaa, *Écrans d'abondance ou Cinéma de libération en Afrique ?* (Tunis: SATPEC, 1978); See also, Omar Khlifi, *Le cinéma en Tunisie* (Tunis: Société Tunisienne de Diffusion, 1970); Florence Martin, 'Tunisia', in *The Cinemas of Small Nations*, ed. Hjort Mette et Duncan Petrie (Edinburgh: University Press, 2008), 213–28.

8 A notable exception, Abdelfettah Benchenna et al. (ed.), 'La circulation des films: Afrique du Nord et Moyen-Orient', *Africultures* 101–2 (2016).

9 Morgan Corriou, 'Un nouveau loisir en situation coloniale: Le cinéma dans la Tunisie du Protectorat (1896–1956)', PhD dissertation, Université de Paris 7, 2011; Nolwenn Mingant, 'Un public aux mille visages: Identifier l'expérience des spectateurs du cinéma américain dans le Maghreb de l'ère coloniale', *Regarder des films en Afriques*, dir. Patricia Caillé and Claude Forest (Villeneuve d'Ascq: PU du Septentrion, 2017).

10 Marie-Claude Bénard, *La sortie au cinéma: palaces et ciné-jardins d'Égypte (1930–80)* (Marseille: Éditions Parenthèses, 2016).

11 The online exhibit by Stephan Zaubiter of cinemas in Tunisia that captures the cinema culture of a past era. http://www.stephanzaubitzer.com/albums/tunisie/content/labc-tunis/ (checked on 30 April 2020).

12 Dina Iordanova and Stefanie Van de Peer (ed.), *Festival Yearbook 6: Films Festivals and the Middle East* (St Andrews: St Andrews Film Studies, 2014).

13 Anaïs Farine, 'Imaginaires cinématographiques du "dialogue euro-méditerranéen" (1995–2017): formes festivalières, formes institutionnelles, formes alternatives', PhD dissertation, Université de Paris 3, 2019.

14 See Patricia Caillé and Claude Forest (ed.), *Pratiques et usages des films en Afriques francophones. Maroc, Tchad, Togo, Tunisie* (Villeneuve d'Ascq: PU du Septentrion, 2019).

15 According to the manager who agreed to the tour of the multiplex, Pathé was still working on developing its marketing strategy and business model.
16 Corriou, *Nouveau loisir*, 355–67, 367.
17 As a French protectorate from 1881 to 1956, Tunisia like Morocco was given more local autonomy than a fully colonized Algeria that was divided in three French counties (départements).
18 Tahar Cheriaa claims that spectatorship in the 1970s in Tunisia was 7 million in regular cinemas and 4 million in non-commercial venues. 'Africa: Rivista trimestrale di studi e documentazione dell'Instituto italiano per l'Africa et l'Oriente', *Anno* 28, no. 3 (September 1973): 431–8.
19 Interview of Ridha Behi by Patricia Caillé in la Marsa, Tunisia, on 17 February 2020.
20 See Patricia Caillé, 'Amateur filmmaking in Tunisia: A Political Film Culture Eliding Contradictions in National Cinema', in *Cinema in the Arab World: Contemporary Directions in Theory and Practice*, ed. Terri Ginsberg and Chris Lippard (Palgrave MacMillan, 2020), 89–123.
21 This figure is the outcome of the survey conducted with the film exhibitors and distributors across Tunisia, as there is no official count of admissions in Tunisia in spite of the desire of the CNCI and a few distributors to collect official data.
22 The Cinémathèque tunisienne has not yet put into a place a much-needed programme of preservation for Tunisian film heritage.
23 Mohamed Frini, interview with Patricia Caillé at HAKKA Distribution, on 13 February2020.
24 See Caillé and Guiga, 'Pratiques des films'.
25 Tour of the Pathé-Gaumont in Tunis City and observation on Saturday, 13 April 2019.
26 Kais Zaied, online interview with Patricia Caillé on 28 December 2018.
27 Artify, a VOD platform for Tunisian film, is certainly the most recent example in March 2020. https://artify.tn/

10

Gatekeepers or facilitators?

MAD Solutions and other film distribution networks for Arab cinema

Stefanie Van de Peer

National and international distribution of Arab films

Production has been the touchstone of cultural policy for national film cultures and for the academic study of film, whether through the lens of national or transnational cinema. Distribution and exhibition, on the other hand, have historically been underexplored, except perhaps in film festival studies. Since the 1970s, the focus in film studies has been on textual analysis, and in policy work focus has consistently been on (co-)production. As this volume and other New Cinema Histories projects show, however, there is now a steady growth in this branch of film studies. The way films move across international circuits and networks in particular has gained the interest of scholars, due to the increased recognition of the power of the global political economy and the debates around the transnational life of film. This is so in spite of, or perhaps precisely because, distribution and exhibition are the key areas of profit in the industry. It is the sensitivity of financial data that makes discussing the distribution and exhibition of film harder: This data can remain a closely guarded secret for commercial reasons. Certainly, in the study of global cinema, the 'problems' of production (i.e. no state investment, censorship, etc.) receive much more attention, in particular in studies by Western-based scholars. As a scholar of Arab and African film, and as a film festival organizer committed to the exhibition of the films from these areas, I have experienced the competition for seeing a film before anyone else, and for getting access to films, whether through legal or questionable means. With current global debates on intersectional representation firmly in mind, I ask: How have global distributors shaped the accessibility of Arab cinema? Beyond

Euro-American trade routes, the directions and speeds of film distribution can – like film festival networks – enable us to think in a more transnational way about audiences and their tastes. The study not solely of the production but of the circulation of cinema can lead to more effective cultural policies that may assist in a more open and receptive perception of world cinema and its value.

When it comes to Arab cinema, its increasing visibility globally has been celebrated but not critically investigated in any great detail, except perhaps in the trade press. Indeed, the arrival of distinctly and confidently regional distribution companies such as MAD Solutions (since 2010) has turned around the visibility of Arab cinema globally. Starting as a marketing company, MAD has expanded both its content and its business reach: from United Arab Emirates it has moved into the centrally located Cairo, the so-called 'Hollywood on the Nile',[1] where the company also refocused its strategy towards a pan-Arab cinematic vision in visibility and distribution. The historical dominance of European and Hollywood distribution networks has significantly impacted the accessibility of Arab films in the Arab world. Under French colonial rule and the Laval Decree, creatives were not only prevented from making films, they also never saw their own identities reflected on their screens.[2] With the independence movements of the 1960s and 1970s, increasing anti-colonial sentiments in the Arab world and elsewhere saw filmmakers keen to 'shoot back' at the oppressor, and co-productions started to steer the distribution and exhibition networks of Arab and African films, but neocolonial ties continued to bind colonized to colonizer in a bond that has continually been perceived as productive. And yet it remains a real detective task to find the European distributors or sales agents of films from the Global South. Even when one does find a distributor of, for example, a Tunisian film, it may not always be straightforward or even possible to project this film onto a European screen, due to the division of national, regional and global rights held by distributors or sales agents.

On top of that, the distinction between regionally popular films and films deemed 'good' enough to 'fit in the catalogue' of individual distributors continues to define the reception of Arab cinema.[3] Visiting the cinema in Marrakech is rather different from visiting a festival or a venue in Edinburgh, to see a Moroccan film. For example, the film *La Isla de Perejil* (*Parsley Island*, Ahmed Boulane, 2016) was hugely popular in Moroccan cinemas, in large part due to its star actor, Abdellah Ferkous, but also because of its slapstick comedy genre classification associated with this actor. The historical and geographical setting of the film is likewise relevant to the film's success in Morocco. The island is a small barren rock off the coast of Morocco that is still owned by Spain, the previous colonizer. In 2002 there was a short-lived international conflict between the two countries when a group of Royal Moroccan Navy marines occupied it for ten days. Spain quickly evicted them. Moreover, in the film, Ibrahim (played by Abdellah Ferkous) is a Moroccan soldier who is sent on duty to the island to monitor the movements of smugglers and illegal immigrants. Ibrahim encounters Mamadou, a very sick refugee, and nurtures him back to health. While the references to the international incident of 2002 are thin, they are there, and the Spanish are ridiculed thoroughly by a hapless and clumsy Ibrahim and a sub-Saharan Rastafari refugee. The film screened only once in the UK, in the context of Film Africa, the London-based African film festival. Because audiences in Europe typically see Arab films as arthouse films, distributors aiming at a European market would not necessarily associate slapstick humour with 'good quality'. And its particularly niche content equally precludes the film from a receptive European audience, except in Spain. With Spanish co-production money from Maestranza Films in Seville, the film was shown on cinema screens in the country, and Canal Sur obtained broadcasting rights for TV.

Another anecdote that illustrates the different perceptions of 'good quality' films can be found in the displays of street vendors whose aim is to pirate and make available the most popular films on (bad quality) DVDs, in order to make a small profit in illegal markets. During the National Film Festival in Tangiers, in Morocco, in 2018, I found a particularly interesting street vendor selling films that were being screened at the festival, while these films were inaccessible to the average Moroccan as the festival works on invitation-only principle. Out of curiosity I asked him about an older film, *Door to the Sky* (Farida Benlyazid, 1989), and a more recent but very controversial film, *Much Loved* (Nabil Ayouch, 2015). He had neither for sale but told me to come back the next day. He gave me both films on DVD and – most interestingly – did not want me to pay for *Much Loved*. That was a present he said, and he quite meaningfully put that DVD underneath the one of *Door to the Sky* so that it was not visible. This is a consequence of *Much Loved* having been banned and the actress controversially threatened with death, that street vendors do not want to sell it, even as it was one of the most widely seen and critically acclaimed Moroccan films internationally in at least a decade. This marked imbalance between what does well in Europe and which films are a success with audiences in the Arab world, reveals perhaps the central difficulty distributors of Arab cinema contend with. And as such, the so-called 'distributors' film' appears as an acquaintance of the much disputed 'festival film'.

Though the age of so-called post-cinema has now been firmly established, Arab distribution companies have flourished in the last decade. This led to some Arab distribution companies making full use of the online possibilities to exhibit their films during the coronavirus crisis: it is not just filmmakers and producers that made their films available online for free streaming, distributors and other exhibition platforms did the same. An example is Abbout Productions[4] working with Aflamuna,[5] who screened, at the time of writing, *A World Not Ours* (*Alam Laysa Lana*, Mahdi Fleifel, Lebanon, 2012), *A Perfect Day* (Hadjithomas and Joreige, Lebanon, 2006) and other Lebanese films. Likewise, the Palestine Film Platform[6] streamed *Ghost Hunting* (Raed Andoni, 2017) and *Amreeka* (Cherien Dabis, 2009). Aflamuna means 'Our Films' – emphasizing ownership as well as a collectivity among Arab streaming platforms. Indeed, some of the films were geo-blocked and available only to audiences in the Middle East and North Africa (MENA) region, while others could be streamed globally.

These platforms and distributors, like exhibitors, act as curators of cinema and provide a means through which films acquire a specific categorization to pique the interests of transnational consumers. Just like other related activities, distribution and exhibition are subject to at least some projection. The 'intuition' of some is better than that of others. So, whether we call distributors gatekeepers or facilitators, we are in essence acknowledging the human factor in their roles. At the same time, distributors facilitate an easier, more streamlined process for exhibitors to access the growing catalogues of Arab cinema, while their marketing and public relations acumen likewise open up to networks of exhibition worldwide. I focus here on distribution strategies, both outside and within the Middle East, to illustrate the rapidly changing conditions of film distribution and the way in which Arab distributors increasingly serve a meta-cultural function to facilitate the circulation of films. How has the establishment of a regional vertically integrated company like MAD Distribution changed the landscape and visibility of Arab film distribution globally? The company's '360-degree' approach (which reflects Golden Age Hollywood studio's 'vertical integration' of production, distribution and exhibition) plays a huge role in its success. Through in-depth interviews with the two directors of MAD Solutions (that took place in person, over the phone and on email on several occasions, including at the Berlinale in 2020, and in March, April and May of the same year), I argue that in the Middle East distribution and exhibition are no longer dominated by foreign knowledge, but have thrived through regionally based, transnationally oriented companies with clear policies and visions for the facilitation of Arab cinema worldwide.

Festival films, distributor films

MAD Solutions[7] was founded in 2010 as a marketing and creative consultancy firm dedicated to the Arab film and entertainment industry. Its founders saw a gap in the market, where the regional and international success of Arab film led to increased production but not to increased visibility. Within three years the company branched out into distribution under its subsidiary MAD Distribution. The company emphasizes that it 'addresses an urgent market problem faced by the growing number of award-winning independent Arab and international filmmakers whose works face major challenges in being seen in theaters outside the festival circuit where they have achieved acclaim and collected numerous prizes'.[8] This symptom – characteristic for world cinema – is mirrored in so-called festival films, seemingly made for festivals and then not reaching a wider audience beyond the network of festivals, in particular in the European festivals network.[9] It is usually curators and programmers who decide how, when and where international audiences can see Arab cinema. In their turn, these programmers and curators are dependent on distributors and sales agents. If a film does not have a distributor or sales agent, the programmer has to try and contact the producer or filmmaker themselves, but this is not always straightforward. Festival professionals take decades to slowly build up a solid network to fall back on to find contact details of producers and filmmakers, sometimes before they have negotiated a deal with a distributor or sales agent. But networks such as these are closely guarded due to intellectual or commercial interests.

Festivals that have markets attached to them include another dimension to their role in accessibility. As Kay Dickinson shows, film markets are increasingly important in a world where global film culture is developing into a business. In her case study on the Dubai International Film Festival, she compares the role of the festival and its market to the logistics industry Dubai is so well known for. At its best, Dubai specializes in bouncing and accelerating an already-existing product onwards. At its worst, Dubai is a service provider in the movement of goods, as it moves away from the costs of owning products and carrying any of the culpability.[10] Rather, Dickinson says, DIFF is a platform that acts as a go-between, a broker, ensuring that films continue to hop between festivals increasingly quickly, rather than land those distribution deals that can ensure wider visibility.[11] I would add that it is a broker with a specific taste and sensibility, that gatekeeps the type of cinema it accelerates. Importantly, Dickinson shows how the continued over-production of films exceeds the number of screens and spaces available in the marketplace,[12] and that distribution needs more attention, both in policies and in the industry.

Nevertheless, there are some more evident 'centralized' distributors programmers can rely on to find specific types of what I call 'distributor films'. North Americans interested in Arab cinema can turn to Arab Film Distribution or AFD, located in Seattle since the 1990s. Their catalogue is educational in focus, and they specialize in political documentaries. As such, their emphasis is on countering the trend to portray Arab characters as stereotypically limited in American cinema.[13] In that sense, rather than gatekeepers, AFD are champions of anti-racist discourse, working with a limited catalogue that promotes an activist agenda. In Europe, in many instances, the links between previously colonized and colonizing countries retain its significance. When it comes to Maghrebi films, for example, more often than not the distributors will be France-based. In the case of Palestine, Germany is the country with the strongest interest in distributing these films. Indeed, Irit Neidhardt, who runs mec film, a German distribution platform dedicated to Arab films,[14] observes that the co-production financing system often determines that these films are only distributed in the Global North, and not at all in the Global South, due to the Middle East's relative lack of exhibition spaces and the fact that filmmakers from the Global South adapt their storytelling techniques to the tastes of these Northern distributors.[15] She asserts that these co-produced Middle Eastern films have little to no commercial value, and that they remain relegated to the film festivals networks, never to be seen in their home countries. Likewise, she is convinced that Egyptian popular cinema for example – not (co-)funded abroad and entirely produced within the borders of its home country – does not have any international appeal.[16] But what if we define the word 'international' not as automatically referring to the Global North, but rather as the region where these films travel, that is the entire Middle East? It is in that context that MAD Distribution has found its market niche, combining an interest in the 'festival films' that circulate in the Global North with an interest in productions that are popular regionally. Their growing reputation and the sense of centralization that comes with their business model reveal the pitfalls of the 'distributor film'. Marketing and promoting the perceived arthouse Arab films often co-produced with Europe and circulating on the festival network *as well as* the locally popular Egyptian productions, MAD Distribution brings together and combines platforms of and for two very distinct types of Arab films for diverse global audiences. It makes a certain type of Arab film more visible while they attempt to broaden their catalogue.

In 2009, Najib Harabi showed that Arab countries had experienced a sharp decline in creative and artistic venues and activities which, in turn, led to a decline in the output of creative industries in those countries.[17] Looking at the scale of the creative industries in the Arab world, his study concluded that while Egypt was the most consistently productive country when it comes to cinema, Lebanon had the most active and engaged audiences. Nevertheless, in most of the countries under consideration the film industry contributed less than 0.1 per cent to GDP. The study concluded that the creative industries in Arab countries were 'substantially underdeveloped' in and before 2009.[18] It also showed that, while production seemed to be healthy (even though it contributes very little to the countries' overall industries), distribution and exhibition were the weakest links in the creative industries. The number of production companies far exceeded distribution companies or exhibition spaces. In Egypt in 2009 there were eleven distribution companies responsible for both domestic and international films and 218 cinemas, while in Morocco there were seven companies serving a spectacularly low number of active cinemas (Harabi claims there were 96 cinemas left in Morocco in 2009, but in 2018, only 28 cinemas remained).[19] In Lebanon, production was also very low, while seven distribution companies serviced a large amount (150) of very well-equipped cinemas that showed mostly foreign productions. In Tunisia, one of the most well-respected film cultures of the Arab region, 'attendance and cinema capacity have also shown sharp downward trends. Box offices declined from about 1.6 million viewers in 1994 to less than 300,000 in 2005. In 2006 Tunisia had a total number of cinemas of 22'.[20]

The study, however, also pointed out the region's 'immense potential', as markets are growing and opening up, and people are becoming more interested in increasingly competent and accomplished home-grown productions. Expanding skillsets and a growing professional workforce, as well as relative economic stability or growth for the middle classes, show that there are very positive demand conditions, even for regional export. In fact, there is a flourishing of skillsets being developed, with many countries specializing in different genres and forms (e.g. Syrian tragedies, Egyptian melodramas and Tunisian political cinema). However, fierce financial and cultural competition (both domestic and foreign) and the absolute lack of public policy by (some) corrupt governments have adverse effects on possibilities for growth and development, and for a long-term vision for the future. The 'great potential' identified by Harabi can only really be achieved with the investment not only in infrastructure but also, importantly, with the aid of public policy: 'governments should encourage upgrading and innovation with the aid of rules, regulations and incentives',[21] through 'regulations, tax policies, [. . .] expansions of interregional and international trade and investment by opening markets, promoting exports and attracting appropriate foreign investment'.[22] The investment of time, money and dedication to the underdeveloped distribution and exhibition sectors in the Arab world has been crucial to ensure a long-term and sustainable future for the otherwise thriving film cultures.

In a more global context, Lauren Carroll Harris confirms and strengthens Harabi's argument that policy is central to the expansion and growth of the film industry, particularly on the side of distribution and exhibition. She asks why policy support for the production sector has prevailed, when distribution is the film industry's key zone for profit. She compares different interventions in national distribution policies, including direct state measures such as subsidies, levies, quotas and import restrictions, indirect state aid, and cultural initiatives by film funding bodies, that stimulate audience engagement in the distribution and exhibition sectors. For her, 'the nature of policy, in any arena, is about pushing with and against the inertia of the status quo – change is slow and imagined as unthinkable until it occurs'.[23] Even though film distributors are in more immediate and direct contact with film audiences, for too long, 'audience engagement has been seen through the lens of film content rather than the lens of distribution'.[24] This policy split between film production and the market makes no sense from the audience's perspective, and so she proposes the following:

> to create demand by improving distribution of the supply, to encourage better market access for [home-grown] productions, to support smaller distributors in assisting audience development, and to create commercial incentives for the widespread distribution and exhibition of [. . .] films in both conventional (multiplex and art-house) and unconventional venues by reducing the risk to distributors in acquiring specialised films.[25]

According to Harris, these measures should lead to an increase in size, diversity and geographical spread of distribution and therefore also of audiences. In fact, she claims, 'audiences are an effect of distribution circuits rather than of texts'. In this sense, film policy is a political phenomenon with far-reaching effects: diversity in film culture, creative alternatives to national or regional production, and imaginative employment in a sector of the industry with actual economic potential.[26] In cultural terms, quite simply, guaranteeing distribution guarantees audiences and a return on investment.

But the problem of distribution remains an invisible one: it manifests as an apparent disinterest from audiences. Rather, distribution should be seen as a megaphone, directed towards audiences to engage them and develop them. Indeed, in the Arab world the potential of the audience is huge, and investment in developing distribution and accessibility is crucial in achieving or reaching that audience. As Harabi shows, the potential and scale of the Arab region are vast, also due to the fact that 'Arab countries share a common language, common religions, a common history and largely a common cultural heritage, all important ingredients for [. . .] consuming common creative goods'.[27]

MAD Solutions, MAD Distribution

In my interview with the artistic director of MAD Solutions in 2020, he identified the same issues and gaps in the market as those that were indicated in Harabi's project in 2009. MAD was an initiative responding exactly to issues with the visibility and exhibition of Arab films, and to the need for more support for and investment in this aspect of the industry. In our interview, Maher Diab emphasized that MAD started as a service focused on the marketing of Arab cinema, specifically to enhance the visibility and stature of Arab films in the region and globally. He is a Lebanese visual artist, who started his career in the advertising industry. With Alaa Karkouti, he founded an Egyptian film magazine with the title *Good News Cinema*, and he was responsible specifically for the magazine's visual identity. Together they started attending film festivals and realized the underdevelopment of an audience dedicated to Arab cinema. Rather than resign to the situation, they saw the potential in developing a promotional approach to Arab film culture. The core business of MAD Solutions, then, is augmenting the perception of Arab films, and even when MAD Solutions (sometimes) branches out into co-production, it is with a view to streamline the promotion and distribution of Arabic entertainment content to the Arab world and beyond, along the lines of what Neidhardt explores above. In our interview, Maher Diab testified that they believe that in focusing on promotion, marketing and distribution, MAD has 'helped usher in a new era of filmmaking and entertainment in the Arab world. The purpose of the company is to set a structure and standards for the film and entertainment industry in the Arab world'. This may be so in terms of their successful establishment as a visible 'accelerator' or 'broker' of popular Arab cinema in Europe, to use Dickinson's terminology. Indeed, their aesthetically very pleasing, colourful and energetic style of marketing is both modern, accessible and enthusiastic. With their brand of bright, fluorescent colours and young members of staff, MAD's presence at international film festival markets is always very visible. This brand, which he calls a 'mad' and fun approach to Arab cinema, and their many streamlined subsidiary brands and events, ensure that they maintain a constant channel of communication with and presence at global festivals, in order to keep audiences everywhere aware of the talent and production in the Arab world. Calling themselves a 360-degree company, with a broad and dedicated focus on all aspects of the industry, reveals a vertically integrated structure. This has enabled MAD to become a dominant powerhouse in the Arab film industry and its visibility globally. Diab said: 'we don't want to say we were the first distributors in the region that gave a platform for "festival-circuit films" to be screened commercially, but I could comfortably and humbly say we created a need for these films to be seen and exhibited'. This confirms the idea that festival films work in tandem with distributor films, which funnel a certain type of film to a certain type of audience, and as such both facilitate access and gatekeep the type of films that are accessible.

This emphasis on understanding the audience, and doing the research – finding out about audience statistics and publishing these in their own publications[28] – shows how MAD responded to that need to develop an audience with a taste for Arab cinema, not only abroad at the many festivals they attended but also at home in Egypt, Lebanon and across the Arab world. The way forward for them was to develop a brand, so that a sense of brand loyalty could be established. In an interview with Karkouti, he confirms that 'It was clear there was a gap in the Arab film market, and we had to develop a new approach, to start making films that Arab audiences could relate to. To do this we needed to better understand the Arab film market and Arab audiences. That was the only way we were going to develop a cinema culture in the region'.[29] Reaching out to and understanding what the 'Arab audience' could be is at the core of MAD's business: 'For far too long, people have built film budgets around fake markets with no idea of the numbers. But if you are going to succeed in this business, attract investors, build credibility, and track progress, you need to understand the size of your market, and your target audience'. Indeed, for MAD's directors this implies looking at the bigger picture and steadily building up international and regional credibility and a long-term, sustainable view in the service of the potential of Arab cinema: 'We want to change perceptions about Arab cinema and create the space for Arab films.'

Likewise, both Diab and Karkouti emphasize that a crucial responsibility in changing perceptions of and attitudes towards Arab cinema lies with governments and their film policies. Just as audiences need to be understood and productions need to be marketed in an integrated manner, so policymakers and regulators need to take the film industry more seriously and recognize its huge economic potential. Once they do that, Karkouti asserts, MAD can move towards thinking beyond development and start to think through strategies for the future, creating a financially sustainable Arab film *industry*, where before there has been a film *culture*. Viola Shafik already showed in 1997 that the difference between a film industry and a film culture is crucial in our understanding of cinema production and audiences in the Arab world. She explains how colonialism and other diverse forms of oppression long hampered the development of film industries, even though film as a cultural product has thrived in the Arab region.[30] Karkouti says: 'The region needs a sustainable film financing and distribution system supported by an investor community that recognizes the talent base as one of the region's great natural resources.'[31] This is so important in their eyes, that MAD Solutions themselves have already offered dedicated film distribution and marketing grants to filmmakers at festivals worldwide, where their presence as MAD and its subsidiaries the Arab Cinema Center[32] and the Arab Cinema Lab[33] are noticed, among other reasons, because of their colourful, vibrant logos and other visual marketing tools. In that respect, they confirm that festivals are crucial meeting places for promoters and distributors to meet and create an interest in their products. This needs to be constantly and flexibly analysed and developed, which is why the ACC and MAD Solutions do not only attend 'the usual suspects' such as Cannes, Venice and Berlin, but, says Diab, 'we also need to look at festivals that don't necessarily have a strong Arab presence but seem receptive to Arab content, be it for sheer curiosity, or via support from the Arab diaspora community. It's a matter of finding possibilities, and not just competing in markets that are already saturated'. Curiosity about Arab culture and cinema globally has grown exponentially in the last decade. Perhaps the revolutions in the region since 2011 have evoked a new, different kind of interest in the Arab world that has finally moved the perceived Western audience beyond its typical Orientalism and into an era of consideration and respect. The explicit requests by film festival organizers for Arab content have been problematized elsewhere,[34] but the wider interest from audiences and the increased critical reception of Arab films is notable in international prize winners (e.g. *For Sama*, Waad al-Kateab, Syria, 2019), members of juries (e.g. Nadine Labaki and Annemarie Jacir), programmers and festival directors (e.g. Orwa Nyrabia, International

Documentary Festival in Amsterdam, IDFA) and transnational stardom (e.g. Amr Waked and Hiam Abbass). It is also changing in the presence and visibility of increasingly knowledgeable programmers, including high-profile Arab programmers, for example at Toronto and Berlin, and their contributions to the movement to decolonize film festivals as institutions.

This also shows how film festival audiences, diverse and global as they are, are stakeholders that need to be understood and serviced by distributors. Even if they find it crucial to move away from 'festival films' or 'distributor films' and give those films a wider platform, it remains important to understand how global tastes develop and what those sophisticated audiences want, in order to continue to be able to speak to and market Arab content for international audiences. One of MAD's strategies complimentary to this vast global and diverse audience is that they work with a wide variety of platforms, in order to reach those many different types of audiences. Not only do they look at the professional big screen events and venues (festivals and cinemas) but also, increasingly, 'airplanes, TV networks, digital platforms, you name it. Wherever we identify an audience for our films, we try and make it happen'. As such, Diab concedes that there can be no one-size-fits-all strategies in the film distribution business:

> Countries respond to films differently, and sometimes unexpectedly. So, things are really explored on a case-by-case basis: each film, each format and each story should be shared with a customized audience. For every single film we have in our library, short or feature – fiction or documentary, we have a screening committee, internal meetings with different departments to discuss the pros and cons, etc.

This acknowledgement of the individuality of films and of their audience is part of a tightly controlled and integrated but considerately curated catalogue of distributor films.

So perhaps we can compare distributors' catalogues to festivals' programmes. Apart from the race to buy and represent the film festival prize winners, there is a curatorial aspect to the way in which they select the films they represent. Distributors determine who gets to see which films, where and under what circumstances. For Jonathan Risner, distributors are gatekeepers who decide which of the 1,000s of films that are made every year we get to see on our cinema screens, a prioritized subset of consumers. Indeed, one criticism that could be aimed at MAD Solutions is their sole focus on contemporary, new, recent films. Their catalogue lacks a sense of the rich history of Arab cinema, and the opportunities presented to them to represent and make more visible and accessible old or classic films are often bypassed.[35] Risner says: 'Distributors circulate particular films, and this particularity holds out the possibility of coming up short in one's pursuit of film consumption.'[36] He shows very interestingly how 'not all cinema is distributed and not all films are distributed equally'.[37] Already in 1987, Roy Armes asserted that distributors' commercial interests result in the companies taking the lion's share of a film's revenue, rather than acknowledging the intellectual property of the artists.[38] This tendency continues today. In fact, as Lobato confirms, distributors also shape films textually, in that distributors' preferences frequently result in changes to scripts, casting and marketing plans, regulate flows of money and meaning that constitute contemporary film culture. As such, distribution circulates cultural capital unevenly (diverse classes and genders have different experiences of accessibilities to venues and events), and this production of difference at the point of distribution deserves greater attention.[39]

Risner says that 'the way in which a distributor conceives its catalogue and how it positions a [. . .] film within that catalogue, enable a film to possess continuity with other films that precede it within that particular catalogue'.[40] The types of films that end up on distributors' catalogues are often classified as 'good', as 'fitting with our catalogue', or along the lines of 'genre' cinema. MAD's Maher Diab acknowledges that

> film genres and sub-genres are so diverse, it would be wrong to make selections based on personal tastes or pure commercial sense. We have several factors that we need to take into consideration, such as the quality of the film, what kind of content it is delivering, how it is adding to the plethora of content present across the region, where is the ideal audience base located for this film and how can they be reached, etc.

While MAD's catalogues have the audience firmly in mind, there is also a limit to what they are willing to represent. They remain tied to commercial interests, which translate into current, new and possibly even post-2011 films. The educational or historical aspect of Arab cinema is lost in that way. As a marketing team, they analyse the product as well as their audience and bring these elements together for a short-term vision for Arab cinema rather than a long-term one.

Nevertheless, for Western festival and theatrical programmers and for the audiences for Arab cinema, MAD Distribution offers a point of centralization, a one-stop space where a variety of modern Arab content can be found. The danger of highly effective companies like MAD, which claim to be filling a void in global appreciation of the potential of Arab cinema, is that it remains the only '360-degree' company that is successful in the region. Its visibility and its dominance of the market are such that programmers could become complacent and stop looking elsewhere for other films. As such, it may become a victim of its own success, in that a lack of competition or MAD's hyper-visibility may, in the short term, put MAD in pole position, but in the long term it may become the sole reference point for Western programmers. At that point, MAD would actually become a gatekeeper. For now, it is a marketing-focused facilitator, pushing for more investment in the distribution and exhibition of Arab cinema, in order to accelerate its response to the potential so clearly displayed by the increasing production of Arab films. With bases in Egypt and UAE, the hubs of classic and hyper-modern Arab cinema, MAD has answered calls for making modern Arab films more visible in and beyond the region, but its vertical integration needs spreading out if it wants to avoid the purely brokerage function so typical of that hyper-modern city of Dubai.

Notes

1. 'Hollywood on the Nile' is a widely used term for popular Egyptian cinema. Most of the studios of early Egyptian films were located in Cairo or in its suburbs, along the banks of the Nile.
2. Olivier Barlet, 'The Ambivalence of French Funding', *Black Camera* 3, no. 2 (2012): 205.
3. Jonathan Risner, 'Constellated Gatekeepers: Distribution as Metaculture and Distributors as a "Real" Audience', *New Cinemas* 16, no. 2 (2018): 138.
4. http://abboutproductions.com
5. https://www.aflamuna.online
6. https://www.palestinefilminstitute.org/
7. The name MAD Solutions comes from the three original founders of the company: Maher Diab, Alaa Karkouti and Dina (M, A and D). When Dina left, Maher told me, they kept the name as it 'represents us and our way of working really well'.
8. http://mad-distribution.film/about.php
9. Tamara L. Falicov, 'The Festival Film: Film Festivals as Cultural Intermediaries', in *Film Festivals: History, Theory, Method, Practice*, ed. Marijke de Valck, Brendan Kredell, and Skadi Loist (London: Routledge, 2016), 209–29.
10. Kay Dickinson, *Arab Cinema Travels: Transnational Syria, Palestine, Dubai and Beyond* (London: BFI, 2016), 141.
11. Dickinson, *Arab Cinema Travels*, 144.
12. Dickinson, *Arab Cinema Travels*, 147.

13 Jack Shaheen, *Reel Bad Arabs: How Hollywood Vilifies a People* (Northampton, MA: Interlink Publishing, 2012).
14 https://mecfilm.com
15 Irit Neidhart, 'Untold Stories', *Westminster Papers in Communication and Culture* 7, no. 2 (2010): 37.
16 Neidhardt, 'Untold Stories', 45.
17 Najib Harabi, 'Creative Industries: Case Studies from Arab Countries', paper prepared for an event on *Developing Knowledge Economy Strategies to Improve Competitiveness in the MENA Region by the World Bank Institute*, 17–21 May 2009, in Alexandria Egypt. Accessible online on Munich Personal RePEc Archive, MPRA Paper No. 15628, 3, https://mpra.ub.uni-muenchen.de/15628/
18 Najib Harabi, 'Creative Industries: Case Studies from Arab Countries', 11.
19 Will Higbee, Florence Martin and Jamal Bahmad, *Moroccan Cinema Uncut. Decentred Voices, Transnational Perspectives* (Edinburgh: Edinburgh University Press, 2020): 177.
20 Harabi, 'Creative Industries: Case Studies from Arab Countries', 15.
21 Harabi, 'Creative Industries: Case Studies from Arab Countries', 19.
22 Harabi, 'Creative Industries: Case Studies from Arab Countries', 21.
23 Lauren Carroll Harris, 'Film Distribution as Policy: Current Standards and Alternatives', *International Journal of Cultural Policy* 24, no. 2 (2018): 236.
24 Harris, 'Film Distribution as Policy', 246.
25 Harris, 'Film Distribution as Policy', 248.
26 Harris, 'Film Distribution as Policy', 252.
27 Harabi, 'Creative Industries: Case Studies from Arab Countries', 21.
28 *Arab Cinema Magazine*, http://acc.film/
29 Catherine Jewell, 'Transforming Arab Cinema with MAD Solutions', *WIPO Magazine*, October 2017, Available online: https://www.wipo.int/wipomagazine/en/2017/05/article0004.html
30 Viola Shafik, *Arab Cinema: History and Cultural Identity*. Revised and Updated Edition (American University of Cairo Press, 2016 [1997]).
31 Catherine Jewell, 'Transforming Arab Cinema with MAD Solutions'.
32 http://acc.film/index.php
33 http://acc.film/acclab-about.php
34 Alisa Lebow, 'Filming Revolution: Approaches to Programming the "Arab Spring"', in *Film Festivals and the Middle East*, ed. Dina Iordanova and Stefanie Van de Peer (St Andrews: STAFS, 2014), 61–74.
35 I was involved in the brokering of a deal with MAD to represent a classic film from 1989, *Door to the Sky* by Farida Benlyazid (Morocco), a classic film of feminist Islamic sensibility, restored and re-subtitled, which although it was initially received with much enthusiasm by MAD, was ultimately rejected from their catalogue due to its age.

36 Risner, 'Constellated Gatekeepers', 134.
37 Risner, 'Constellated Gatekeepers', 136.
38 Roy Armes, *Third World Film Making and the West* (California: University of California Press, 1987).
39 Ramon Lobato, 'Subcinema: Theorizing Marginal Film Distribution', *Limina* 16 (2007): 116.
40 Risner, 'Constellated Gatekeepers', 137.

11

A new online cinema audience?
An interview on Aflamuna with Jad Abi Khalil

Anaïs Farine

Aflamuna // أفلامنا ('our films' in Arabic) is an online platform which aims to bring for free and to a diverse audience 'some of the best, most thought-provoking and independently-minded works of contemporary Arab cinema'. The website www.aflamuna.online was launched on 25 March 2020 by Beirut DC, in partnership with mec film, Abbout Productions and MAD Solutions (see Stefanie Van de Peer's chapter on MAD Solutions in this volume). After a break beginning in October 2020, the website was revived in March 2021 as a space more clearly designed for curated programmes. Beirut DC collaborated with film director and cinema historian Hady Zaccak to present his programme 'Are we all Fedayeen?' and invited 'Cinematheque Beirut'[1] and Cinema al Fouad[2] to curate programmes in May and June, for example.

The following interview with Jad Abi Khalil was conducted in Beirut on 27 July 2020, during the first phase of the Aflamuna's service. Jad Abi Khalil is Beirut DC's chairman. Beirut DC was founded in 1999. Since then, the organization has developed various initiatives such as *Ayam Beirut Al-Cinema'iya* – a biennale Arab Film Festival – as well as DOCmed and Beirut Cinema Platform, two programmes dedicated to film production[3]. Before this conversation, I had already conducted an interview with Jad Abi Khalil when I was working on my PhD thesis. In 2015, as part of a research project which sought to question the imaginary around the 'Euro-Mediterranean dialogue' through the analysis of festivals as well as programmes dedicated to 'Mediterranean cinema' and the films funded by them, I contacted Jad Abi Khalil to ask him about DOCmed (a training programme on documentary filmmaking). Part of my research then focused on the analysis of *This Little Father Obsession* (Selim Mourad, 2016) and *A Feeling Greater than Love* (Mary Jirmanus Saba, 2017), two films developed within the training programme of DOCmed. The first of these two films was screened on Aflamuna in June 2020 while the second was available in 2021 as part of the 'Spotlight on Beirut DC' programme.[4]

Despite my strong reluctance to watch films at the beginning of Covid-19, I was interested by the model in-progress offered by Aflamuna. I felt that, while adapting gradually to multiple challenges, Beirut DC was trying different options to programme films. As a teacher, I began using Aflamuna alongside cinema history books and film festivals to source films for my classes.

In keeping with the broader themes examined by other authors in this volume, the following conversation I had with Jad Abi Khalil mainly focuses on audiences and programming. It reminds us that 'technical issues' are political issues. Technological inequalities, for example, can make it very difficult to see a movie online with a slow internet connection. The current economic crises in Lebanon also makes it practically impossible to buy anything with a bank account in the country. The geo-blocking practice used by some Video on Demand (VOD) platforms and digital edition's of film festivals dedicated to the exhibition of the same kind of films as Aflamuna (re)produces issues of accessibility and borders in the digital world.[5] The interview also points out how material conditions within which films are distributed and seen contribute to the erasure of some cinema histories.

The creation of 'Aflamuna' and the Covid-19 pandemic

Anaïs Farine (AF): Aflamuna was born during the Covid-19 pandemic and quarantine. Films were uploaded online via streaming platforms directly or earlier than what was planned. However, in January 2020 a few months before the launch of Aflamuna – and as a result of the neoliberal policies adopted since the 1990s, and the Lebanese economy plunging into a financial crisis – the Metropolis Empire Sofil Theatre – an arthouse cinema in Beirut programmed by the Metropolis Art Cinema Association which for example hosted the *Ayam Beirut Al-Cinema'iya* Festival – announced its closure.. How did you conceive Aflamuna, in terms of purposes and form, in relation to that context?

Jad Abi Khalil (JAK; for Beirut DC): The idea to create an online platform for Arab independent author films was there before the launch in March 2020. It's true that the pandemic pushed us to accelerate the decision because it was an idea that we wanted to develop in 2021 or 2022. But the idea to create Aflamuna is part of an ongoing restructuring of Beirut DC. The question of the diversification of our audience is one of the most important parts of this restructuring, so Aflamuna is central to the strategy we are building. With the pandemic, we thought that it was urgent to give the people the opportunity... to see those films and to see them now. That's why we went online a few weeks after the beginning of the pandemic in Lebanon. Also, the revolution and then the financial crisis put the country on a very critical path and it became crucial for us to have Aflamuna in March, even if Beirut DC is working in and for the Arab world. And as you mentioned, Metropolis closed during the revolution, and then everything closed. So the idea to make independent Arab movies available free of charge in Lebanon became a very important and urgent point for us.

AF: Long before 2020, Beirut DC participated in many events where different people were invited to talk about their experiences with Video on Demand (VOD). I am curious to know if you had some statistics about the number of Netflix users in Lebanon for example, or about the number of people watching films on Cinemoz[6] in mind when thinking of creating Aflamuna? Also, how can you describe your place, your ambition and your specificity in terms of programming in relation to Cinemoz – which presents for free some films that could be streamed on Aflamuna, such as *The Last Days of the Man of Tomorrow* (2017) by Fadi Baki and *Kindil el Bahr* (2014) by Damien Ounouri?

JAK: We were not at all creating a VOD platform. The creation of the website was really coming from Beirut DC's way of thinking about how to make independent Arab content available. The other platforms have been working for years now, but most of the films that we put online were still not available. So in terms of statistics, it's not comparable with other platforms' results because the content is completely different. Aflamuna is coming from an NGO kind of proposal with the aim to empower filmmakers and also to make the films available for the audience. The idea is not to generate any kind of profit. The only profit which can be generated will not be for Aflamuna but for the filmmakers, besides the fact that their films will be visible to a larger audience. I like what Cinemoz did and if there are titles that already exist on Cinemoz, we are open to collaboration. But I think that Aflamuna is more specialized and focused in terms of the choice of films.

Connections

AF: How did you conceive of your model bearing in mind that the internet in Lebanon is so slow?

JAK: For the internet connection, we opted for Vimeo because it allows us to integrate the films within the website. In the second step, which will start in September, Aflamuna will have more flexible video embedded, making it more user-friendly for the low internet connection in Lebanon and also in other Arab countries. Actually, until now it was difficult to see the films with very low internet connection but we are working on it for the next stage of Aflamuna.

AF: Do you have statistics of the number of views by countries or cities, for each film, or each week? What reflections do you have on these results? Did something in particular strike you as something unexpected?

JAK: What was really amazing was the result of the first month. It was 100,000 visits and 50,000 viewers. For now I think we are around 300,000 website visits and 150,000 viewings. Honestly we were not expecting to have millions of views for those films. The numbers of viewings are already really huge compared to anything else we have done before. In general those films are screened at festivals where a few hundred people can see them, then they will have a few weeks at the cinema, and that's it. We are talking about multiplying the numbers by ten thousand. So it is a very important way of rethinking distribution of independent Arab movies. Another important point is that we are not releasing new films. The films are two, three, four and sometimes ten or fifteen years old. So it is giving them another life, and in this perspective we discovered that Aflamuna is really relevant. It confirmed that we should continue with this platform.[7]

Decentralization

AF: Do you think about Aflamuna in terms of decentralization? Do you think the platform gives wider accessibility to these films, to an audience that did not necessarily have the opportunity to see them earlier? Or do you think it is more accurate to say that Aflamuna is attracting the same viewers as festivals, just shifting them from the cinema to the internet?

JAK: I think it's opening up [the films to people] outside the city (Beirut) and the country, and it's also opening [them up] to another audience, not necessarily the arthouse usual suspects. We have a few statistics by cities and by countries. Most of the viewers are from the Arab world. There is a big number from Australia, from the United States, from Italy during the lockdown and the pandemic, and from Spain. There is also a big number of views from France and from the UK but this is not surprising. The majority of the viewers are from the Arab world and sometimes not from the main cities. If we fix the internet problem and work more on promotion, I think we will be more accessible in the rural countryside, which is one of our targets. The idea is not to have the same audience than the one who would be already seeing these films in the cities. The implementation of the second phase of Aflamuna will take more time. We are continually searching to find the best way to be more efficient and to reach more people outside the big cities.

AF: Most of the films which were presented on Aflamuna so far have been by Lebanese filmmakers. In the meantime the website presents itself as an initiative that exhibits contemporary Arab cinema to audiences. Do you think this had an influence in terms of the number of people who visited Aflamuna from different countries, and would you like to have more films from countries other than Lebanon in the future?

JAK: Of course you will get more people from Egypt if you have an Egyptian film, but actually it's a very technical problem. Until now we were working without paying any fees because of the bank lockdown. We will be fixing this by September (2020) and we will have more Arab titles that we will be able to pay for, alongside Lebanese titles. We've got more Lebanese films because we are in Lebanon and it's easy to ask for the films. We are talking about feature-length films, so if you receive the film via a file-sharing site and you want to download a high-resolution film in Beirut you can spend a whole day doing that. The idea was to make available for this period the titles that we could access. In the meanwhile, we did screen some Arab titles from close friends from Egypt, Algeria, Morocco, Tunisia and Jordan.

AF: Some films are available in all countries, while others in the Arab region only. Is it linked to the partnership you have with mec film for example – or with MC Distribution even if they are not partners in this project – and the rights that they have?

JAK: It's also a technical issue. It actually depends because sometimes the director has the rights and sometimes there are sales agents. In general when there are sales agents we talk to them, not the director. Sometimes the seller has the right for the Arab region so we cannot put the film for worldwide access. For example, when MC Distribution has the rights for some films, they only have the rights for the Arab region and the world rights belong to another sales agent. Ideally we would love to put the films up for worldwide access, but in the meantime the main focus of Aflamuna is on Arab people.

Relations with other initiatives

AF: What are the links between Aflamuna and other initiatives by Beirut DC like the Ayam Beirut Al-Cinema'iya and Docmed for example? How are these other projects helping in terms of network and inspiration of film titles you would like to share? Are they an obstacle in the sense that Beirut DC is already identified more with some films and filmmakers than others?

JAK: As with other Beirut DC activities, the idea of Aflamuna is to help Arab filmmakers and to help Arab audiences have access to Arab films. That being said, when you participate in one of the Beirut DC activities, it's easier to have access to the other projects because we know every step about your film. If you developed your film in one of our workshops, it will be easy to identify the process and to invite the film when it's done to Ayam Beirut Festival for example. But through the years it was never mandatory. I mean a film can pass through one of the Beirut DC activities and not be selected for another one. Also, the selection committees are so different from one programme to another that it's impossible to have a closed circle.

AF: How is the selection committee of Aflamuna composed?

JAK: For the first months it was internal decisions of people working at Beirut DC. But now we are building a real programme team composed mostly of professionals from outside the association, as we do for the other activities we lead.

Selection and the writing of cinema history

AF: At the beginning Aflamuna presented a diversity of content and all films were introduced individually. It is still mostly the case but you also introduced some curated collections of films with the 'Love and Identity in Arab Cinema' programme, presented by Cinema al Fouad, Mawjoudin[8] and Jeem,[9] as well as with the retrospectives of Mohamed Soueid and Ghassan Salhab. As a scholar and teacher in cinema studies, I am thinking a lot about film festivals and the circulation of movies in relation to how cinema history was and is written. When Aflamuna was launched I was giving classes and the platform gave me the opportunity to change the way I was working. I was not coming with films I collected through years and introducing excerpts, but proposing the students to watch some of the films you were sharing fully to then talk about them during online classes. It changed both the titles I chose and the way we were discussing cinema.

During Covid-19, Beirut DC did amazing work on its website, uploading the archive of Ayam Beirut for example. However, it is not possible to go back to titles of films when they are taken off the website.

JAK: It's also a technical problem. We ask for the rights for fifteen days. The day we will create an archive of the films shown through Aflamuna, it will be something on demand. The films will be available for a period and then if someone wants to watch it, this person should pay.

AF: My question was not about the films themselves but about the titles because you can't go back to the programme in itself. And sometimes the issue is not that the content is not available but that we don't know what to look for. So an archive of the titles can give one the idea to look for a film you didn't know anything about before, even outside Aflamuna. Also this sort of memory of the titles allows us to reflect on what sort of narrative of Arab cinema Aflamuna is building through the selection of films shown.

JAK: This will be fixed in the second phase and we will most probably create a kind of Video on Demand for the films that were shown on the platform for free. If they are available elsewhere on demand, we will put the link.

Curation

AF: Would you like to feature more curated programmes like 'Love and Identity in Arab Cinema' or in a form like the one Ashkal Alwan (The Lebanese Association for Plastic Arts established in Beirut in 1993) developed with aashra[10] by inviting curators to select films and videos for their open-access video streaming platform, for example?

JAK: We are trying a lot of forms to see what's the best way to present the films. At the beginning, we had the idea to put five films online every two weeks. We are not sure about the number for the next step yet, nor if we should go thematic or by a director or a mix of both. There are a lot of ideas and options. Of course, it's an added value in terms of the number of views to have a curated programme and to work with different people, but at the same time, sometimes you need to put some films as a statement, as a proposal of an idea you have about human rights for example. And sometimes it's also a statement to show a film and to put it in the sense of saying this is a film, we are bringing you cinema first of all. The statistics gave us an idea about what will be the response for each form, but we don't know yet what the final decision will be for the next step in terms of programming.

Notes

1. 'Cinematheque Beirut' is a platform by Metropolis Cinema Association dedicated to the art and conservation of cinema in Lebanon: https://cinemathequebeirut.com/cinematheque/home/
2. Named after a 1993 film by filmmaker and author Mohamed Soueid, Cinema Al Fouad is a queer film festival first organized in Beirut in June 2019.
3. For more information about Beirut DC programmes: https://www.beirutdc.org/programs.
4. *A Feeling Greater than Love* was also made available on Shasha, a paying streaming platform for South-West Asian and North African cinema launched in March 2021. Mary Jirmanus Saba was interviewed by Suyin Haynes as part of an article focusing on that website. 'Films From the Middle East and North Africa Often Struggle to Reach Viewers in the Region. A New Streaming Service Aims to Bring Them Home', *Time*, 1 March 2021, https://time.com/5943142/shasha-streaming-movies-middle-east-north-africa/.
5. To give only two examples in the French context, I'm thinking of Tënk (a VOD platform for independent documentaries available in France, Switzerland, Belgium and Luxembourg whose aim is to ensure that these kinds of films can be seen despite their lack of distribution outside festivals) and of the last edition of the PCMMO-Panorama des cinémas du Maghreb et du Moyen-Orient (a film Festival based in Saint-Denis dedicated to films from the MENA region) whose online 2021 edition was restricted to viewers based in France.
6. See https://www.cinemoz.com/.
7. According to Beirut DC 1,000 people subscribed to the platform in the first week of its launching. At the beginning of the second phase of Aflamuna, most subscribers were based in Lebanon (20 per cent), while 10 per cent of them were based in the United States of America, 7 per cent in France, 7 per cent in Egypt, 5 per cent in the United Kingdom and 5 per cent in Palestine.

8   Mawjoudin is a Tunisia based NGO that works towards achieving equality, human rights, bodily rights and sexual rights for the LGBTQI+ community and other marginalized groups and individuals.
9   *Jeem* is a website that produces knowledge as well as critical and cultural content about gender, sex and sexuality. To read their work on cinema, see for example the dossier, https://jeem.me/مشاهدات-كويرية-للسينما-العربية
10 *aashra* was launched in 2018 by Ashkal Alwan, https://aashra.ashkalalwan.org/.

12

A taste for cinema

Saudi Arabia's mediated transitional public film culture

Anne Ciecko

In the case of Saudi Arabia, cinema is a heterogeneous phenomenon that has become associated with persuasive possibilities of soft power and entertainment capital, accumulation of wealth, and civic restrictions and freedoms.[1] The nexuses, processes and products of film production, exhibition and distribution are influenced by state regulatory mechanisms and cultural attitudes in a monarchy that has maintained authority while also promoting consumer desires. In the Saudi context, fundamentalism and capitalism coexist.[2] Saudi Arabia asserts its geocultural, transnational and global centrality in 'multiple "realms": the Middle East, the Arab world, Islamic world, and the world of energy production'.[3] Cinema's history in Saudi Arabia is rife with strategic geopolitical alliances, local exclusions and revisionism. In this chapter, I focus on film cultural initiatives in Saudi Arabia during the past two decades and the palimpsestic and recursive ways re-introductions of cinema have been discursively constructed.[4] Introductions and re-introductions of cinema in the Saudi public sphere, and related formations of taste, have involved constant struggle and contradictions, as well as mediated film cultural events and landmarks.[5]

Earlier 'public' relations

The establishment of the modern Kingdom of Saudi Arabia and the discovery of petroleum in the region were roughly contemporaneous, linking the nation-state and oil in the Saudi cultural imagination and the global mediascape. The residential compounds for expatriate workers in the oil industry became the locations for the first film screenings in Saudi Arabia. Based on archival evidence, it seems likely that the first film to be shown in Saudi Arabia was a pre-Code Hollywood drama called *The Gallant Lady* (Gregory LaCava, USA, 1934), screened in a newly established compound for Western oil workers, while local Saudis attempted to access the flickering images through outside windows.[6] The first feature-length film made in Saudi Arabia was a curious docufiction hybrid, produced by Saudi Aramco (Arabian American Oil Company), the company formed from a concession agreement between Saudi Arabia and Standard Oil Company of California. *Jazirat al-'Arab* (Island of the Arabs, 1955) is a propagandistic celebration of the heroism of the first king of Saudi Arabia, Abdulaziz bin Abdul Rahman Al Saud, who oversaw the development of the nascent oil industry. Demonstrating the entwinement of film and television in Saudi Arabia since the inception of the latter medium, this was also the first film that was shown on air when Aramco began Arabic-language television broadcasting.[7]

In an analysis of the emergence of film culture in Bahrain, Firat Oruc writes, 'The core political issue of the emergence of a cinema culture in the Gulf was the restriction of cinematic medium and space to certain populations. As such, policing cinema was linked to the question of managing the social forces of hydrocarbon modernity that the discovery of oil unleashed.'[8] Saudi film history navigates the problematics of an inaugural exclusionary and segregated exhibition model in the residential oil compounds. Film culture subsequently took domestic root in varied venues in cities across the country, enabling wider Saudi exposure to cinema. The absence of licensing requirements for film screening initially afforded related entrepreneurial and film cultural activity without official government approval. Adapted film exhibition practices reflected and refracted the normalization of gender segregation in Saudi public spaces that privileged the male spectator (with women-only screenings considered 'private'). Films were edited to conform to local cultural codes, especially in terms of representation of sexuality and religion. An array of makeshift, repurposed or designated theatres developed, along with a micro-distribution economy circulating films among clubs, foreign embassies, small movie houses and so-called 'backyard' cinemas.[9] A 1960s UNESCO report identifies Saudi Arabia as a significant market with the purchase of films (mainly Egyptian) 'meant not for public performance, but for presentation in the private auditoria owned by the Arabs, as it is highly doubtful that the Europeans and the Americans living there would ask for such films'.[10] In the 1970s, the Egyptian film industry became increasingly dependent on Saudi distribution companies.[11] An appetite for cinema was cultivated as the dominant Egyptian films were often screened along with Hollywood, Italian, Turkish and/or Indian movies. While such screenings met with some disproval by Islamic clerics (as did television), they were not prohibited.[12] According to documentary producer Jomanah Khoja, the small theatrical venues in Saudi Arabia eventually suffered because of increased mediated access to movies and the experience of home-viewing, especially through the rising popularity of VHS tapes.[13] More cataclysmically, Khoja argues that after the 1979 seizure of the Grand Mosque in Mecca by insurgents, conservative Saudi religious leaders cracked down with restrictions on movies and their perceived corrupting influence, with a subsequent ban on public exhibition of film.

This ban caused cinema to necessarily become what I have termed a 'non-public' concept/phenomenon, an adaptation of the concept of the public sphere defined by Jürgen Habermas (1989):

> In the absence of cinema halls and with recurring bans on film exhibition, the participation in a film-going public as a discursive space to congregate, is an embattled concept at best. Counter-publics of a sort have emerged with semi-clandestine filmmaking and screening groups, repurposed exhibition contexts, transnationally mobile spectators, new and expanded media technologies and formats, and everyday consumer subversions.[14]

Non-public cinema restricted or altered the practices that openly enable the experience of cinema *in situ*: 'where people go to take their place as spectators in front of a spectacle'.[15] However, it also contributed to the expanded, flexible, relational discursive imagination of audiovisual moving-image media products and experiences in Saudi Arabia as vehicles for art, education, rhetorical persuasion and entertainment commodity.

From the 1980s onward, the proliferation of shopping malls in Saudi Arabia selling all sorts of commodities enabled Saudi consumer participation in an architecturally modern public space with bountiful products on display.[16] New multi-screen megaplexes after the lifting of the ban in 2018 emphasize the proliferation of cinematic products. They underscore the illusion of seemingly infinite consumer choices in a hierarchical society with uneven distribution of wealth, power, rights, opportunities and time for leisure activities. According to industry insiders, a dominant characterization of the contemporary Saudi filmgoer is someone who goes to the cinema for the experience of movie-going without the initial intention to see a particular film, desiring an expanded menu of choices.[17] Arguably, one of cinema's most-valued state-recognized functions in contemporary Saudi Arabia is 'modeling modernity and progress'.[18]

Film culture in transition

Transition is a shifting concept, delineated by myriad perceived moments of rupture and conceptual markers of periodization. Periods of transition can retrospectively demonstrate continuities, contradictions, closures, lack of reform, limits on modernization efforts and containment of resistance (all addressed in the interdisciplinary and transdiscursive work of scholars on Saudi society, politics, economics and religion in transition).[19] I refer broadly here to Saudi film culture in the first two decades of the twenty-first century and, more specifically, to an attenuated period of transition of film exhibition (as well as distribution and production), subject to further refinements, revisions and extensions. For example, Arab media expert Naomi Sakr, conceptualizing the political economy of Saudi cinema, identified a transitional period from the mid-2000s through the rest of the decade. She interprets the public screening of programmes of Arabic-dubbed cartoons at the Intercontinental Hotel in Riyadh in 2005 to an audience of women and children as an apparent signal of 'the possibility that cinemas might be permitted in Saudi Arabia'.[20] The proliferation of such signals of the possibility of cinema – and citizens – entering into more public and less restricted realms in Saudi Arabia continued through the subsequent decade. The permission for cinema was ostensibly realized with the official lifting of the exhibition ban by royal decree, but the public nature of cinema continued to be negotiated afterward.

When the contemporary Saudi monarchy outlined plans for change with ambiguous timelines and details for implementation, such spectacular, publicity-generating deliverables such as the opening of cinemas in 2018 served the dual functions of garnering Saudi public support and attracting global media attention.[21] As Rosie Bsheer illustrates in her work on Saudi archives, patterns of historical effacement/erasure and architectural rebuilding/urban redevelopment/upscale megaprojects demonstrate the dynamics of state influence in Saudi Arabia.[22] I contend that the bourgeoning post-ban cinematic multiplex landscape makes visible Saudi and international investment in manifesting power through material culture and built environment. Television, video, internet, cellphones and digital technologies enabled expanded home and mobile viewing experiences and the emergence of new talents and restructured markets, 'rendering national borders more permeable' in this 'hitherto protected and excluded society'.[23] Additionally, Saudi film festivals and circulation of films in the international image market, and the presentation of a modern public cinema as a consumer smorgasbord, have all enabled constant regenerative narratives of so-called 'first' and 'better' film cultural achievements in Saudi Arabia.

Festivals

The concept of festivals as aggregations of films, showcases and competitions of multiple short films has been essential in this transitional period of Saudi film culture, with a central cultivation goal of introducing the Saudi public to the locally produced films that have been shown abroad, and also expanding the possibilities of what a Saudi or regional film should look like, in terms of quality, genres and themes, and cultural codes and conventions. Local Saudi festivals emerged starting in the 2000s. The privately financed Jeddah Visual Show Festival, launched in 2006, was held at the Jeddah Science and Technology Center and touted as the first Saudi Arabian film festival, screening documentary, narrative and animated shorts from Saudi Arabia, as well as the United Arab Emirates and Kuwait.[24] Assiduously avoiding film in its name, Jeddah Visual Show Festival became an annual event until its cancellation in 2009.[25] A separate 2008 multi-day event was once again announced by the press as Saudi Arabia's first film festival.[26] The Dammam Literary Club in Saudi Arabia's Eastern province had reportedly been hosting private gender-segregated film screenings; and this multi-day film festival was organized by Dammam Literary Club with the Saudi Society of Arts and Culture (the first such civil organization in the country established in 1973) to screen and award prizes to short films and documentaries from around the Gulf.

These festivals, their organizers and related press coverage rhetorically addressed issues of cinematic visibility, taste and quality while the cinema ban was still in place. Jeddah Visual Show Festival's organizer, still a major player in the Saudi film scene, participating in local branding and production of Saudi film content and distribution of international films in the Kingdom, publicly deferred to the morality-based determinations of taste and 'meaningful' messages in a festival held at an educational venue. The Jeddah Visual Show Festival's format, context and nomenclature enabled a flexible definition of cinema: 'mainly experiments by amateurs who wanted to express themselves through movies'.[27] Noting that many cafés in Jeddah already regularly showed movies via satellite television, Saudi journalists readied for public cinema to re-emerge in Saudi society, positing a problematic disconnect between choice and taste in nascent public film culture versus the larger Saudi entertainment-scape: 'Will people flock to the auditorium eager to watch whatever movie available, or will they prefer to stay in the comfort of their homes watching Hollywood movies on satellite channels?'[28]

Before the announced lifting of the cinema ban by royal decree, Crown Prince Mohammad bin Salman also tested the waters of public film exhibition within the context of a 'pioneering' festival event in August 2017 at the Riyadh International Conventions and Exhibitions Center.[29] Hakaya Misk Festival, an initiative for bin Salman's youth foundation, featured intense media convergence and commercial possibilities, as it promoted Snapchat, Wikipedia, YouTube and LinkedIn. Youth-oriented content creation in this context included story-writing and storytelling, painting, animation and production, and other forms of art. While film/cinema was not mentioned by name, animation was emphasized as an interartistic and technocentric storytelling vehicle and a promoted model of cultural production, with connotations of youth, family and dissemination of positive messages. Local media announced, as part of the Hakaya Misk Festival's cultural programming, a 'grand film screening to take place for the first time in recent history' with *Bilal: A New Breed of Hero* (2015), a CGI-animated biopic of Bilal ibn Rabah, prayer caller during the time of Prophet Mohammad.[30] While *Bilal: A New Breed of Hero* was made by Barajoun Entertainment, an animation and visual effects studio based in Dubai, the film was also celebrated for its Saudi credentials, as it was co-written, co-produced and co-directed by Saudis.[31]

Home-grown productions and home-viewing

The claim of the first Saudi films to be produced in the Kingdom is generally given to documentaries about the city of Riyadh and the civil war in Beirut made in the 1970s by Abdullah Al-Muhaisin, a Saudi-born filmmaker who has received some international film festival recognition throughout his career.[32] Provenance and genre have also been central to discourses on the authenticity of Saudi filmmaking during the contemporary transitional period. *Keif al-Hal?* [How Are You?] (2006) was a pioneering commercial venture produced by Riyadh-based company Rotana International, then owned by Saudi mega-investor Prince Al-Waleed bin Talal and positioned as the Arab world's largest entertainment group. The comedy-romance about an aspiring Saudi filmmaker (played by the Saudi winner of a pan-Arab singing competition show) was written, directed and acted by pan-Arab talent and filmed in the United Arab Emirates. The so-called first Saudi-produced movie was also hailed as Saudi Arabia's 'first popular release movie'.[33] While it could not be shown theatrically in Saudi Arabia, *Keif al-Hal* began showing on Eid in October 2006 at movie theatres across the Middle East, including other countries in the Gulf region. Even before *Keif al-Hal*'s release, the BBC was using scare quotes around '"first" Saudi feature film' given the lack of exhibition infrastructure in Saudi Arabia.[34] *Keif al-Hal* and Rotana's entrance into feature film production functioned as another step towards making a Saudi film industry possible and visible, without capitulating to a conservative panoptic gaze. It whetted interest in Saudi-themed stories and challenged the limits of representation, especially of women, through the infusion of comedic elements, progressive characters and scenes of 'driving in the desert far away from the peering eyes of the religious police'.[35] A second film produced by Rotana, the 2009 comedy *Menahi*, about a Saudi Bedouin farmer, adapted a TV character for the big screen, in a get-rich-quick scheme/culture clash narrative taking place in Dubai.[36] Given the public visibility of the project, it sparked global headlines like trade paper *Variety*'s premature pronouncement: 'Saudi Arabia lifts ban on cinemas.'[37] After months of negotiations, and despite religious protests, the producers got *Menahi* screened at government-run cultural centres in Riyadh, Jeddah and Taif.[38] *Keif al-Hal?* and *Menahi* confirmed Saudi taste for local movie content and exhibition, the potential for developing pan-Arab audiences for Saudi films, and global interest in the Saudi film sector.

The currency of *Keif al-Hal?* and *Menahi* as ground-breakers was discursively adjusted with the performance of the international festival and arthouse favourite, *Wadjda* (2012), a co-production of Saudi Arabia (Rotana), the Netherlands, Germany, Jordan, the United Arab Emirates and the United States. Written and directed by Saudi filmmaker Haifaa al-Mansour, *Wadjda* was well positioned to be considered a revolutionary exemplar of a new Saudi cinema of quality and global reach. It was acclaimed as the first Saudi film to be shot entirely in Saudi Arabia, the first Saudi feature directed by a woman (al-Mansour previously made short films and also had an associate producer credit on *Keif al-Hal?*) and the first Saudi film to be submitted for consideration for the Best Foreign Language Film category of the Academy Awards. Deftly crafting a Saudi-located narrative, milieu and characterizations with universally intelligible, affective resonance and a window-into-a-closed-society appeal, *Wadjda* focuses on a spunky young Saudi girl who decides to participate in a Quran recitation contest so that she can win prize money to buy a bicycle.

Wadjda's script, shooting and fiscal profile were developed in the laboratories of the Sundance Rawi Screenwriters workshop in Jordan, the International Film Festival Rotterdam's Hubert Bals award, and through the collaboration of multiple German private and public funders, necessitating the obfuscation of global brands such as Starbucks during part of the filming process in a Riyadh shopping mall.[39] *Wadjda* narratively foregrounded the liberating possibilities of breaking free from the restrictive constraints of traditional gender roles. Haifaa al-Mansour was able to guide her cameramen and actors in public outdoor spaces, while also exercising caution given cultural codes, by using two-way radio from the inside of a van navigating the streets of Riyadh.[40] Prominent media attention focusing on al-Mansour as a globally mobile female Saudi filmmaker demonstrated profound disconnections in Saudi society, given the persistence of gender segregation, unequal rights and limited progress in Saudi women's status across areas of public life.[41] Despite *Wadjda*'s international recognition, the film was exclusively screened by invitation only in cultural centres in Saudi Arabia.

The history of film exhibition in Saudi Arabia is further complicated by other negotiations of taste and ideology, media convergence and specificity and perceptions of regulated and democratized viewing. The introduction of television was justified as a means of communication controlled by the state, with TV, as well as viewing of movies on videotape, ostensibly contained within the family home; however, Saudi Arabia was unique in allowing television while forbidding public film screenings in the 1980s.[42] Television, according to Marwan Kraidy, did not apparently pose the same risk of potential illicit social interaction and dangerous gender-mixing as projected movies in darkened spaces.[43] Home-viewing expanded with satellite television, and the internet also fed film and transmedia fandom. Saudi television companies such as Rotana and the Arab Radio and Television Network (ART) became involved in film production.[44] The film and television symbiosis in Saudi Arabia is recognized in the ongoing development of a production and post-production support infrastructure in Saudi Arabia. However, such a 'new regime of accessibility' can be viewed as having a limited impact on societal change because of connections between media ownership and Arab political leadership, content control and dissemination of 'government-molded discourse'.[45]

Cultural and educational experiences

By the time the official decree lifting the cinema ban was issued, official public screenings outside the residential compounds were limited to an IMAX dome theatre in the Sultan Bin Abdulaziz Science and Technology Center, located in Khobar in the Damman metropolitan area in Saudi Arabia's Eastern province within 10 km of the main administrative centre of the Saudi oil industry in Dhahran. There, screenings were presented as educational documentaries rather than premium cinematic experiences and spaced out so as not to overlap with daily prayer.[46]

For a decade before Mohammad bin Salman lifted the cinema ban, the oil company Saudi Aramco in 2008 announced the planning of a state-owned cultural megaplex, complete with a cinema, in Dhahran. Designed by a Norwegian architectural team selected after a global competition, the Saudi Aramco's King Abdulaziz Center for World Culture (also known as Ithra which means 'enrichment') included an auditorium with the primary purpose of 'screening original works from the emerging Saudi film industry, as well as educational and insightful documentaries from across the globe'.[47]

In negotiations of the concession agreement between Saudi Arabia and Standard Oil Company of California in 1933, King Abd al-Aziz Al Saud insisted on including a clause directing the company to provide opportunities for Saudi citizens.[48] However, as mentioned in the introduction to this chapter, Saudi Aramco had its own complicated roles in the development of film culture in Saudi Arabia's Eastern province, and beyond, which did not include the participation of Saudi citizens. Expat memoirs offer idyllic portraits of consuming a steady supply of Hollywood releases, from live-action features to Disney animations, on the gated compounds before the advent of television in the Kingdom.[49] These privileges were afforded to Western and, in some cases, to South Asian and non-Saudi Arab workers, but Saudi workers were excluded. In 1956, Saudi workers demonstrated at the Ras Tanura camp, demanding to be let into the company movie theatres and were dealt with brutally.[50] In contrast, during the contemporary transitional period, the primarily state-owned Aramco, one of the world's most profitable companies, positioned itself as a leader in cultivating home-grown film production in Saudi Arabia and participation in film cultural activities and related publicity, leveraging corporate and political clout to raise the profile of emerging Saudi filmmakers abroad.[51] Events such as Saudi Film Days in Los Angeles created red carpet press exposure, with screenings of Saudi films and appearances of emerging Saudi filmmakers in constructed Hollywood environments.[52]

The official announcement of the lifting of the exhibition ban by Mohammad bin Salman Al Saud was given an interconnected educational and cinephilic backstory, as the crown prince supposedly claimed to have learned English by watching Hollywood movies.⁵³ Transnational film cultural investment has figured significantly in bin Salman's Saudi Vision 2030, and international media and potential fiscal partners perceived an extraordinary financial and public relations opportunity. Opening cinemas promised, and made visible, a commitment to change and modernity and recognition of Saudi hunger for movies. Such ventures also potentially reduce oil dependency and open possibilities for economic diversification and access to new potential sources of revenue through film exhibitions. Towards building film industry infrastructure under Vision 2030, the General Culture Authority (GCA) of Saudi Arabia announced a plan for a secularized strategic development of film talent, regulatory structures, production, funding and Saudi brand-promotion with the formation of the Saudi Film Council.⁵⁴

Yet the timing of such celebrations of Saudi public cinema seemed to function also as means to deflect attention away from issues of accountability, justice and the murkiness of Saudi-US alliances. Human rights organizations and the international press have treated the proliferation of governmental film initiatives in Saudi Arabia with increasing scepticism and wariness about public relations strategies, especially in light of Saudi participation in the ongoing war in Yemen, detention and punishment of women's rights activists and the October 2018 assassination of the prominent Saudi dissident journalist Jamal Khashoggi in the Saudi consulate in Istanbul.⁵⁵ Khashoggi had worked for many Saudi news publications and was an active presence on social media. And he also assisted Princes Al-Waleed bin Talal and Turki bin Faisal towards the expansion of Saudi television news and in the capacity of a media consultant.⁵⁶ Living in self-imposed exile outside Saudi Arabia during the last part of his life and career because of restrictions on public critical discourse in the Kingdom, Khashoggi advocated for democracy and wrote persuasively about the role of cinema in shaping the public image. Indeed, as I will detail in a few pages, he became an important voice in the dialogue about cultural meanings of a key programming choice in the 'new' public cinema in Saudi Arabia.

New public cinema and the Cola wars

In haste to be the 'first', the post-ban public presentation of film in Saudi Arabia in January 2018 raised eyebrows abroad about curious criteria of judgement and apparent violations of taste. The historic double-bill, largely mocked by the US media, included two 2017 animated features, DreamWorks Animation's *Captain Underpants: The First Epic Movie* and the critically reviled *The Emoji Movie* from Sony Pictures Animation. The films were shown in a makeshift theatre in Jeddah, at the state-run Culture and Arts Society with a week of screenings of the animated films as a family movie festival, complete with red carpet and popcorn machine, supported by the General Entertainment Authority, established by Mohammad bin Salman in 2016.[57] The film's organizer was an outfit called Cinema 70, advertised as Saudi Arabia's first cinema brand, whose CEO, Mamdouh Salem, had previously overseen the organization of one of the aforementioned first Saudi film festivals, Jeddah Visual Shows Festival.[58] The screening of these animated films and global press coverage of the event inadvertently set up a scenario whereby the next Saudi public cinema move would look more professional and tasteful and reflect favourably on the new regime.

Central to this launch of Saudi public film culture was AMC, the largest theatre chain in the world, an American company with Chinese conglomerate Wanda Group owning a controlling stake at the time.[59] Singapore's *Straits Times* newspaper heralded the post-ban screening with a headline about 'Chinese-controlled AMC' opening the first cinema in the country in decades.[60] AMC was granted the first licence to operate movie theatres in Saudi Arabia, with the first stage of this development being a single-screen theatre in a refurbished former symphony hall in King Abdullah Financial District, a new development in northern Riyadh.[61] AMC and the Saudi Development and Investment Entertainment Company announced the goal of achieving approximately a 50 per cent market share of the Saudi Arabian movie theatre industry, with expectations of 40 new cinemas in Saudi Arabia within five years and up to 100 theatres in Saudi Arabia by 2030.[62] As the second theatre chain to get granted a licence in Saudi Arabia, the Dubai-based exhibitor Vox also quickly racked up several 'firsts' while multiplying opportunities for experiencing diversified multi-screen entertainment, including the first movie theatre complex to offer luxury amenities, the first non-educationally dedicated IMAX venue in the Kingdom, the first 3D movie shown in Saudi Arabia, the first horror film to be screened in KSA, the first Egyptian film to be shown in a Saudi multiplex and the first Indian film (a Tamil movie) to be shown in a Saudi multiplex, and the so-billed first Saudi film developed, written and produced with an all-Saudi crew.[63] In a bourgeoning multiplex landscape dominated by global companies, a new company, Muvi, established itself as Saudi Arabia's first domestic multi-screen theatre chain, heralding its technological advancements and attractions with the first Dolby movie experience in Saudi Arabia.[64]

Black Panther was the 'first film' shown post-ban in a designated commercial movie theatre in Saudi Arabia, the concert hall in Riyadh's King Abdullah Financial District repurposed by AMC.[65] The multivalent choice of superhero film as a global commodity, branded by both Disney and the Marvel Universe, was both celebrated and critically deconstructed, given the apparent grandiosity and inconsistencies of Mohammad bin Salman's vision of reform and modernization. Following a US tour by the crown prince to attract investors, the first screening of *Black Panther* in Saudi Arabia in April 2018 also functioned as elaborate, VIP/invitation-only photo opportunities.[66] Global brands and products such as Lexus and Coca-Cola were on conspicuous – and socially mediated – display, commingling discourses of modernity and consumer culture, showcasing corporate partners committed to investing in the Saudi market and apparently aligned with Vision 2030.[67] A Coca-Cola commercial screened before *Black Panther* depicts a Saudi daughter getting a desert driving lesson and a bottle of the iconic soda from her proud father to help steady her steering under his watchful gaze. This commercial had already premiered on Coca-Cola's YouTube channel, met with a mixed reception due to its corporatized paternalistic cooptation of the struggle for women's right to drive, and further complicated by the realities of gender inequities and abuses, including the detention of Saudi women activists.[68]

The commercial's tagline 'Change has a taste' declared a timely but vague Saudi variant/addition to Coca-Cola's global 'Taste the feeling' campaign, resonant of a populist application of a synesthetic tautology of 'structures of feeling'.[69] This multi-sensory cultural experience of consumption linked cinema with the advertisement of a refreshing fizzy soft-drink treat with corporate clout, presented as an integral part of the audiovisual landscape and emblematic of modern film-going and/as cultural change. The red-and-white logos for Coca-Cola and AMC made for a consistent colour scheme, uncannily repeated in the crimson colour of popcorn containers, and the red-and-white checked shemagh headdresses worn with traditional white thobes by the photographed Saudi male spectators as active agents at the invitation-only screening; many of them were pictured documenting the experience through the screen of their cellphones.[70] Bourdieu's social critique of the judgement of taste is evident in a film cultural milieu and dress codes (with the majority of photographed women in attendance wearing black abayas), demonstrating institutional legitimization of such cultural practices of consumption, while also clearly reinforcing gender difference. The AMC movie theatre in Riyadh also included large-scale black-and-white photographs of Hollywood movie stars, as photo-op backdrops.[71]

The privileged positioning of Coca-Cola also signalled a new strategic positioning in a country with a huge, competitive market for non-alcoholic beverages, with Pepsi the long-time soft-drink leader in the Middle East region. Coca-Cola was formerly subject to Saudi boycott after the Arab-Israeli war because of Israeli bottling connections, and both Coke and Pepsi (and other US corporations/brands) were boycotted in Saudi Arabia in the early 2000s because of anti-Saudi rhetoric after 9/11, Israel's invasion of Gaza and the US's invasion of Iraq. Muslim-associated brands offering a challenge to Western hegemony were introduced into the Saudi market, most notably Iranian Zamzam Cola, which became the official soft drink of the Hajj pilgrimage to Mecca in 2002. The Coca-Cola partnership, and audiovisual assertion of Coke as the soft drink of the new public cinema in Saudi Arabia, also made manifest the recent breakdown of Saudi-Iranian diplomatic relations and closer connections of an outwardly increasingly secular Saudi Arabia with the United States.[72] The branded convergence of Coca-Cola, Disney, the Marvel Universe and AMC Theatres contributed to the presentation of Saudi film culture as very closely aligned with Hollywood and global capital.

Public opinions

The inaugural version of *Black Panther* screened in Saudi Arabia required glocalized remediation. Acquired through Disney's distributor-partner in the Middle East, the film screened at the premiere retained all the violent scenes but imposed the logic of regional censorship, with edits including the removal of the final kiss.[73] The recontextualization of *Black Panther* in the Saudi cinema public was likewise ripe with polysemic possibilities for allegorical reading and critique. Adam Aron, CEO of AMC Entertainment Holding, presented *Black Panther* as 'the story of a young prince who transforms a great nation'.[74]

Saudi filmmaker Haifaa al-Mansour, now based in Los Angeles and recruited to serve on the board of directors for the newly established Saudi GCA, praised the choice of *Black Panther* in a *New York Times* op-ed for its status as the first film screened in the Kingdom, and as a cinematic attraction: 'It represents everything I love about cinema, and provides the audience with conversations about identity, politics and diversity, through an action-movie thrill ride. To experience a phenomenon like this in public, with friends and family, to laugh and cringe along with strangers, is a privilege.'[75]

The late Saudi exilic journalist Jamal Khashoggi offered up a powerful opinion piece in *The Washington Post* amidst a wave of arrests of Saudi intellectuals, clerics, social media influencers, women's rights activists and journalists, asserting that the screening and the reinstituting of cinemas in Saudi Arabia was a huge step towards normalization in negotiating the authority of the state and personal choice of citizenry.[76] Yet given the uncanny selection of this particular film, Khashoggi wondered whether there is space for critical public discourse at all in Saudi Arabia, let alone dissent. Comparing affluent and insular Saudi Arabia with the fictional African nation Wakanda, he pointed out that, finally, strong oil-rich KSA lacks intellectual, scientific and technological assets on a par with the film's Afrofuturist superheroes and the kinetic energy of Wakanda's precious resource, vibranium. Khashoggi's article, published less than six months before his tragic assassination at the Saudi consulate in Istanbul, activated a moral argument, espousing not just good taste but good will as well, particularly in terms of developing resources. Rhetorically employing the landmark film of the official inauguration of public cinema in Saudi Arabia as a central metaphor, Khashoggi recognized the need to build regional peace and foreign relations and to use extraordinary power for the greater good.

Conclusion: Screens, streams and vaccines

Saudi film culture and the circulation of Saudi films, having developed tributaries outside theatrical exhibition, are clearly not exclusively bound by it. Online platforms for content creation and distribution, social media, film streaming, television and theatrical movie exhibition continue to coexist, flow together and generate new 'firsts'. YouTube as a contemporary video-sharing platform, for example, has been successfully utilized by countless makers, including Saudi-based C3 Films, the start-up/creative media studio, Telfaz11, a multi-channel digital entertainment production and distribution network.[77] Such content creation and sharing were especially vital to amplify, mediate and transmute protest during and in the aftermath of the Arab Spring, when Saudi censorship and watchdog regulation of social and audiovisual media intensified. In 2013, Saudi women courageously used online spaces to post videos protesting the unwritten ban on driving and documenting acts of public defiance; and 'No Woman, No Drive', Telfaz11 creator Hisham Fageeh's satirical video performance, based on the classic Bob Marley song 'No Woman, No Cry', became a global viral hit.[78] Scholar Sean Foley, who has extensively examined artistic production in Saudi Arabia as a change agent, effuses that by 2016, 'the kingdom's online and artistic communities had merged into a vibrant artistic movement that drew on talent around the kingdom and had no equal in the Gulf or the wider Arab world'.[79]

The Saudi film *Barakah Meets Barakah* (2016), filmed entirely in Jeddah and featuring YouTube-cultivated talent, premiered on the international film festival circuit at Berlinale before securing theatrical distribution in European and Middle Eastern markets, and becoming Saudi Arabia's second-ever official Oscar submission after *Wadjda*.[80] Further, it would break new ground by becoming the first Saudi film to be acquired for streaming by Netflix.[81] The Aramco/Ithra-funded production, *Joud* (2018), an experimental documentary without spoken dialogue, became the first Saudi film to premiere at the Cannes Film Festival, where Saudi officials actively promoted the country as a viable venue for filmmaking with an extraordinary domestic talent pool.[82]

According to recent reports by the British Council and other research institutes on capacity building in the growing film sector in Saudi Arabia and media consumption in the MENA countries, 'Saudi Vision 2030 has the potential to drastically shift the relationship between the state and citizens'.[83] In order to expand the talent pool and promote inclusivity in film culture, more training and educational opportunities in film are critically needed in a country with a median age under thirty years old, where many related skills have been self-taught or learned abroad. Under-representation and gender equity issues continue to plague the film sector and society at large.[84] Quantitative data cited in the British Council report indicates that most of the surveyed Saudi consumers would prefer to watch Saudi film content but have had limited opportunity to do so.[85]

After Saudi Arabia's unprecedented growth in multiplex movie theatres in a country with a well-established shopping mall culture, the novel coronavirus/Covid-19 pandemic in 2020 necessitated temporary closure, a hiatus of theatrical film exhibition and postponement of film festival plans during the lockdown, followed by limited capacity (and ultimately, expanded) reopenings and implementation of new security measures.[86] In September 2020, during the ongoing crisis, Saudi Arabia's Ministry of Media hosted a film premiere at AMC Cinema in Riyadh, the cinema that had been publicly inaugurated by the superhero blockbuster *Black Panther*. This high-profile special screening of a documentary about the everyday heroism of Saudi workers and citizens throughout KSA combatting the coronavirus was attended by princes, cultural ministers and members of the media. Demonstrating mediated intervention in a national and global crisis, the documentary was subsequently shared on the Center for Government Communication (CGC)'s YouTube channel and broadcast on Saudi television.[87] During the global pandemic, Saudi Arabia's multi-screen theatres ultimately defied the downward trend in film exhibition receipts/revenue stream. The country emerged as the Middle East's top theatrical market and a vital global player, given Hollywood's urgent need to recoup losses in a time of crisis.[88] As I have argued throughout this chapter, the cultivation of a taste for cinema in transitional Saudi Arabia demonstrates an interplay of ever-shifting mediations and discursive revisions. These include geopolitical and economic alliances, entertainment attractions and sites of consumption, and promotion of branding strategies through glocalized public film exhibition. The study of the contemporary film scene in Saudi Arabia shows us how official state endorsement of such spectacular audiovisual 'evidence' of modernity and reform can function as a deflection of, or inoculation against, criticism of absolute power and repressive societal restrictions. However, the bourgeoning Saudi cinema nexus also reveals creative resilience and ongoing development, in a country which may have heretofore looked to the world like a film cultural desert.

Notes

1 See Joseph S. Nye, Jr., *Soft Power: The Means to Succeed in World Politics* (New York: PublicAffairs, 2005). The concept of soft power, along with 'small nation' cinema, has been effectively applied to world cinema studies. See Song Hwee Lim, 'Taiwan New Cinema: Small Nation with Soft Power', in *The Handbook of Chinese Cinemas*, ed. Carlos Rojas and Eileen Cheng-yin Chow (Oxford: Oxford University Press, 2013), 152–69. In contrast with Taiwan, I find the emergent and resurgent film culture of Saudi Arabia largely resists the useful model of small nation cinema proposed by Mette Hjort and Hjort and Duncan Petrie. See Mette Hjort, *Small Nation, Global Cinema* (Minneapolis, MN: University of Minnesota Press, 2005) and Mette Hjort and Duncan Petrie (eds), *The Cinema of Small Nations* (Bloomington, IN: Indiana University Press, 2007). However, a comparative analysis of related global dispersion of film production in the United Arab Emirates and New Zealand by Alfio Liotta presents some related concerns about film culture in the Arab Gulf region. Alfio Liotta, 'Small Nations and the Global Dispersal of Film Production: A Comparative Analysis of the Film Industries in New Zealand and the United Arab Emirates', *The Political Economy of Communication* 2, no. 2 (2014), https://www.polecom.org/index.php/polecom/article/view/36/234 (accessed 14 April 2021).

2   Lina Khatib, *Filming the Modern Middle East: Politics in the Cinemas of Hollywood and the Arab World* (London; New York: I.B. Tauris, 2006), 170.
3   Hassan Ismaik, 'Four Reasons Why Saudi Arabia's Soft Power Eclipses All Others', *al-Arabiya News*, 4 December 2020, https://english.alarabiya.net/views/news/middle-east/2020/12/04/Four-reasons-why-Saudi-Arabia-s-soft-power-eclipses-all-others (accessed 14 April 2021).
4   I focus primarily on critical analysis of public-facing disseminated information in English-language media sources within and outside Saudi Arabia, including journalistic coverage, mediated public acts such as inaugural post-ban film screening, reports and 'official' website content.
5   Such processes, according to Bridget Fowler in a Bourdieuian analysis of cinema as cultural production, are endemic to the making of cinema as a legitimate, autonomous or restricted artistic field. Bridget Fowler, 'Bourdieu, Field of Cultural Production and Cinema: Illumination and Blind Spots', in *New Uses of Bourdieu in Film and Media Studies*, ed. Guy Austin (New York; Oxford: Berghahn Books, 2016), 18. I contend that such film cultural processes have been embattled in the Saudi case.
6   Robert Vitalis, *America's Kingdom: Mythmaking on the Saudi Oil Frontier* (Stanford, CA: Stanford University Press, 2007), 60.
7   Vitalis, *America's Kingdom*, 123.
8   Firat Oruc, 'Petrocolonial Circulations and Cinema's Arrival in the Gulf', *Film History* 32, no. 3 (Fall 2020): 32.
9   Deema Al-Khudair, 'Saudi National Day Turns Spotlight on Cinema's Golden Years', *Arab News*, 22 September 2019, https://www.arab news.com/node/1558166/saudi-arabia
10 Georges Sadoul, *The Cinema in the Arab Countries* (Beirut: Interarab Centre of Cinema and Television, 1966), 191.
11 Viola Shafik, *Arab Cinema: History and Cultural Identity* (Cairo: American University in Cairo Press, 2016), 27.
12 Valerie Anishchenkova, *Modern Saudi Arabia* (Santa Barbara, CA: ABC-CLIO, 2020), 309.
13 Khoja, producer of al-Arabiya's documentary about the backyard cinemas, *Cinema Al-Ahwash*, is quoted in Al-Khudair, 'Saudi National Day Turns Spotlight on Cinema's Golden Years'.
14 Anne Ciecko, 'Cinema "of" Yemen and Saudi Arabia: Narrative Strategies, Cultural Challenges, Contemporary Features', *Wide Screen* 3 no. 1 (June 2011): 5.
15 See Robert Arnold's essay, 'The Architecture of Reception', *Journal of Film and Video* 37, no. 1 (Winter 1985): 47; quoted in Ina Rae Hark, General Introduction, *Exhibition: The Film Reader*, ed. Ina Rae Hark (London; New York: Routledge, 2002), 10.
16 For a fascinating discussion of gendered consumerism and social practices in Saudi shopping malls, see Amélie Le Renard, 'Engendering Consumerism in the Saudi

Capital: A Study of Young Women's Practices in Shopping Malls', in *Saudi Arabia in Transition: Insights on Social, Political, Economic and Religious Change*, ed. Bernard Haykel, Thomas Hegghammer, and Stephane Lacroix (Cambridge: Cambridge University Press, 2015), 314–31. Le Renard explores broader questions of women in Saudi society in her book, *A Society of Young Women: Opportunities of Place, Power, and Reform in Saudi Arabia* (Stanford, CA: Stanford University Press, 2014).

17 See Nick Vivarelli, 'Saudi Arabia Becomes Top Middle East Theatrical Market, Bucking Covid-Era Downward Trend', *Variety*, 9 November 2020, https://variety.com/2020/film/global/saudi-arabia-top-middle-east-theatrical-market-1234824347/. Vivarelli includes exhibition figures released at the META Cinema Forum exhibitors' conference, and quotes Cameron Mitchell, CEO of prominent Middle East exhibitor VOX Cinemas and David Hancock, an analyst at London-based Omdia.

18 Noha Mellor, 'Arab Cinema', in *Arab Media*, ed. Noha Mellor, Muhammad Ayish, Nabil Dajani, and Khalil Rinnawi, (Cambridge; Malden, MA: Polity Press, 2011), 103.

19 See Bernard Haykel, Thomas Hegghammer, and Stephane Lacroix, ed. *Saudi Arabia in Transition: Insights on Social, Political, Economic and Religious Change* (Cambridge: Cambridge University Press, 2015).

20 Naomi Sakr, 'Placing Political Economy in Relation to Cultural Studies: Reflections on the Case of Cinema in Saudi Arabia', in *Arab Cultural Studies*, ed. Tarik Sabry (London: I.B. Tauris, 2012), 221.

21 Ellen R. Wald, *Saudi, Inc.: The Arabian Kingdom's Pursuit of Profit and Power* (New York: Pegasus Books, 2018), 285.

22 Rosie Bsheer, *Archive Wars: The Politics of History in Saudi Arabia* (Paolo Alto, CA: Stanford University Press, 2020), 229.

23 Shafik, *Arab Cinema*, 342.

24 Scott Macauley, 'The Jeddah Visual Show Festival', *Filmmaker Magazine*, 17 July 2006, https://filmmakermagazine.com/2426-the-jeddah-visual-show-festival/#.YgjjLVVBwrg (accessed 13 February 2022).

25 Ben Child, 'Saudis in Riyadh Enjoy First Taste of Filmgoing in Three Decades', *The Guardian*, 9 June 2009, https://www.theguardian.com/film/2009/jun/09/riyadh-screening (accessed 14 April 2021).

26 Ali Jaafar, 'Saudi Arabia Unveils First Film Festival', *Variety*, 19 February 2008, https://variety.com/2008/film/markets-festivals/saudi-arabia-unveils-first-film-festival-1117981119/ (accessed 14 April 2021).

27 These qualifications are from Mamdouh Salem, executive manager of the Ruwaad media company for audio and visual production, the organizer of the event, quoted in Ebtihan Mubarek, 'Jeddah Hosting First Saudi Arabian Film Festival from Today', *Arab News*, 12 July 2006, https://www.arabnews.com/node/287659 (accessed 14 April 2021).

28 This specific question is asked by Mubarek, 'Jeddah Hosting First Saudi Arabian Film Festival From Today'.
29 See 'Hakaya Misk Festival Sheds Light on Youth Creativity Once More', a post on the MiSK Foundation blog.
30 'Bilal Movie to Screen in Riyadh Today', *Saudi Gazette*, 17 August 2017, https://saudigazette.com.sa/article/515245 (accessed 14 April 2021).
31 Credited Saudi talent includes Ayman Jamal (co-director, co-producer, story credit and founder of Barajoun Entertainment) and Yassin Kamel (co-author of the screenplay, who came to fame with his YouTube show, 'E7thar Khalfak Matab').
32 Ruba Obaid, 'The Rise, Fall, and Rebirth of Saudi Cinema', *Arab News*, 12 December 2017, https://www.arabnews.com/node/1207671/saudi-arabia (accessed 14 April 2021).
33 See Marwan Kraidy, *Reality Television and Arab Politics: Contention in Public Life* (Cambridge: Cambridge University Press, 2009), 97fn.20. Hisham Abdulrahman, the star of *Keif al-Hal*, was the 2005 winner of the pan-Arab musical competition reality show, Star Academy (Arabia) on Lebanese Broadcasting Company's satellite channel.
34 Vincent Dowd, 'First Saudi Feature Film Aims High', *BBC News online*, 26 May 2006, http://news.bbc.co.uk/2/hi/middle_east/5019116.stm (accessed 14 April 2021).
35 Motez Bishara, 'Arab Films at Cannes Tackle Taboos', *Al Jazeera (online)*, 26 May 2006, https://www.aljazeera.com/news/2006/5/26/arab-films-at-cannes-tackle-taboos (accessed 10 September 2021).
36 Ali Jaafar, 'Saudi Business Beats the Odds', *Variety*, 14 March 2008, https://variety.com/2008/scene/markets-festivals/saudi-business-beats-the-odds-1117982467/ (accessed 14 April 2021).
37 Ali Jaafar, 'Saudi Arabia Lifts Ban on Cinemas', *Variety*, 5 December 2008, https://variety.com/2008/more/news/saudi-arabia-lifts-ban-on-cinemas-1117996919/ (accessed 14 April 2021).
38 In Riyadh, the film was screened at the King Fahd Cultural Centre, reportedly attracting near capacity audiences of men, boys and girls under the age of ten; women were prohibited from attending. See Ben Child, 'Protests as Saudi film screened in Riyadh', *BBC*, 8 June 2009, http://news.bbc.co.uk/2/hi/middle_east/8089763.stm (accessed 11 February 2022), and Child, 'Saudis in Riyadh Enjoy First Taste of Filmgoing in Three Decades' (accessed 11 February 2022).
39 Beth Hanna, 'Talking "Wadjda" Firsts: Film Shot Entirely in Saudi Arabia and By a Woman', *Indiewire*, 9 September 2013, https://www.indiewire.com/2013/09/talking-wadjda-firsts-film-shot-entirely-in-saudia-arabia-and-by-a-woman-trailer-196159/ (accessed 14 April 2021).
40 Dan Zak, '"Wadjda" Director Haifaa Al Mansour Gives Female Perspective of Life in Saudi Arabia', *The Washington Post*, 19 September 2013, https://www

.washingtonpost.com/lifestyle/style/wadjda-director-haifaa-al-mansour-gives-female-perspective-of-life-in-saudi-arabia/2013/09/19/ff9b15f6-1bd5-11e3-8685-5021e0c41964_story.html (accessed 14 April 2021).

41 See Naomi Sakr, 'Women and Media in Saudi Arabia: Rhetoric, Reductionism and Realities', *British Journal of Middle Eastern Studies* 35, no. 3 (2008): 385–404. In addition to Haifaa Al-Mansour, other high-profile women filmmakers in Saudi Arabia include Shahad Ameen, whose feature *Scales* (2019) was the Saudi submission for the Academy Awards for the revamped 'Best International Feature' category (formerly 'Best Foreign Language Film'), and award-winning actress and filmmaker Ahd Hassan Kamel, who studied filmmaking in the United States and is one of the stars of *Wadjda*.

42 Viola Shafik, *Arab Cinema* (Cairo: American University in Cairo Press, 1998), 49.

43 Marwan Kraidy, 'Saudi-Islamist Rhetorics about Visual Culture', in *Visual Culture in the Modern Middle East*, ed. Christiane Gruber and Sune Haugbolle (Bloomington, IN: Indiana University Press, 2013), 288.

44 Alexander Hammond, *Popular Culture in the Arab World: Arts, Politics, and the Media* (Cairo: The American University in Cairo Press, 2007), 152.

45 Ouidyane Elouardaoui, 'The Crisis of Contemporary Arab Television: Has the Move Towards Transnationalism and Privatization in Arab Television Affected Democratization and Social Development?', *Global Societies Journal* 1, no. 1 (2013): 101.

46 Siddhant Adlakha, 'The Ramifications of Saudi Cinemas Opening Their Doors', *The Village Voice*, 8 January 2018, https://www.villagevoice.com/2018/01/08/the-ramifications-of-saudi-cinemas-opening-their-doors/ (accessed 14 April 2021).

47 Aramco 'Ithra' report/website: https://www.aramco.com/en/making-a-difference/people-and-community/ithra (accessed 13 February 2022). The institution now hosts the Ithra Film Society, Ithra Film Production initiative focusing on Saudi culture, and the Saudi Film Festival.

48 Aramco 'Ithra' report/website.

49 See, for example, Rick Snedeker, *3,001 Arabian Days: Growing up in an American Oil Camp in Saudi Arabia 1953-1962* (New York: Station Square Media, 2018)

50 Vitalis, *America's Kingdom*, 159.

51 Ellen R. Wald, 'Behind the Scenes of Saudi Cinema', *Forbes*, 11 December 2017, https://www.forbes.com/sites/ellenrwald/2017/12/11/behind-the-scenes-of-saudi-cinema/#3942dab0a8d3 (accessed 13 February 2022).

52 Sharon Swart, 'Hollywood Flocks to Paramount Lot for Saudi Arabian Film Days', *The Hollywood Reporter*, 11 November 2016, https://www.hollywoodreporter.com/rambling-reporter/hollywood-flocks-paramount-lot-saudi-arabian-film-days-945489 (accessed 14 April 2021).

53 Ryan Faughnder, 'Hollywood Rolls Out the Red Carpet for Saudi Arabia's Crown Prince, Hoping to Cash in on a New Market', *Los Angeles Times*, 2 April 2018,

https://www.latimes.com/business/hollywood/la-fi-ct-saudi-arabia-hollywood-20180402-story.html (accessed 14 April 2021).
54 Charles Gant, 'In Focus: Saudi Arabia's Bourgeoning Exhibition Sector', *Screen Daily*, 13 December 2018, https://www.screendaily.com/features/in-focus-saudi-arabias-burgeoning-exhibition-sector/5135256.article (accessed 14 April 2021).
55 Alex Ritman, 'Saudi Arabia is Quietly Trying to Salvage Its Plan to Build a Film Industry', *The Hollywood Reporter*, 10 May 2019, https://www.hollywoodreporter.com/news/saudi-arabia-quietly-trying-salvage-plan-build-a-film-industry-1208262 (accessed 14 April 2021).
56 Susanne Koelbl, *Behind the Kingdom's Veil: Inside the New Saudi Arabia under Crown Prince Mohammad Bin Salman* (Coral Gables, FL: Mango Publishing, 2019), 100–2.
57 Amid Amidi, 'Saudi Arabia Lifts 35-Year Movie Theater Ban with the Emoji Movie and Captain Underpants', *Cartoon Brew*, 15 January 2018, https://www.cartoonbrew.com/business/saudi-arabia-lifts-35-year-movie-theater-ban-emoji-movie-captain-underpants-155992.html (accessed 14 April 2021).
58 Nancy Tartaglione, 'Saudi Arabia: 'The Emoji Movie' & 'Captain Underpants' Are First Films to Screen', *Deadline.com*, 16 January 2018, https://deadline.com/2018/01/saudi-arabia-the-emoji-movie-captain-underpants-first-films-screened-1202243833/ (accessed 14 April 2021).
59 Wanda's stake in AMC changed in in 2021. See Rebecca Rubin, 'Wanda Group No Longer Majority Shareholder in AMC Theatres', *Variety* (blog), 12 March 2021, https://variety.com/2021/film/news/china-wanda-group-amc-theatres-1234929145/ (accessed 14 September 2022).
60 'Chinese-Controlled AMC to Open Saudi Arabia's First Cinema in Decades on April 18', *Straits Times*, 5 April 2018, https://variety.com/2018/film/news/amc-movie-theaters-saudi-arabia-1202743116/ (accessed 14 April 2021).
61 Brent Lang, 'AMC to Open Saudi Arabia's First Movie Theater', *Variety*, 4 April 2018, https://variety.com/2018/film/news/amc-movie-theaters-saudi-arabia-1202743116/ (accessed 14 April 2021).
62 Nick Vivarelli, 'Exhibitors at Dubai Forum Show No Sign of Pulling Back from Saudi Arabia', *Variety*, 29 October 2018, https://variety.com/2018/film/news/exhibitors-dubai-forum-saudi-arabia-jamal-khashoggi-killing-1203009133/ (accessed 14 April 2021).
63 Nick Vivarelli, 'Vox Cinemas to Open 110 Screens in Saudi Arabia This Year', *Variety*, 7 February 2019, https://variety.com/2019/film/news/vox-cinemas-110-screens-saudi-arabia-1203131137/ (accessed 14 April 2021).
64 Nick Dager, 'Muvi Opens Saudi Arabia's First Digital Cinema', *Digital Cinema Report*, 3 August 2020, https://www.digitalcinemareport.com/article/muvi-opens-saudi-arabias-first-dolby-cinema (accessed 14 April 2021).
65 Lang, 'AMC to Open Saudi Arabia's First Movie Theater'.

66 Tasneen Alsultan, 'Reality Breaks Up a Saudi Prince's Charming Media Narrative', *The New York Times*, 14 October 2018. https://www.nytimes.com/2018/10/14/business/media/reality-saudi-prince-media-narrative.html (accessed 14 April 2021).

67 Sara Townsend, 'Coca-Cola to build $100 million bottling plant in Saudi Arabia', *Arabian Business*, 6 October 2016. https://www.arabianbusiness.com/coca-cola-build-100m-bottling-plant-in-saudi-arabia-647973.html (accessed 14 April 2021).

68 Ben Hubbard, 'Saudi Arabia Agrees to Let Women Drive', *The New York Times*, 26 September 2017. https://www.nytimes.com/2017/09/26/world/middleeast/saudi-arabia-women-drive.html (accessed 14 April 2021).

69 See alternative readings of Raymond Williams and Pierre Bourdieu in Ben Highmore's 'Taste as Feeling', *New Literary History* 47, no. 4 (2016): 547–66 and John Blewitt's 'Film, Ideology, and Bourdieu's Critique of Public Taste', *The British Journal of Aesthetics* 33, no. 4 (October 1993): 367–72.

70 One striking example is the Reuters file photo by Faisal Al Nasser with the caption 'Two Saudi men take a selfie at Saudi Arabia's first commercial movie theater in Riyadh, Saudi Arabia April 18, 2018' that illustrated the article, Stephen Kalin and Sarah Dadouch, 'Saudis Flock to *Black Panther* as First Public Cinema Premieres', *Reuters*, 20 April 2018, https://www.reuters.com/article/us-saudi-cinema-idUSKBN1HR33G

71 One notable exception to a whitewashed pantheonic display of screen talent at the AMC Black Panther event, including portraits of Meryl Streep, Robert Downey Jr., Al Pacino, Julia Roberts and Michael Douglas, was the beloved late Egyptian superstar, Omar Sharif (1932–2015), who worked in Egyptian, American and European popular and art cinema, including David Lean's historical epic, *Lawrence of Arabia* (1962) and other Hollywood blockbusters.

72 According to a report published in *The New York Times*, the Saudi Coca-Cola boycott and Arab League blacklist of the company was initiated in 1965 and eased in 1989, with new agreements struck in 1993. See 'Resuming Regular Sales in Saudi Arabia', 27 January 1993, 4, https://www.nytimes.com/1993/01/27/business/company-news-coca-cola-resuming-regular-sales-in-saudi-arabia.html. Saudi Arabia is considered the largest soft drinks consumer base in the Middle East. The proliferation of brands targeting the Muslim consumer also included the transnational Arab venture, Mecca Cola. Zamzam Cola, formerly established as a subsidiary of Coca-Cola in Iran in 1954 (and named after a sacred well in Mecca), broke away from the parent company and rebranded as an Islamic product after the 1979 Islamic Revolution. Because of disintegration of diplomatic relations between Saudi Arabia and Iran since 2016, after the execution of Shia cleric Sheikh Nimr al-Nimrin Riyadh, prompting subsequent protests. Amira Al Hussaini and Mahsa Alimardani, 'Zam Zam Cola, A Symbol of Happier Diplomatic Ties Between Iran and Saudi Arabia', *Global Voices*, https://globalvoices.org/2016/01/11/zam-zam-cola-a-symbol-of-happier-diplomatic-times-between-iran-and-saudi-arabia/ (accessed 11 February 2022).

73. Rex Santus, 'Here's What Was Censored from "Black Panther" in Saudi Arabia', *Vice.com*, 19 April 2018, https://www.vice.com/en/article/gymnjm/black-panthers-40-second-kiss-scene-censored-in-saudi-arabia (accessed 14 April 2021).
74. See Kalin and Dadouch, 'Saudis Flock to *Black Panther* as First Public Cinema Premieres'. Such affinitive constructions of transmedia charisma were also evident at music concerts and comic conventions introduced in Saudi Arabia in 2018. For example, at Egyptian superstar's first-ever Saudi Tamir Hosni concert in Jeddah in March 2018, Prince Mohammed Bin Salman was projected on a screen like the ultimate popstar. For some journalistic insights into this process, see Susanne Koelbl, *Behind the Kingdom's Veil: Inside the New Saudi Arabia Under Crown Prince Mohammad Bin Salman* (Coral Gables, FL: Mango, 2020).
75. Haifaa al-Mansour, 'A Day at the Movies in Saudi Arabia', *The New York Times*, 30 April 2018, https://www.nytimes.com/2018/04/30/opinion/saudi-arabia-movies-women.html (accessed April 14, 2021).
76. Jamal Khashoggi, 'What Saudi Arabia Can Learn From "Black Panther"', *The Washington Post*, 17 April 2018, https://www.washingtonpost.com/news/global-opinions/wp/2018/04/17/what-saudi-arabia-can-learn-from-black-panther/ (accessed 14 April 2021).
77. Telfaz11 YouTube channel is still active and has 3.26 million subscribers as of April 2021: https://www.youtube.com/user/telfaz11
78. For a discussion of the video's virality, see BBC Trending, 'Trending: The Story behind No Woman No Drive', 28 October 2013, https://www.bbc.com/news/magazine-24711649 (accessed 14 June 2022).
79. Sean Foley, *Changing Saudi Arabia: Art, Culture, and Society in the Kingdom* (London; Boulder, CO: Lynne Rienner Publishers, 2019), 151.
80. Maria Cavasutto, 'Saudi Arabia Submits Second Ever Film, 'Barakah Meets Barakah' for Oscar Foreign Language Race', *Variety*, 24 August 2016, https://variety.com/2016/film/news/saudi-arabia-2017-oscars-foreign-language-barakah-meets-barakah-1201843201/ (accessed 14 April 2021).
81. Olivia Cuthbert, 'Barakah Meets Barakah' Stars Say Cinema Move Will Help Bring Saudi Stories to World', *Arab News*, 23 February 2018, https://www.arabnews.com/node/1252451/lifestyle (accessed 14 April 2021).
82. Foley, *Changing Saudi Arabia*, 176.
83. See the British Council report with research conducted by Nordicity titled 'Saudi Film Skills', 10. https://www.britishcouncil.sa/sites/default/files/saudi_film_skills_research_-_english_version.pdf (accessed 13 February 2022).
84. British Council/Nordicity, 'Saudi Film Skills', 8, 18.
85. British Council/Nordicity, 'Saudi Film Skills', 32 fn 6 and 7. The report cites research from Northwestern University in Qatar, Harris Poll, Pan Arab Research Center and Doha Film institute.

86 Tuqa Khalid, 'Saudi Arabia Reopens Cinemas with Coronavirus Protocols', *al Arabiya*, 22 June 2020, https://english.alarabiya.net/en/coronavirus/2020/06/22/Saudi-Arabia-re-opens-cinemas-with-coronavirus-protocols-The-Dos-and-Don-ts (accessed 14 April 2021).
87 'Media Ministry Launches Saudi Documentary Film Difficult Stage', *Saudi Press Agency*, 21 September 2020, https://www.spa.gov.sa/viewfullstory.php?lang=en&newsid=2136587 (accessed 13 February 2022).
88 Vivarelli, 'Saudi Arabia Becomes Top Middle East Theatrical Market, Bucking Covid-Era Downward Trend'.

13

The multifunctional cinema exhibition space at the turn of the century

A dialogue

Nour El Safoury and Jowe Harfouche

Founded in 2009, the Network of Arab Alternative Screens (NAAS) is a regional network for Arab film exhibitors. To date, it counts twenty-one cinema spaces in eleven Arab countries as members. NAAS illustrates a global trend, namely to build networks that bring together often small and mid-sized exhibitors. Other examples include EU-funded Europa Cinemas, founded in 1992; Arthouse Convergence in the United States, founded in 2006, and Independent Cinema Office, founded in 2003 in the UK. NAAS also illustrates context-specific concerns. Within a pan-Arab film market, this coalition among exhibitors aims not only to circulate films that are artistically different from the ones that saturate the market but also to share resources and skills. Through their membership in NAAS, exhibitors can get access to new pools of money as well as skill development modules and workshops.

The network members are a diverse group of exhibitors. Among NAAS members are film clubs such as the Tunisian Federation of Cine-Clubs, cinemas such as Zawya Cinema in Cairo and spaces that combine filmmaking, education and exhibition, such as Comra Films in Yemen. While some charge tickets, other spaces do not, a few members get governmental funding but the majority relies on a mix of donations, grants and ticket sales, some have a distribution arm while others raise funds to cover screening fees. A common factor among them, however, is that they define their function as exceeding that of a traditional exhibitor. They are spaces to gather around films and to grow and nurture a film culture. In countries that lack cinemas such as Yemen, NAAS members carve out a space for cinema on the cultural landscape. In others like Egypt where there is a century-old film culture, NAAS members challenge the mainstream film market by screening artistically adventurous old and new films that might not be profitable but are critically valuable.

Film exhibitors have typically depended on the market to sustain their business. They sell tickets, cover their expenses and make a profit. In the case of a new kind of multifunctional cinema exhibition space, this traditional financial model proved limiting. Some of the activities NAAS members undertake cannot be monetized within the exhibition market. Some members even choose to fulfil an educational mission and do not charge tickets at all. As a result, the lack of sufficient government funding contributes to economic precarity among this group of exhibitors.

Hope for a less strained financial structure came at the turn of the twenty-first century when new pools of cultural funding became available, and we begin this conversation with a description of the changes which led to that. Jowe Harfouche, to whom I speak in the following conversation, has been working for the past four years since his appointment as NAAS's executive director to articulate the possibilities presented by changes in cultural funding to reconfigure the cinema exhibition space and align it with civil society organizations that vanguard social change. Now twenty years into the twenty-first century, there are even more changes impacting the economic infrastructure supporting cultural work in the region. More than ever before, the contested relationship that this strand of cinema exhibitors has to the market is the subject of debate with different solutions proposed. NAAS is one of these proposed solutions.

Arab alternative screen culture

NES: Let us begin by speaking about the context and needs that motivated NAAS's founding as a regional network of film exhibitors at the turn of the twenty-first century.

Jowe Harfouche (JH): NAAS was started by a group of people – mostly representing arthouse cinema initiatives – who met at regional and international cinema events and through a string of personal connections. The initial desire to establish a network stemmed from a need to come together and figure out what we can do collectively. This need then turned out to be shared by a greater number of cinema initiatives than the original founding members of the NAAS.

The regional scope of the network's geography was inevitable since a large number of NAAS's current members act as the sole alternative cinema initiative in the community, town or city they serve. Sometimes they are even the sole alternative cultural initiative. When elaborating the perimeters of this network, and the bounds of its inclusion and exclusion criteria, it was important to focus primarily on film exhibition initiatives in order to highlight the value of this often invisibilized final link in the classic chain of the filmmaking process, the one that ensures access to the audience. A decades-long focus by donors, foundations and practitioners on production and skill development in the industrial art of making films across the region has marginalized film exhibition. The fringes became a place suitable for the development and growth of an alternative culture of film screenings and independent film exhibition.

It took time to identify the members of the NAAS network, and this slowness, we have come to learn, is quite essential in the process of network-building and community-making. For example, it took long conversations to crystallize the vision for a network gathering cinema exhibitors whose activities would position them, beyond circulating film copies as commodities, as active supporters of a growing alternative film culture. This was effectively translated into eligibility criteria for NAAS membership. For example, one of the eligibility requirements is that the applicant maintains a community around film throughout the year.

I mention this because we also soon realized, and I think we are still realizing, the full political potential of this exercise of network-building as a practice: delineating an existing community, in our case around shared skills and interests, and then clarifying its mandate or shared mission. If you were to ask me today to categorize NAAS's work in a field or discipline, I would say it fits best under cultural policy.

NES: In 2016, NAAS replaced the word 'arthouse' in its title with 'alternative'. This shift was driven by a realization that members not only are committed to developing a market for arthouse films – as another type of film commodity – but work with a total view of the function of the cinema institution. They develop a film-going culture and create new publics. Architecturally even these exhibition spaces include gathering areas, a coffee shop for example, a library or a roundtable to host workshops.

JH: The mission of local cultural initiatives, cinemas or otherwise, is already highly political in nature: organizing physical gatherings and championing critical thinking through their proposed programming. The availability of and access to parallel arts and culture productions that are neither monetized nor mediated by media conglomerates is already an act of counter-programming that goes against hegemonic trends of cultural consumption. Further, creating the space to engage critically with artistic and cultural productions – films or otherwise – and to question the issues they raise and the conditions of their making is also a practice contrarian to that with which the audience is reduced to passive receiving consumers.

This important role – whether or not we are conscious of it – positions us in a larger equation where we, as cultural practitioners, are fulfilling a role whose parameters we did not always take part in defining. To me, our awareness of our role and our positioning, which then inspires our programming and activities, in addition to the role of the cultural institution and its relationship to the audience, is what I am referring to as cultural policy in practice.

Starting in the early 1990s, new pools of money became influential mainly by way of multinational foundations that set out to build a civil society in countries where the infrastructure for citizenry and collective organizing was dismantled by years of colonial rule and subsequent regimes of oppression. Cultural diplomacy was the name of the game, and it brought about a wealth of neo-colonial undertones that inevitably seep(ed) into and reproduce(d) themselves in cultural practice. It was in this climate that a number of grant-making organizations, such as Culture Resource (*Al-Mawred Al-Thaqafy*), Arab Fund for Arts and Culture (AFAC) and NAAS among others, came to exist. NAAS has been supported for example since its beginning by generous grants from the Ford Foundation and the Open Society Foundations, both with significant involvement in the development sector in the region.

In this landscape, funding models prioritized the monetization of cultural work and the instauration of meritocracy-based forms of support, which both led to gatekeeping as a natural byproduct. Today, I find the all-important term 'cultural policy' eerily missing from the discourse around the work which we do, particularly in relation to grant-making organizations that have played an undeniable role in guiding and shaping the cultural modus operandi of the region. This critical field of practice is generally relegated to 'advocacy' or 'lobbying' efforts with states and governments, which limits it to the realm of policymaking. And since we have long been disillusioned by policymakers in our region, the impact and resonance of such work mainly serve in my opinion to maintain a status quo shaped primarily by capital and the channels in which this capital flows.

A non-hierarchical governance cooperative model

NES: Let us then speak more about what it means to say that NAAS as a network of exhibitors plays a role in crafting cultural policy by influencing the modus operandi of a significant number of alternative cinema institutions. This is a key difference in positioning compared to other distributor or exhibitor alliances that primarily aim to more effectively and profitably move films across borders. How is the work of this network different from other sorts of alliances that aim to carry films across geography?

JH: The exercise of network-building that is NAAS – like-minded cinema institutions coming together across borders to work in coalition – is by and large an exercise in unionizing that challenges gatekeeping models for example. The aim of organizations like NAAS is not only to source new pools of income and grow parallel channels for distribution, exhibition and support in the long term but also to draw and learn from the existing funding systems in order to question, repurpose and rethink the way we do things. Umbrella organizations have a vital role to play as a buffer between international funding bodies and local organizations, liberating the latter from the effects the policies of the former have on them. That is in addition to the vital role of knowledge production in framing, documenting and disseminating cumulative non-hegemonic cultural practices.

I see our job as a way to disarm these monies and rid them slowly of their dominion over shaping the type of work that we do in arts and culture. The onus is on us cultural practitioners to be introspective and self-critical, to be the pioneers of organizing and collectivizing, all the while drawing on comparative perspectives (both historical and geographical) as this particular struggle is not novel nor is it specific to our region or our sector.

I also find hope in this moment of crisis of structures both economic and organizational, to nudge us towards rethinking our grant-making schemes whose limitations and inequities are now evident more than ever before. In NAAS we like to imagine what money can do instead of just what it is doing now. What can we achieve by slowly dissociating our cinema institutions from bureaucratic rule and actively challenging the neoliberal laws of the market in our cultural economies and organizational models? What would art and film communities look like in the presence of more equitable access and distribution?

NES: Following the economic changes in the early 1990s which you have spoken about, in the past ten years or so there seems to be a more visible shift taking place towards an entrepreneurial, market-driven cultural economy, sometimes supported by the grant-making organizations you refer to. A marketplace that does not value their non-monetizable activities is limiting to cinema spaces. Yet for many small and mid-sized film exhibitors, to whom survival is a daily concern, outside of the funder-funded economy, the market seems like the only other viable financial option. There seem to be no other sustainable economic models outside of these two options.

JH: Our model is that of a cooperative. We think within a non-hierarchical governance model, cultivate a long-term and inclusive approach to network activities and aim to learn from and inhabit parallel economies. Cinapses Labs for example is one iteration of our approach and shows how it impacts the work our members do on the ground. As part of Cinapses, a group of fifteen institutions during the eighteenth Marrakech Film Festival allocated financial resources among themselves in a completely horizontal process. It was a landmark moment for a network that envisions communities taking ownership of their available resources and their allocation. Another example is a network-wide workshop around governance models that suggested sociocracy as a non-democratic alternative. We are looking into the potential of such integrative models to inform decision-making within our organizational structure instead of the classic top-down hierarchical administration. These governance models affect programme designs as well as the decision-making process around the allocation of resources.

Our work consists primarily of a lot of facilitation and moderation, making partnerships and cross-disciplinary alliances, proposal writing and donor management, in addition to administration, information management and producing training opportunities and networking events. It is a type of work that requires slowness, deep investment and kinship with one another. The NAAS members wear at least two hats: one that represents each individual institution, and one that is part of a larger body of institutions. A position that allows for a much richer engagement with each other, but is not without its complexities.

The belief in network-building, especially networks of solidarity, is materializing in a growing support for organizing cultural activities and rethinking cultural practice, even more so after Covid-19. Moving towards parallel economies in cultural work, more belief in collectivity, in degrowth, a move towards slower institutions, more initiatives veering culture away from the hegemonic rules of the market are all directions that are amalgamating.

Making space

NES: I believe that to understand changes on both the level of organizational structures and the type of films screened at these multifunctional exhibition spaces, one has to turn to audiences. Are contemporary cinema audiences seeking new types of cinemas that do not function like the traditional theatre? Of course, there are also cultural operators, for example film programmers and critics, who feel limited by the organizational and operational structures of the traditional film theatre. Especially after the dissolution of many film clubs – because of the absence of state support among other reasons – these cultural operators have fewer exciting and accommodating outlets for their work. So in rethinking the MO of exhibitors, can we say that some exhibitors, cultural operators and audiences are together drawing up, or reviving, a relationship that exceeds the transactional ticket-sale one?

JH: I agree that this is an aspiration for some exhibitors. That said, I would like to draw attention to the burden of fundraising which makes engaging with audiences a more formatted and cumbersome affair, limited in possibility. Both governments and donor foundations have historically projected onto alternative cultural centres a model of financial self-sustainability parachuted from the business world onto cultural institutions. This model pressured them to generate income in the name of cultural entrepreneurship and conditioned every fundraising strategy and income-generating activity. Yet, we know from practice that those concepts are neither compatible nor feasible in our contexts unless you monetize your service (i.e. your relationship with audiences). We need to liberate alternative cinemas and cultural institutions from a for-profit model, in my opinion.

The infrastructure that a network provides exposes alternative cinemas to different institutional models and possibilities. Exhibitors exchange experiences with one another and gain access to knowledge and praxis on the international level. Not only highlighting the vital role that these exhibitors play, networks also allow cultural practitioners the frameworks, time and space to rethink the governance models of their institutions which would go hand in hand with rethinking the relationship to the audience and the role the cinema institution plays in serving its community and the dynamics that go with that role.

The deepening rift between commercial and not-for-profit cinemas (i.e. for-profit vs. mission-driven) is inevitably redefining the role that these cinemas play in relation to their audiences. How it is being redefined depends on each context. But some directions that already reverberate across the network include a deeper focus on open community screenings, both inside the cinema space (for youth, people with hearing loss, the elderly, focus group screenings, issue-related screenings, etc.) and outside (open-air screenings, town squares, community centres, prisons, schools, with focus on rural areas or urban peripheries); film programmes that creatively respond to timely political and social matters and partnerships with local networks and organizations for specialized and sustained programming. A cultural initiative is typically mandated by the community it serves and is implicated in its politics and concerns, while a commercial cinema space exists to fulfil a market need that is more often than not manufactured.

NES: It is true that the new multifunctional cinema space offers another mode of engagement with audiences but I would argue that it is not one that is by default more inclusive or critical. There are similarities between the type of experience offered by the traditional theatre and the one offered by this new cinema exhibition space. Now even more so because some mission-driven exhibitors are already shifting towards the economies of creative cultural entrepreneurship. I agree that there remains a distinction between the two experiences at the cinema, it is just harder for me to associate it with a divide or a deep rife.

JH: In a community-funded cinema the relationship to the audience is intrinsic. An integrative governance model leads to audience engagement on the grass-roots level. These models are ones of transparency, equity and inclusion. I believe that once you start questioning how you do the work that you do, you would logically also question what it is that you're doing and for whom. This is the goal for where we want the network to be in ten years.

The deepening rift I speak about is a result of the diverging visions of the purpose or *raison d'etre* of cinemas. Our bet is on the unique role that the NAAS members play which we hope would become even more vital and essential. Some of the cinema members double as cultural centres, a space for communities to gather and for critical discourses to be harvested. Examples range from Tangier where the 'School at the Cinema' programme invites hundreds of young Moroccan students to interact with the cinema archive of the Cinémathèque de Tanger, all the way to Samawa Cinema in Iraq where media literacy workshops engage with audiences across generations outside the capital and urban centres, to the role Sudan Film Factory played in mass organizing and mobilizing during the revolution in and around Khartoum by offering up physical and discursive spaces and then engaging in consultations around drafting a new cultural policy with the new ministerial body. Until these societal and political needs are rendered obsolete, the work that the network members offer cannot find a substitute channel, online for example.

NES: Gathering and meeting others is partly how the people maintaining these cinema spaces understand their function. 'Making space' is an essential feature of the multifunctional cinema exhibitor. Comra Films and Samawa Cinema joined NAAS recently. Comra is in Yemen and Samawa in Iraq. Both help us understand, in addition to the other spaces you mention in Sudan and Morocco, why the narrow role of the traditional film exhibitor – to show films – is insufficient in some contexts. This is true also in countries that might not have just gone through wars or social upheaval like Iraq, Sudan and Yemen have. 'Making space' to gather around films is a need that exists in many countries in the region, as a result of our cinema archives being hardly accessible or non-existent, our cinema heritage being rarely historicized and harder to activate in the present and contemporary Arab cinema practices needing more critical attention and support.

JH: Of course, there is a sustained threat to the survival of our spaces, as the existence of (for lack of a better word) civic space in general is under threat. I am not only referring to the dialectic between physical screenings and online screenings – which have and will continue to co-exist – but I mean more importantly the larger context of the data capitalism age into which we are being ushered. I question the possibility of a civic space online. When I say that the work the network members offer cannot find a substitute channel online, I am refusing the possibility of digital civic engagement, at least in the context of the cinema institution and its role towards its audience.

The digital migration in film exhibition has been picking up steam for a while now. But I do think – perhaps naively – that the current pandemic has valorized the function of alternative film exhibition beyond merely programming content. I do not believe we are going back to funding that centres skill development rather than the work of exhibition, circulation and audience engagement. On the contrary, in fact I see some doubled-down belief in the importance of reaching and engaging communities and developing a substantive and rich film(-going) culture. The current public health crisis has unveiled a much deeper crisis of systems, structures and policies; this is a reality that is becoming evident to more donors and stakeholders.

NES: I like that we found ourselves as a matter of course referring to data capitalism. A typical mistrust of the network model is around data and the use of it. Cinema exhibition networks that operate regionally or internationally are often fed information by their members on activities such as ticket sales, number of screens, audience admissions, number of staff. These networks would then become powerful holders of data and information about cinema audiences, their tastes, habits and behaviours and also about the infrastructure of film exhibition on a regional or an international level. This might already upset the horizontal relationship with the members because the administrative body in the network would know a lot more than the network members.

JH: I absolutely echo the concerns you raise around data collection. The measures of transparency and accountability that we have established as a network to prevent exploitative and extractionist approaches to data collection include a collective approach to creating the very tool (an annual membership form) used for data gathering and accumulation; restricting the use of collected data for administering and managing the participation within the network; consent-based access by members to each other's data; and a network-wide commitment to deep contextualization and seeking consent when using compiled data for purposes outside the direct scope of the network.

It is important to note that NAAS is mandated by the network members to represent their interests and support their missions, therefore data collection tools are created by the members in order to tabulate and catalogue their work and are owned by them. The role of the NAAS staff to moderate and facilitate is more of a secretariat role. And thus, when such a mandate for NAAS is no longer valid, the organization would automatically dissolve.

14

The visual nation

Film, soft power and Egypt as a community of spectators

Iskandar Abdalla

Prologue: The passage

It is Egypt post-1967. The ramifications of the so-called Six-Day War are devastating. The army has been almost entirely destroyed. Even worse, it seems to have lost people's respect. Yet both officers and soldiers are determined to restore their dignity and by implication to repair the wounded honour of the defeated nation. This is the backdrop against which the plot of Sharif 'Arafa's film *al-Mamar* (*The Passage*) produced in 2019 unfolds. The title designates a purgatory metaphor: a passage from despair to hope, from defeat to victory, that the protagonists and the whole nation have to pass through.[1] Journalist and photographer Ihsan volunteers to document a secret military mission: an ironic incongruity. Besides his misfitting physical appearance – especially in contrast to the masculine jacked bodies of the army officers – Ihsan is introduced to us as a feminized loser, whose only qualification is a passion for Egyptian films. His future boss ridicules him for this, noting that 'what one sees in films has nothing to do with reality'. But then the camera takes us to a key scene: an open-air cinema amidst the desert. Soldiers are gathered watching in great excitement an Egyptian film, the 1956 *Rasif Nimra Khamsa* (*Platform 5*). The main protagonist of this film is Khamis (played by actor Farid Shawqi), a soldier too, but in the maritime forces of the police (Figure 14.1).

The gathering becomes a stage to demonstrate the regional, ethnic and religious diversity within the army in specific and in Egypt in general; Copts, Nubians, upper Egyptians, urban middle-class Egyptians are aligned in a half

Figure 14.1 Lobby card of *Rasif Nimra Khamsa* (*Platform 5*, 1956) featuring Khamis (Farid Shawqi).

circle, eagerly following the film and interactively engaging with the struggle of its courageous protagonist (Figure 14.2).

In euphoric elation, Ihsan observes the scene and features it in the first photograph he takes from the front. His passion for Egyptian films seems not to be out of place.

It seems that even during a war, films are not futile; they have power: a task to accomplish and a message to convey and it is not just about entertaining soldiers. The gathered men can *see* themselves in Khamis, they can relate to his patriotism and virility, they feel remorse for his shame when defeated and rejoice in his joy when he eventually wins the heart of the beautiful Nuzha (Huda Sultan), saving her from the grip of a villain. The cinema screen refers to the viewers and aligns them at once. Its power to refer lies in the modes of identification it offers; in its ability to represent the viewers and reimagine their reality. Its power to align lies in the happy futures it foreshadows; in its ability to captivate the viewers and keep them waiting for a rewarding resolution.

Interestingly, *The Passage* has been praised by its fans for its assumed ability to represent people's realities and focus on the bright sides of Egypt's history, thus giving people hope.[2] The president of Egypt ʿAbd al-Fattah al-Sisi personally praised the film. He saluted how the film celebrated 'the *ʾiltifaf* (alignment) of the people around the army' and the alignment of both

Figure 14.2 The gathered soldiers watching *Rasif Nimra Khamisa (Platform 5)* in *The Passage* by Sharif ʿArafa.

'around the state' stressing the urgency of this idea in times when Egypt faces many attempts 'to deprive its people from hope'.[3] *The Passage* is regarded as a film that refers to the people, aligns them, gives them hope and thus embodies what is often described as Egypt's 'soft power', understood here in terms of Egyptian films' power to convince and impress.[4] Featuring *Platform 5* as a film in film, *The Passage* reminds us of the power of films and by proxy refers to itself; to the same form of power it hopes to embody. This chapter dwells on this specific form of power; it attempts to understand how within and through filmic representations *referring* to viewers' lives and *aligning* them as a community of spectators operate in a joint venture to maintain and manifest power.

The analysis transcends *The Passage* as an exemplary case going beyond the notion of films as bearers of distinct meanings to be interpreted in terms of the intentions of their authors. In other words, I put no stock in reading *The Passage* – nor any other Egyptian films – as *sui generis* film creation with particular characteristics. My interest in films is only demonstrated in so far as they stand in relationship to the viewer; in so far as they establish discursive spaces through which the subjectivity of viewers unfolds and power can take shape. In the following, I will look at the discursive afterlives of films in a visual format that enables them to exist quasi off-screen: a TV show.

The perspective offered here avails itself of the scholarly work on film reception, cinema and memory that garnered considerable attention over the last thirty years.[5] If scholars like Robert Allen have garnered our attention to the conditions under which viewers watch films and the practices 'surrounding the confrontation between the semiotic and the social',[6] the perspective offered here will keep the screen as an interface between the semiotic and the social or the image and the viewer intact, while surpassing the physical space of viewing films. I inquire about how Egyptian films are rendered embodiments of 'soft power' in the course of recalling their memories on TV and how soft power of films is configured in such context as a power to refer and to align.

To bring the realms of viewing films under scholarly attention, Robert Allen ventured also to think of cinema screenings, in terms of performances, mutually shaped by the films' content and the multifaceted experiences of moviegoers.[7] By extension, I adopt the notion of performance in relation to films yet deploying it beyond both cinemas and the immediate time of viewing, attending to the performativity of remembering films; to the rhetorical and affective structures of enacting film memories to shore up national sentiments (Figure 14.2).

The performance of memory

The Passage was one of many iconic Egyptian films to be honoured by the TV show *Sahibet al-Saʿada* (*The Owner of Happiness*). Conductor Nadir ʿAbbasi was commissioned by the show to notate, re-orchestrate, comment and conduct the live performance of the scores on TV, in two separate episodes titled '123 Years of Cinema'.

Sahibet al-Saʿada has been running on TV since 2014.[8] It has a format similar to the late-night talk shows popular in the United States. It not only regularly features celebrities but is also animated by the celebrity status of its presenter ʾIsʿad Yunis, who is a prominent actress, producer and writer. *Sahibet al-Saʿada* hosts public personalities active in different fields, but most prominently film and TV professionals: actors, directors, screenplay authors, film composers and critics.

'We are not nostalgic. We live in times where some try to shake the grounds we stand upon, to steal it from beneath our feet so that we get lost in a vacuum [. . .] but we will never give up our grounds, nor our nature or history, holding onto them is what pushes us forward', elaborates Yunis on the idea behind the special episodes honouring Egyptian cinema.[9]

While ʿAbbasi is conducting the scores' performance, film posters are projected on the stage's background. Yunis takes up the role of an attentive spectator fully touched by the music. She communicates her affection with poignant facial expressions and bodily movements. Each performed score is followed by a conversation with guests. During these conversations, the dramatic qualities of the scores are analysed, while evoking memories about films and reassessing their historical value, the circumstances of their production and exhibition: a performance of memories simulated by music, images, bodily gestures and embedded in a narrative of a collective identity.

Scholars have shown that remembering is performative. Memory activation can take the shape of a performance and allows spectators to experience the past in the present through myriad cultural practices, including films.[10] Cinematic experiences transform narratives about history and identity into a sensational spectacle by which the viewers are not only intellectually addressed but are also invited to sensuously engage with through their bodies.[11] While keeping these effects intact, the re-enactment of cinematic experiences through memories shifts their boundaries beyond the realms of the personal. By virtue of performative remembering, viewing films is evoked in *Sahibet al-Saʿada* as a social experience that signifies commonalities. The repertoire at stake is not only performative but also affective. Spectators are expected to respond in a certain way; they are called upon to remember emotionally. The public performance of film memories and their integration into a narrative of identity incorporate personal memories of films into a collective experience of viewing: a collective history that lays grounds for the nation, attach people to it and manifest its power.

'I hope you can be confident that we stand on steady grounds [. . .] that we have a history that propels us to move forward, not just to look behind [. . .] we want to move forward armed with our culture and soft power.' These were Yunis's closing words for the episodes of '123 Years of Cinema'.[12]

Associating Egyptian cinema with soft power is by no means Yunis's invention. Coined by political scientist Joseph Nye in the context of the rising anxieties about American decline after the Cold War, 'soft power' designates a mode of power that dwells on persuasion rather than coercion; that aims at changing the behaviour of others, not through direct control or blatant aggression, but by rendering the own culture or ideology attractive so that others willingly follow.[13] Often appropriated and sensationalized, the notion of soft power made a public career in Egypt in the last two decades while being constantly associated with films, TV dramas, singers and literary figures in numerous popular accounts.[14]

To trace how Egyptian cinema became linked to soft power as one of the major sites of its manifestation, two aspects should be noted. First, the discourse of Egypt's soft power is one of a waning power with relinquishing reach and capacities.[15] It is often endowed with nostalgic undertones invoking good old times, rather than demonstrating a real existing grandeur. At the same time, it dwells on future visions, employing a vocabulary of revival and restoration. Second, soft power here is not merely meant to be a configuration of state's power – Egypt in this case – in relation to other states or an outline of its external influence on others, inasmuch as its sheer utterance is a matter of enforcing internal cohesion and conjuring national sentiments. The nation's soft power might make it attractive to others, but what counts here most is how the performative uttering and public recitation of soft power make the nation an object of love for its subjects. Consequently, I suggest understanding soft power here in performative and affective terms. First, it is realized as power when uttered: when it is attributed to things and when things refer to it. Second, it is a power that seeks to attach to objects by investing the latter with signs of love and happiness. Along these lines, I will assess how Egyptian cinema became an edifice for the nation's soft power.

On allegory, nostalgia and the power to refer

When Yunis asserted in 2019 that her show wants to propel people to 'move forward' not just to 'look behind', that it is also 'about the future', not just about the past, she wanted to refute the assumption that her content is sheerly nostalgic.[16]

But if we want to argue with Svetlana Boym that nostalgia is Janus-faced, at once retrospective and prospective, a fantasy of the past at the behest of contemporary preoccupations and future visions, then a nostalgia to the past would not necessarily stand in contradiction with moving forward to the future.[17] Nevertheless, it bears consideration here to inquire about present perspectives imbricated in the postulations of looking back and in the hopes to move forward.

In effect, when *Sahibet al-Sa'ada* started, five years before the celebration of '123 Years of Cinema', moving forward was not the main concern. The show invited Egyptians rather to feel loss, to realize absence, to figure out a condition of a troublesome amnesia; it was rather a call for a halt as moving forward under such a condition must have unpleasant consequences:

> Do you know this when you are about to travel, and you feel all the time like missing something? You know when you then try hard to remember what you miss, but in vain? [. . .] I feel that I forgot someone so important.[18]

The introduction's text of the very first episode explicitly exhibits the new show as a quest against absence: a journey to look for something or rather someone that suddenly got lost, someone whose features become unrecognizable, but whose loss is ubiquitously felt.

> I still feel *her* absence. The question is not anymore where *she* is going. The question is where we have lost her. [...] We need to look for *her* together. [...] [*She*] is a friend of mine, but about 7000 years older. [...] We were together for a whole life. In the last few years though, things happened, and we drifted apart for a while. I am here to remember, but not alone. We will remember her all together: The owner of happiness.[19]

Recognizing loss does not suffice; one is rather urged to end the condition of absence, to re-identify and locate the object of loss, not by holding it in place – as the question is not where it goes – but rather by keeping after it all the while by the virtue of remembering.

The 'things that happened' are the revolution of 25 January and its aftermath. 'She' or 'the owner of happiness' is Egypt; a nation that has been popularly imagined as a woman in diverse contexts.[20] Constructing the nation as a feminine object not only evokes desire and admiration but also implies the protection of a masculine agency. Loss is exacerbated when gendered, as has been convincingly demonstrated by Rim Nagiub.[21]

According to Nagiub nationalist narratives in the post-coup era produced two types of gendered dichotomies. The first one is between a masculine militarized saviour – embodied in the figure of Sisi himself – and a feminized nation in need for love and protection. The second dichotomy is between a pure, loyal femininity of a unique ancient nation that deserves love, and an ungrateful femininity of a populace who failed to embody the ideal of love,[22] who is amnesic and thus responsible for the drift that had taken place; for breaking ancient bonds, webs of recognition and identifications; for the distortion of view.

The launching of the show in April 2014 – a few weeks after colonel al-Sisi announced his candidacy for the presidential elections – comes to mark a point of reorientation towards the nation; to repair the drift and recognize loss; or rather to recognize the past few years as a puzzling conundrum and the troubles of the present as predominantly symptoms of loss and amnesia. In doing so, it pleads for imagination as the domain in which realities can be envisioned differently.

'What happened to us lately? Was it all real or imagined? Or has imagination fallen victim to reality?' These are the main questions the first episode poses. To answer them, Yunis solicits the opinion of experts, whose profession is imagination: a group of authors who write for film and TV. The most prominent among them was the journalist and public intellectual Ibrahim 'Issa, who is asked to offer an explanation for the purported 'state of confusion', and the 'distortion of view' since the revolution.

Of a compelling interest for our context is not primarily the content of what 'Issa says, but rather how he says what he says: the images summoned and rhetorical devices deployed in his conversation with Yunis.

'Issa invokes the Egyptian film classic *al-Layla al-Akhira* [The Last Night] by Kamal al-Shaykh from the year 1963 as a narrative vehicle to elaborate his arguments on what he perceives as the prevailing dilemma facing Egyptians since 2011.

In the film Nadia (played by Fatin Hamama) wakes up one day to find herself living in a house that is not her own, being a mother at a young age and a wife of a man she does not know. Tormented by suspicions, she refused to believe what is professed to her as her reality and adheres to a thin thread of memories that suggest a different identity and a life story. Eventually, she finds out that she has been deceived for years. An airstrike killed her sister Fawziyya and destroyed her family house many years ago, subsequently she developed amnesia. Her brother-in-law decided to use the situation for his benefit and imposed on her a false identity; she became her dead sister (Figure 14.3).

In the film's protagonist, Nadia, 'Issa and Yunis see millions of Egyptians, or they are calling Egyptians to see themselves in relation to her story. In many

Figure 14.3 Nadia (Fatin Hamama) and Shakir (Mahmud Mursi), her brother-in-law, in *al-Layla al-Akhira or The Last Night* (1963) by Kamal al-Shaykh.

episodes that will follow, Yunis and her guests endow films with referential power to comment on political events, to illustrate social conditions and to set models for thought and conduct. Film images and stories serve above all to re-tell the history of the nation, to contrast its past with its present, to envision its future and at the same time to personify its timeless character: its 'true' identity.

If nations are fictitious narratives, Egyptian films serve as tropes to narrate the nation and invest it with mythical character.[23] Since its early years, Egyptian cinema has functioned as a site for moulding a national culture, in which predominantly middle-class visions of authenticity and modernity are prescribed.[24] Maintaining civic belonging, filmic representations have figuratively characterized and contrasted 'good' versus 'bad' citizens, thus demarcating the legitimate boundaries of the national community. They delineated role models, reconfigured class and gender affiliations, adapting them to the changing logics of power over time.[25]

The story of Nadia personifies here the collectivity of Egyptians; it allegorizes the nation. The plot offers a template not only to narrate what happened to the nation but also to allegorically highlight the possibilities of a way out of what the conversation partners perceive as a puzzling conundrum or a collective amnesia.

Despite the plausible objections against his theoretical generality in conceiving of 'third-world literature',[26] Frederic Jameson's notion of 'national allegories' might be useful here. Jameson claims that in literary texts of the so-called third world the private individual destiny of literary figures always becomes an allegory of the nation, or 'of the embattled situation of culture and society'.[27] In the case under scrutiny, it is important to note that the reference at work correlates with the film text without any attempt to envisage its intention. It is a reference that dwells on transference and translation rather than interpretation, and that is precisely where the allegorical qualities of the reference reside.

Lexically, an allegory is often understood as a linguistic device that enables one to say something and mean another or communicate one thing under the mask of another.[28] An allegorical reading of *The Last Night* pushes the film beyond the confinements of meaning and time to say something else, to communicate national sentiments. What is at stake is not what the film explicitly or implicitly wanted to say, but rather how, against the grain of its text and context, it can be meaningful for the contemporary realms of circulation in which it has been evoked. As Brian Larkin has noted in his reassessment of Jameson, an allegory is not necessarily immanent to (film) texts, it is something 'placed upon them through the act of circulation'.[29] If realities of the revolution and its aftermath have 'killed imagination',[30] films as allegorical templates reactivate imagination and democratize it as a common good. Imagination is central for allegorical formations but not the imagination of the writer or director of the film, rather one that is derived 'from the movement of the text in and out of different publics'.[31] The incorporation of 'publics' as constitutive to allegoric formations would even bring us closer to the etymological origins of the term 'allegory' that combines two Greek words: '*allos*' meaning 'other' or 'different' and the verb '*agorreuin*' meaning to speak publicly or in the *agora*.

Allegories imply, moreover, a disposition towards history and time. Allegories free texts from contexts to perpetuate the former and endow it with renewing referential power. They conquer the past to reintroduce it into the present. Removed from its particularities, the past becomes, on the one hand, all-present and omnirelevant and, on the other hand, so flattened and diluted so that it can be easily penetrated by present concerns and ambitions of restoration. Films in this vein might cease to speak for their own past, or only do so in so far as their past concerns the present, to borrow Walter Benjamin's notion in the *Theses on the Philosophy of History*.[32] Nevertheless, allegorical invocation of films might bestow them with future lives that are not their own. Allegories allow one to see in a text from the past the future it would never have unfolded otherwise.[33] In a similar vein, Nadia's amnesia and loss of identity prefigure a collective loss after the revolutionary turmoil of 2011: the reality to which imagination has fallen victim. Allegories in this sense feed on imagination. Yet imagination is only set free when the past becomes malleable to allegorization; when references can be smoothly extracted from it to validate scripts of restoration and claims of identity. *Sahibet al-Sa'ada* hopes to free imagination from a confusing reality by reintroducing films as allegorical markers of identity that resist the lapse of time and prefigure the future. Jameson would call that an 'ideological function of allegory' by which subjectivities are constructed, and a utopian narrative of history is being revealed.[34] Boym would rather call it a 'restorative nostalgia', one that does not perceive itself as nostalgia, but as 'truth and tradition',[35] and 'proposes to rebuild the lost home and patch up the gaps of memories'.[36]

Finally, if nostalgia is a dialectical move that looks back to the past to envision the future while anchored in the present, the reinvention of the past is not solely about remembering but also about forgetting.

Let's go back to Nadia and take her as a reference. After living with a false identity for fifteen years, Nadia wakes up one day haunted by suspicions: How come that all of this can be real? This was the same moment when she started to regain her memories: her lost identity. Paradoxically, this same moment of reconciliation with her 'true' self marks the erasure of fifteen years of memories of her life as Fawziyya, the Cairene mother and wife. Benjamin here is again instructive. For if the past is remembered as far as it concerns the present, then every image of the past that is not recognized as such 'threatens to disappear irretrievably'.[37] Forgetting is not about producing absence but about repeatedly multiplying presence.[38] Projects of restoration are often afflicted with erasure concealed as the promise to owe happiness.

On happiness and the power to align

In Arabic, the term '*Sahibet al-Sa'ada*' is polysemic. Grammatically it is a construct state that combines two nouns: the first, *sahibet*, a feminine agent noun derived from the verb *sahaba* (to accompany) and literally means owner, friend or companion and the second is *al-sa'ada*, which means happiness. Idiomatically, the term is equivalent to the honorific designation 'excellency' given to statesmen or women, ambassadors or members of the aristocracy. *Sahibet al-Sa'ada* can thus be also translated as Her Excellency. The ambiguity conveyed in the show's name should not be taken for granted, as it allows several layers of overlapping meanings to coalesce in drawing the image of the signified object: Egypt.

The choice of happiness as a predicate for the owner – Egypt – is not arbitrary. If the first episode of the show makes clear that *sahibet al-sa'ada* is Egypt, the second episode elaborates on why Egypt owes happiness or is accompanied by happiness.[39]

The episode begins with a seemingly improvised discussion on laughter, comedy and happiness. Again, Egyptian films and filmed stage productions are evoked to exemplify forms and styles of humour and to remind us of prominent Egyptian comedians, whom Yunis calls the 'makers of happiness'. The main guest of the show is one of those, Samir Ghanim, who featured in numerous films, theatre plays and TV productions since the early 1960s. What is deemed as Egyptians' genuine capability to relish laughter and to respond to tragedies with a witty sense of humour is the central theme of the discussion. No matter how bleak the events since 2011 have been, Egyptians are cunningly able to embrace happiness in the face of misfortunes, according to Yunis and her guests. This is not to claim that Egyptians are living happily in the here and now, the argument is rather about their willingness to be happy amidst troubles. Happiness is not something they own in actuality; happiness is a promise guaranteed by an enduring sense of humour that connects their past with their future.

> Since the times of the Pharaohs [. . .] all issues are handled with laughter [and] the most strenuous sorrows trigger irony [. . .] It is the nature of our people to laugh about everything.[40]

Humour then authenticates Egypt as a nation by virtue of its resilience as a notable feature of its people. Humour characterizes a national behaviour and guarantees the continuity of a national identity over time. Nations are not only narratives but also affective practices.[41]

As scholars have previously shown, humour can have the social function of forging cohesiveness within a community whose members agree on its targets and content.[42] In the episode under scrutiny, this function is brought about in performative acts of remembering film stories and stars associated with laughter and carried out jointly by the conversation's partners who engage themselves in paroxysms of giggling while re-enacting film memories.

Yet the affective cohesiveness at work should not be conceived of in terms of an investment or a cultivation of feelings among laughers, but rather in terms of setting a common *direction* towards happiness and its makers. Sara Ahmed might be helpful here when she suggests inquiring about the *direction* of happiness: its imagined or real geographies, where it locates us and where it directs us to, as happiness is more about following and less about finding.[43] Happiness articulates as something to be expected, as a promise whose fulfilment is guaranteed when one turns towards those things that embody happiness. The promise of happiness aligns us with others in a certain way; it straightens us across established lines and around things pre-defined as objects or makers of happiness. It allows proximity and social bonding, but it does so not necessarily by disseminating feelings of compassion or attentiveness to others; rather by directing feelings to the same things that have accumulated the value of conveying happiness or making it.

An affective community is then constructed as one that shares the same feelings of the same things[44] and thus shares the same view and direction. But for us to share the same view, we must first be placed somewhere, positioned in a certain way. Ahmed also is attentive to that when she notes that happiness can become 'a stopping point' or 'provide us with a full stop', in the sense that the tautology of happiness as something self-evidently good and fundamentally necessary blocks further thoughts and questions: I desire this or that because it makes me happy, or this or that makes me happy, therefore I must desire it.[45] To turn towards those things that embody happiness, we are urged to stop and contemplate, to be seated. Another allegory from the first episode of the show encapsulates this idea. In his attempt to illustrate what went wrong after the revolution of 2011, 'Issa brings up the example of a cinema:

> You come inside the cinema, lights are off and it's dark everywhere. You need an usher to let you in, to guide you to your seat so that you don't fall. In Egypt our

problem is the usher. Our usher [since the revolution] is blind] [. . .] We are a society with no avant-garde to show you the way.⁴⁶

For ʿIssa, the blind cinema usher stands for the political elites after the revolution, the cinema for the nation and the film viewers for its people. If we want to follow up on that image, then people need to be directed, seated and placed somewhere so that the spectacle can go on.

The happy nation is a community of spectators; each needs to be in her/his proper place so that the direction can be fixed and the view can be shared. The idea of the nation as a community of spectators is also demonstrated in the visual schemes deployed in the show from the outset. The conversations with the show's guests in the main studio are often interrupted by short clips, displaying scenes from films pertinent to the conversation.

The film sequences are sometimes projected onto a graphically animated frame that resembles a cinema screen (Figures 14.4 and 14.5) and sometimes are displayed as if they are playing on an old television set. Sometimes, the television

Figure 14.4 Two animated frames from *Sahibet al-Saʿada*. At the top Hussein Fahmi in *al-Liʿb Maʿa al-Kibar* (Playing with Giants, 1991) by Sharif ʿArafa. At the bottom, the opening credits of *Wa Saqatat fi Bahr al-ʿAsal* (Caught in a Honey Trap, 1977) by Salah Abu Seif.

Figure 14.5 Two animated frames from *Sahibet al-Sa'ada*. At the top, the opening credits of *Hadduta Masriyya* (An Egyptian Story, 1982) by Youssef Chahine. At the bottom, Dalal (Huda Sultan) and Fatima (Nadia al-Gindi) in *Zawga min al-Shari'* (A Wife From The Street, 1960) by Hasan al-Imam.

sets themselves are located in public spaces; in the midst of a street, in a rural field, on a bridge, in a traditional coffee shop, or on a rooftop of a house where we can see the city in the background (Figures 14.6 and 14.7). These images preassume or imagine a specific spatial configuration; they arrange bodies in the setting of viewers aligned around the screen, directing their gazes to it, seated to share the same view. But they are also establishing screens exhibiting films as public monuments, as quotidian anchor points of public life that give orientation and conjure a sense of familiarity.

Performing memories in this sense requires a spatial imaginary that enables mediation on the one hand and emplacement and viewing on the other hand. The relationship between the nation and its subjects is figuratively reproduced as the relationship between a screen and its spectators. Cinemas become a spatial trope for the nation and TV sets showing films in public spaces summon the image of happy citizens. Indeed, the introduction of the first episode mentioned

Figure 14.6 Two animated frames from *Sahibet al-Sa'ada*. At the top Sanaa'(Mirvat Amin) in *Tharthara Fawqa al-Nil* (Chitchat on the Nile, 1971) by Husyan Kamal. At the bottom, the opening credits of *Wahda bi Wahda* (Tit for Tat, 1984) by Nadir Galal.

earlier shows Yunis happily seated in a cinema, engaging in admiration with footage of Egyptian film classics, while telling us about her relationship to Egypt, her personal friend, with whom she 'used to take photos', and at the same time she used to watch her 'on TV'.

So, if we are urged to take a seat, to align around the screen and share the view so that the promise of happiness can be fulfilled. What is the view like? Who are the makers of happiness, its friends, companions or owners, in whose bodies the soft power of the nation resides and manifests?

When Yunis describes Samir Ghanim as one of the greatest jesters and makers of happiness, she inevitably includes herself in the industry of laughter and happiness, as an actress whose major roles were in comedies. In her conversations with Ghanim – and with many other celebrities – she recalls mutual travels, mutual film shootings and other joint encounters. Egypt is not the only friend Yunis has and 'takes photos with'; or rather this friendship with Egypt implies a friendship with hundreds of stars and film professionals who featured with

Figure 14.7 Two animated frames from *Sahibet al-Sa'ada*. At the top Noha (Nadia al-Gindi) in *'Imr'ah Hazat 'Arsh Misr.* (A Women who Shook the Throne of Egypt, 1995) by Nadir Galal, at the bottom, the opening credits of *al-Sahir* (The Magician, 2001) by Radwan al-Kashif.

Yunis in numerous films and TV productions. Egypt's past and Yunis's biography intermingle in the course of recalling and performing film memories. Like *The Passage* when featuring *Platform 5*, Yunis reminds us of a film history and by proxy refers to herself; to a secular urban elite of film professionals in whose bodies the nation's soft power is manifested. We are encountered not only with film references but also with the referees. If the show unequivocally refers to *sahibet al-sa'ada* as Egypt, the title becomes the by-name of Yunis herself, given to her by her audience and guests.

Strikingly, Is'ad, the first name of Yunis, literally means 'making happy'. *Sahibet al-Sa'ada* blends the nation together with the figure of its female celebrity presenter. Such blending becomes interesting for highlighting – as previously demonstrated – the function of gendered imaginaries in constructing the nation and foregrounding the ways by which its 'soft power' manifests and maintains itself. If the nation blends in Yunis's body by the very naming of *sahibet al-sa'ada*, other female bodies of film professionals bear the features of the nation as well. One of the 2019's episodes, for example, praises the beauty of several Egyptian actresses from different generations for inheriting the eyes of old Egyptian queens and goddesses, for having 'the eyes of Egypt' in their faces.[47]

In fact, the sheer differentiation between a soft and a hard power is gendered; soft power convinces and arouses desire, whereas hard power defends and protects.

Informed and secured by such gendered dichotomy, another dichotomy or rather a split in the body of the nation in the case under scrutiny is demonstrated: the split between the viewed and the viewer; the imagined and the real; an ideal embodied in the nation's cinematic legacy, and an amnesic populace trapped in its confusing present.

By juxtaposing both the viewed and the viewer, imagination and reality *Sahibet al-Saʿada* tries to fix the same split it constantly creates. Reconciling people's present with the nation's past becomes the promise of a happy future unfolding as a spectacle of a visual nation around which the people are aligned. 'Let's fall into the arms of *sahibet al-saʿada*, tomorrow will be happier.'[48]

Conclusion: Mirrors

Ancient Nation voicing its youth.
A new age of hope where everyone had a place at the table.
[. . .] Cinema becomes reality.
Mirrors society and moulds it.
The drama of everyday life follows the script.[49]

This chapter aimed to focus on the way a certain form of power takes shape, less on the agents through which or upon which this power is exercised. It grapples with the reifications of this power in spatial imaginaries, in embodiments, in narratives about time and history that articulate national identity. In doing so, it does not necessarily take notice of possible ideological ends or political interests of certain agents.

The question posed here is on how power unfolds as a performance, how the nation draws its power to attach and align by demonstrating its tangibility as a visual nation whose fiction is capable of representing realities and offering scripts of identification.

Bringing affects and the notion of performativity into play allows the relationship between memories and discourses of identity to remain propelled by power without necessarily flattening it by linear or unidimensional conceptions.

My argument is neither to dispute the veracity of certain memories nor to suggest a 'false consciousness' of reality. It is also not about how mass culture is deployed to deceive or oppress the masses. My endeavour is rather to show how perceptions of time, reality and the nation are performatively and affectively mediated through film references.

* * *

The previous quotation stems from the editorial note of an illustrated book titled *The Golden Years of Egyptian Film* and published by the American University of Cairo in 2008. The book contains printed film stills in black and white from notable Egyptian films between 1936 and 1967. As it is evident from the quotation, the power endowed to Egyptian cinema lies in how the latter mirrors and shapes people's realities. In doing so, or rather for being able to do so, it reverses the relation between the screen and its viewers. Realities follow the (mirror) images and not vice versa, or when realities become too baffling to grasp, the screen reflects the clearer images, fixes position and gives direction. How does it become possible to mirror the same reality one shapes? Certain tricks must be enabled to resolve such a dilemma: doubling and coupling.

In *The Passage*, the screen is doubled through a film in a film, a doubling that doubles reality itself into a direct one, off-screen and a mediated one, quasi off-screen. At the same time, we are coupled with the viewing soldiers by the virtue of common film references. Despite the screen, the soldiers become a part of our reality as witnesses of the same film history, or we become all characters in a bigger spectacle.

The same counts for *The Owner of Happiness*. There, Yunis's presence itself is doubled; one resides in memories, and the other is a remembering present; one is on-screen and the other pretends to be off-screen. We are coupled with her by virtue of remembering. We are all a community of spectators, sharing or remembering the same visual references. When we are coupled with the characters of *The Passage*, we let them live a reality on our behalf, or we imagine ourselves figures in their reality. Reality when doubled is uncoupled from both the present and the claim of truth. The lived reality is not necessarily the 'true' one, as it was the case in *The Last Night*. What the screen mirrors is not reality as it is but rather as it is imagined, having been like in the past and as it is hoped to be like in the future. At the same time, our present reality remains identifiable as far as we recognize it as loss and distortion. The screen mirror at work reflects to correct; when we look at it, we do not see ourselves as we are, but as we should be; it resembles a Lacanian mirror[50] for a collective body, whose reflection brushes away fragmentation and confusion, and recognizes the nation as a powerful timeless and 'true' identity. Let's end with how the show begins. We see Yunis behind the scenes walking through corridors decorated with photographs of Egyptian film stars, before she enters her room. There she sits faced by a mirror contemplating her reflection and saying:

> This time I am not here to talk to people, I am here to talk with them. You will see both, what we are doing and what we have done [...] we will talk about our memories, but also about our baffling present, our all too baffling present that we don't know any more if it is real or imagined.[51]

Notes

1. 'Imad Safwat, 'Muntj Film *al-Mamar* Yakshif Sabab 'Ikhtiyar 'Ismuh' (The Producer of *The Passage* Reveals the Reason Behind Choosing Its Name), *al-Youm al-Sabi'*, 17 February 2019.
2. Sayyid Salam, '*al-Mamar* wa Tajdid al-Khitab al-Sinima'i' (*The Passage* and the Renewal of the Cinematic Discourse), *al-Ahram*, 17 October 2019; Muhammed al-Shamma', 'Najah al-'Ikhtiar wal-*Mamar* Namudhaj. Awdat al-Ruh lil-Quwa al-Na'ima al-Misriyya' (The Success of *The Choice* and *The Passage* is Exemplary. The Spirit of Egyptian Soft Power Returns), *Akhbar al-Youm*, 31 December 2020.
3. OnDrama, 'al-Sisi Yuwajih al-Shukr li Abtal Film *al-Mamar*' (al-Sisi Thanks the Cast of *The Passage*), *YouTube*, 13 October 12019, youtube.com/watch?v=F1M3s dtGe3s&ab_channel=ONdrama (accessed 22 December 2021).
4. Ayat al-Hadad, 'al-Mamar Tafra fi Tarikh al-Sinima' (*The Passage* is a Breakthrough in the History of Cinema), *al-Wafd*, 13 June 2019, alwafd.news/essay/43705 (accessed 22 December 2021).
5. Daniel Biltereyst, Richard Maltby and Philippe Meers, 'Cinema, Audiences and Modernity: An Introduction', in *Cinema, Audiences and Modernity: New Perspectives on European Cinema History*, ed. Daniel Biltereyst, Richard Maltby and Philippe Meers (London: Routledge, 2012), 2–3; Annette Kuhn, Daniel Biltereyst and Philippe Meers, 'Memories of Cinemagoing and Film Experience: An Introduction', *Memory Studies* 10, no. 1 (2017): 5–9.
6. Robert Allen, 'From Exhibition to Reception: Reflections on the Audience in Film History', *Screen* 41, no. 4 (Winter 1990): 394.
7. Allen, 'From Exhibition', 352.
8. It was first broadcast on the private channel CBC (2014–18) and then in DMC (since October 2018).

9   DMC, 'Sahibet al-Sa'ada, Nadir 'Abbasi, 4-11-2019', 5 November 2019', *YouTube*, https://www.youtube.com/watch?v=ATxkdLc2vDA&t=756s (accessed 22 December 2021).
10 Liedeke Plate and Anneke Smelik, 'Performing Memory in Art and Popular Culture: An Introduction', in *Performing Memory in Art and Popular Culture*, ed. Liedeke Plate and Anneke Smelik (London: Routledge, 2013), 3.
11 Alison Landsberg, *Prosthetic Memory: The Transformation of American Remembrance in the Age of Mass Culture* (New York: Columbia University Press, 2004), 31.
12 DMC, 'Sahibet al-Sa'ada. al-Naqid al-Sinma'i Kamal Ramzi, 5-11-2019' (The Owner of Happiness. Film critic Kamal Ramzi), *YouTube*, 6 November 2019, https://www.youtube.com/watch?v=zg7Ako0fWPE (accessed 22 December 2022).
13 Joseph Nye, 'Soft Power', *Foreign Policy* 80 (Autumn, 1990): 153–71.
14 Ahmad Muhammad Abu Zaid, 'al-Quwa al-Na'ima al-Misriyya bayn al-S'ud wal-taragu'' (Egyptian Soft Power Between Rise and Recession), in *Siyasat 'Arabyya* 5, November 2003, Arab Center for Research and Policy Studies, Doha, 77–8; Mahmud Duwair, *Quwat Misr al-Na'ima. al-Badayat wal-Mukawinat* (Egypt's Soft Power. Beginnings and Components) (Cairo: al-Hay'a al-'Ama lil-kitab, 2019), 30–42.
15 Abu Zaid, 'al-Quwa', 78.
16 DMC, 'Sahibet', 11 November 2019.
17 Svetlana Boym, *The Future of Nostalgia* (New York: Basic Books, 2001), xviii.
18 CBCtwo, '18.04.2014. Bid' Rihlat al-Bahth 'an Sahibet al-Sa'ada' (Beginning of the Journey to Search for the Owner of Happiness), *YouTube*, 19 April 2014. https://www.youtube.com/watch?v=BnkbOtQT9BI&list=PLFnwKc_-O1C1xnPL_R0DX3yOece8Ozl6q&index=10 (accessed 22 December 2021).
19 CBCtwo, '18.04.2014'. Italicization added.
20 Beth Baron, *Egypt as a Woman: Nationalism, Gender and Politics* (California: University of California Press, 2005); Walter Armbrust, 'Manly Men on National Stage (and the Women Who Make Them Stars)', in *Histories of the Modern Middle East. New Directions*, ed. Israel Gershoni, Hakan Erdem and Ursula Woköck (Boulder, CO: Lynne Rienner Publishers, 2002), 248–9.
21 Rim Naguib, 'The Leader as Groom, the Nation as Bride: Patriarchal Nationalism under Nasser and Sisi', *Middle East – Topics and Arguments* 14 (Gender, 2020): 52.
22 Naguib, 'The Leader as Groom', 59–60.
23 Homi K. Bhabha, 'Introduction: Narrating the Nation', in *Nation and Narration*, ed. Homi K. Bhabha (London: Routledge, 1990), 1–7.
24 Walter Armbrust, *Mass Culture and Modernism in Egypt* (Cambridge: Cambridge University Press 1996), 99–100.
25 A similar role has been also played by Egyptian *musalsalat* or TV dramas. See Lila Abu Lughod, *Dramas of Nationhood: The Politics of Television in Egypt* (Chicago: The University of Chicago Press, 2005).

26 Aijaz Ahmad, *In Theory: Class, Nations Literatures* (New York: Verso Books, 1992), 95–122.
27 Fredric Jameson, 'Third-World Literature in the Era of Multinational Capitalism', *Social Text* 15 (1986): 69.
28 Morton. W. Bloomfield, 'Varieties of Allegory and Interpretation', *Revue international de Philosophie* 41, no. 162/163 (1987): 330.
29 Brian Larkin, 'National Allegory', *Social Text* 27 (2009): 164–8.
30 CBCtwo, '18.04.2014'.
31 Brian Larkin, 'National Allegory', 165.
32 Walter Benjamin, *Illuminations, Essays and Reflections*, trans. Harry Zohn (New York: Schocken Books, 2007), 255.
33 This brings us back to the theological origins of allegorized narratives as Christian readings to the Old Testament that prefigure Christ in the chronicles of the Jewish biblical history.
34 Fredric Jameson, *Allegory and Ideology* (London: Verso Books, 2019), 36.
35 Boym, *The Future of Nostalgia*, xviii.
36 Boym, *The Future of Nostalgia*, 41.
37 Benjamin, *Illuminations*, 255.
38 Umberto Eco, 'An *Ars Oblivionalis*? Forget It!', *PMLA* 103, no. 3 (May 1988): 260.
39 CBCtwo, '25.04.2014 | Hiwar Ma'a Sani' al-Dihka Samir Ghanim # Sahibet al-Sa'ada' (A conversation with Samir Ghanim, the maker of laughter), *YouTube*, 26 April 2014, https://www.youtube.com/watch?v=kRzByRfo4Pk&t=1478s (accessed 22 December 2021).
40 CBCtwo, '25.04.2014'.
41 Michael Epp, 'The Imprint of Affect: Humor, Character and National Identity in American Studies', *Journal of American Studies* 44, no. 1 (February 2010): 48.
42 Villy Tsakona and Diana Elena Popa, 'Humour in Politics and the Politics of Humour. An Introduction', in *Studies in Political Humour: In Between Political Critique and Public Entertainment*, ed. Villy Tsakona and Diana Elena Popa (Amsterdam: John Benjamins, 2011), 46; Michael Billig, *Laughter and Ridicule. Towards a Social Critique of Humour* (London: Routledge, 2005), 194–5.
43 Sara Ahmed, *The Promise of Happiness* (Durham, NC: Duke University Press, 2010), 32.
44 Ahmed, *The Promise*, 38.
45 Ahmed, *The Promise*, 203.
46 CBCtwo, '25.04.2014'.
47 DMC 'Sahibet al-Sa'ada, Al-Nagma Safiya al-'Imary' (The Owner of Happiness | Star Safiya al-'Imary), *YouTube*, 27 February 2019, https://www.youtube.com/watch?v=7eV-MVZE41c (accessed 22 December 2021).
48 CBCtwo, '18.04.2014'.

49 Sherif Boraïe, 'Cinema Cairo', in *The Golden Years of Egyptian Film. Cinema Cairo 1936-1967*, ed. Sherif Boraïe (Cairo: AUC, 2008), 6.
50 With the 'mirror stage', French psychoanalyst Jacques Lacan designates the phase in which an infant through his/her identification with the apparently unified imago of the mirror's reflection recognizes him/herself as an 'I' or as an 'ideal ego', in contrast to a condition of bodily fragmentation and vulnerability. See Jacque Lacan, 'The Mirror Stage as Formative of the *I* Function as revealed in Psychoanalytic Experience', in *Écrits*, trans. Bruce Fink (New York: Norton, 2006), 47-81.
51 CBCtwo, 18.04.2014.

Selected Bibliography

Historical periodicals

al-Ahram
al-Jadid
al-Kashkul
al-Kawakib
al-Musawwar
al-Suwar al-Mutaharrika
Fan al-Sinima
Film Trade
Jrayed – (Arabic Newspaper Archive of Ottoman and Mandatory Palestine)
Kawakib al-Sinima
Le Progrès égyptien
Motion Picture Herald
The Moving Picture World
Variety

Online news sites

Akhbar al-Youm
Al Jazeera
AlArabiya News
al-Wafd
al-Youm al-sabi'
Arab News
Arabian Business
BBC News online
Forbes
Global Voices,
Indiewire
Jadaliyya
Khuyut
Los Angeles Times
Mada Masr

Reuters
Saudi Gazette
Saudi Press Agency
Screen Daily
The Guardian
The Hollywood Reporter
The New York Times
The Washington Post
Vice

Project websites

Aflamuna https://www.aflamuna.online/
Comra Films https://www.comrafilms.com
Metropolis Art Cinema Association https://www.metropoliscinema.net/page/home/
Network of Arab Alternative Screens (NAAS) https://www.naasnetwork.org/
The Palestinian Museum, Digital Archive. https://palarchive.org/
Parallax Haifa http://parallaxhaifa.com/

Books and articles

Aaron, Sushil J. *Straddling Faultlines: India's Foreign Policy Toward the Greater Middle East*. New Delhi: Centre de Sciences Humaines, 2003.

Abaza, Mona. *Changing Consumer Cultures of Modern Egypt: Cairo's Urban Reshaping*. Leiden; Boston: Brill, 2006.

'Abd al-Fattah, Ahmad al-Sayyid. 'al-Tabi' al-'Imrani li-Mudun al-Qana: Mirasa li Madinat al-Isma'illiya fi Qarn al-'Ishrin'. MA dissertation, Faculty of Fine Arts, Alexandria University, Alexandria, 2010.

'Abd al-Majid, Ibrahim. *Ana wal-Sinima*. Cairo: al-Dar al-Misriya al-Lubnaniya, 2018.

'Abd al-Shakur, Mahmud. *Kuntu Sabiyan Fi Al-Sab'iniyat: Sira Thaqafiya Wa-Ijtima'iya*. Cairo: al-Karma lil-Nashr wa-al-Tawzi', 2015.

'Abd al-Shakur, Mahmud. *Sinima Misr: Ziyara Jadida li Aflam Qadima*. Cairo: Tanmia, 2021.

'Abd al-Wahhab, Lutfi. *al-Masrah al-Misri, al-Mawsim al-Masrahi: 1917–1918 [The Egyptian Theatre: 1917–1918 Season]*. Cairo: National Center for Theater, Music & Folklore, 2001.

Abou Shadi, Aly, Fadel el-Aswad, and Marie-Claude Bénard. *Le Caire et le Cinéma égyptien des Années 80*. Le Caire: CEDEJ, 1990.

Selected Bibliography

Abu Jawda, 'Abudi. *Hadha Al-Masa', Al-Sinima Fi Lubnan, 1929–1979*. Beirut: al-Furat lil-Nashr wa-al-Tawzi' 2015.

Abu-Lughod, Janet L. *Cairo: 1001 Years of the City Victorious*. Princeton, NJ: Princeton University Press, 1971.

Abu Lughod, Lila. 'The Interpretation of Culture(s) After Television'. *Representations* 59 (1997): 109–34.

Abu Lughod, Lila. *Dramas of Nationhood: The Politics of Television in Egypt*. Chicago: University of Chicago Press, 2005.

Abu Zaid, Ahmed Mohamed. 'al-Quwah al-Na'imah al-Misriyya Bayn al-S'ud wa al-Taragu". *Siyasat 'Arabiyya*, Arab Centre for Research and Policy Studies, Doha 5 (November 2003): 76–91.

Abu Zayd, Rajiya Isma'il. *Tarikh Madinat al-Isma'iliya: Min al-Nash'a ila Muntasaf al-Qarn al- 'Ishrin*. Cairo: Maktabat al-Adab, 2012.

Adlakha, Siddhant. 'The Ramifications of Saudi Cinemas Opening Their Doors'. *The Village Voice*, 8 January 2018. https://www.villagevoice.com/2018/01/08/the-ramifications-of-saudi-cinemas-opening-their-doors/ (accessed 14 April 2021).

Ahmad, Aijaz. *In Theory: Class, Nations Literatures*. New York: Verso Books, 1992.

Ahmed, Sara. *The Promise of Happiness*. Durham, NC: Duke University Press, 2010.

al-Hadari, Ahmad. *Tarikh al-Sinima fi Misr: al-Juz' al-Awwal (Vol.1) min Bidayat 1896 li- Akhir 1930*. Cairo: Nadi al-Sinima, 1989.

al-Susha, Muhammad. *Ruwwad wa Ra'idat al-Sinima al-Misriyya*. Cairo: Mu'assasa Ruz al-Yusuf, 1993.

'Ali, AbdulAmeer. 'Fi Madih Dar lil-Sinima bi Baghdad'. *Jadaliyya*, 23 January 2013, https://www.jadaliyya.com/Details/27866 (accessed 15 February 2022).

'Ali, Mahmoud. *Fajr al-Sinima fi Misr [Dawn of the Cinema in Egypt]*. Cairo: Egypt Ministry of Culture, Cultural Development Fund, 2008.

'Ali, Mahmoud. 'al-Shaykh Hasan: Awal Azma Fanniyya Tuwajih Thawrat Yuliu'. *Shari'a al-Fann*, 28 October 2003.

Ali, Sahar. 'Statistical Data Collection on Film and Audio-Visual Markets in 9 Mediterranean Countries, Country Profile, 1. Egypt'. Tunis/Strasburg: Euromed Audiovisuel / Observatoire Européen de l'Audiovisuel, 2012.

Allen, Robert. 'From Exhibition To Reception: Reflections on the Audience in Film History'. *Screen* 41, no. 4 (winter 1990): 347–56.

Anishchenkova, Valerie. *Modern Saudi Arabia*. Santa Barbara, CA: ABC-CLIO, 2020.

Aramco. 'Ithra'. Report/Website: https://www.aramco.com/en/making-a-difference/people-and-community/ithra (accessed 14 April 2021).

Armbrust, Walter. 'New Cinema, Commercial Cinema, and the Modernist Tradition in Egypt'. *Alif: Journal of Comparative Poetic*, Arab Cinematics: Towards the New and the Alternative 15 (1995): 81–129.

Armbrust, Walter. *Mass Culture and Modernism in Egypt*. Cambridge, England: Cambridge University Press, 1996.

Armbrust, Walter. 'When the Lights Go down in Cairo: Cinema as Secular Ritual'. *Visual Anthropology (Journal)* 10, no. 2–4 (1998): 413–42.

Armbrust, Walter, *Mass Mediations New Approaches to Popular Culture in the Middle East and Beyond*. Berkeley, CA: University of California Press, 2000.

Armbrust, Walter. 'The Golden Age Before the Golden Age: Commercial Egyptian Cinema Before the 1960s'. In *Mass Mediations: New Approaches to Popular Culture in the Middle East and Beyond*, edited by Walter Armbrust, 292–329. Berkeley, CA: University of California Press, 2000.

Armbrust, Walter. 'Colonizing Popular Culture or Creating Modernity? Architectural Metaphors and Egyptian Media'. In *Middle Eastern Cities, 1900–1950*, edited by Hans Chr. Korsholm Nielsen and Jakob Stovgaard-Petersen, 20–43. Gylling: Aarhus University Press, 2001.

Armbrust, Walter. 'Manly Men on the National Stage (and the Women who make them stars)'. In *Histories of the Modern Middle East: New Directions*, edited by Israel Gershoni, Hakan Erdem and Ursula Woköck, 247–79. Boulder, CO: Lynne Rienner Publishers, 2002.

Armbrust, Walter. 'The Rise and Fall of Nationalism in the Egyptian Cinema'. In *Social Constructions of Nationalism in the Middle East*, edited by Fatma Müge Göçek, 217–50. Albany, NY: State University of New York, 2002.

Armbrust, Walter. 'Audiovisual Media and History of the Arab Middle East'. In *Middle East Historiographies: Narrating the Twentieth Century*, edited by Israel Gershoni, Amy Singer and Y. Hakan Erdem, 288–313. Seattle and London: University of Washington Press, 2006.

Armbrust, Walter. 'The Ubiquitous Nonpresence of India. Peripheral Visions from Egyptian Popular Culture'. In *Global Bollywood: Travels of Hindi Song and Dance*, edited by Sangita Gopal and Sujata Moorti, NED-New edition, 200–20. University of Minnesota Press, 2008.

Armbrust, Walter. 'Political Film in Egypt'. In *Film in the Middle East and North Africa*, edited by Josef Gugler, 228–53. Austin, TX: University of Texas Press, 2011.

Armes, Roy. *Third World Film Making and the West*. Berkeley, CA: University of California Press, 1987.

Armes, Roy. *New Voices in Arab Cinema*. Bloomington, IN: Indiana University Press, 2015.

Armes, Roy. *Roots of the New Arab Film*. Bloomington, IN: Indiana University Press, 2018.

Arnold, Robert. 'The Architecture of Reception'. *Journal of Film and Video* 37, no. 1 (Winter 1985): 36–47.

Askari, Kaveh and Samhita Sunya. 'Introduction: South by South/West Asia: Transregional Histories of Middle East–South Asia Cinemas'. *Film History* 32, no. 3 (2020): 1–9.

Asseraf, Arthur. *Electric News in Colonial Algeria*. Oxford: Oxford University Press, 2019.

Athique, Adrian, and Douglas Hill. *The Multiplex in India: A Cultural Economy of Urban Leisure*. New York: Routledge, 2010.

Ayman, Alia. 'The Artist as Bureaucrat: Documentary Filmmaking in Egypt, 1960–1980s'. *American Ethnological Society*, 18 August 2019, https://americanethnologist.org/features/reflections/the-artist-as-bureaucrat (accessed 15 February 2022).

Azab, Rasha and Sherif Boraie. *Dream Factory on the Nile: Pierre Sioufi Collection of Egyptian Cinema Lobby Cards*. New York: American University in Cairo Press, 2020.

Bahout, Joseph. 'Dubaï-Beyrouth: l'ombre et son double'. *Esprit* 11 (2006): 76–85.

Barbara, Hiba and Tamás Molnár. 'Towards Understanding the Colonial Heritage in Algeria: The Case of the Sheridan Villa'. *Pollack Periodica: An International Journal for Engineering and Information Sciences* 14, no. 1 (2019): 223–34.

Barlet, Olivier. 'The Ambivalence of French Funding'. *Black Camera* 3, no. 2 (2012): 205–16.

Baron, Beth. *Egypt as a Woman: Nationalism, Gender and Politics*. Oakland, CA: University of California Press, 2005.

Battegay, Alain. 'Dubaï : Économie Marchande et Carrefour Migratoire. Étude de Mise En Dispositif'. In *Mondes En Mouvements: Migrants et Migrations Au Moyen-Orient Au Tournant Du XXIe Siècle*, edited by Françoise Métral and Hana Jaber. Beyrouth: IFPO, 2005.

Bayram al-Tunisi, Mahmud. *Bayram al-Tunisi: al-A'mal al-Kamila*. Cairo: Maktabat Madbuli, 2002.

Behi, Ridha. Interview by Patricia Caillé in la Marsa, 17 February 2020.

Bel Hédi, Habib. Interview by Patricia Caillé in Tunis, 12 November 2017.

Ben Achour, Mohammed El-Fadhel. *Le mouvement littéraire et intellectuel en Tunisie*. Tunis: Alif, 1998.

Bénard, Marie-Claude. *La Sortie Au Cinéma : Palaces Et Ciné-Jardins d'Égypte: 1930–1980*. Marseille: Éditions Parenthèses, 2016.

Benchenna, Abdelfettah, Patricia Caillé, Nolween Mingant (ed.). 'La circulation des films: Afrique du Nord et Moyen-Orient'. *Africultures* 101–102 (2016).

Benjamin, Walter. *Illuminations: Essays and Reflections*, trans. Harry Zohn. New York: Schocken Books, 1968.

Bhabha, Homi K. 'Introduction: Narrating the Nation'. In *Nation and Narration*, edited by Homi K. Bhabha, 1–7. London: Routledge, 1990.

Billig, Michael. *Laughter and Ridicule: Towards a Social Critique of Humour*. London: Sage, 2005.

Biltereyst, Daniel and Daniela Treveri Gennari. *Moralizing Cinema: Film, Catholicism, and Power*. London: Taylor and Francis, 2014.

Biltereyst, Daniel, Richard Maltby and Philippe Meers. 'Cinema, Audiences and Modernity: An Introduction'. In *Cinema, Audiences and Modernity: New Perspectives on European Cinema History*, edited by Daniel Biltereyst, Richard Maltby and Philippe Meers, 1–17. London: Routledge, 2012.

Biltereyst, Daniel, Richard Maltby and Philippe Meers. *Cinema, Audiences and Modernity: New Perspectives on European Cinema History*. London: Routledge, 2012.

Biltereyst, Daniel, Richard Maltby, and Philippe Meers (eds). *The Routledge Companion to New Cinema History*. London; New York: Routledge, 2019.

Blewitt, John. 'Film, Ideology, and Bourdieu's Critique of Public Taste'. *The British Journal of Aesthetics* (October 1993): 367–72.

Bloomfield, Morton W. 'Varieties of Allegory and Interpretation'. *Revue international de Philosophie* 41, no. 162/163 (1987): 329–46.

Boraïe, Sherif. 'Cinema Cairo'. In *The Golden Years of Egyptian Film: Cinema Cairo 1936–1967*, edited by Sherif Boraïe, 6–7. Cairo: AUC, 2008.

Bornkamm, Henriette. *Orientalische Bilder und Klänge: Eine transnationale Geschichte des frühen ägyptischen Tonfilms*. Marburg: Schüren Verlag, 2021.

Boym, Svetlana. *The Future of Nostalgia*. New York: Basic Books, 2001.

British Council/Nordicity. 2020. *Report: "Saudi Film Skills"* https://www.britishcouncil.sa/sites/default/files/saudi_film_skills_research_-_english_version.pdf (accessed 14 April 2021).

Bruslé, Tristan, and Aurélie Varrel. 'Introduction. Places on the Move: South Asian Migrations through a Spatial Lens'. Edited by Tristan Bruslé and Aurélie Varrel. *South Asia Multidisciplinary Academic Journal* 6 (December 28, 2012).

Bsheer, Rosie. *Archive Wars: The Politics of History in Saudi Arabia*. Paolo Alto, CA: Stanford University Press, 2020.

Caillé, Patricia. 'Amateur Filmmaking in Tunisia: A Political Film Culture Eliding Contradictions in National Cinema'. In *Cinema in the Arab World: Contemporary Direction in Theory and Practice*, edited by Terri Ginsberg and Chris Lippard, 89–123. London: Palgrave MacMillan, 2020.

Caillé, Patricia and Lamia Guiga. 'Pratiques des films au regard de l'offre et de la demande dans la Tunisie urbaine aujourd'hui'. In *Pratiques et usages du film en Afriques francophones: Maroc, Tchad, Togo, Tunisie*, edited by Patricia Caillé and Claude Forest, 33–100. Villeneuve d'Ascq : Septentrion, 2019.

Carlier, Omar. 'Medina and Modernity: The Emergence of Muslim Civil Society in Algiers Between the Two World Wars'. In *Walls of Algiers: Narratives of the City Through Text and Image*, edited by Zeynep Çelik, Julia Clancy-Smith, and Frances Terpak, 62–84. Los Angeles: The Getty Research Institute; Seattle, WA: University of Washington Press, 2009.

Çelik, Zeynep. 'Colonial/Postcolonial Intersections: *Lieux de mémoire* in Algiers'. *Historical Reflections/Réflexions Historiques* 28, no. 2 (2002): 143–62.

Centre Interarabe du Cinéma et de la Télévision. *Cinéma et Cultures Arabes: IVème Conférence de La Table Ronde Organisée Avec l'aide Technique de l'UNESCO*. Beirut: n/a, 1965.

Cheriaa, Tahar. 'Africa: Rivista trimestrale di studi e documentazione dell'Instituto italiano per l'Africa et l'Oriente'. *Anno* 28, no. 3 (September 1973): 431–38.

Cheriaa, Tahar. *Écrans d'abondance ou Cinéma de libération en Afrique ?* Tunis: SATPEC, 1978.

Ciecko, Anne. 'Cinema "of" Yemen And Saudi Arabia: Narrative Strategies, Cultural Challenges, Contemporary Features'. *Wide Screen* 3, no. 1 (June 2011): 1–16.

Clancy-Smith, Julia. 'Exoticism, Erasures, and Absence: The Peopling of Algiers, 1830–1900'. In *Walls of Algiers: Narratives of the City Through Text and Image*, edited by Zeynep Çelik, Julia Clancy-Smith, and Frances Terpak, 19–61. Los Angeles: The Getty Research Institute; Seattle, WA: University of Washington Press, 2009.

Cohen, Jean-Louis. 'Architectural History and the Colonial Question: Casablanca, Algiers, and Beyond'. *Architectural History* 49 (2006): 349–72.

Cormack, Raph. *Midnight in Cairo: The Divas of Egypt's Roaring '20s*. New York: W. W. Norton & Company, Inc., 2021.

Corriou, Morgan. 'Des ciné-clubs aux Journées Cinématographiques de Carthage. Entretien avec Tahar Cheriaa'. *Maghreb et Sciences Sociales 2009–2010* (2010): 163–74.

Corriou, Morgan. 'Un nouveau loisir en situation coloniale : le cinéma dans la Tunisie du protectorat'. PhD dissertation, Université Paris Diderot-Paris 7, Paris, 2011.

Corriou, Morgan. 'Un nouveau loisir en situation coloniale: Le cinéma dans la Tunisie du Protectorat (1896–1956)'. PhD dissertation, Université de Paris 7, 2011.

Corriou, Morgan. '"Le choix entre l'Orient et l'Occident?" Les Tunisiens et le cinéma dans les dernières années du protectorat français (1946–1956)'. In *Cultures d'Empires: Échanges et affrontements culturels en situation coloniale*, edited by Romain Bertrand, Hélène Blais and Emmanuelle Sibeud, 171–96. Paris: Karthala, 2015.

Corriou, Morgan. 'La France coloniale et le spectateur "indigène": histoire d'une incompétence cinématographique'. *MEI – Médiation et information* 49 (2020): 63–77.

Crisp, Colin. *The Classic French Cinema, 1930–1960*. Bloomington, IN: Indiana University Press, 1997.

Dager, Nick. 'Muvi Opens Saudi Arabia's First Digital Cinema'. *Digital Cinema Report*, 3 August 2020. https://www.digitalcinemareport.com/article/muvi-opens-saudi-arabias-first-dolby-cinema (accessed 14 April 2021).

Darwish, Mustafa. 'al-Riqaba wa al-Sinima al-'Ukhra: Shahada Raqib'. *Alif: Journal of Comparative Poetics* 15 (1995): 91–8.

Dewhurst Lewis, Mary. *Divided Rule: Sovereignty and Empire in French Tunisia, 1881–1938*. Berkeley, CA: University of California Press, 2013.

Dickinson, Kay. *Arab Cinema Travels: Transnational Syria, Palestine, Dubai and Beyond*. London: BFI, 2016.

Dickinson, Kay. *Arab Film and Video Manifestos Forty-Five Years of the Moving Image Amid Revolution*. Cham: Springer International Publishing, 2018.

Dimitris, Eleftheriotis and Dina Iordanova. 'Introduction'. *South Asian Popular Culture* 4, no. 2 (2006): 79–82.

Dönmez-Colin, Gönül. *The Cinema of North Africa and the Middle East*. London: Wallflower Press, 2007.

du Roy, Gaétan. 'Union des Corps et Civilités Urbaines : Shubrā ou le Cosmopolitisme au Petit écran'. In *Culture Pop en Egypte: Entre Mainstream Commercial et Contestation*, edited by Frédéric Lagrange and Richard Jacquemond, 129–56. Paris: Riveneuve, 2020.

Dwyer, Rachel. 'Bollywood's Empire: Indian Cinema and the Diaspora'. In *Routledge Handbook of the South Asian Diaspora*, edited by Joya Chatterji and David A. Washbrook, 407–16. London: Routledge, 2013.

Eco, Umberto. 'An *Ars Oblivionalis*? Forget It!'. *PMLA* 103, no. 3 (May 1988): 254–61.

Ehrlich, Evelyn. *Cinema of Paradox: French Filmmaking Under the German Occupation*. New York: Columbia University Press, 1985.

El Khachab, Chihab. 'The Sobky Recipe and the Struggle over "the Popular" in Egypt'. *Arab Studies Journal* (2019): 34–61.

El Khachab, Chihab. *Making Film in Egypt: How Labor, Technology, And Mediation Shape The Industry*. Cairo: American University in Cairo Press, 2021.

El Shakry, Omnia. 'History without Documents'. *The American Historical Review* 120, no. 3 (2015): 920–34.

Elouardaoui, Ouidyane. 'The Crisis of Contemporary Arab Television: Has the Move towards Transnationalism and Privatization in Arab Television Affected Democratization and Social Development?'. *Global Societies Journal* 1, no. 1 (2013): 100–14. https://escholarship.org/uc/item/13s698mx (accessed 14 April 2021).

Elsadda, Hoda. *Gender, Nation and the Arabic Novel in Egypt: 1892–2008*. Edinburgh: Edinburgh University Press, 2012.

El Safoury, Nour (ed.). *Mapping Cinema Audiences*. Cairo: Network of Arab Alternative Screens, 2018.

Elsaket, Ifdal. 'Projecting Egypt: Cinema and the Making of Colonial Modernity, 1896–1952'. PhD dissertation, University of Sydney, 2013.

Elsaket, Ifdal. 'Sound and Desire: Race, Gender, and Insult in Egypt's First Talkie'. *International Journal of Middle East studies* 51, no. 2 (2019): 203–32.

Epp, Michael. 'The Imprint of Affect: Humor, Character and National Identity in American Studies'. *Journal of American Studies* 44, no. 1 (February 2010): 47–65.

Erdogan, Nezih. 'The Making of Our America: Hollywood in a Turkish Context'. In *Hollywood Abroad: Audiences and Cultural Exchange*, edited by Melvyn Stokes and Richard Maltby. London: BFI, 2007.

Fahmy, Ziad. *Street Sounds: Listening to Everyday Life in Modern Egypt*. Stanford, CA: Stanford University Press, 2020.

Fair, Laura. *Reel Pleasures: Cinema Audiences and Entrepreneurs in Twentieth-Century Urban Tanzania*. Athens, OH: Ohio University Press, 2018.

Falicov, Tamara L. 'The Festival Film: Film Festivals as Cultural Intermediaries'. In *Film Festivals: History, Theory, Method, Practice*, edited by Marijke de Valck, Brendan Kredell, and Skadi Loist, 209–29. Routledge, 2016.

Farid, Samir. *Tarikh al-Raqaba ʿala al-Sinima fi Misr*. Cairo: al-Maktab al-Misri li-Tawziʿ al-Matbuʿat, 2002.

Farine, Anaïs. 'Imaginaires cinématographiques du ' dialogue euro-méditerranéen ' (1995–2017): formes festivalières, formes institutionnelles, formes alternatives'. PhD dissertation, Université de Paris 3, 2019.

Fathi, Samih. *The Art of Egyptian Film Posters*, trans. Siham 'Abd al-Salam. Cairo: The American University in Cairo Press, 2014.

Fathi, Samih. *Classic Egyptian Movies: 101 Must-See Films*, trans. Sarah Enany. Cairo: The American University in Cairo Press, 2018.

Fathi, Samih. *Ihsan 'Abd al-Qaddus Bayna al-Adab wa-al-Sinima*. Cairo, 2018.

Fawzi, Naji. *Al-Markaz al-Kathuliki al-Masri li-l-Sinima wa Khamsun 'Aman min al-Thaqafa al-Sinima'iyya*. Cairo: al-Markaz al-Kathuliki, 1999.

Fiske, John. *Understanding Popular Culture*. London: Routledge, 1989.

Flibbert, Andrew J. 'State and Cinema in Pre-Revolutionary Egypt, 1927–1952'. In *ReEnvisioning Egypt: 1919–1952*, edited by Arthur Goldschmidt, Amy J. Johnson, and Barak A. Salmoni, 448–65. Cairo: American University in Cairo Press, 2005.

Flibbert, Andrew J.. *Commerce in Culture: States and Markets in the World Film Trade*. New York: Palgrave Macmillan, 2007.

Foley, Sean. *Changing Saudi Arabia: Art, Culture, and Society in the Kingdom*. London; Boulder, CO: Lynne Rienner Publishers, 2019.

Fowler, Bridget. 'Bourdieu, Field of Cultural Production and Cinema: Illumination and Blind Spots'. In *New Uses of Bourdieu in Film and Media Studies*, edited by Guy Austin. New York; Oxford: Berghahn Books, 2016.

Gennari, Daniela Treveri, Danielle Hipkins and Catherine O'Rawe. *Cinema Outside the City: Rural Cinema-Going from a Global Perspective*. New York: Palgrave, 2018.

Gershoni, Israel. 'The Reader-"Another Production": The Reception of Haykal's Biography of Muhammad and the Shift of Egyptian Intellectuals to Islamic Subjects in the 1930s'. *Poetics Today* 15, no. 2 (1994): 241–77.

Gershoni, Israel and James P. Jankowski. *Redefining the Egyptian Nation, 1930–1945*. Cambridge: Cambridge University Press, 2002.

Ghannam, Farha. *Remaking the Modern Space, Relocation, and the Politics of Identity in a Global Cairo*. Berkeley, CA: University of California Press, 2002.

Ghawanmeh, Mohannad. 'Entrepreneurship in a State of Flux: Egypt's Silent Cinema and Its Transition to Synchronized Sound, 1896–1934'. PhD dissertation, UCLA, Los Angeles, 2020.

Ginsberg, Terri, and Chris Lippard. *Historical Dictionary of Middle Eastern Cinema*. Lanham, MD: The Rowman & Littlefield Publishing Group, 2010.

Ginsberg, Terri, and Chris Lippard. *Cinema of the Arab World: Contemporary Directions in Theory and Practice*. Cham: Springer International Publishing, 2020.

Goerg, Odile. 'Les films arabes, une menace pour l'Empire ? La politique des films arabes à la veille des indépendances en Afrique Occidentale française'. *Outre-mers* 100, no. 380–381 (2013): 295–7.

Goerg, Odile. *Tropical Dream Palaces: Cinema in Colonial West Africa*. London: Hurst & Company, 2020.

Gonzales-Quijano, Yves and Guaaybess Tourya (eds). *Les Arabes parlent aux Arabes: La révolution de l'information dans le monde arabe*. Arles: Actes Sud, 2009.

Gordon, Joel. 'Pop Culture Roundup'. *International Journal of Middle East Studies* 50, no. 4 (2018): 787–94.

Grabar, Henry S. 'Reclaiming the City: Changing Urban Meaning in Algiers after 1962'. *Cultural Geographies* 21, no. 3 (2014): 389–409.

Graebner, Seth. 'Contains Preservatives: Architecture and Memory in Colonial Algiers'. *Historical Reflections/Réflexions Historiques* 33, no. 2 (2007): 257–76.

Guaaybess, Tourya. 'Les bouquets satellitaires et le développement du système télévisuel arabe'. *INA, la Revue des Médias*, 4 November 2011.

Guaaybess, Tourya. *Les médias arabes: Confluences médiatiques et dynamique sociale*. Paris: CNRS, 2012.

Gürata, Ahmed. 'Tears of Love: Egyptian Cinema in Turkey (1938–1950)'. *New Perspectives on Turkey* 30 (2004): 55–82.

Habermas, Jürgen. *The Structural Transformation of the Public Sphere: An Inquiry into a Category of Bourgeois Society*. Cambridge: Polity Press, 1989.

Hammond, Alexander. *Popular Culture in the Arab World: Arts, Politics, and the Media*. Cairo: The American University in Cairo Press, 2007.

Harabi, Najib. 'Creative Industries: Case Studies from Arab Countries'. *Developing Knowledge Economy Strategies to Improve Competitiveness in the MENA Region*, World Bank Institute, 17–21 May 2009, Alexandria Egypt. Accessible online on Munich Personal RePEc Archive, MPRA Paper no. 15628: https://mpra.ub.uni-muenchen.de/15628/

Hark, Ina Rae (ed.). *Exhibition: The Film Reader*. London: Routledge, 2001.

Harris, Lauren Carroll. 'Film Distribution as Policy: Current Standards and Alternatives'. *International Journal of Cultural Policy* 24, no. 2 (2018): 236–55.

Hasan, Manar and Ami Ayalon. 'Arabs and Jews, Leisure and Gender, in Haifa's Public Spaces'. In *Haifa Before & After 1948 - Narratives of a Mixed City*, edited by Mahmoud Yazbak and Yfaat Weiss, 69–98. Dordrecht: Republic of Letters.

Hayek, Ghenwa. 'Where to? Filming Emigration Anxiety in Prewar Lebanese Cinema'. *International Journal of Middle East Studies* 51, no. 2 (May 2019): 183–201.

Hayek, Ghenwa. 'Locating the Lost Archive of Arab Cinema'. *Regards – Revue Des Arts Du Spectacle* 26 (30 October 2021): 15–19.

Haykel, Bernard, Thomas Hegghammer, and Stephane Lacroix (eds). *Saudi Arabia in Transition: Insights on Social, Political, Economic and Religious Change*. Cambridge: Cambridge University Press, 2015.

Hayoun, Massoud. *When We Were Arabs: A Jewish Family's Forgotten History*. New York: The New Press, 2019.

Herf, Jeffrey. *Nazi Propaganda for the Arab World*. New Haven, CT: Yale University Press, 2009.

Higbee, Will, Florence Martin and Jamal Bahmad, *Moroccan Cinema Uncut: Decentred Voices, Transnational Perspectives*. Edinburgh: Edinburgh University Press, 2020.

Highmore, Ben. 'Taste as Feeling'. *New Literary History* 47, no. 4: 547–66.
Higson, Andrew. 'The Concept of National Cinema'. *Screen (London)* 30, no. 4 (1989): 36–47.
Hjort, Mette. *Small Nation, Global Cinema*. Minneapolis, MN: University of Minnesota Press, 2005.
Hjort, Mette and Duncan Petrie (eds). *The Cinema of Small Nations*. Bloomington, IN: Indiana University Press, 2007.
Iordanova, Dina with contributions from Juan Goytisolo, Ambassador K. Gàjendra Singh, Rada [Sbreve]e[sbreve]ić, Asuman, Suner, Viola Shafik and P.A. Skantze. 'Indian Cinema's Global Reach'. *South Asian Popular Culture* 4, no. 2 (2006): 113–40.
Iordanova, Dina and Stefanie Van de Peer (eds). *Film Festivals and the Middle East*. St Andrews: St Andrews Film Studies, 2014.
Irving, Sarah. 'Gender, Conflict, and Muslim-Jewish Romance: Reading 'Ali Al-Muqri's The Handsome Jew and Mahmoud Saeed's The World through the Eyes of Angels'. *Journal of Middle East Women's Studies* 12, no. 3 (2016): 343–62.
Jameson, Fredric. 'Third-World Literature in the Era of Multinational Capitalism'. *Social Text* 15 (1986), 65–88.
Jansen, Jan C. 'Celebrating the "Nation" in a Colonial Context: "Bastille Day" and the Contested Public Space in Algeria, 1880–1939'. *The Journal of Modern History* 85, no. 1 (2013): 36–68.
Jansen, Jan C. 'Fête et ordre colonial: Centenaires et résistance anticolonialiste en Algérie. Pendant les années 1930'. *Vingtième Siècle: Revue d'histoire* 121 (2014): 61–76.
Jewell, Catherine. 'Transforming Arab Cinema with MAD Solutions'. *World Intellectual Property Organization, WIPO Magazine*, October 2017. https://www.wipo.int/wipo_magazine/en/2017/05/article_0004.html (accessed 15 February 2022).
Keller, Kathleen. *Colonial Suspects: Suspicion, Imperial Rule, and Colonial Society in Interwar French West Africa*. Lincoln, NE: University of Nebraska Press, 2018.
Khalili, Laleh. 'The Politics of Pleasure: Promenading on the Corniche and Beachgoing'. *Environment and Planning: Society & Space* 34, no. 4 (2016): 583–600.
Khashoggi, Jamal. 'What Saudi Arabia Can Learn From 'Black Panther''. *The Washington Post*, 17 April 2018. https://www.washingtonpost.com/news/global-opinions/wp/2018/04/17/what-saudi-arabia-can-learn-from-black-panther/ (accessed 14 April 2021).
Khatib, Lina. 'The Orient and its Others: Women as Tools of Nationalism in Egyptian Political Cinema'. In *Women and Media in the Middle East: Power Through Self-expression*, edited by Naomi Sakr, 72–89. London: Bloomsbury, 2004.
Khatib, Lina. *Filming the Modern Middle East: Politics in the Cinemas of Hollywood and the Arab World*. London; New York: I.B. Tauris, 2016.
Khidr, Muhammad. *al-Kiyanat al-Sinimaiyah al-Kubra fi Misr Ba'da al-Khaskhasah*. Giza: Akadimiyat al-Funun, 2006.
Khlifi, Omar. *Le cinéma en Tunisie*. Tunis: Société Tunisienne de Diffusion, 1970.

Kholoussy, Hanan. 'Stolen Husbands, Foreign Wives: Mixed Marriage, Identity Formation and Gender in Colonial Egypt'. *Hawwa* 1, no. 2 (2003): 206–40.

Kholoussy, Hanan. 'Interfaith Unions and Non-Muslim Wives In Early Twentieth-Century Alexandrian Islamic Courts'. In *Untold Histories of the Middle East: Recovering Voices From the 19th and 20th Centuries* edited by Amy Singer, Christoph Neumann and Selçuk Aksin Somel, 54–70. London: Routledge, 2011.

Khouri, Malek. *Arab National Project in Youssef Chahine's Cinema*. Cairo: American University in Cairo Press, 2010.

Kirtikar, Margo. *Once Upon a Time in Baghdad*. Bloomington, IN: Xlibris, 2011.

Koelbl, Susanne. *Behind the Kingdom's Veil: Inside the New Saudi Arabia Under Crown Prince Mohammad Bin Salman*. Coral Gables, FL: Mango Publishing, 2019.

Koning, Anouk de. *Global Dreams: Class, Gender, and Public Space in Cosmopolitan Cairo*. Cairo: The American University in Cairo Press, 2009.

Kraidy, Marwan. *Reality Television and Arab Politics: Contention in Public Life*. Cambridge: Cambridge University Press, 2010.

Kraidy, Marwan. 'Saudi-Islamist Rhetorics about Visual Culture'. In *Visual Culture in the Modern Middle East*, edited by Christiane Gruber and Sune Haugbolle, 275–92. Bloomington, IN: Indiana University Press, 2013.

Kuhn, Annette. *An Everyday Magic: Cinema and Cultural Memory*. London: I.B. Tauris, 2002.

Kuhn, Annette. 'Heterotopia, Heterochronia: Place and Time in Cinema Memory'. *Screen (London)* 45, no. 2 (2004): 106–14.

Kuhn, Annette, Biltereyst, Daniel, and Meers, Philippe. 'Memories of Cinemagoing and Film Experience: An Introduction'. *Memory Studies* 10, no. 1 (2017): 3–16.

Laachir, Karima. 'Sectarian Strife and "National Unity" in Egyptian Films: A Case Study of Hassan and Morqos'. *Comparative Studies of South Asia, Africa and the Middle East* 31, no. 1 (2011): 217–26.

Lacan, Jacques. 'The Mirror Stage as Formative of the / Function as Revealed in Psychoanalytic Experience'. In *Écrits*, trans. Bruce Fink, 47–81. New York: Norton, 2006.

Landau, Jacob. *Studies in the Arab Theater and Cinema*. Philadelphia, PA: University of Pennsylvania Press, 1958.

Landsberg, Alison. *Prosthetic Memory: The Transformation of American Remembrance in the Age of Mass Culture*. New York: Columbia University Press, 2004.

Lang, Robert. *New Tunisian Cinema*. New York: Columbia University Press, 2014.

Larkin, Brian. 'National Allegory'. *Social Text* 27 (2009): 164–8.

Le Renard, Amélie. 'Engendering Consumerism in the Saudi Capital: A Study of Young Women's Practices in Shopping Malls'. In *Saudi Arabia in Transition: Insights on Social, Political, Economic and Religious Change*, edited by Bernard Haykel, Thomas Hegghammer, and Stephane Lacroix, 314–31. Cambridge: Cambridge University Press.

Lebow, Alisa. 'Filming Revolution: Approaches to Programming the 'Arab Spring''. In *Film Festival Yearbook 6: Film Festivals and the Middle East*, edited by Dina Iordanova and Stefanie Van de Peer, 61–74. St Andrews: STAFS, 2014.

Lerner, Daniel. *The Passing of Traditional Society, Modernizing the Middle East*. Glencoe: Free Press, 1958.
Leveratto, Jean-Marc. 'Histoire du cinéma et expertise culturelle'. *Politix* 16, no. 61 (2003): 17–50.
Lim, Song Hwee. 'Taiwan New Cinema: Small Nation with Soft Power'. In *The Handbook of Chinese Cinemas*, edited by Carlos Rojas and Eileen Cheng-yin Chow, 152–69. Oxford: Oxford University Press, 2013.
Limbrick, Peter. *Arab Modernism as World Cinema: The Films of Moumen Smihi*. Berkeley, CA: University of California Press, 2020.
Lindeperg, Sylvie. *Les écrans de l'ombre: La Seconde Guerre mondiale dans le cinéma français, 1944–1969*. Paris: Éditions Points, 1997.
Liotta, Alfio. 'Small Nations and the Global Dispersal of Film Production: A Comparative Analysis of the Film Industries in New Zealand and the United Arab Emirates'. *The Political Economy of Communication* 2, no. 2 (2014). https://www.polecom.org/index.php/polecom/article/view/36/234 (accessed 14 April 2021).
Lobato, Ramon. 'Subcinema: Theorizing Marginal Film Distribution'. *Limina* 16 (2007): 131–20.
Lobato, Ramon. *Shadow Economies of Cinema: Mapping Informal Film Distribution*. London: Palgrave Macmillan BFI, 2012.
Maatouk, Tamara Chahine. *Understanding the Public Sector in Egyptian Cinema: A State Venture*. Cairo: American University in Cairo Press, 2019.
Macauley, Scott. 'The Jeddah Visual Show Festival'. *Filmmaker Magazine*, 17 July 2006, https://filmmakermagazine.com/2426-the-jeddah-visual-show-festival/#.YgpBG1VBwrg (accessed 14 February 2022).
Maingard, Jacqueline. 'Cinemagoing in District Six, Cape Town, 1920s to 1960s: History, Politics, Memory'. *Memory Studies* 10, no. 1 (1 January 2017): 17–34.
Maltby, Richard. 'How Can Cinema History Matter More?' *Screening the Past* 22 (2007), http://www.screeningthepast.com/issue-22-tenth-anniversary/how-can-cinema-history-matter-more/ (accessed 27 February 2022).
Maltby, Richard, and Melvyn Stokes (eds). *Hollywood Abroad: Audiences and Cultural Exchange*. London: BFI Publishing, 2004.
Maltby, Richard, Daniel Biltereyst and Philippe Meers. *Explorations in New Cinema History: Approaches and Case Studies*. Malden, MA: Wiley-Blackwell, 2011.
Maltby, Richard, Melvyn Stokes and Robert C. Allen (eds). *Going to the Movies: Hollywood and the Social Experience of Cinema*. Exeter: University Press, 2014.
Mankekar, Purnima. 'National Texts and Gendered Lives: An Ethnography of Television Viewers in a North Indian City'. *American Ethnologist* 20, no. 3 (1993): 543–63.
Mar'i, Farida. *Sihafat al-Sinima fi Misr: al-Nisf al-Awwal min al-Qarn al-'Ishrin*. Cairo: Egyptian Film Centre, 1996.
Mar'i, Farida. *Turath al-Nuqqad al-Sinima'iyyin fi Misr: Kitabat al-Sayyid Hasan Jum'a, 1–3*. Cairo: Markaz al-Qawmi lil-sinima, 1997.

Mar'i, Farida and May al-Tilmisani. 'Majallat "Kawakib al-sinima"'. In *Sahafat al-Sinima fi Misr: al-Nisf al-awwal min al-Qarn al-'Ishrn*, edited by Farida Mar'i, 249–62. Cairo: Egyptian Film Center, 1996

Marchal, Roland, Fariba Adelkhah, and Sari Hanafi. *Dubaï: Cité Globale. Espaces et milieux*. Paris: CNRS, 2001.

Markovits, Claude François. *The Global World of Indian Merchants (1750–1947): Traders of Sind from Bukhara to Panama*. Cambridge; New York: Cambridge University Press, 2000.

Martin, Florence. 'Tunisia'. In *The Cinemas of Small Nations*, edited by Hjort Mette and Duncan Petrie, 213–28. Edinburgh: University Press, 2008.

Mattelart, Tristan (ed.). *Piratages Audiovisuels : les Voies Souterraines de la Mondialisation Culturelle*. Bruxelles, Belgique, France: De Boeck, 2011.

Mayeur-Jaouen, Catherine. 'Le Vatican II des Catholiques Égyptiens: Au temps de Nasser, l'Espoir d'un Monde Meilleur'. *Archives de Sciences Sociales des Religions* 175 (2016): 361–86.

Mayeur-Jaouen, Catherine. *Voyage en Haute-Egypte: Prêtres, Coptes et Catholiques*. Paris: CNRS Éditions, 2019.

McDougall, James. *A History of Algeria*. Cambridge: Oxford University Press, 2017.

Mehrez, Samia. *Egypt's Culture Wars: Politics and Practice*. London: Routledge, 2008.

Mellor, Noha. 'Arab Cinema'. In *Arab Media*, edited by Noha Mellor, Muhammad Ayish, Nabil Dajani, and Khalil Rinnawi, 103–22. Cambridge; Malden, MA: Polity Press, 2011.

Melnick, Ross. 'A Long Ride on the Metro: Metro News, Hearst Metrotone Inc., and U.S. Studio-Government Relations'. In *Rediscovering U.S: Newsfilm: Cinema, Television, and the Archive*, edited by Mark Cooper, Sara Levavy, Ross Melnick, and Mark Williams, 186–203. New York: AFI Film Readers; Routledge, 2018.

Memmi, Albert. *Portrait du colonisé; précédé de Portrait du colonisateur*. 1957. Paris: Gallimard, 2002.

Mérigeau, Pascal. *Jean Renoir: A Biography*, trans. Bruce Benderson. Philadelphia, PA: Ratpac Press; Running Press, 2017.

Mernissi, Fatima. *Dreams of Trespass: Tales of a Harem Girlhood*. Cambridge: Perseus Books, 1995.

Mingant, Nolwenn. 'When the *Thief of Bagdad* Tried to Steal the Show: The Short-Lived Dubbing of Hollywood Films into Arabic in the 1940s'. In *Reassessing Dubbing: Historical Approaches and Current Trends*, edited by Irene Ranzato and Serenella Zanotti, 42–61. Amsterdam: John Benjamins, 2019.

Montebello, Fabrice. 'Films égyptiens et ouvriers algériens dans la Lorraine industrielle. Analyse d'un cas de 'diaspora des publics''. In *Publics et spectacle cinématographique en situation coloniale*, edited by Morgan Corriou, 273–316. Tunis: IRMC, CERES, 2012.

Motadel, David. *Islam and Nazi Germany's War*. Cambridge: Belknap Press of Harvard University Press, 2014.

Mubarak, Salma and Walid al-Khachab. *Al-Iqtibas: Min al-Adab ila al-Sinima*. Cairo: Dar al-Maraya, 2021.

Mzali, Mohamed Salah. *Au fil de ma vie: souvenirs d'un Tunisien*. Tunis: H. Mzali, 1972.

Naguib, Rim. 'The Ideological Deportation of Foreigners and "Local Subjects of Foreign Extraction" in Interwar Egypt'. *Arab Studies Journal* 28, no. 2 (2020): 6–44.

Naguib, Rim. 'The Leader as Groom, the Nation as Bride: Patriarchal Nationalism under Nasser and Sisi'. *Middle East – Topics and Arguments* 14 (2020): 40–56.

Neidhardt, Irit. 'Untold Stories'. *Westminster Papers in Communication and Culture* 7, no. 2 (2010): 31–50.

Nizami, Khaliq Ahmad. 'Early Arab Contact with South Asia'. *Journal of Islamic Studies* 5, no. 1 (1994): 52–69.

Nolwenn, Mingant. 'Un public aux mille visages: Identifier l'expérience des spectateurs du cinéma américain dans le Maghreb de l'ère coloniale'. In *Regarder des films en Afriques*, edited by Patricia Caillé and Claude Forest. Villeneuve d'Ascq: PU du Septentrion, 2017.

Nye, Joseph. 'Soft Power'. *Foreign Policy* 80 (Autumn, 1990): 153–71.

Nye, Joseph S. *Soft Power: The Means to Succeed in World Politics*. New York: Public Affairs, 2005.

Olsen, Pelle Valentin. '*Al-Qahira-Baghdad*: The Transnational and Transregional History of Iraq's Early Cinema Industry'. *Arab Studies Journal* 29, no. 2 (Fall 2021): 8–33.

Olsen, Pelle Valentin. 'Iraqi Cinema Beyond the Screen and the Archives of Leisure'. *Regards–Revue des arts du spectacle* 26 (2021): 129–41.

Oruc, Firat. 'Petrocolonial Circulations and Cinema's Arrival in the Gulf'. *Film History* 32, no. 3 (Fall 2020): 10–42.

Oruc, Firat. '"Cinema Programmes" of the British Public Relations Office in the Persian Gulf, 1944–1948'. *Film History (New York, N.Y.)* 32, no. 3 (2020): 197–209.

Oualdi, M'hamed, and Noureddine Amara (ed.). 'La nationalité dans le monde arabe des années 1830 aux années 1960. Négocier les appartenances et le droit'. *Revue des mondes musulmans et de la Méditerranée* 137 (2015).

Patil, S. K. 'The Year in Retrospect. An Annual Survey of the Film Industry by Leading Spokesmen'. *Filmfare*, 16 March 1956.

Plate, Liedeke and Smelik, Anneke. 'Performing Memory in Art and Popular Culture: An Introduction'. In *Performing Memory in Art and Popular Culture*, edited by Plate, Liedeke and Smelik, Anneke, 1–22. London: Routledge, 2013.

Rashid, Rawiya. *Yusuf Wahbi: Sanawat al-Majd wa al-Dumu*. Cairo: Dar El Shuruq, 2016.

Reynolds, Nancy. *A City Consumed: Urban Commerce, the Cairo Fire and the Politics of Decolonization in Egypt*. Stanford, CA: Stanford University Press, 2012.

Risner, Jonathan. 'Constellated Gatekeepers: Distribution as Metaculture and Distributors as a 'Real' Audience'. *New Cinemas*, 16, no. 2 (2018): 131–42.

Risso, Patricia. 'India and the Gulf: Encounters from the Mid-Sixteenth to the Mid-Twentieth Centuries'. In *The Persian Gulf in History*, edited by Lawrence G. Potter. 189–206. New York: Palgrave Macmillan, 2009.

Rosenberg, Clifford. 'The International Politics of Vaccine Testing in Interwar Algiers'. *The American Historical Review* 11, no. 3 (2012): 671–97.

Ryad, Umar. *Islamic Reformism and Christianity: a Critical Reading of the Works of Muhammad Rashid Rida and his Associates (1898–1935)*. Leiden: Brill, 2009.

Ryzova, Lucie. *The Age of the Efendiyya: Passages to Modernity in National-Colonial Egypt*. Oxford: Oxford University Press, 2014.

Ryzova, Lucie. 'The Good, the Bad, and the Ugly: Collector, Dealer and Academic in the Informal Used-paper Markets of Cairo'. In *Archives, Museums and Collecting Practices in the Modern Arab World*, edited by Sonia Mejcher-Atassi and John-Pedro Schwartz, 93–120. London: Ashgate Press, 2016.

Sadoul, Georges (ed.). *Les Cinémas des Pays Arabes*. Beyrouth: Centre Interarabe du Cinéma et de la Télévision, 1966.

Sadoul, Georges. *The Cinema in the Arab Countries*. Beirut: Interarab Centre of Cinema and Television, 1966.

Saglier, Viviane. '"Not-Yet" an Industry: The Temporalities of Contemporary Palestinian Cinema'. In *Cinema of the Arab World: Contemporary Directions in Theory and Practice*, edited by Terri Ginsberg and Chris Lippard, 125–46. Cham: Springer International Publishing, 2020.

Said, Edward. 'In Memory of Tahia'. *London Review of Books* 21, no. 21 (28 October 1999); https://www.lrb.co.uk/the-paper/v21/n21/edward-said/in-memory-of-tahia (accessed 15 February 2022).

Sakr, Naomi. 'Women and Media in Saudi Arabia: Rhetoric, Reductionism and Realities'. *British Journal of Middle Eastern Studies* 35, no. 3 (2008): 385–404.

Sakr, Naomi. 'Placing Political Economy in Relation to Cultural Studies: Reflections on the Case of Cinema in Saudi Arabia'. In *Arab Cultural Studies*, edited by Tarik Sabry, 214–33. London: I.B.Tauris, 2012.

Salah al-Din, Muhammad. *Al-Din wa-l-Aqida fi al-Sinima al-Misriyya*. Cairo: Maktaba Madbouli, 1998.

Salah, Nahed. *Husayn Sidqi al-Multazim*. Cairo: Mahragan al-Qahira al-Sinima'iyya, 2014.

Segrave, Kerry. *American Films Abroad: Hollywood's Domination of the World's Movie Screens From The 1890's To The Present*. London: McFarland, 1997.

Segrave, Kerry. *Piracy in the Motion Picture Industry*. Jefferson, NC: McFarland and Co. 2003.

Shafik, Viola. *Popular Egyptian Cinema: Gender, Class and Nation*. Cairo: The American University in Cairo Press, 2006.

Shafik, Viola. *Arab Cinema: History and Cultural Identity*, revised and updated edition. Cairo: American University in Cairo Press, 2016.

Shaheen, Jack. *Reel Bad Arabs: How Hollywood Vilifies a People*. Northampton, MA: Interlink Publishing, 2012.

Sharkey, Heather. *American Evangelicals in Egypt: Missionary Encounters in an Age of Empire*. Princeton, NJ: Princeton University Press, 2008.

Singerman, Diane, and Paul Amar. *Cairo Cosmopolitan: Politics, Culture, and Urban Space in the New Globalized Middle Eas*. Cairo: American University in Cairo Press, 2006.

Smoodin, Eric. *Paris in the Dark: Going to the Movies in the City of Light, 1930–1950*. Durham, NC: Duke University Press, 2020.

Snedeker, Rick. *3,001 Arabian Days: Growing up in an American Oil Camp in Saudi Arabia (1953–1962)*. New York: Station Square Media, 2018.

Srour, Némésis. 'Bollywood Film Traffic: Circulations des films hindis au Moyen-Orient (1954–2014)'. MA dissertation, Ecole des Hautes Etudes en Sciences Sociales (EHESS), 2018.

Starr, Deborah A. *Togo Mizrahi and the Making of Egyptian Cinema*. California: University of California Press, 2020.

Stoler, Ann Laura. *Along the Archival Grain: Epistemic Anxieties and Colonial Common Sense*. Princeton, NJ: Princeton University Press, 2010.

Sunya, Samhita. 'On Location: Tracking Secret Agents and Films, between Bombay and Beirut'. *Film History* 32, no. 3 (2020): 105–40.

Suwayd, Muhammad. *Ya Fu'adi: Sirah Sinima'iyah 'an Salat Bayrut al-Rahilah*. Bayrut, Lubnan: Dar al-Nahar, 1996.

Tallima, Essam. *Hasan Al-Banna wa Tajrubat al-Fann*. Cairo: Maktaba Wahba, 2008.

Tamam, Hussam. *Tahawwulat al-Ikhwan al-Muslimin: Tafakkuk al-Idiyuluji wa Nihayat al-Tanzim*. Cairo: Maktaba Madbouli, 2010.

Thomas, Martin. *Empires of Intelligence: Security Services and Colonial Disorder after 1914*. Berkeley, CA: University of California Press, 2008.

Thompson, Elizabeth F. 'Politics by Other Screens: Contesting Movie Censorship in the Late French Empire'. *Arab Media and Society*, no. 7 (Jan. 2009), https://www.arabmediasociety.com/politics-by-other-screens/ (accessed 15 February 2022).

Thompson, Elizabeth F. *Colonial Citizens: Republican Rights, Paternal Privilege and Gender in French Syria and Lebanon*. New York: Columbia University Press, 2000.

Thompson, Elizabeth F. 'Sex and Cinema in Damascus: The Gendered Politics of Public Space in a Colonial City'. In *Middle Eastern Cities, 1900–1950*, edited by Hans Chr. Korsholm Nielsen and Jakob Stovgaard-Petersen, 89–111. Gylling: Aarhus University Press, 2001.

Thompson, Elizabeth F. 'Scarlett O'Hara in Damascus: Hollywood, Colonial Politics, and Arab Spectatorship during World War II'. In *Globalizing American Studies*, edited by Brian T. Edwards and Gaonkar Dilip Parameshwar, 184–208. Chicago: University of Chicago Press, 2010.

Thompson, Elizabeth. 'Boycott d'un cinéma à Fès en 1948'. In *Publics et spectacle cinématographique en situation coloniale*, edited by Morgan Corriou, 181–200. Tunis: IRMC, CERES, 2012.

Thompson, Kristin. *Exporting Entertainment: America in the World Film Market, 1907–1934*. London: British Film Institute, 1985.

Tsakona, Villy and Elena Popa, Diana. 'Humour in Politics and the Politics of Humour. An Introduction'. In *Studies in Political Humour: In Between Political Critique and Public Entertainment*, edited by Tsakona, Villy and Elena Popa, Diana, 1–32. Amsterdam: John Benjamins, 2011.

Unesco. *Importation of Films for Cinema And Television In Egypt: A Study*. Communication and Society 7. Paris: Unesco, 1981.

Vande Winkel, Roel and David Welch (eds). *Cinema and the Swastika: The International Expansion of Third Reich Cinema*. New York: Palgrave Macmillan, 2007.

Vermeulen, Pieter, Stef Craps, Richard Crownshaw, Ortwin De Graef, Andreas Huyssen, Vivian Liska, and David Miller. 'Dispersal and Redemption: The Future Dynamics of Memory Studies – A Roundtable'. *Memory Studies* 5, no. 2 (2012): 223–39.

Vitalis, Robert. 'American Ambassador in Technicolor and Cinemascope: Hollywood and Revolution on the Nile'. In *Mass Mediations: New Approaches to Popular Culture in the Middle East and Beyond*, edited by Walter Armbrust, 269–91. Berkeley, CA: University of California Press, 2000.

Vitalis, Robert. *America's Kingdom: Mythmaking on the Saudi Oil Frontier*. Redwood, CA: Stanford University Press, 2006.

Wahbi, Yusuf. *Ishtu Alf 'Am: Mudhakkirat Fannan al-Sha'b Yusuf Wahbi*. Cairo: Dar al-Ma`arif, 1973.

Wald, Ellen R. *Saudi, Inc.: The Arabian Kingdom's Pursuit of Profit and Power*. New York: Pegasus Books, 2018.

Walters, Meir M. 'Censorship as a Populist Project'. PhD dissertation, Graduate School of Arts and Sciences, Georgetown University, Washington DC, 2016.

Zekkour, Afaf. 'Les lieux de sociabilité islahistes et leurs usages: la ville d'Alger (1931–1940)'. *Le Mouvement Social* 236 (2011): 23–34.

Index

14 January revolution   179, 192
'123 Years of Cinema' (episode)   257–9
1973 war   140, 143
2011 revolution   184

Aan (*Pride*, 1954)   121, 123
aashra   217, 219 n.10
Abbasi, Nadir   257, 258
Abbass, Hiam   206
Abbout Productions   198, 211
'Abd al-Aziz, Karim   144, 146
Abd al-Aziz Al Saud (king)   228
'Abd al-Magid, Mahmud   150, 160, 163
'Abd al-Quddus, Ihsan   168
'Abd al-Shakur, Mahmud   150, 154, 158, 169, 173 n.17
Abdi, Nidam   37
'Abdin, Hurriya   124
Abu-Lughod, Janet   173 n.28
Abyad, Dawlat   104
Abyad, George   84
Academy Awards   226
A.C.E.   74
Actualités Françaises   34
Adhoua: Lumières du cinéma   183
advertisements   16, 123, 231
aesthetics   28, 52, 53, 95, 188
   visual   109
affective community   265
Afghanistan   63
Aflamuna   10, 14, 198, 211–17
African films/cinemas   184, 196
AfricArt   177, 179, 188
Afrique française du Nord (AFN, French North Africa)   30, 32, 33, 35
Afrita Hanim (Little Miss Devil, 1949)   36, 39
Agence tunisienne de films (Tunisian Film Agency)   32
Agora   185
Agricultural Development Bank   136

Ahmed, Sara   265
Akhir Kidba (*The Last Lie*, 1950)   36
al-Abriya' (*The Innocent*, 1944)   96
al-Afrang (foreigners) neighbourhood   135, 138
al-Ahli Cinema   137
al-Ahram   99, 100
al-'Amil (*The Worker*,1943)   96
al-Arabia Cinema Company   144
al-Azhar   99, 107
al-'Azima (*Resolution*, 1939)   96
Alexandria   64, 84, 87, 93, 123, 151, 160, 163
al-Express   85
al-Fanfar Club   136
Algeria   30, 32–4, 37, 47, 48, 51, 54, 55, 57, 58, 63
   Algiers   32, 33, 35, 47–51, 182
   cinema bureau   33
   Communist party   54
   Muslims   27, 37
Alhambra cinema   49, 56, 57, 67, 160, 163
Al Hamra cinema   188
al-Hurriya (Liberty) Cinema   137, 138, 141, 142, 147
'Ali, Mahmud   84
al-Jumhuriyya Cinema (the Republic Cinema)   139
al-Kashkul   83, 89
al-Kawakib   97, 99
al-Layla al-Akhira (The Last Night, 1963)   261–3, 271
allegory   112, 259–65
Allégret, Marc   50
Allen, Robert   257
Alliance Israélite Universelle   44 n.57
Allied and Axis   12, 62–4, 66–71, 76, 78
al-Limbi (2002)   149 n.12
All Quiet on the Western Front (1930)   56
al-Mahhta al-Jadida neighbourhood   139, 142

al-Mamar (*The Passage*, 2019)   254–7, 269, 271
al-Mu'ayad   85
al-Musawwar   89
al-Muthalath (Triangle) Café   137
al-Nasr (Victory) Cinema   142
al-Sabah   89
al-Sinima al-Sharqi (Eastern Cinema)   90 n.5
al-Ta'awun Cinema (The Co-operative Cinema)   135–7, 142–3
al-Ta'awun Garden Cinema (The Co-operative Garden Cinema)   136–7, 139, 141, 142
al-Ta'mir (Construction) Club Cinema   141
Amar circus   56
amateur films   183
AMC
  Cinema   234
  Entertainment Holding   232
  Theatres   230–2
American Cosmograph   85
American films. *See* Hollywood
American University of Cairo   271
Amilcar   188
Amir, Aziza   9
Amman   128
Amreeka (2009)   198
Andoni, Raed   198
Andrews, Julie   165
Anglo-Egyptian treaty (1936)   67
animation   225
  animated films   51, 224
Ankara   72
Annales Africaines   47
Antar bin Shadad   168
anthropology   94
anti-Allied sentiment   68
anti-Semitic films   75
anti-Semitism   44 n.57, 68, 73, 75
Arab alternative screen culture   245–7, 250, 252
Arab cinema   6, 10, 137, 147, 184, 199, 217, 252
  Arabic-speaking region   63, 65, 67
  audiences for   65, 129, 204, 207, 216, 252

centralized distributors   200
contemporary   208, 215
culture   203, 205
distribution and exhibition   14, 195, 196, 198, 200–3, 208, 246, 252
DOCmed   211
exhibitors   198, 244, 245, 248–50
history   206
independent   212, 214
industry   204, 205
market   127–9, 204
national and international distribution of   195–8, 208
production   208
studies   10–16
Arab Cinema Center (ACC)   205
Arab Cinema Lab   205
Arab Film Distribution (AFD)   200
Arab Fund for Arts and Culture (AFAC)   247
Arabian American Oil Company   221
Arabic Acting House (*Dar al-Tamthil al-'Arabi*)   84
Arabic language   30, 31, 39
Arabisance   51
Arab-Israeli conflict (1967)   123
Arab-Israeli war (1948)   97, 232
Arab modernism   52
Arab neighbourhood (al-Mahatta al-Jadida)   135, 139
arabophone Levantines   103, 104
Arab Radio and Television Network (ART)   227
Arab-speaking public sphere   38–9
Arab Spring   177, 233
'Arafa, Sharif   254
'Arayshiyat al-'Abid (slave quarters)   139, 149 n.6
'Arayshiyat Misr   139
archives   3, 5, 7, 8, 12, 42 n.31, 94, 106, 107, 111, 119 n.55, 217, 221, 223, 251, 252
'Are we all Fedayeen?' programme   211
Armbrust, Walter   6, 116 n.11, 151
Armes, Roy   207
Aron, Adam   232
arrêté résidentiel   30–1
Ar-Sinemasi   76
Artaud, Antonin   50

Arthouse Convergence 244
arthouse films 197, 212, 246
Artify 191
Art Nouveau Colisée 185
Ashkal Alwan (The Lebanese Association for Plastic Arts) 217, 219 n.10
Asseraf, Arthur 8
Association of Catholic Schools 110
al-Atrash, Farid 36, 137
Attia, Mohamed Ben 181
audience(s). *See also under* Arab cinema; Egyptian film(s); Egyptian women; European; film(s); foreign (*khawaja*); metropolitan; North Africa(n); Turkish cinema/film(s); Western
   community-making 246
   community of spectators 226, 256, 258, 267, 271
   family 30
   film festival 206
   German 74
   indigenous 31
   Maghrebi 29
   mixed-gender 87
   stigmatization 31
   TV 147
Au fil de ma vie: souvenirs d'un Tunisien (Mzali) 44 n.62
auteur films 185, 188, 189
authenticity 94, 262
Awlad al-Dhawat (*Sons of Aristocrats*, 1932) 102–4, 112
Ayam Beirut 211, 212, 216, 217
Ayouch, Nabil 197
Ayub, Ibrahim 136
Azbakiya Theatre 82

Bab al-Hadid (*Cairo Station*, 1958) 39
Bab al-Luq 156, 170
Baccar, Selma 181
Bachchan, Amitabh 124, 127
Badi 'Subhi 124
Baida family 35, 38
Baker, Josephine 50
Baki, Fadi 213
balconies 52, 53, 85, 87, 135, 143, 144, 153, 161, 162
Barajoun Entertainment 225

Barakah Meets Barakah (2016) 234
Barbette 50
Bastille Day events 54
Baur, Harry 50
Bavaria 74
Behna Brothers 32, 34
Beirut 121, 122, 125, 127–9, 225
Beirut Cinema Platform 211
Beirut DC 14, 211–13, 216, 217, 218 n.7
Bella, Ahmed Ben 37
belly dances 36, 39
Ben Ali, Zine El Abidine 177
Ben Ammar, Hichem 187, 188
Bénard, Marie-Claude 150
Ben Chaabane, Tarek 188
Benjamin, Walter 263
Benlyazid, Farida 197, 209 n.35
Bennani, Mohamed 40 n.5
Bensimon, André 33
Bensimon, Pierre 33
Benzakour 35
Berlin 63, 72
Bernard, Raymond 56
Bilal: A New Breed of Hero (2015) 225
bin Faisal, Turki 229
bin Salman, Mohammad 225, 228–31
bin Talal, Al-Waleed 225, 229
Black Panther (2018) 231, 232, 234
Black Scorpion, The (1957) 1, 2
Blanche-Neige et les sept nains (*Snow White and the Seven Dwarfs*, 1937) 51
blockbuster films 147, 234
Blum-Byrnes agreements (1946) 30
BluRays 185, 193 n.4
Bollywood films 10, 13, 128
   Arab film market and Dubai monopoly 127–9
   circulation, Arab merchants' circuits and shadow economies in Gulf 125–7, 129, 130
   in Egypt 122–4, 128, 129
   industry 121, 122
Boman Sinema Filmleri 73
Bombay 126, 129
Bombay film company 121, 128
Bonjour Alger (1930) 50
Bonnafous, Jean-Marie 40 n.5
Bornkamm, Henriette 65

298 Index

Bouazizi, Mohamed   177
Bouchnak, Abdelhamid   181
Bouhid, Jamila   168
Boulane, Ahmed   196
Bourdieu, Pierre   231
box-office hits   31, 57, 128, 145, 191, 192, 201
Boym, Svetlana   259, 263
Breathless (1983)   164
Britain   62–4, 71, 78, 83
British colonial rule   65
British Council   234
British film(s)   66, 68, 69, 76, 123
  companies   64
  industry   66
British Mandate   66
British military   93
British Troops camp   139
Broadway Cinema   137–9, 142, 143
Brothers troupe   84
Bulgaria   77

Cairene American Cosmograph cinema   87
Cairo   47, 64, 65, 84, 85, 87, 89, 93, 122, 123, 128, 129, 140, 141, 145, 151, 159, 163
Canal Sur   197
Cannes Film Festival   126, 234
Captain Underpants: The First Epic Movie (2017)   230
Carioca, Tahia   7
Carthage Film Festival (JCC)   39, 184, 188
cartoons   155, 156, 223
Casablanca   47, 51, 57
Casbah   48, 49
casinos   47, 52, 53, 56, 57
Catholicism
  Catholic attitudes   105
  Catholic ethics   106
  Catholic Film Center (CFC)   12, 94, 105–7, 111–14, 119 n.54(55) 120 n.61
  Catholic Youth Association   119 n.56
  Lay Catholics   105
Cemberli-tasch   74
censorship   12, 27, 31, 33, 42 n.31, 75, 94, 95, 105–8, 110, 111, 114, 119 n.51, 232, 233

Center for Government Communication (CGC)   235
Centre national du cinéma et de l'image (CNCI)   179, 185, 187, 191
C'est Paris (1930)   50
Cette vieille canaille (1933)   50
Chaabini, Hamouda   32
Chahine, Youseff   39, 168
Chaplin, Charlie   47, 88
Chbabek El Janna (*Borders of Heaven*, 2014)   181
Cheriaa, Tahar   36, 181, 184
Chikhaoui, Tahar   183
childhood memories   154–5
Chopra, Yash   128
Chor Bazaar   125
Christian (*masihi*)   103, 107, 111
  education   106
  indigenous   104
  missions   104, 106, 111
  and Muslim differences   93
  women   112
Christianity   103, 108, 111, 112
Cinapses Labs   249
Ciné7èmeArt   185
Cine 350   187
cine-clubs   188
Cinécrits   183
Cinefils   188
cinema(s). See also film(s)
  backyard cinemas   221
  clean cinema   136
  commercial   187, 250, 251
  commercialism   96
  community-funded   251
  Dolby   230
  downtown   124, 151, 164, 186, 187
  Fascist   69
  first-class   123, 146, 160
  Grand Rex   47
  Mediterranean cinema   211
  non-Western   29
  not-for-profit cinemas   250
  one-screen cinemas   179, 184
  online   211, 252
  pan-Arab   14, 196, 244
  paraphernalia   7
  popular   137, 200
  provincial   52

summer   141, 142, 160, 161
theatre owners   144, 145
travelling   182
upper-market   155, 162
Cinema al Fouad   211, 216
Cinema al-Hadaiq   161
Cinema and I, The ('Abd al-Magid)   150
Cinema and the Swastika: The International Expansion of Third Reich Cinema (Vande Winkel and Welch)   62
'Cinema Audiences' (poem)   158
Cinema Club   164
Cinema Concordia   165
CinéMadart   184, 188
Cinema Diana   162
Cinema di Partito Nazionale Fascista (Cinema for the National Fascist Party)   63
Cinema Dunya   138, 143, 147
Cinema Exhibition Manager   181
cinema-going   10, 187, 189
   children   153–6
   cultures   151
   experiences   12, 152, 153, 159, 167, 170, 257
   memories   150, 152, 154–5, 158, 160, 167–70
   practices   151
   as secular ritual   151
Cinema Karim   124
Cinema Modern   124
Cinema Odeon   164
Cinema of the Arab World (Ginsberg and Lippard)   7
Cinema Planets (*Kawakib al-Sinima*)   84, 89
Cinema Plaza   165
Cinema Radio   159
Cinema Rivoli   162, 165
cinémas d'exclusivité   57
Cinematheque Beirut   211, 218 n.1
Cinémathèque de Tanger   251
Cinémathèque tunisienne   187
cinematic
   cinematographic exchanges   122
   convoy   154
   experiences   151, 161, 171, 228, 258
   hegemony   39

ideology   64
independence   27, 32
infrastructure   62, 65
literacy   153
movement   47
products   222
propaganda   62, 64
realism   95
representations   112, 114
visibility   224
Cinemoz   213
Cinephilia
   community   36
   film culture   188
Ciné-Soir   32
Cité de la culture   179, 181, 187, 188
civic space   252
Civil War   127
Clair, René   48, 49
class distinctions   151
Coca-Cola   231, 232, 241 n.72
code du cinéma   182
Cold War   78, 258
Colisée cinema   49, 182, 184
colonialism   4, 12, 30, 54, 55, 69, 205
   administration   27–9, 33, 37
   anti-colonial cinema   97
   anti-colonial movement   104
   anti-colonial nationalism   107
   anti-colonial struggles   96, 97
   anti-missionary sentiment   104
   anti-Nazi films   65
   archives   9
   cinema   49–51
   colonization   67, 182
   control   54, 77
   discourse   29
   domination   94
   economics   32–5, 39
   legacies   62, 68
   power   29, 36, 58, 112
   project   53–5
   quasi-colonial status   48
   repression   38
   violence   103
Commissaire Général du Centenaire   55
communism
   films   78
   passion   29

Comœdia 54
Comra Films 9, 244, 252
Confessions of a Nazi Spy (1939) 65
Constituent National Assembly 177
Continental 74
co-production 196, 200, 226
Coptic Church 120 n.57
    Coptic Catholic Patriarch of
        Alexandria 110
    Coptic Christians 93, 104
    Orthodox Church 95, 110, 111,
        114
copyright issues 179
Cormack, Raphael 8
Corriou, Morgan 182
Covid-19 pandemic 147, 148, 172 n.11,
    179, 184, 190, 191, 198, 212–13,
    217, 234, 249
creative industries 201
Crédit Lyonnais 55
Crémieux decree 44 n.57
Croy, Homer 90 n.5
culture(al)
    affinity 72
    Arab culture 55, 205
    Arab-Muslim culture 28
    control 53
    diplomacy 247
    disqualification 36
    economy 249
    entrepreneurs 184, 185
    entrepreneurship 250, 251
    events 50, 51, 54
    films 74
    imperialism 27
    initiatives 202, 220, 246, 251
    magazines 88
    policy 195, 196, 247, 248
    politics 95
    proximity 130 n.3
    relations 28
    representation 111
    studies 27, 94
Culture and Arts Society 230
Culture Resource (*Al-Mawred
    Al-Thaqafy*) 247
curation 217–18
currency issue 32
customs duties 32

Dabis, Cherien 198
Dachra (2017) 181
Dammam Literary Club 224
Dar al-Salam 82
Darfeuil, Colette 102
debates 12, 94, 102, 111, 114, 118 n.38,
    183, 195
decentralization 214–15
decolonization 94, 95, 106
Délégation générale 33
DeMille, Cecil B. 100
Der Postmeister, Madame Bovary
    (1940) 75
Der Unsterbliche Walzer (1939) 75
Desai, Manmohan 121, 124
Deutsche Soldatenkinos (German Soldier
    Cinemas) 63
Deutsche Wochenschau (German Weekly
    Newsreel) 68, 75
dhikr 99
Dhoom 3 (2013) 128, 129
Diab, Maher 203–7
diaspora 128, 129, 205
    pro-diaspora policy 128
Dickinson, Kay 8, 199
digital technology 185
    DCP projector 185
    digital exhibition practices 10
D III 38 (1939) 75
al-Din, Muhammad Salah 117 n.28
Direction de la Sûreté publique
    (Directorate for Public
    Security) 28
Disney 155–6, 231, 232
Disney, Walt 51
distribution 1, 62, 64, 68, 70–2, 75,
    106, 122. *See also* Tunisian film
    distribution and exhibition
    Arab cinema 14, 195–8, 200–3, 208,
        246, 252
    channels 32
    direct state measures 202
    distributor films 199–203, 206
    Egyptian film 27, 32–6, 39, 144
    European 196
    German cinema 73
    Indian cinema 122, 129
    Nazi cinema 62, 64
    Saudi cinema 220–3, 225–9, 233, 235

documentaries 224, 225, 234, 235
Dollar Film Production Company 143, 144
domestic
  film 28, 82
  market 32
  politics 107
Dönme 73
Door to the Sky (1989) 197, 209 n.35
Douglas, Kirk 165
Douglas Fairbanks 16
DreamWorks Animation 230
Dubai 121, 122, 127-9, 208
Dubai film market 128
Dubai International Film Festival (DIFF) 127, 199
Dubai Media City (DMC) 127
Dubai media industry 127, 130
dubbed films 65, 76, 185
Du Plessy, Armand 88
Durchhaltepropaganda (perseverance propaganda) 75
du Roy, Gaétan 114
Duvivier, Julien 50
Dyer, Kevin 7

early cinema 82
  early industrial era 12, 82, 83, 87, 88
  magazines 87-9
early Islamic history (*islamiyyat*) 100
Écrans d'abondance (Cheriaa) 181
EDAC 188
Eden Cinema 16
education 84-6
  films 72
  mission 245
Egypt 15, 29, 30, 33, 36, 63-7, 95, 98, 103, 106, 114, 121, 151, 152, 167, 169, 201, 208, 215, 244, 254, 256, 259, 264, 265, 268, 269
  Christian churches 110
  cosmopolitanism 64
  government 65, 123, 124
  Hindi films in 122-5, 128, 129
  Liberation Committee 123
  press 82, 110
  studios 39
  theatres (*al-Tiyatru al-Misri*) 83-6, 88, 123, 124, 146, 151

Egyptian Chamber of Cinema 124
Egyptian Christians 103, 104, 110-12
Egyptian film(s) 11, 16, 37, 38, 43 n.41, 64, 67, 94, 96, 100, 106, 111, 124, 127, 140, 162, 165, 170, 182, 183, 189, 215, 222, 254-7, 262, 264, 271
  audiences 29, 30, 82, 83, 86, 95, 150
  development 29
  distribution 27, 32-6, 39, 144
  early 95, 96
  exhibition 31, 136-41
  feature 28
  genre 179, 185
  history 134, 150, 167
  industry 6, 27, 30, 66, 221
  performance of memory 257-9
  productions 27, 33, 89, 144, 147
  trade 33-6, 38, 39
  Ufa Wochenschau footage 64
Egyptian Gazette 131 n.15
Egyptianization 96, 113
Egyptian Railway Company Cinema 141
Egyptian women 82, 102
  as audiences 12, 83-9
  empowerment 83, 84
  morals and virtue 88
  patronage 83, 85, 88, 89
  as stage performers 87
El Jaida (2017) 181
El Khadra 182
Elsadda, Hoda 101, 102
Elsaket, Ifdal 102, 112, 114, 123
El Sobky Company 144
Emo, E. W. 75
Emoji Movie, The (2017) 230
Empire cinema 49, 51-3
Empire Entertainment 128
entertainment 30, 39, 57, 66, 68, 72, 75, 78, 84, 86, 88, 140, 152, 153, 168, 169, 184, 203, 222
Erbil 128
Erdogan, Nezih 77
Erses, Necip 73-6
Ethiopia 68
ethnographic approach 94, 114
Euro-American domination 4
Euro-Mediterranean dialogue 211
Europa Cinemas 244
Europe 47, 51, 53, 62, 70, 151, 200

European
  audiences 52, 135
  colonial elites 65
  culture 96
  distribution networks 196
  festivals network 199
  film(s) 29, 30, 37, 189
  women 103
exhibition 46, 47, 49–51, 57, 58, 62, 64, 68, 71, 72, 82–5, 122, 135, 222, 245. *See also* Tunisian film distribution and exhibition
  Arab cinema 14, 195, 196, 198, 200–3, 208, 246, 252
  Egyptian cinema 31, 136–41
  German cinema 72–5
  governmental funding 244, 245
  Indian 122
  Saudi cinema 220–3, 225–9, 233, 235
expatriate workers 220
export market 27

Fageeh, Hisham 233
Fahmi, Mansi 104
Fahmy, Ziad 8
El Fani, Nadia 177
Farah, Iskandar 84
Faranzidis, Boutros 105
Farine, Anaïs 212–17
Faruq (king) 31, 97, 136
Faruq Cinema 136, 138
fascism 57
  cinema 69
  Italy 62–4, 67–9, 71
Fawzi, Layla 104
feature films 64–6, 68, 74, 75, 93, 184, 215
Feeling Greater than Love, A (2017) 211, 218 n.4
Ferkous, Abdellah 196, 197
Film Africa 197
Film du Centenaire 55
Film History: South by South/West Asia 9
Film Industry Seminar (1955) 122
film(s). *See also specific titles*
  Asian 124
  audiences 106, 135, 139–41, 143, 146, 148, 170, 171, 182, 184, 185, 202, 203, 250

ban 14, 222–5, 227, 228
class division 135
clubs 250
colour motion pictures 84
comedy 168
control 31
credits 167
culture 48, 49, 122, 179, 183, 187, 189–92, 202, 221, 223–4
distribution 1, 62, 64, 68–72, 75, 106, 122
distributors 31–3, 35, 37, 38, 46–7, 198, 202, 206, 207
duty-free 32
DVDs 197
economy 190
educational role of 151, 152
entertainment 185
epic 99, 168
exhibitions 46, 47, 49–51, 57, 58, 62, 64, 68, 71, 72, 82–5, 122, 135, 222, 245
exhibitors 134–6, 190
for families 156–7
festival 183, 191, 192, 195–7, 199–206
fiction 66–7, 69, 77, 78, 184
and foreign policy 122
history 1, 27, 46, 212, 216
illegal markets 197
industry 32, 35, 36, 39, 46, 47, 57, 58, 76, 113, 124, 129, 168, 201, 202
legislation 182
literature and 167–9
management 185
market 37, 38, 63, 70–7, 122, 199
memories 257, 258, 261, 263, 265, 267, 269–72
morality 136
narrative 89
nonfiction 67, 69, 77, 78
non-Hollywood 27
as playground 154–6
policy 202, 205
production 1, 83, 95, 114, 124, 136
programming 2, 4, 5, 9, 16, 114, 123, 185, 187, 189, 212, 213, 218, 229, 247, 251, 252
as public good 53

quality   36
rentals   75, 76, 134, 138, 140–2, 148, 149 n.14
romance and sex   163–5
in service of Islam   112–14
social and cognitive impact of   106
stars in television series   147
studies   195
studios   58
taste for   220, 224–7, 229, 231, 233, 235
textual analysis   3, 94, 114, 195
theatres   137, 147, 148, 250
tickets   139–40, 145, 147, 162, 170, 185, 189, 244, 245
for women   158–60
Films Régence   28, 32–4, 36–9, 40 n.5
Film Trade   123
financial crisis   212, 213
Finland   75
'The First Hebrew City: Early Tel Aviv through the Eyes of the Eliasaf Robinson'   16
First World War   27, 71, 72, 86
flagship productions   74
Flaubert, Gustave   75
flea markets   125, 129
Fleifel, Mahdi   198
Foley, Sean   233
food consumption   157–8
forced displacement   140–1
Ford Foundation   247
foreign (*khawaja*)   103, 104, 110
audiences   97–8, 137
films   27, 28, 30, 32, 73, 76, 106, 137, 140, 142, 147, 165
foreign investment   202
For Sama (2019)   205
Forst, Willi   74
Forum des images   190
Fouad cinema   64
France   28, 30, 32–5, 37, 38, 46–51, 53–5, 57, 58, 62, 63, 67, 69, 71, 74, 182
Franciscan Canadian Sacred Land Foundation   106
Franciscan community   106
francophone sources   46–8, 53
Francorexfilms   33
Franko, Fernando   72

Free Officers   93, 94, 97, 99, 112, 113
French
administration   33
authorities   27, 29–31, 46, 51, 54, 58, 59 n.11
cinema/film(s)   12, 28, 31, 33, 47, 48, 50, 54, 58, 64, 67, 74, 182
colonial empire   27, 28, 34, 38, 46
embassy   33
Equatorial Africa   34
language   29
literary works   50
nationality   44 n.57
propaganda   33
West Africa   31, 34
Frini, Mohamed   188, 190
Fritsch, Willy   74
Fu'ad, Nagwa   137
funding models   247
fundraising strategy   250
fusha (outing)   156

galarie (balcony) seats   85
Gallant Lady, The (1934)   221
gamahir al-tirsu (terso audience)   162
Gamal, Samia   36
Ganga Jamuna (*Mother India*, 1957)   126
Gasmelbari, Suhaib   15
gender
dichotomies   260, 270
dynamics   151
imaginaries   269
mixing   86–9, 227
relations   95
representation   94, 95
segregation   221, 227
General Culture Authority (GCA)   229
General Entertainment Authority   230
genre films   179, 185, 187–9
geo-blocking practice   212
German cinema/film(s)   63, 66, 71, 74–7
D.F.E.   74
distribution   74
exhibition   72–5
industry   64, 73
production   64, 74
in Turkey   69–70
German culture   72
German-Egyptian co-productions   64

German Federal Archives 63, 78 n.2
Germany 58, 62, 65, 70, 71, 74, 76, 77, 200
    Kaiserreich 72
    supremacy 77
Ghadr wa 'Adhab (*Treachery and Misery*, 1947) 96
Ghanim, Samir 264, 268
Gharam wa Intiqam (*Love and Revenge*, 1944) 31, 37, 42 n.31
Gharib, Asmaa 136, 138–48
Ghost Hunting (2017) 198
Ghweba Cinema 135–8, 141, 142, 148
Ghweba family 134
    Abbas Ghweba 13, 136–41
    Hasan Ghweba 136, 138, 141, 142, 144, 149 n.14
    Tareq Ghweba 13, 141–8
Ginsberg, Terri 7
Global North 200
Global South 196, 200
Goha 183
Golden Age of Hindi cinema 124
Golden Years of Egyptian Film, The 271
Good News Cinema 203
Goubantini, Lassaad 185, 187, 190, 191
Goubantini brothers 182
grant-making organizations 247, 248
Great Love 1942 74
Greece 70, 71
Greek Melkite Catholics 119 n.49
Greek Orthodox 104
guerrilla warfare 93
Gulf countries 121, 125, 126, 128–30, 179
Guns of Navarone (1961) 187

Haathi Mere Saathi (*Elephants Are My Companions*, 1971) 121
Habermas, Jürgen 222
Hadjithomas, Joana 198
Hafiz, 'Abd al-Halim 137, 163, 164, 167
Haïk, Jacques 32, 34–6, 39, 43 n.35, 46–7
Hakaya Misk Festival 225
HAKKA Distribution 190, 191
al-Halim Mahmud, Abd 99

Hamama, Fatin 261
Hammad, Hanan 8
Hammam al-Malatili (*The Bathhouse of Malatili*, 1973) 144, 149 n.10
Hanoune, Georges 57, 58
Hansen, Rolf 74
Harabi, Najib 201–3
harem 90 n.5
    boxes 84
Harfouche, Jowe 245–53
Harlan, Veit 75
Harris, Lauren Carroll 202
Hayek, Ghenwa 7–8
Hayoun, Massoud 30
Hebdo 46, 53, 54
Hédi, Habib Bel 179, 188
Helmi, Ahmad 144
Hepburn, Audrey 165
Herf, Jeffrey 68
Hersch, Hermann 72
Hijazi, Salama 84
Hikayat Hubb (1959) 163
Hinaydi, Muhammad 146, 149 n.12
Hindi cinema. *See* Bollywood films
Hinduja, Deepchand 126
Hinduja family 126, 127
historical films 72
Hollywood 12, 27–9, 31, 48, 50, 56, 57, 70, 71, 73, 76, 77, 123, 141, 151, 179, 187, 189, 196, 228, 232, 235
    distribution 68
    films 9, 30, 39, 42 n.33, 50, 64–7, 69, 165, 225, 229
    free-market film companies 76
    genre films 185
    movie stars 231
    musicals 30
    newsreels 68
    productions 65, 67
    studios 127, 198
Hollywood Cinema 137, 138, 141
Hollywood studios 127
Home Cooperative Association 137
Hong Kong 124
    films 124
horror films 230
Hubert Bals award 227
hubus 36

Human Rights League   177
human rights organizations   229
humour   265
Husayn, Taha   100
Husni, Suʿad   142

Ibn al-Walid, Khalid   168
Ibn Rabah, Bilal   225
Ibrahim, Mina   114
Ibrahim, Sayyid   156
ʿid al-fitr   32, 155, 226
   ʿidiya   155
Idris, Yusuf   167, 168
Imam, Adil   124
IMAX dome theatre   227–8, 230
Imbaba Cinema   161
immigrants   77
import-licensing process   32
Independent Cinema Office   244
independent films   185, 188, 246
India   122, 126
India-Egypt Association   122, 123
Indian cinema/film(s)   123, 124, 126, 165, 230
   archives   9
   distribution   122, 129
   exhibition   122
   industry   122, 130
Indian government   122, 123, 128
Indian Trade Exhibition (1954)   122
Information and Broadcasting Ministry   123
intercommunal relations   93
Intercontinental Hotel   223
interfaith
   love   114
   marriage   111, 112, 118 n.38
   unity   109
International Amateur Film Festival in Kelibia (*Festival international du film amateur de Kélibia*, FIFAK)   183
International Colonial Exhibition (1931)   54
International Congress of Educational Cinema   53
international co-productions   192
International Documentary Festival (IDFA)   205–6

International Film Festival Rotterdam   227
international films   27, 183, 224
international funding bodies   248
internationalization   27
international market   128
international trade   27
internet
   connection   213–14
   problem   215
Intisar al-Islam (*Victory of Islam*, 1952)   100
Iran   63, 121, 126
Iranian film market   127
Iraq   63, 65, 70, 128, 252
Islam(ic)   101, 111, 112
   ethics   98, 103
   identity   101, 103
   modernity   103
   norms   100, 112
   'official Islam'   99
Islamist movements   111
Ismailia   134–7, 142, 143
Ismailia Rayih Gay (*Round Trip to Ismailia*, 1997)   146, 147
ʿIssa, Ibrahim   261, 265, 266
Istanbul   71, 72, 75, 76
Istiqlal Party   35
Italian films   76
I Was a Boy in the 1970s (ʿAbd al-Shakur)   150, 158
ʿIzz, Ahmad   146
ʿIzz al-Din, Ibrahim   100

Jacir, Annemarie   205
Jameson, Frederic   262, 263
al-Jazayirli, Fawzi   82
Jazirat al-ʿArab (*Island of the Arabs*)   221
Jeddah Science and Technology Center   224
Jeddah Visual Show Festival   224, 225, 230
Jeem   216, 219 n.9
Jews   66
   boycott   64–6
   traders   39
Joreige, Khalil   198
Joud (2018)   234
judenrein (free of Jews)   73
Jud Süß (1940)   75

Kamil, Mustafa 99
Kapoor, Raj 121, 126, 127
Karaoui, Nabil 179
Karim, Muhammad 89, 102
Karkouti, Alaa 203–5
Kassab, Boutros 119 n.56
al-Kateab, Waad 205
Kay-Bee studio 47
Keif al-Hal? (*How Are You?*, 2006) 225, 226
Kelada, Mariz 6
Keystone studio 47
El-Khachab, Chihab 6
Khalil, Jad Abi 211–18
Khalili, Laleh 174 n.34
Khan, Mehboob 121, 123
Khashoggi, Jamal 229, 233
Khayat, Edmond 33
Khayat, Édouard 33
Khayat, Théodore 35
Khedival Opera House 82
Khoja, Jomanah 222
Kholoussy, Hanan 114
Kindil el Bahr (2014) 213
King Abdulaziz Center for World Culture (Ithra) 228, 234
King Abdullah Financial District 230, 231
Kirtikar, Margo 15
Kraidy, Marwan 227
Kramp, Fritz 64
KSA 230
Kuwait 69, 224

Labaki, Nadine 205
Lac aux dames (1934) 50
LaCava, Gregory 221
L'Afrique du Nord illustrée 46, 47, 50, 54
La garçonne (1923) 88
Laïcité Inch'Allah (2012) 177
La Isla de Perejil (*Parsley Island*, 2016) 196–7
Lait, George 66
Lamprecht, Gerhard 75
La Passion de Nancy (1930) 49
La République 72
La revue du Centenaire 55
Larkin, Brian 262
Lashin (1938) 65

Last Days of the Man of Tomorrow, The (2017) 213
La Tranchée (*The Trench*) 56
Laval Decree 196
La Vie artistique 51
Laylat al-Qadr (*Night of Power*, 1952) 12, 93–5, 97, 106, 111
 CFC's rating 105–7
 coloniality 99–104
 report of al-Mazawi 107–12
Leander, Zarah 74
Leasim, Harry 71
Lebanese cinema/film(s) 198, 215
 Golden Age of 127
 market 127
 screens 121
Lebanese Civil war 127
Lebanese economy 212
Lebanese traders 39
Lebanon 15, 62, 63, 121, 127, 129, 201, 212–14
Le Bled (1929) 54–5, 58
Lebrati, Moïse 56–7
L'Echo d'Alger 46, 51, 55, 57
Le cinéphile 183
Legion of Decency 105
legitimacy 36
 theatre 56
leisure activity 151–4, 156, 159, 160, 168–71, 182, 186, 187, 222
le Majestic 185
Le Métropole 188
Le Petit Marocain 57
Le Petit Roi (1933) 50
Le Progrès égyptien 131 n.15
Lerner, Daniel 37
'le roi du cinéma' (the king of cinema) 46, 58
Les Chantiers nord-africains (*North African Building Sites*) 52, 53
Les Croix de Bois (1932) 56
Les Misérables (1934) 50
Levantines 106, 111
Leveratto, Jean-Marc 28, 36
Liberation Rally health scheme fund 123
Library of Congress 16
Libya 34, 63, 68, 69, 78
Lippard, Chris 7

Liqa' Hunak (*A Meeting There*,
    1979)   120 n.61
literary fiction   94
literature   100, 167–9
Litvak, Anatole   50
live
    entertainment   155
    performances   50, 56, 257
Lobato, Ramon   39, 207
Loew   66
loges   84, 85, 87, 157, 162
'Love and Identity in Arab Cinema'
    programme   216, 217
Lowe, Al   66
Luce, Giornale   68
al-Luz, 'Abd al-Rahman   36

Maadi Club   155
Maadi constituency   99
Maasri, Mounir   15
Maatouk, Tamara Chahine   8
Mabrouka Films   33
McBrian, Julie   114
Madam Loretta (1919)   82
MAD Distribution   198–200, 203–8
MAD Solutions   14, 196, 198, 199,
    203–8, 208 n.7, 211
Maestranza Films   197
magazines   3–6, 8, 16, 84, 87–9, 102, 153,
    154
Maghreb   11, 27–9, 32–5, 38–9
Maghrebi films   200
Mahfouz, Naguib   167, 168
Maisch, Herbert   75
Majestic cinema   36, 49, 50, 54, 55
Majestic studio   47
Making Film in Egypt (El-Khachab)   6
Malayalam films   128
Maltby, Richard   3
Manifestations du Centenaire   55
Manshiyat al-Shuhada' (*Martyrs*)   139
al-Mansour, Haifaa   226, 227, 232
Mapping Cinema Audiences (El
    Safoury)   7
al-Maraghi, Mustafa   99
Mard (*Man*, 1985)   121, 124
Markos II Khouzam   113
Markovits, Claude   125
Marley, Bob   233

Marrakech Film Festival   249
marriage   94, 102, 109
    interracial   94, 102
    Muslim-Christian   120 n.57
martial arts films   124
Marvel Universe   231, 232
masculinity   94, 95, 101–3, 112
*Mass Mediations: New Approaches to
    Popular Culture in the Middle East
    and Beyond* (Armbrust)   6
M. A. Thirumugham   121
matinees   85
Mawakib al-'Izz   42 n.31
Mawjoudin   216, 219 n.8
al-Mazawi, Farid   105–7, 109–11, 113,
    118–19 n.48
MC Distribution   215
mec film   200, 211
media literacy workshops   251
Meknes   31
Melkite Catholic Church (*Rum
    Katolik*)   104, 106
melodrama   93, 97, 100
Memmi, Albert   35, 44 n.57
Menahi (2009)   226
Mera Naam Joker (*My Name Is Joker*,
    1970)   126
'*métis* of colonization'   35
Metro Cinema   66, 162
    kids raffles   155
    live entertainment   155
Metropolis Art Cinema Association   212
Metropolis Empire Sofil Theatre   212
Metropolis Project   15
metropolitan
    audiences   50
    cinemas   33
    distribution companies   32
Metro Super Market   141
MGM   66
Miami Cinema   123, 162
middle-class   151, 153, 159, 161, 162,
    169, 201
    childhood   153
    countries   64, 234
    at war and movies   64–9
Milestone, Lewis   56
Mingant, Nolwenn   9, 40 n.5, 42 n.33
Minister of Religious Endowments   99

Ministry of Cultural Affairs   184, 187
Ministry of Enlightenment and
    Propaganda   70
Ministry of Information   76, 182
Ministry of Interior   106–8, 110
Ministry of Media   234
Ministry of Propaganda   73
Ministry of Social Affairs   106
Misr (Egypt) Cinema   136–8, 143
missionary education   104
Mistinguett   50
Mizrahi, Togo   8
MK2 Bibliothèque   190
Moderne   49, 53
modernity   94
    Arab-Muslim   28
    Egyptian cinema   262
    Islam   101
    Saudi Arabia   223, 229, 235
modernization   37, 83, 101, 231
Moors, Annelies   114
moral
    cinema   107
    panic   27, 30
    pedagogy   106
    responsibility   107
Moroccan cinema/film(s)   196, 197
Morocco   30, 31, 34, 35, 44 n.57,
    47, 54, 63, 65, 69, 182, 192,
    201, 252
Motadel, David   69
Motion Picture Daily   69
Motion Picture Herald   69, 70
*Motion Pictures (al-Suwar
    al-Mutaharrika)*   83, 87, 88
Moulin Rouge cinema   49
Mourad, Selim   211
Moving Picture World, The   84, 85, 87
Mubarak, Hosni   124, 143
Much Loved (2015)   197
Al-Muhaisin, Abdullah   225
Muhammad, Amina   96
multi-day film festival   224
multifunctional cinema exhibition
    space   244–53
multi-sensory cultural experience   231
Munib, Marie   168
Murad, Layla   8
Mursi, Ahmad Kamal   117 n.27

music   35, 49
Muslim Brotherhood   95, 100
Muslim-Christian
    difference   110
    marriage   120 n.57
    romance   114
Muslim(s)   35, 111
    societies   28
    Tunisians   182
    women   29
Muvi   230
My Fair Lady 1964   165
Mzali, Mohamed Salah   36, 44 n.62

Naana, Fares   181
Nabab of Palanpur (Muslim
    Maharajah)   122
al-Nabulsi, 'Abd al-Salam   163
Naga Hamadi   154
Nagiub, Rim   260
Naguib, Muhammad   99, 113, 122
Nahas   34
Naksa (loss of the six-day war)   152,
    168–9, 174 n.34
Nasser, Gamal Abdel   99, 113, 123, 134,
    152
nation   254, 258–60, 262, 265–72
national
    culture   184, 262
    discourse   106
    identity   28, 94, 95, 265
    liberation   97
    nationalism   94, 95, 100, 134, 135
    nationalization   127
    security   95, 111
    unity   107, 112, 114, 122
National Archives and Records
    Administration (NARA)   40 n.5
national cinema/film(s)   5, 27, 66, 96, 97,
    124, 181
    cultures   195
    production   1
National Film Festival   197
National Liberation Front   37
National Library of Israel   16
National Party Club   141
National Security Agency   94, 107
National Security Directorate   110
Nawadi cinema   183

Naya 128
Nazi cinema/film(s) 12, 67, 70, 76
  distribution 62, 64
  industry 63
  Universum Film AG (Ufa) 62–5, 70–7
Nazi Germany 62–4, 75
Nazis 47, 58, 62–70, 75, 77
  pro-Nazi films 67
  pro-Nazi ideology 69
  propaganda 68–70, 72, 76
Neidhardt, Irit 200, 203
neoliberal laws 248
neoliberal policies 212
neorealism 183
  films 39
Nessma 177, 179
Netflix 147, 213, 234
network-building 246, 248
Network of Arab Alternative Screens (NAAS) 7, 9, 14, 244–8, 251, 252
new cinema
  historians 3
  new cinema history (NCH) 2–4, 8, 11, 13, 17, 27, 195
New Egypt (*Misr al-Haditha*) 96
newsreels 64–8, 74, 75, 78, 182
New York Times 232
Nhebek Hedi (Hedi, 2016) 181
Noguès, Charles 42 n.33
non-aggression pact 71
Non-Aligned Movement 122, 129
non-Europeans 59 n.11
non-hierarchical governance cooperative model 248–9
non-public
  cinema 222
  concept/phenomenon 222
North Africa(n) 27, 28, 31–3, 37, 39, 46–50, 53–5, 57, 58, 62, 66, 69, 179, 182
  audiences 27–9
  cinema exhibition 12
  culture 51
nostalgia 14, 95, 114, 257, 259–64
  restorative 263
'No Woman, No Cry' (song) 233
Nye, Joseph 258
Nyrabia, Orwa 205

Occupied Zone 57
Office Catholique International du Cinéma (OCIC) 105
Office of War Information (OWI) 69
Official Board of Cinema 124
off-screen 6–9, 11, 15, 257, 271
oil industry 220
Olympia Cinema 49, 84, 85
online platforms 147, 211, 212, 233
  LinkedIn 225
  Vimeo 214
open-air cinemas 136–7, 139, 152, 153, 155–7, 170, 254
  and class 161–2
  and geographical memory 160–1
Open Society Foundations 247
Operation Torch 57
oral histories 3, 7, 8, 15, 151, 152
Oran Spectacles 46
Organization of the Islamic Conference 113
Oruc, Firat 221
Oscar Company 144
Ottoman Empire 70, 72
Ounouri, Damien 213
Overseas Film Division 69

Palace cinema 49
Palestine 66, 67, 78, 107, 200
Palestine Film Platform 198
Palestinian Museum Digital Archive 16
Palestinian Oral History Archive 15
pan-Arab identity 28–30, 38
parafilmic archives 8
Parallax Haifa 15
Paris 39, 47–51, 55, 57
Parisian-style streets 51
Paris Ki Ek Shaam (*An Evening in Paris*, 1967) 127
paternalism 88, 107, 112
Pathé Cinématographe 85
Pathé-Gaumont multiplex 179, 181, 188
Pathé-Rural 53–4, 58
Pearl Harbor 67, 70
Pepsi 232
Pera 72, 73, 76
Perfect Day, A (2006) 198
Persepolis (Marjana Satrapi, 2007) 177

personal status laws (PSL)   111, 112, 120 n.59
petromodernity   9
pieds noirs   48
piracy   126, 129, 140, 185
Pius XI (Pope)   105
Place d'Armes   51
playhouses   82–4, 86
political
   activism   187, 190
   autonomy   29
   demonstrations   29
   documentaries   200
   economy   195, 223
   films   167
   history   168
   instability   169
   relationship   122
Popcorn   179
Popular Revolution (1919)   87, 93, 109
Port Said   64, 65, 93
posters   153, 154
post–Second World War   95, 182–4
post-war film clubs   36, 39
post-war period   35, 38
pre-colonial economic structures   39
Presley, Elvis   165
printed lyrics   28, 30, 40 n.5
private archives   28, 40 n.5, 43 n.35
promotional campaign   99, 113
promotional films   78, 183
Prophet Muhammad   100
public
   amusement   68
   cinema   224, 229–32
   discourse   104
   film   222, 225, 235
   piety   99
   policy   201
   space   31
   sphere   38–9, 220, 222
   television   113
purposeful art (*al-fann al-hadif*)   95

Questions Man (*Rajul al-As'ila*)   88
Qutb, Sayyid   95

racial
   differences   135
   policies   73

politics   64
purity   77
radio broadcasts   68, 69, 71
Radio Pictures (RKO)   71
radio programmes   68
radio waves   68
Railway Company Cinema   141
Raimu   50
Ramadan   32
Ramadan, Muhammad   146, 149 n.13
Ramses movie house   64
Ramsis Theatre   12, 83–7, 90 n.16
Rashid, Rawiya   84, 86, 87, 91 n.23
Rasif Nimra Khamsa (*Platform 5, 1956*)   254, 256, 269
Ras Tanura camp   228
reform   231, 235
Regard   8
Régence-Algérie   35, 37
Régence-Maroc   35
Régence-Tunisie   35
Régent cinema   49, 51, 53
regional politics   112–14
Reich Film Chamber   70, 73, 74, 76
Reich Ministry of Economics   76
religion(us)
   bigotry   108
   conflict   107
   difference   94–5, 107
   equality   93
   extremism   114
   festivities   32
   film (*film dini*)   99, 100
   identity   100
   institutions   114
   practice   98, 100
Renaissance Cinema   137, 141, 143
Renoir, Jean   54, 55
rental agreements   76
Republican People's Party   70
Résidence générale   182
Revolutionary Command Council   123
revolutionary taxes   37
Revue de culture par le film   183
Rio Cinema   137, 138, 156, 170, 171, 172 n.11
riots   93
Riskin, Robert   69
Risner, Jonathan   206, 207
Rivoli Cinema   1

Riyadh   225, 227, 234
Riyadh International Conventions and Exhibitions Center   225
Roman Catholic churches   110
romance films   100, 137
Roosevelt, Franklin D.   69
Rosenberg, Clifford   48
Rotana International   225–7
Royal Cinema   89, 99, 138, 142
Royale Cinema   107, 137, 141, 142, 146, 147
Rushdi, Fatima   96
Russia   71
Russian films   164
Rusti, Istifan   104
Ryzova, Lucie   102

Sa'ad, Muhammad   146
Saadallah, Amal   190
Saba, Mary Jirmanus   211, 218 n.4
Sadallah, Amel   188
Sadat, Anwar   99, 113
Sadoul, George   130 n.3
El Safoury, Nour   7, 245–53
Saglier, Viviane   6
Sahat al-Shuhada' (Martyr's Square)   1
Sahibet al-Sa'ada (*The Owner of Happiness*, TV show)   14, 257–60, 263, 264, 269–71
   happiness   264–70
Said, Edward   7
Sa'idi Fil Gama'a al-Amrikiya (1998)   149 n.12
Sakarya cinema   74
Sakr, Naomi   223
Salafists   177
Salem, Mamdouh   230
Salhab, Ghassan   216
Salim, Kamal   96
Salle de l'Opéra   188
Salle Tahar Cheriaa   187
Samanta, Shakti   127
Samawa Cinema   251, 252
Sangam (*Confluence*, 1964)   121, 126, 165
al-Saqqa, Ahmed   144, 146
Saray cinema   72
the Sark cinema   74
Al Saud, Abdulaziz bin Abdul Rahman   221

Saudi Arabia   10, 68, 177
   Grand Mosque   222
   multiplex movie theatres   128, 129, 189, 191, 192, 223, 230, 234, 235
   multi-screen megaplexes   222
Saudi Arabia cinema/film(s)   14
   C3 Films   233
   cultural and educational experiences   227–9
   festivals   224–5
   film culture in transition   223–4
   home-grown productions and home-viewing   225–7
   production, exhibition and distribution   220–3, 225–9, 233, 235
   public cinema and Cola wars   229–32
   public opinions   232–3
   public relations   220–3
Saudi Arabian General Entertainment Authority   10
Saudi Aramco   221, 228, 234
Saudi Development and Investment Entertainment Company   230
Saudi Film Council   229
Saudi Film Days   228
Saudi Society of Arts and Culture   224
Saudi Vision 2030   10, 229
Saudi women   227
Schneider Hammam   85
'School at the Cinema' programme   251
school-boy truants   162–3, 170
school films   183
Schwarz, John-Pedro   73, 74
Screen Art (*Fan al-Sinima*)   84, 89
SEAM-Films   35
'second-class' movie house   64, 124, 160
Second World War   29, 32, 48, 54, 62, 65–6, 69–70, 78, 182
Sections administratives spécialisées (SAS)   33
secularism   109
Seibarras, Joseph   12, 46, 47, 49–58
Seif, Salah Abu   39, 149 n.10
Selassie, Haile   68
Ses-Film   74
sex
   prudence   30
   work   165
Sfax   36

Shahid.net 147
El Shakry, Omnia 152
Shaltut, Mahmud 99, 108
Sha'rawi, Huda 82, 87
al-Sharif, Nur 142
Sharjah 125
Shasha 218 n.4
Shawqi, Farid 162, 254
al-Shaykh, Kamal 261
Shaykh Zayid neighbourhood 140
al-Shinawi, Kamal 142
shopping malls 222, 227, 234
shop window theatre 66
short films 65, 68, 224
Shubra Palace Cinema 124
Shwam (Levantine people) 138
al-Siba'i, Yusuf 167
Sidonie Panache (1934) 50
Sidqi, Husayn 93–100, 102, 103, 105, 107, 109–13
silent films 49, 55, 151
al-Sisi, 'Abd al-Fattah 255, 260
Six-Day War (1967) 139, 142, 169, 254
Slouma, Abderrazak 35
Smadj, Joseph 36
Snapchat 225
social
 clubs 161
 conscious cinema 113
 discourses 94
 inequality 93
 injustices 97
 media 233
 problems 97
 realist film 96
socialization 151, 152, 161
société anonyme (public limited company) 35
société anonyme à responsabilité limitée (limited liability company) 35
Societé des cinématographes 57
Societé des Ingénieurs Civils de France 53
sociology 35
soft power 220, 256–9, 268–70
songs 28, 30, 35
Sony Pictures Animation 230
Soueid, Mohamed 216
sound 185
 7.1 Dolby 185
 films 49, 64, 65

Sound of Music, The 1965 165
Sous les toits de Paris (1930) 48, 49, 59 nn.14–15
Southeast Asia 58
South-South cinematographic circuits 121
Soviet Army 77
Soviet Union 78
Spanish co-production 197
spectatorship 27, 39. *See also* audience(s)
Splendid cinema 57
sports 50
 clubs 161
'Spotlight on Beirut DC' programme 212
Sri Hinduja 126
Stafford, Marilyn 1
Standard Oil Company, California 221, 228
Stanford libraries 16
Starr, Deborah 8
state censor 112–14, 120 n.57
stereotypes 37, 129, 135
Straits Times 230
Strand Cinema 123
streaming platforms 212, 217, 233
Studio Misr 34, 64, 82–3
subtitle/dub films 30
Sudan 252
Sudan Film Factory 251
Suez Canal 140
Suez Canal Company 135, 138, 149 n.6
Suez Canal project 134
Suez crisis 33
Suleiman, Lama 15
Sultan, Huda 255
Sultan Bin Abdulaziz Science and Technology Center 228
al-Sultan Husayn Street 135, 138
Sultanic Opera 85, 86
Sundance Rawi Screenwriters 227
Suraj (*Sun*, 1966) 121
Syndicat des distributeurs indépendants 37
Synergy Company 144
Syria 62, 63, 125, 129
Syrian Jesuit Father Ayrout 110

Talking about Trees (2020) 15
Tamil films 128
Tariq al-Shawwak (*Path of Thorns*, 1950) 96

Tartarin de Tarascon (1934)   50
Tarzan film series   137
'Taste the feeling' campaign   231
tax
  policies   202
  relief   184
Tazi, Muhammad Abderrahman   7
technical issues   212, 215, 217
technological inequalities   212
Tehran   125, 127
television   151, 159, 167, 170, 179, 221, 227, 233, 266–7
  BBC   226
  programmes   140
  satellite   225, 227
Telfaz11   233
Tënk   218 n.5
Terra   74
terso   162
Theses on the Philosophy of History (Benjamin)   263
Third Reich   71
third-world literature   262
This Little Father Obsession (2016)   211
Thompson, Elizabeth   31, 65–7, 77
Thompson, Jack Lee   187
Tietz, Fritz   73, 75
Tita Wong (1937)   96
Tobis   74
T. Prakashrao   121
Trade and Payments Agreement (1953)   122
trade journals   28
trade press   63
traditional markets   128
transition   223–4
Transjordan   68, 70
transmedia fandom   227
transnational
  cinema   195, 229
  ethnography   122
  phenomenon   5
  stardom   206
traumatic memories   169
troisièmes (third-rate) seats   85
al-Tukhi, Ahmad   100
Tunis   28, 32, 34, 36, 46, 177, 179, 181, 182, 184, 185
al-Tunisi, Bayram   158
Tunisia   30–4, 44 n.57, 47, 54

Tunisian Association for the Promotion of Film Criticism (*Association tunisienne pour la promotion de la critique cinématographique*, ATPCC)   183
Tunisian Federation of amateur filmmakers (*Fédération tunisienne des cinéastes amateurs*, FTCA)   183, 184
Tunisian Federation of Cine-Clubs (*Fédération tunisienne des ciné-clubs*, FTCC)   183, 244
Tunisian film distribution and exhibition   177–92
  cinema-going since post–Second World War   182–4
  and circulation   190–1
  film consumption, conceptions of   184–90
Tunisian films   13, 179, 184, 185, 187–90, 192
Tunisian Ministry of Cultural Affairs   36
Tunisian Public Company of Film Production and Expansion (*Société anonyme tunisienne de production d'expansion du cinéma*, SATPEC)   182
Turkey   5, 62–4, 69–78
Turkish cinema/film(s)
  audiences   71, 72, 74, 76
  distributor   73
  exhibitors   72, 73
  industry   72
  production   70
Turkish government   71
Tyber, Lyna   50

Ucicky, Gustav   75
'Ukasha, 'Abdalla   84
UNESCO   221
Uniate Coptic-rite churches   110
United Arab Emirates (UAE)   127, 128, 208, 224, 226
United Artists   66, 72
United Brothers   144
United Motion Pictures company   128
United Nations   76
United States   47, 48, 51, 62, 63, 67, 70, 71, 77, 78, 105, 232, 257
  Embassy   42 n.22

Federal Communications
Commission 68
government 69
Information Agency 78
Office of War Information 68
Unshudat al-Fu'ad (*The Song of the Heart*,
1932) 28
upper class 151, 156, 161
tastes 102
upper-middle class 159, 161
UTorrent 179

Variety 66, 67, 75, 76, 226
Vatican 105
Vercel, Pierre 37
VHS 170, 222
Vichy 34, 57, 58, 63, 67, 69, 77
Video on Demand (VOD)
platforms 212, 213,
217
Vigilanti Cura 105, 118 n.46
Vision 2030 231, 234
VOD platform 191
Voilà Paris (1932) 50
Volpe, Mario 31
von Papen, Franz 70, 71, 76
Vox 230

Wadjda (2012) 226, 227, 234
Wafd party 86, 87
Wahbi, Yusuf 31, 64, 65, 83, 84, 86–7, 91
n.23, 96, 102, 103
Wahbi Cinema 64
Waked, Amr 206
Wanda Group 230
Warner Brothers 1, 65
wartime films 74, 78

Washington Post, The 233
Waxman, A. P. 67
Welch, David 62
hegemony 232
neo-colonialism 27–8
westernization 95
Western-ness 30
West-Osteuropäische Warenaustausch
Aktiengesellschaft
(WOSTWAG) 63
White Rose, The (*al-Warda al-Bayda'*,
1933) 89
Widad (1936) 64
Wiener Blut (Vienna Blood) 1942 74
Wikipedia 225
Winkel, Roel Vande 62
World Not Ours (*Alam Laysa Lana*,
2012) 198

Yash Raj Films (YRF) 128, 129
non-traditional markets 128
Yasqut al-Isti'mar (Down with
Colonialism) 1952 97
Yassin, Isma'il 168
Yemen 252
youth-oriented content creation 225
YouTube 225, 231, 233–5
Yunis, 'Is'ad 257–62, 264, 268, 269, 272
Yusab II 113

Zaccak, Hady 211
Zaied, Kais 188, 190
Zamzam Cola 232
Zawya Cinema 244
Zion Hall Cinema 16
Zuhur al-Islam (*The Rise of Islam*,
1951) 100

www.ingramcontent.com/pod-product-compliance
Lightning Source LLC
Chambersburg PA
CBHW052148300426
44115CB00011B/1563